The WINE *of* WISDOM

RELATED TITLES

Rumi: Past and Present, East and West, Franklin D. Lewis, ISBN 1–85168–335–6

The WINE *of* WISDOM

The Life, Poetry and Philosophy of

Omar Khayyam

MEHDI AMINRAZAVI

ONEWORLD
OXFORD

I humbly dedicate this work to the democratic movement of the people of Iran. May Khayyam's spirit of freethinking prevail in our native land.

THE WINE OF WISDOM

Oneworld Publications
(Sales and Editorial)
185 Banbury Road
Oxford OX2 7AR
England
www.oneworld-publications.com

A CIP record for this title is available
from the British Library

ISBN 1-85168-355-0

Typeset by Jayvee, India
Cover design by Design Deluxe
Printed and bound in India by Thomson Press Ltd

Contents

Acknowledgements

I would like to express my gratitude to all those who assisted me with this project. In thanking them chronologically they are: Muḥammad Ismaili, who assisted me in finding rare articles in the libraries of Iran inaccessible to me; for their administrative support, our secretary Cindy Toomey, our skilled interlibrary loan officer Carla Baily and graphic designer June T. Padgett; and our students Gretchen Schwemer, Shahla Chohan, Lindsay Biddinger, Shannon MacMichael, Patrick Shepherd, Stephanie Van Hook and Zeke Kassock who have all been very helpful. I am grateful to Professor Seyyed Hossein Nasr for his suggestions on an early draft of this work, and Professor Suzanne Sumner of our Mathematics Department for her suggestions on Chapter Seven. I am particularly indebted to my dear colleague and friend, Professor David Cain for his most thorough reading of this book and his numerous suggestions. Much of the revisions made in the final edition are due to his diligence. Finally, I am thankful to the University of Mary Washington for a grant that enabled me to complete some of the research pertaining to Chapter Eight.

Mehdi Aminrazavi
University of Mary Washington
Fredericksburg, VA

حدیث مطرب و می گوی و راز دهر کمتر جو
که نگشادست ونگشوید کس بحکمت این معما را

Speak of happiness and wine
and seek not the riddle of the universe,
For no one has, nor will
unveil this mystery through wisdom

(Ḥāfiẓ)

The statue of Omar Khayyam beside the entrance to his tomb.

Introduction

This is a comprehensive introductory work on the life, works, philosophy, science and poetry of Omar Khayyam for the Western reader. In it I propose to reintroduce a remarkable man whose Western exotic image is not an accurate depiction of this mysterious and misunderstood philosopher, poet and scientist of the fifth/eleventh century.[1] This is my attempt to reconstruct, for the first time in the English language, the personality and thought of a figure who is unparalleled in the annals of Islamic intellectual thought, a stranger both in his homeland and in the West, a figure misunderstood by many people, loved by the free spirited and hated by many among the orthodox.

There are very few non-Western figures who rivaled the fame of Omar Khayyam in the West. Just a century ago not only was his poetry taught in schools and colleges but he was regarded to be the representative of the "East" in all its exoticness. Omar Khayyam's significance in the West is twofold; first, his *Ruba'iyyat* (quatrains);

second, his scientific works, especially those in the field of mathematics; the latter however has always been overshadowed by his poetry. His *Ruba'iyyat* became a household name from the 1870's to the 1950's and were discussed by the likes of Mark Twain, Ezra Pound and the public at large.

There are a number of reasons for his fame and cult-like status in England and especially in America, some of which I have discussed in Chapter Eight of this work. On the one hand, the First World War in Europe and the Civil War in America had left deep scars on the soul of Western societies; it is not surprising therefore to see that Khayyam's message concerning suffering and evil resonated deeply with the Western audience. On the other hand, materialism, secularism and spiritual humanism, as is evident in the case of the "New England School of Transcendentalism," was on the rise. The puritanical spirit of the founding fathers was slipping away into what the Christian fundamentalists saw as the rise of a new paganism.

Omar Khayyam's *Ruba'iyyat* became a powerful symbol for the debate between puritanical Christianity and secularism in the West. For the defenders of the Christian West Khayyam became the symbol of the "Other," the pagan heretic poet who was bent on weakening the moral fabric of the society by prescribing hedonism. The moral czars argued that the West in general and America in particular was falling into the abyss of materialism and its inevitable consequence, hedonism, because of its openness to foreign ideas. Khayyam's *Ruba'iyyat* in a sense was a perfect target; in no uncertain terms he advocated drinking wine and making love amidst the uncertainty of life after death. He became the antichrist to the orthodox Christianity, the protagonist in the drama of the Christian West against the secular West.

Omar Khayyam's *Ruba'iyyat* also resonated deeply with the secularists in the West. Khayyam challenged religious doctrines, alluded to the hypocrisy of the clergy, cast doubt on almost every facet of religious rituals and advocated a type of humanism. The new West embraced Khayyam irrespective of whether these *Ruba'iyyat* were his own but because the East contained a wisdom that the West supposedly lacked. The exotic East embodied in the very being of

Omar Khayyam, as represented in his *Ruba'iyyat*, advocated free-thinking, rebellion against religious thought and establishment, spiritualism and living in the here and now. Khayyam's timely message, praised highly by the secularists and condemned by the defenders of God, was captured so eloquently in his *Ruba'iyyat* thanks to the poetic genius of Omar Khayyam and his illustrious translator Edward FitzGerald.

Khayyam is also significant for his scientific views. He was also a mathematical genius whose commentaries on geometry and algebra stimulated much interest among Western mathematicians. His scientific treatises are very brief but nevertheless ground-breaking; his works have been translated in numerous languages and taken seriously by Russian, European and lately American mathematicians. Khayyam was both an original thinker in the scientific domain and an important transmitter and interpreter of Greek mathematical writings to the Islamic world. In the case of Euclidian geometry for instance, he offered major improvements on the Euclidian postulates.

Khayyam's *Ruba'iyyat* in the Western world in the nineteenth and twentieth centuries was a modern revival of Epicurianism. It must have been intriguing to the Victorian audience who saw humanism as the fruit of the Renaissance, to discover that the wise master from the East also advocated the same. The myth was once again reinforced that the wise sages of the East must have known all along what we in the West have just discovered! Omar Khayyam provided a mirror through which the West saw itself; those who liked what they saw praised him and those who did not blamed him for the moral degeneration of Western societies.

There are primarily two reasons for the composition of this work. First, there is a misunderstanding of the nature of Omar Khayyam's thought, perhaps due to the lack of a single volume in the English language[2] devoted to a comprehensive discussion of the thought of this multidimensional personality. Somehow Omar Khayyam has emerged as the prophet of the hedonists, agnostics and atheists; and has been hailed by others as a freethinker, the "Eastern Voltaire"[3] of the Islamic world whose cynical views on religion made him the hero of thirteenth AH/nineteenth-century Europe. The stereotypical picture of this great philosopher-scientist after whose name so many nightclubs have been named in the West is, however, a pure distortion. The image has been solidified by the Victorian sense of the exotic, romantic and often erotic notions that are attached to the East, notions that Khayyam's poetry concerning wine and women tends to strengthen. The introduction of a serious thinker such as Omar Khayyam to the Western reader, and the restitution of his tarnished image, therefore, remains my primary objective.

The second reason for the composition of this book is a personal one. Khayyam has been a source of inspiration throughout my life; his simple and yet profound message concerning temporality puts the universally shared trials and tribulations of daily life and our inner torments in their proper context. Perhaps it is for the above reason that from among the major figures of the colorful spectrum of intellectual thought in Iran, Omar Khayyam resonates with me in a unique way. It would not be inaccurate to say that somehow, I have found myself to have been "Khayyamian" ever since childhood and have come to experience a sense of belonging to all that constitutes what I call the "Khayyamian school of thought."

Some nostalgic reflections from the past may explain my special love for and admiration of Omar Khayyam. I was born in Mashhad, Iran, a city about two hours from Nayshābūr where the old master lived and died. One of my most vivid memories of childhood is my family's repeated visits to his tomb. In the springtime, around the Persian New Year, Norūz, we would take a weekend trip to Nayshābūr, a city whose ethereal presence has left an indelible mark upon my soul. Above all, we would visit Omar Khayyam's tomb, around which we always found people reciting poetry. Certainly, there were other sites to visit,[4] but none stimulated the kind of feeling Khayyam's presence brought about in me. Who was this man whose simple poems had affected the impressionable mind of a young boy and whose poetry has been an enduring source of inspiration for so many centuries? This is a question I have revisited throughout the last four decades of my own tumultuous life; and each time – like the scent of a rose, the intoxication of an aged wine and the sound of a nightingale – his poems send a refreshingly powerful message: to live is to live in an eternal presence. The pain and sorrow of the past and worries for the future, however, prevent us from experiencing the here and now; hence Khayyam's repeated reminder of the temporality of life. Seeing life as a river that is in a constant state of flux, Khayyams tells us, is a remedy to being continuously pounded by the merciless forces of life. Khayyam's mystique which mesmerized me as a young boy and led me to memorize much of his *Ruba'iyyat* (quatrains), gave way to a deeper understanding of him when later on, as I entered the maze of adult life, I kept hearing him whispering in my ears, "*This too shall pass.*"

And so, forty years after my first visit to Khayyam's tomb, I decided to embark upon an endeavor to reintroduce Omar Khayyam to the Western reader and to undertake the daunting task of analyzing and interpreting the intellectual aspects of his life, thought, poetry, science and philosophy.

A survey of the literature in the field of Khayyamian studies reveals several distinct, if not contradictory, interpretations, each of which captures the spirit of one aspect of this multidimensional figure. Was Khayyam the agnostic-hedonist of the Victorian era as presented by his illustrious translator Edward FitzGerald, or was he the devout Muslim he was reported to be by some of his biographers, including his son-in-law, Imām Muḥammad Baghdādī? Or perhaps, as suggested by others, there were several Khayyams, and Khayyam the mathematician and astronomer is misidentified with a poet and a Sufi master of the same name.

While these interpretations will be elaborated upon at some length in the forthcoming chapters, a brief review of them here will assist us in putting such discussions into a proper context.

KHAYYAM THE AGNOSTIC-HEDONIST

This view has had many proponents both in the West and the East. We owe much of this interpretation to Edward FitzGerald, whose free but eloquent translations of Khayyam matched the romantic spirit of the Victorian era as well as views in certain circles in the Eastern part of the world. There is certainly a long tradition of seeing Khayyam as an agnostic whose cynical views of life lead to a form of hedonism. Needless to say, many of Khayyam's *Ruba'iyyat*, if taken literally, lend credence to this perspective.

This interpretation of Khayyam is simply fallacious if one studies thoroughly not only his *Ruba'iyyat* but also his philosophical works which have been usually completely neglected by Western scholarship on Khayyam. Contrary to the *Ruba'iyyat* (the authorship of some of whose poems is somewhat dubious), his philosophical and scientific writings are decisively his own, each beginning with praise to God and the Prophet Muḥammad and ending with salutations and prayers.

Furthermore, the very fabric of his philosophical thought, which generally has received little attention both in the East and the West, clearly indicates that Khayyam was operating well within a monotheistic philosophical paradigm very much like his predecessor Avicenna whom he calls "his teacher." Above all, there is the last day of his life, his death scene, which has been portrayed in some detail. The report has it that Khayyam performed his Islamic prayers throughout the day before he died.

THE TWO-KHAYYAM THEORY

A decade ago, an eminent Iranian scholar, Muḥiṭ Ṭabāṭabā'ī[5], in a work entitled *Khayyam yā Khayyāmī*, argued that there have been a number of Khayyams and that Khayyam the astronomer has been mistaken for Khayyam the poet. Ṭabāṭabā'ī argues that the discrepancy between the theistic nature of Khayyam's thought as reflected in his philosophical treatises and the agnostic-hedonist tendencies presented in his *Ruba'iyyat* clearly indicates that these works belong to different people. Ṭabāṭabā'ī offers extensive evidence in this regard both textually and circumstantially. This view has gained some strength in recent years,[6] as we have come to learn more about the other Khayyams. For instance, there was Abū Ṣālih Khalifah Khayyam who hailed from Bukhārā which, at the time, was part of Khūrāsān; and the second one was Muḥammad ibn 'Alī al-Khayyāmī al-Irāqī from Māzandarān near the Caspian Sea. Is it not possible that their poems were misidentified with the works of Omar Khayyam? In 867 AH/1476 CE, Yār Aḥmad Rashīdī Tabrizī edited over six hundred quatrains, which may have been from all these Khayyams, and titled it the *Tarabkhānah*, only adding confusion to the whole field of Khayyamian studies.

There is another argument that favors this position. In the annals of the Islamic literary genre, there is *no one* else who so openly criticized all aspects of religion and yet lived to be as old as Khayyam! This makes Khayyam almost a unique figure, too good to be true. It is not the case that he lived in a more liberal era of Islamic history, nor did he live in a remote part of the Islamic world. If anything, he lived under the watchful eyes of ultra-orthodox jurists, such as Abū Ḥāmid Ghazzālī who in the early years of his life had no appreciation for Sufism. The question therefore is, "If Khayyam did write the *Ruba'iyyat*, how did he get away with it?"

Perhaps with the exception of Abu'l- 'Alā' al-Ma'arrī, I know of no other poet who survived while preaching skepticism, agnosticism and atheism and yet died of natural causes. The miraculous survival and thriving of Omar Khayyam does strengthen the theory that perhaps there were several other Khayyams, though one of whom at least was a poet.

This argument, as I shall demonstrate, is also fallacious, not because it is propagated by only a very small minority of scholars, but because of the overwhelming number of biographers who have identified Khayyam the astronomer-mathematician as the one who was the author of at least some of the *Ruba'iyyat*.

There is an Arabic proverb which says, "Arabs do not forgive their wives or their horses, but they forgive the poets" which might well have been true in this case. Poetic license may well have saved him from the wrath of the orthodox elements.

KHAYYAM THE SUFI

There are those who have tried to resolve the apparent agnosticism of Khayyam as it appears in his *Ruba'iyyat* by interpreting the poetry within a Sufi context. Accordingly, Khayyam was a mystic who relied heavily on allegory, metaphor and symbolism; and like so many other great Sufi masters, if the esoteric symbolism of his *Ruba'iyyat* is understood properly, a different Khayyam emerges whose mastery of gnosis and esotericism will only dazzle the intellect of those who are familiar with the spiritual tradition of Sufism.

There is some truth to this theory since Khayyam himself unequivocally states in his work, *On the Knowledge Of the Principals of Existence*,

> The Sufis are those who do not seek knowledge intellectually or discursively but by the cleansing of their inner self and purgation of their morals have cleansed their rational soul from the impurities of nature and the corporeal body. When that substance [the soul] is purified and becomes a reflection of the spiritual world, the *forms* in that status are truly unveiled without any doubt or ambiguity. *This path is the best of them all.*[7]

Despite Khayyam's clear endorsement of the Sufi path, seeing him only as a Sufi does a great disservice to the field of Khayyamian studies and is an impediment to allowing a more inclusive picture of this giant figure to emerge. Based on the existing evidence, Khayyam did not have a spiritual master or belong to a Sufi order, nor have any of his biographers ever reported his Sufi affiliation. It is reasonable to conclude therefore that even if he had Sufi tendencies, he was not a practicing Sufi. Finally, his statement in which he considers himself to be a student of Avicenna, and his philosophical treatises written in the Peripatetic style, do not allow us to place him squarely within the Sufi camp. Clearly, he was familiar with Sufism and had esoteric tendencies, but one has to read *into* his *Ruba'iyyat* extensively , as some of the medieval and modern scholars have, in order to see him only as a Sufi. In either case, it is safe to assume that Khayyam was not a Sufi as Ḥallāj, Rūmī, or even Aḥmad Ghazzālī were.

There might be a cultural and even political reason for wanting to see the *Ruba'iyyat* in their esoteric aspects only. But the fact remains that, despite the wide spectrum of Persian and Islamic intellectual thought – even in their most tolerant forms – there is no room for doubt in the modern sense as such, much less a place for an agnostic or perhaps even an atheist perspective. The message of hedonism is equally unacceptable, for it goes against the very grain of the Islamic theocentric worldview. Therefore, it has always been a challenge where to place Khayyam in the annals of the Islamic intellectual and literary tradition in such a way that one of the cultural heroes of Iran can be rescued from the charges of heresy. It is in this context that it becomes hard to resist the project of the "Suficization" of Khayyam, a perspective which allows one to interpret his *Ruba'iyyat* in order to reveal his "true message," which happens to be in complete conformity with the esoteric teachings of Islam.

KHAYYAM THE DEVOUT MUSLIM

The other interpretation which has also tried to rescue Khayyam and repair his image and reputation from heresy, is the more orthodox view which attempts to completely exonerate him from even writing the *Ruba'iyyat*. There are those who have made an attempt to distinguish the pious Omar Khayyam from other heretical poets by the same name and, therefore, distanced our faithful mathematician-astronomer from those who attributed the so-called *Ruba'iyyat* to him. Somehow, the advocates of this project see this endeavor as another way to save one of the cultural heroes of Persians and to preserve the purity of Khayyam's faith, but in reality, they only perpetuate further misunderstanding of a major thinker whose complex views transcend faith and reason, a figure who cannot be placed in a simple model of an "either /or" dichotomy. This view, on which I will elaborate, is simply fallacious and based on a one-dimensional approach to the ideas of a figure who was a one-man university.

KHAYYAM THE PERSIAN NATIONALIST

A discussion concerning Khayyam would not be complete without reference to his alleged membership in the Persian nationalist movement known as *Shu'ubiyyah*. Khayyam is said to have been a member of the disenchanted Persian intelligentsia who were deeply troubled by the fact that non-Persian rulers governed Persia for much of its history since the invasion of the Arabs in the first/seventh century, foreigners who were not sophisticated enough to appreciate the Persian cultural heritage. This situation continued until Khayyam's own time when the Turkish Seljuq dynasty took over the reign of power in Persia. Khayyam, along with many other significant Persian intellectuals such as the poet Ferdawsī, is said to have participated in the revival of the authentic Persian intellectual tradition.

This interpretation sees the *Ruba'iyyat* as a demythologization of the central tenets of the Islamic faith and the central themes upon which the Semitic religions are based. Khayyam not only questions central tenets of Islam such as angels, breaking the religious law, life after death and the purpose of creation, but he does so in a cynical way[8] which is indicative of his nationalistic agenda.

This modern interpretation is as cynical as some of Khayyam's *Ruba'iyyat* and is yet another symptom of reading Khayyam selectively. There is no question that Khayyam was a proud Persian, well aware of the major intellectual and cultural contributions of his civilization, as well as a practicing Muslim; but attributing nationalism in the modern sense of the word to a medieval figure misses the point completely. Omar Khayyam was too profound a thinker and too engaged with the existential riddles of life to entertain nationalism, an implied form of racism. He was the embodiment of a Persian-Muslim, proud and aware of his ancient heritage as is evident in his attempt to keep the Pahlavī names of the months in his new calendar. He was also a believer as is clearly evident in his philosophical writings and yet he maintained a sense of rebellion against orthodoxy, a salient feature of much of Persian intellectual and mystical literature.

KHAYYAM THE WISE SAGE

It is my argument throughout this work that the legendary Khayyam was a philosopher-sage (*ḥakīm*), a spiritual-pragmatist of the highest stature who, like some of his predecessors such as Fārābī and Avicenna, provided us with the leaven of his wisdom. His mature pen, powerful intellect and relentless quest for answers to philosophical and existential questions produced a person whose nectar of wisdom exudes from every fiber of his being both poetically and philosophically.

Khayyam was not a practicing Sufi, though he was not opposed to it; he was not an orthodox Muslim, though he practiced Islam and upheld the religious law (*sharīʿah*) in his personal life; nor was he only a scientist like Birūnī and Khwārazmī since he remained attentive to so many other domains of knowledge. Omar Khayyam was an exemplar of the best gift man possesses – *nous* (intellect) – that he applied so skillfully throughout his scientific works. At the same time, he demonstrated the application of *sophia* (wisdom) not just in its narrow rational sense but as it pertains to life itself and the existential dilemmas that humans face. Khayyam was a philosopher and his *Rubaʿiyyat* were a philosophical commentary upon life and the human condition. He was a man who did not see questioning and quandary as the opposite of faith, but rather as part of the process of being human, an endless process of intellection between the two existential poles of man's life, reason and faith.

Despite all the available textual and biographical sources, a decisive and definite response to the question of and the search for the "real historical Khayyam" is neither possible nor prudent for our purposes. To begin with, we are operating on the basis of an insufficient amount of evidence with regard to much of what is said about Khayyam, not to mention contradictory accounts about him. I am of the opinion that on the basis of the existing evidence, much of which is based on a number of inauthentic poems attributed to Khayyam, one cannot establish with certainty the exact character and thought of the "historical Khayyam." What can be said, however, is that an "either/or" model as a way of approaching Khayyam – whether as an agnostic-hedonist, a devout Muslim or a grand Sufi master – is a fallacious perspective[9] which can be refuted.

Khayyamian studies have become a victim of Victorian romanticism on the one hand and the Persian religious and cultural lenses in which one is either a faithful Muslim or an infidel on the other. The genius of Khayyam's unique intellect and multidimensional personality is simply too complex to fit into an "either /or" model or any other pre-fabricated intellectual structure. It is precisely this multifaceted nature of Khayyam that has allowed so many people to claim him as their own hero; but the reality – even if it means taking the cultural hero of Persians away from them – is that he may have been *all* that is said about him. Perhaps, at times, he was an agnostic and at other times a man of faith, and yet there were moments when he transcended both faith and reason. Khayyam is certainly not the first case of a perplexed thinker who was tormented as he wrestled with the enduring questions of an ultimate existential nature. Naturally, his poetic form of expression has been seen by some as a theology of protest, a loud bemoaning of his bewilderment, and for others as the outer shell of a deeper hidden meaning. An American follower of Khayyam, J. Brigham, reminds us, "To one, he is little more than a tavern drunk; to another, he is a poet whose soul is imbued with Epicurean philosophy; to another still, he is a pagan agnostic peering through the mist in a vain search for God; to still another, he is like the distracted one who in anguish cried out, 'Lord, I believe, help thou mine unbelief!' "[10]

Finally, there is the thorny question regarding the authenticity of Khayyam's poetry, a subject of considerable debate among the scholars of Khayyam and Persian literature in general. As I will discuss in Chapter Four, despite all the various methods and techniques developed by scholars, it is virtually impossible to distinguish the authentic poems from the inauthentic ones. Whereas ideally it would have been prudent to have access to his "real" *Ruba'iyyat*, I am of the opinion that by focusing on the question of authenticity, we miss the Khayyamian message which lies at the heart of the *Ruba'iyyat*. The late Henry Corbin, one of the most eminent Western scholars of Islam, in a conversation with the late great Shi'ite scholar, 'Allāmah Ṭabāṭabā'ī, posed a question concerning the authenticity of the authorship of Imām 'Alī's work, *The Path of Eloquence*. 'Allāmah responded by saying "he who has written *The Path of Eloquence* 'is' for us 'Alī."[11] I like to adopt this rather phenomenological approach and suggest that he who has composed the *Ruba'iyyat* is for us Khayyam.

The fact remains that we have a large number of quatrains that are attributed to a man called Omar Khayyam. We can indulge ourselves in endless discussions about the authenticity of these poems or we can stand back and look at what is before us. Those who are obsessed with the historical-textual methodology and see some value in finding the "real Khayyam" will undoubtedly be frustrated with the present work since it begins with the following questions: if there were to be an Omar Khayyam who was simultaneously the author of the scientific treatises and much of the *Ruba'iyyat*, what type of a person would he have been? Is a reconstruction of this half-mythical half-real person possible based on *all* the available evidence? Is an attempt to read between the lines in order to infer some of the original fragrance of Khayyamian thought possible, given the fact that many of the *Ruba'iyyat* are not his? Finally, can we postulate that even though much of the *Ruba'iyyat* we use in this work are not Khayyam's, do they not reveal *something* about the spirit of the "real Khayyam"? While I think it is possible and prudent to do this, one may not lay an absolute claim to such findings.

A.E. Christensen, the eminent Danish scholar of Khayyam, in a treatise he gave to V. Rozen, a distinuished Khayyam scholar, mentions that within 350 years after Khayyam's death, the authentic and inauthentic *Ruba'iyyat* were inseparable. So intertwined had they become that distinguishing them remains impossible.[12]

The search for the historical Khayyam in light of the existing evidence therefore is a futile attempt that should be abandoned in favor of a more befitting and useful model which, if adopted adequately, addresses the question – not who Khayyam was, but what is the message of the existing *Ruba'iyyat*? The above scheme suspends the search for the messenger in order to open the door for the message and is as a model which is fitting for our mysterious poet. This model, often referred to as a phenomenological approach, abandons the search for the "real historical Khayyam" and puts the emphasis on the immediate encounter between what is available, which are the *Ruba'iyyat* and their readers throughout the ages. It is true that there are some poems that are truly Khayyam's, while there are others, the numbers of which add up to several hundred, which are clearly inauthentic. Despite this, even some of the *Ruba'iyyat* that are widely regarded to be inauthentic, bear a resemblance to the so-called authentic ones both in form and content. Even though most of these poems are clearly later developments and are attributed to him, the "family resemblance" among them allows us to conclude the following:

1. Khayyam represents a school of thought, a *weltanschauung*, a voice of protest against what he regarded to be a fundamentally unjust world. Many people found in him a voice they needed to hear and, centuries after he had died, he became a vehicle for those who were experiencing the same trials and tribulations as Khayyam combined with a fear of persecution.

2. More than a person, Khayyam is the representative of a particular world-view which traditionally has not had a prominent place in the Islamic religious universe. Theodicy was put to rest in the early period of the Islamic theological debate and even to raise the question of why evil exists is often seen as a sign of weakness in faith. Khayyam had no problem raising and pondering the issue[13] using his poetic license.

Therefore I suggest that we focus on the "Khayyamian school of thought" rather than Khayyam the person, thereby making the question of who was the real Khayyam as well as the authenticity of his poems somewhat irrelevant to the message of this school of thought attributed to Khayyam. Furthermore, the question of whether there were several Khayyams or not becomes equally irrelevant to our message-based inquiry. Even if we have misidentified Omar Khayyam with a poet by the name of 'Alī Khayyāmī, as some have suggested, we are still left with a particular world-view that is reflected in the *Ruba'iyyat* which we can identify with the Khayyamian school of thought.

Finally, relying on a combination of historical textual methods of criticism where possible, and a phenomenological one where necessary, a more balanced view of the Khayyamian message can be presented without involving the reader in the long and arduous scholarly debate concerning such open questions as those regarding the authenticity of Khayyam and his own identity. For the same reason,

The tomb of Omar Khayyam in Nayshābūr.

I have avoided introducing a discussion concerning different editions of the *Ruba'iyyat* scattered throughout the libraries of Iran and Western countries. My emphasis has been to produce a work that introduces for the first time a comprehensive picture of a historical figure who has come to be known as Omar Khayyam.

Having said the above, since our project here is to reconstruct the life and thought of Omar Khayyam *as much as* possible, I have relied on a two-fold methodology to elaborate upon the mission impossible. First, I have accepted the 178 *Ruba'iyyat* which the eminent and life-long scholar of Khayyam, Muḥammad 'Alī Furūghī has accepted to be authentic. Having compared and contrasted various editions and versions of the *Ruba'iyyat* and their place in the early and later sources, Furūghī considers a number of them to be "acceptable" realizing that ultimately, in the absence of concrete evidence, one can not be certain regarding the authenticity of any of the *Ruba'iyyat.* It is imperative to realize that in analyzing and interpreting Khayyam's thought in this work, I have first and foremost made use of Furūghī's accepted *Ruba'iyyat.* Second, where and when I have used other *Ruba'iyyat* to shed light on *Khayyam's* thought, I have made sure their content is consistent with and supportive of Furūghī's version. I have avoided using those versions of the *Ruba'iyyat* whose theme and message radically clashes with the content of Furūghī's *Ruba'iyyat*, as well as other acceptable quatrains by such scholars as Dashtī, Malik and Foulādvand.

Despite taking such care in using the *Ruba'iyyat*, the reader is encouraged to focus on the Khayyamian school of thought as representative of a world-view rather than an individual. The fact that there are hundreds of quatrains which have been attributed to Khayyam throughout the centuries, in my view, is not a liability but an asset. Khayyam had become the voice of many voiceless poets who, fearing persecution, used him as a shield, a veil; those poets who shared Khayyam's views found him to be a suitable vehicle in whom they could take refuge. Our Khayyam therefore, should not be viewed only as a historical figure but also as a school of thought which, as it will be demonstrated, proclaims the irreconcilability of faith and reason, respecting and questioning both simultaneously. This unique figure makes a sincere attempt not to reconcile faith and reason but to acknowledge these two irreconcilable poles of human existence, the eternal struggle between the heart and the mind. The question for him was not how these two discourses can be reconciled but how one can live amidst such a tension, while not giving in to easy pre-fabricated answers or falling into nihilism and heresy.

For the purposes of this study, I have avoided extensive textual analysis and comparison of different editions of the *Ruba'iyyat.* Lengthy discussions concerning the question of the authenticity of the quatrains and the type of discussions that are more prevalent in literary circles have been kept to a minimum.

Even though this book is written for a wide readership, some chapters might be of interest to the specialist only. I highly recommend that readers begin the text by reading the quatrains (*Ruba'iyyat*) first; these poems included in Appendix B constitute the heart and soul of the Khayyamian message. Chapter Six and the six translations of Khayyam's philosophical treatises included in Appendix A contain highly technical language and require some familiarity with Aristotelian philosophy.

All the translations are mine unless otherwise stated and, in some cases where I have adopted other translations, they have been modified for accuracy and duly noted. Diacritic marks have not been placed on certain words such as "Omar Khayyam" which are repeated throughout the work and others, such as "Sufi," which have entered into the English language.

Mehdi Aminrazavi
Norūz 1383/501 March 2004

1

Khayyam's Life and Works

Of knowledge naught remained I did not know,
Of secrets, scarcely any, high or low;
All day and night for three score and twelve years,
I pondered, just to learn that naught I know.[1]

OMAR KHAYYAM'S LIFE

Birth and family

His full name was Abu'l Fatḥ Omar ibn Ibrāhīm Khayyam, born in the district of Shādyakh of the old city of Nayshābūr in the province of Khūrāsān in the Eastern part of Iran sometime around 439 AH/1048 CE,[2] and he died there between 515 and 520/1124 and 1129. The precise date of his death is a mystery, especially in light of the fact that upon his death, Khayyam was a famous man. There are reasons to believe that he died in or before 515/1124,[3] but most contemporary scholars seem to think that 517/1126 is a more likely date. Some have reported the place of his birth to have been Isterābād and others, Lawkar; but Bayhaqī, his contemporary biographer who actually met him, states that his forefathers all came from Nayshābūr.[4]

Student years and teachers

The title "Khayyam" – meaning "tent maker" – in all likelihood was inherited from his father, Ibrāhīm, an illiterate tent maker who realized the keen intelligence of his young son Omar and the need for him to study under the great masters of his time.

Raḥīm R. Malik in his work[5] mentions that Khayyam's father may have been a convert, presumably from the Zoroastrian religion to Sunni Islam, and so Khayyam was a first generation Muslim. Malik also claims that because Khayyam was referred to by so many as "Abu'l-Fatḥ" (father of Fatḥ) he must have had a son by that name. Neither of these two claims have been substantiated by other biographers of Khayyam.

Being uncertain if the masters would agree to tutor the son of a poor tent maker, Ibrāhīm asked the Imām of the Mosque, Mawlānā Qāḍī Muḥammad, to accept his son as his student. He arranged a meeting in which the master asked the young Omar a few questions concerning religious sciences, and it did not take much for Qāḍī Muḥammad to realize how gifted this child was since Omar had memorized much of the Qur'an already. Legend has it that Omar asked the master why every chapter in the Qur'an begins with the verse, "In the Name of God, Most Merciful, Most compassionate" to which Qāḍī replied that the Qur'an is the word of God and every chapter must begin accordingly. Young Omar then asked, "Why does Allah need to begin every chapter by calling upon his own name and whether this implies a duality?" The story may well be part of the cult of personality which has developed around this legendary figure. Omar Khayyam studied Qur'anic sciences, Arabic grammar, literature and other introductory religious sciences, and he quickly learned what Qāḍī Muḥammad could teach him. The teacher then asked Omar to continue his studies with a different master,[6] Khāwjah Abu'l-Ḥasan al-Anbārī. Under the direction of his new teacher, Omar studied various branches of mathematics, astronomy and traditional cosmological doctrines, in particular, the major work of Ptolemy, *Almageste* (*Majisṭā*). As is indicated in the *Tatimmah ṣiwān al-ḥikmah*, "Abu'l-Ḥasan al-Anbārī al-Ḥakīm: Despite his knowledge of discursive sciences, he was learned in geometry and the philosopher (*ḥakīm*) Omar ibn Khayyam was benefiting from him and learned *Almageste* from him."[7]

Khayyam, who was quiet and reserved with a humble character and an eagerness with which he pursued his advanced studies, was quickly recognized as the most gifted student of Khāwjah. Soon Omar was ready to study with the well-known master, Imām Muwaffaq Nayshābūrī, who taught only the best of the best. He was somewhat of a court philosopher who tutored the children of the nobility. Once again, in a meeting between them, Omar had convinced the new master of his worthiness to study with him. With Imām Muwaffaq, Khayyam studied advanced Qur'anic studies and jurisprudence but did not show great interest for the latter area of study. Finally, Omar studied philosophy, with Shaykh Muḥammad Manṣūr, under whose direction he became familiar with the writings of Avicenna, particularly the *Ishārāt*, a work which he studied until the last day of his life.

Khayyam himself refers to Avicenna as his master and some have interpreted this to mean he studied with Avicenna, which is almost an impossibility. Khayyam wrote one of his philosophical treatises, *Being and Necessity*, when he was in Iṣfahān in response to a series of questions that 'Abū Naṣr ibn 'Abd al-Raḥīm Nasawī, one of the students of Avicenna, had posed to him. In this treatise, he states:

> Know that this problem is one of the (philosophical) complexities which most people are bewildered by ... Perhaps I and my teacher, the noblest of the later (*ḥakīms*), Shaykh al-Ra'is, Abū 'Alī Ḥusayīn ibn 'Abdallāh Bukhārī [Ibn Sīnā], have reflected upon this particular problem.[8]

It is not clear when and where Khayyam could have been Avicenna's student because Khayyam would have to have been born much earlier if he were to have met Avicenna. It is entirely possible that he studied with Bahmanyār, the famous pupil of Avicenna. Except for a brief reference by Niẓāmī 'Aruḍī Samarqandī, who tells us that Avicenna went to Nayshābūr, there is no evidence of this.[9] In either case, Khayyam's respect and reverence for Avicenna remained categorical until the last day of his life when he was allegedly reading the *Ishārāt* just hours before he died. This is also indicated in his spirited conversation with 'Alā' al-Dawlah, the governor of Ray,[10] who was a follower of Abu'l Barakāt al-Baghdādī. 'Alā' al-Dawlah asked Khayyam what he thought about Abu'l Barakāt's criticisms of Avicenna, to which he replied, "Abu'l Barakāt did not even understand Avicenna, much less to criticize him." The conversation which followed and Khayyam's passionate defense of Avicenna clearly indicate that he was an avid supporter of Avicennian philosophy.[11]

It is entirely possible that he studied with Bahmanyār, or at least met him in Isfahān during his stay in that city. There are several references to this possibility. Ṣafadī in *al-wafī bi'l-wafiyāt*[12] and Qoṭb al-Dīn Maḥmūd Shirāzī in *Tuḥfat al-shāhiyyah*,[13] mention that Khayyam and Lawkarī, a colleague and classmate of Khayyam, were students of Bahmanyār.

The other major figure with whom Omar may have studied was the famous theologian and teacher of Abū Ḥāmid Ghazzālī, Imām al-Ḥaramayīn Juwaynī who taught in Nayshābūr. If this were true, Khayyam would have been a fellow classmate of Ghazzālī, a point none of his biographers have mentioned. However, given Juwaynī's fame, it is hard to imagine that Khayyam would not have benefited from him and his scholarly circle in Nayshābūr.

Khayyam the teacher and his students

Khayyam soon established himself as a one-man university whose fame went far and wide. He has been referred to with honorary titles such as "Ḥujjat al-Ḥaqq" (The Evidence of Truth), "Ghiyāth al-Dīn" (The Patron of Faith) and "Imām," all of them indicative of the respect he had in the community and the recognition of him as a religious authority.

He wrote very little, but what he wrote was of great significance. He accepted few students, but was scrupulous in his teaching. It is said that once Ghazzālī asked Khayyam a question concerning geometry in the morning, and Khayyam elaborated on the question until Ghazzālī reminded him that it was time for the noon prayer. Khayyam did not participate much in the scholarly debates and circles of Nayshābūr, which by this time had become one of the greatest centers of learning in the Islamic world. He is said to have been shy and sensitive, with a bad temper, an impatient man with little interest in sharing his knowledge with others. Some have attributed this lack of interest in teaching to a desire not to be intellectually conspicuous. There are two accounts concerning his remarkable memory, from two trips, one to Balkh and the other to Iṣfahān. In both instances, he came upon a book in which he was keenly interested, and the owners only allowed him to read it, but not to make a copy of it. In each case, Khayyam read the book carefully, and upon his return to Nayshābūr, dictated it to a student. Later his dictated version was compared with the original, revealing almost a perfect match.

In another story, Khayyam traveled to Balkh in search of books; in particular, he wanted to find a copy of Apollonius of Perge's *The Book of Conics*. On the way, he arrived at a village that had been swarmed by birds who ate the crops and left their waste everywhere. Khayyam was asked to assist the villagers whom he asked to make two large, clay hawks which they placed in strategic locations with a number of dead birds surrounding them. The birds migrated from the village at once.

Whereas the authenticity of these stories can always be questioned, they do bear testament to the power of his intellect as perceived by his students and the people. These are stories which no doubt have contributed to the creation of a legendary figure. The unverifiable nature of these stories also makes scholarship about him rather difficult since one can neither simply dismiss all of them as false nor can one verify their sources.

Despite his withdrawn and somewhat monastic existence, Khayyam associated with a number of well-known scholars and had a few exceptional students, among whom were Aḥmad al-Ma'murī al-Bayhaqī, Muḥammad Ilāqī, Imām Muḥammad Baghdādī, (who also became his son-in-law), Niẓāmī 'Aruḍī Samarqandī (who benefited from Khayyam's presence though he was not trained by him), Abu'l-Ma'ālī 'Abdallāh ibn Muḥammad al-Miyānjī (also known as 'Ayn al-Qoḍāt Hamadānī),[14] and Muḥammad Hijāzī Qā'nī. Also, one can mention 'Abd al-Rafi' Hirawī who may have been the author of *Norūz nāmah*, a treatise usually attributed to Khayyam himself. From the figures mentioned above who may have studied with Khayyam, 'Ayn al-Qoḍāt Hamadānī is the least likely of them.[15] There are no references made to either figure in their works. Hamid Dabashi in his major work on 'Ayn al-Qoḍāt Hamadānī interprets their association as "the metanarrative of Persian Sufism,"[16] arguing their association is somewhat wishful thinking that "fits" well among those who like to see Khayyam as a Sufi.

The encounter of Khayyam with other masters

While scholars in Nayshābūr were abundant,[17] Khayyam associated with only a few of them, the most famous of whom were the poet Sanā'ī, the great theologian Zamakhsharī, Maymūn ibn Najīb and Imām Muẓaffar Isfizārī with whom he collaborated to make a new calendar, and finally the most famous of them all, Abū Ḥāmid Ghazzālī with whom he had a difficult relationship.

As I will investigate in the forthcoming chapters, Ghazzālī's relationship with Khayyam reveals much about the intellectual milieu of the time and the rise of dogmatic theology against which perhaps Khayyam was reacting. It is said that Ghazzālī studied with Khayyam for a number of years, but due to the orthodox and austere reputation of Ghazzālī and the controversial views of Khayyam, Ghazzālī went to Khayyam's home early in the morning before anyone would see him. Khayyam, intending to reveal Ghazzālī's hypocrisy, asked a man with a drum to stand on the rooftop and to beat on it when Khayyam gave the sign. One day upon Ghazzālī's departure, Khayyam signaled the man to beat on his drum whereby people gathered to see that Ghazzālī, who apparently questioned Khayyam's faith privately, was nevertheless studying with him.[18] Perhaps Ghazzālī's *The Incoherence of the Philosophers* (*Tahāfat al-falāsifah*) was written at least partially in response to Khayyam's philosophical perspective.

The other master with whom Khayyam had an encounter was the famous literary figure Sanā'ī. Shortly before Khayyam's major trip to Iṣfahān in 467/1076, Sanā'ī came to visit Khayyam in Nayshābūr.

The discussion concerning literature, philosophy and subjects of mutual interest continued for a while and created a profound friendship between the two giants, one a literary genius and the other a philosopher-scientist. While in Nayshābūr, some money was stolen from a money exchanger, and the suspect claimed that Sanā'ī's servant had stolen the money. The servant, who was arrested and mistreated, had expected the master to intervene on his behalf; but Sanā'ī decided to leave Nayshābūr. Disappointed with his master's lack of interest in saving him, the servant said that he had given the money to Sanā'ī who was on his way back to Herat. Upon receiving a letter from the money exchanger asking for the return of his money, Sanā'ī was greatly saddened. He wrote a letter to Khayyam which is regarded as one of the most sublime examples of Persian literature.[19] In it, he asked him to intervene on his behalf and to vouch for his innocence. Khayyam resolved the matter skillfully.

A careful analysis of the content and the language of the letter is indicative of Khayyam's stature and the respect he enjoyed in the community as well as the sphere of his influence. Clearly, he must have been a well-known figure in good standing with the authorities. If doubts concerning Khayyam's faith were even partially an issue, Khayyam would not have enjoyed the kind of respect and power that Sanā'ī attributes to him in his letter.

Finally, there is the other unlikely story concerning Khayyam mentioned in the *Tarabkhāneh*, which addresses an encounter between him and the famous Ismā'īlī poet-philosopher, Nāṣir Khusraw. Allegedly, Nāṣir Khusraw sent a copy of his treatise, *Rawshanā'ī nāmah*, to Khayyam who was pleased by it. Tabrizī gives the following account of this story:

> Sayyid Nāṣir Khusraw, may paradise be his, composed the *Rawshanā'ī nāmah* and sent it to *ḥakīm* [Khayyam] for review. He used his withdrawn nature as an excuse [not to comment upon it] and he [Nāṣir Khusraw] requested [Khayyam] for a long poem[20] or at least a quatrain since the eloquence of quatrain is the completion of sublimity. He [Khayyam] composed a few *Ruba'iyyat* and them sent to him and gave the excuse that since eternity it was my destiny to write these words, I had no choice in the matter.[21]

When Nāṣir Khusraw returned from his numerous trips to Egypt, he spent a few years as an itinerant preacher in Khurāsān before he was off on his exile and it is almost certain that he spent some time in Nayshābūr. Nāṣir Khusraw considered himself qualified enough in mathematics to write a book about it and was already famous for his poetry. Nāṣir Khusraw tells us that he wrote the book "even though there is no one around who understands mathematics. I have written this for scholars of the future." So whether Nāṣir Khusraw would have sent his philosophical work *Rawshanā'ī nāmah* (also known as *Shish faṣl*) to the younger astronomer Omar Khayyam for review and comments, remains to be verified. This story, however, is not corroborated by other biographers of Khayyam[22] and is highly dubious.

The Three Musketeers and The Sweet Tale of a Friendship

Few stories have captured the imagination of Persians more than the friendship that allegedly existed between Omar Khayyam, Ḥasan Ṭūsī (who was later given the title "Niẓām al-Mulk," the Order of Nation, and became the Chamberlain of the Seljuq court) and Ḥasan Ṣabbāḥ (the founder of the order of assassins). This story, too, is highly unlikely since, on careful examination of the dates and the personalities involved, such a friendship as stipulated in the story is unlikely.[23]

This story of friendship may have been based on several similar stories. In *Mu'jam al-'udabā'*, Yāqut Ḥamawī describes the famous poet, Bākhizrī, reporting that the *vizir* al-Kondorī and Bākhizrī were both students of Imām al-Muwaffaq. In 434/1043, al-Kundurī and Niẓām al-Mulk were both *vizirs* of Sulṭān Alp Arslān, and Khayyam and Bākhizrī were both poets. Another similar story takes place during the reign of Manṣur when several men came to be known as the "companions of the fig." A.M. 'Abdus al-Jahshiyarī in *Kitāb al-wuzarā'* tells us that 'Abidallāh Nu'mān, 'Abd al-Mālik ibn Ḥamīd and two other men made a vow under a fig tree to assist one another in political and administrative matters if any of them achieved a high status in the government.[24] As it turned out, 'Abd al-Mālik became the secretary of the Sulṭān and kept his promise by appointing his friends to high offices.

The earliest source where an account of Khayyam's friendship with Ṭūsī and Ṣabbāh can be found is in Rashīd al-Dīn Faḍlallāh's *Jāmi' al-tawārikh*. According to this account of the story, Khayyam, Niẓām al-Mulk and Ḥasan Ṣabbāh were all classmates in Nayshābūr studying with Imām Muwaffaq. Khayyam was more reserved, an introvert whose life was completely dedicated to academic inquiries and the pursuit of knowledge. Ḥasan, a Shi'ite, claimed to be an Arab from the tribe of Ṣabbāh Ḥumayrī, but is believed to have been from the city of Ray near today's Tehran. Unlike Khayyam, he was more interested in socio-political issues. There was also Ḥasan Ṭūsī, the son of a prominent government official who knew at an early age that he was destined to be a politician. The three boys made a vow that whoever came to a position of power and was aggrandized should help the other two; as it turned out, all three became prominent in their respective fields. Khayyam became a well-known scholar whose advice was sought by various sulṭāns. Niẓām al-Mulk became the grand vizir of the King. Ḥasan Ṣabbāh became a greatly feared revolutionary bent on overthrowing the King and ameliorating the conditions of life. As fate had it, Ḥasan Ṣabbāh may have had something to do with the murdering of Niẓām al-Mulk, his alleged friend from his school years. In the *Jāmi' al-tawārikh*, Rashīd al-Dīn Faḍlallāh describes their friendship:

> Our master [Ḥasan Ṣabbāh] and Omar Khayyam and Niẓām al-Mulk were close companions. As it is the habit of the time of youth and tradition of children, they adhered to the principle of friendship, companionship until they became blood brothers and promised that whoever among us achieves a great status and exalted rank, should assist and strengthen others. As is written and stated in the history of the dynasty of the Seljuqs, it happened that Niẓām al-Mulk became the grand *vizir*.
>
> Omar Khayyam came to him [Niẓām al-Mulk] and reminded him of the promise of childhood and he recognized and honored the past and said, "The governorship of Nayshābūr and its vicinities is yours." Omar Khayyam who was a great *ḥakīm*, learned and

rational minded, said "I have no ambition for ruling and commanding the people to do what is right. By way of patronage, assign a stipend for me." Niẓām al-Mulk assigned ten-thousand Dinārs [for him] from the taxes of Nayshābūr to be given to him without any shortcoming or discriminatory consideration.[25]

Some of the Europeans such as Edward FitzGerald, who mentioned the story in the introduction to his translation of Khayyam's *Ruba'iyyat*, and many who took this story to be true, contributed to make this myth into a reality in the West. A thorough examination of the dates in this regard, however, clearly indicates that such a friendship could not have been the case though these three men may have met on different occasions.

Some have argued that a possible motive for creating this story may well have been Persian nationalism, and that these three men may have been members of a Persian nationalistic movement known as *Shu'ubiyyah*. Persians who had come under the domination of Arabs first and then a succession of non-Persian dynasties had reacted to their domination by producing a literary, intellectual and political movement to combat foreign domination. Politically, the Turkish Seljuqs were seen by Persians as "foreigners" who had taken over the country, and notable figures such as Khayyam and his friends may have been members of this movement. Niẓām al-Mulk may have decided to work from within the system to increase the influence of Persians, while Ḥasan Ṣabbāh may have engaged in an arms struggle against the central government. Khayyam simply refused to cooperate fully with them and preferred not to represent the foreign rulers in an official capacity.

Journeys to Iṣfahān and Ray

One of the major events of Omar Khayyam's life was his trip to Iṣfahān at the invitation of his friend, Niẓām al-Mulk. In 455/1064, Tughrul the Seljūq Sulṭān died and was succeeded by Alp Arslān who replaced the grand vizier, 'Amid al-Mulk Kondorī, with Ḥasan Ṭūsī, known as Niẓām al-Mulk. Niẓām al-Mulk had established throughout the Islamic world a series of prestigious schools named

Niẓāmiyyah, the most famous of which were in Baghdād, Iṣfahān and Nayshābūr and Khayyam must have been eager to visit the scholars of the *Niẓāmiyyah* in Iṣfahān.

Following Niẓām al-Mulk's appointment, Khayyam, whose fame as a mathematician and astronomer had spread widely, decided to accept an invitation from a group of scientists in the city of Ray and to travel to this thriving center of learning. He was not in Ray for long before he received an invitation from Niẓām al-Mulk, who invited him to go to Iṣfahān, the capital of the Seljuqs. Khayyam and his entourage arrived in Iṣfahān in 467/1076 where they found themselves amidst opulent palaces, the ceremonies of the imperial court and a luxurious life to which they were unaccustomed. Khayyam preferred solitude to crowds, simplicity to luxury and, with his background of having come from a poor family, must have felt uncomfortable in Iṣfahān; but his friend, Niẓām al-Mulk, saw to it that he was provided for. While in Iṣfahān, Khayyam benefited from the rich libraries of the royal court of Seljuqs which offered among other treasures the writings of Euclid.

Khayyam had extensive discussions with Niẓām al-Mulk concerning philosophy, literature, politics and perhaps even Ḥasan Ṣabbāh, who by now was a legendary figure known for his piety and feared by the authorities. Niẓām al-Mulk, whose patronage of the learned was well-known, extended the same courtesy to Khayyam by granting him the estate of Shādyākh in Nayshābūr, Khayyam's favorite neighborhood, with an annual stipend of 10,000 Dinār.

When the Sulṭān and Niẓām al-Mulk had to leave Iṣfahān for matters pertaining to the state, Khayyam stayed on until he decided to return home to Khurāsān in 470/1079. Perhaps Khayyam had sensed some tension at the court exacerbated by the riots in various parts of the country. In addition, there may have been some rivalry between Khayyam and other learned scholars.

A few months later Sulṭān Alp Arslān was assassinated, and his son, Jalāl al-Dīn Malik Shāh, came to the throne. The young king wanted to commemorate his inauguration every year but had difficulty determining an exact date. In 467/1076, Niẓām al-Mulk arranged a meeting between Khayyam and the new Sulṭān,

Malik Shāh, in the city of Marv where Khayyam was commissioned to work on a new calendar. Khayyam requested several assistants among whom were the philosopher, mathematician and astronomer, Maymun ibn Najīb Waseṭī from Herat; Abu'l-Muzaffar Isfizārī; Ḥakīm Abu'l-Abbās Lawkarī, who was the student of Bahmanyār, himself a student of Ibn Sīnā; and 'Abd al-Raḥmān Khāzanī. Under the direction of Khayyam, they traveled to Iṣfahān where the Sulṭān had promised to build an astronomical observatory for them. Following three years of hard work, a new calendar was made, known as the "*taqwīm Jalālī*."[26] One of the most thorough calendars ever produced, it remains the official calendar of Iran today.

During Khayyam's second journey to Iṣfahān, which was even more intellectually fruitful than the first, he was able to study the works of Euclid, Apollonius and other Greek masters. Khayyam's days in Iṣfahān, however, were shortened by Niẓām al-Mulk's demise from power and his subsequent assassination while on his way to perform his pilgrimage. Following the tragedy concerning the death of his friend, Niẓām al-Mulk, Khayyam decided to go to Bukhārā where the Sulṭān was headed, but on his way Khayyam received more bad news that the Sulṭān himself had died – hence began the rivalry between the two sons. Khayyam decided to go to Mecca instead to perform his pilgrimage. There may have been ulterior motives for his pilgrimage since Qifṭī in *Tārikh al-ḥukamā*'[27] tells us that some of Khayyam's contemporaries had accused him of having heretical tendencies, and others privately questioned his faith. Khayyam decided to perform his pilgrimage as a way of demonstrating his faith and to exonerate himself of such allegations.

Khayyam returned to his native land, but he had hardly settled down before he was invited by the new Sulṭān to go to Marv. His fame as the leading scientist of his time and his service to the two previous kings were the reasons Sulṭān Sanjar had invited him to stay at the court. Khayyam accepted the offer and moved to Marv where he enjoyed the patronage of the Sulṭān even though his relationship with Sulṭān Sanjar was not as cordial as with the king's two predecessors.

The following story about Khayyam and Sulṭān Sanjar may very well be true, but, as with other accounts, cannot be substantiated. Sulṭān Sanjar wished to go hunting and asked Khayyam to select a day when the weather would be suitable. Khayyam, who did not believe in predicting the weather, reluctantly was forced to do so. The Sulṭān, who made all the necessary preparations on the specified day, ran into stormy weather and called upon Khayyam. To everyone's surprise, Khayyam assured him that all would soon be well. Sure enough, the weather cleared, and the Sulṭān went into the desert with an increased respect for his chief astronomer.

Return to Nayshābūr, old age and the end of a remarkable life

Declining in health, Khayyam asked the Sulṭān if he could return to Nayshābūr. His request was granted, and he returned to his native land amidst the happiness of his family and a hero's welcome. The rest of Khayyam's life was dedicated to scientific and scholarly activities, and even though he was not a prolific scholar, what he did write was original, dense and ground-breaking, particularly in the field of mathematics.

Sometime around 517/1126, Khayyam reached "the winter of his life," as Persians say, and his health continued to decline. In a recently published treatise entitled *Response to Three Philosophical Problems*, there is a brief reference to his health problem not noted in previous studies.

> The concepts and states to be enumerated are many but my time is limited and I am unable to [comment on them] since I am suffering from a terrible illness which has caused my handwriting and speech to falter. May God grant us and our brothers a good ending.[28]

It is probable that he may have suffered from Alzheimer's disease from which he may have died. Khayyam's last day of life is reported in some detail by his son-in-law, Imām Muḥammad Baghdādī.

> He was studying the *Shifā'* while he was using a golden toothpick until he reached the section on the "unity and multiplicity." He marked the section with his toothpick, closed the book and asked his

> companions to gather so he could state his will of testament. When his companions gathered, they stood up and prayed and Khayyam refused to eat or drink until he performed his night prayer. He prostrated by putting his forehead on the ground and said "O Lord, I know you as much as it is possible for me, forgive me for my knowledge of you is my way of reaching you" and then died.[29]

Niẓāmī 'Aruḍī Samarqandī, in his *Chahār maqālah*, composed in 550/1159 and dedicated to Prince Hishām al-Dīn Ghurrī, states that in 530/1139, "It was a few years since Khayyam had died" when Samarqandī went to visit his grave and had this to say:

> In the year 500/1109, in the quarter of slave traders of Amir Bū Sa'id, I saw Imām Omar Khayyamī and Imām Muẓaffar Isfizārī and I heard from Ḥujjat al-Ḥaq Omar (the evidence of truth) that he said, "my grave will be in a location that every Spring the north wind will spread flowers upon my grave." When in 533, I arrived in Nayshābūr, that noble soul was buried and the corporeal world had become an orphan due to his absence. Since he was my teacher, one Friday, with a companion, I went to visit his grave in the cemetery of *Ḥayrah*, I turned left and at the bottom of the walls of the garden saw a grave with pears and apricot trees whose blossoms had covered Khayyam's grave just as he had predicted. This reminded me of the conversation I had heard from him in the city of Balkh, I wept, for in the four corners of the world I had seen no one like him.[30]

Omar Khayyam died, but surviving the test of time, there remains a legacy of a man whose posthumous existence and message did not have the rightful ears, for his message was too advanced for his time.

THE WORKS OF OMAR KHAYYAM

Up to date, there are fourteen treatises that are known to have been written by Omar Khayyam. The problem of elaborating on most of them is that they are of a scientific nature and are simply too technical for the non-specialist to understand. Despite this challenge, I will attempt to offer a brief summary of each of his works. A complete translation of his philosophical treatises, some of them for the first time, will be included in the appendices.

As one can see, Khayyam wrote little but his works are dense, original and written in very concise language. With regard to some of his works, we know the exact date of their composition, whereas with others we know their approximate date in terms of their priority and posterity to his other works. Brief accounts of Khayyam's books are as follows:

On the proposition that asserts genera are of four types
(Al-qawl 'alā ajnās al-ladhi bi'l-arba'ah)[31]

This five-page treatise is probably part of a different book by the name *Sharḥ al-mushkil min kitāb al-musiqī* which has not survived. This treatise provides highly technical commentary on music theory that discusses the mathematical relationship among notes, minor, major and tetrachords. Khayyam makes references to the views of Fārābī and Avicenna with regard to music and offers a reclassification of musical scales.

On the elaboration of the problems concerning the books of Euclid
(Risālah fī sharḥ mā ashkāl min muṣādarāt kitāb uqlidus)[32]

This treatise consists of three parts. In the first part, Khayyam refutes the possibility of doubt concerning Euclidian postulation of parallels. In the second part, he undertakes a discussion of ratios and proportions criticizing what Euclid has presented in the fifth chapter of the *Principles of Euclidian Geometry*. Khayyam offers mathematical proof as to why these principles are incomplete and calls for a philosophical investigation of the principles that underlie Euclidian geometry. This work can be regarded as a treatise on the philosophy of science and mathematics. In the third section, Khayyam discusses the problem of ratios, particularly the types of relationships that can exist between any three separate entities.[33]

On the division of a quadrant of a circle
(Risālah fī qismah rub' al-dā'irah)[34]

This treatise, whose subject is mathematics nevertheless, contains references to both mathematical and philosophical achievements of Muslims while mentioning a number of mathematicians. These references point to the specific achievements of particular mathematicians and are significant as far as the history of science is concerned.[35]

On proofs for problems Concerning Algebra
(Risālah fī barāhīn 'alā masā'il al-jabr wa'l-muqābalah)

Khayyam dedicates this treatise to Imām al-Sayyīd ibn Ṭāhir, a well-known jurist of his time, and complains of the status of scientific research.

> I always had an insatiable appetite for research and to know possible and impossible proofs ... we live at a time when the few scientists we have live with thousands of difficulties in order to use the opportunities to conduct research and to actualize and strengthen the foundations of knowledge. The pseudo-scientists of our time, present truth as falsehood and do not step further beyond pretending to know.[36]

Khayyam goes on to say that before he would comment on truth in the philosophical sense, he would comment on the introductory issues in Algebra. In the *Treatise on the Division of a Quadrant of a Circle*, he tells us that he intends to write the book under discussion, and it appears that this treatise is precisely what he had promised to compose. He describes his own work as follows:

> ... and these equations, the learned masters before us have solved. From the other ten types [of proofs] in their works and particularly with my [type of] commentary, nothing has reached us. If I get a chance and succeed in doing so, I intend to gather all the fourteen types with their various branches and show how "possible" can be distinguished from "impossible." So a treatise with introductory materials can be gathered which would be of great benefit in this field.[37]

This work, which was well-known throughout the Middle Ages, contains one of the first attempts to classify and discuss equations of type X^2 and X^3.[38]

On the deception of knowing the two quantities of gold and silver in a compound made of the two (Risālah fi'l- iḥtiyāj lima'rifat miqdaṛī al-dhahab wa'l-fiḍḍah fī jism murakkab minhā)[39]

As its name suggests, the central theme of this short work is to decipher different quantities of precious metals in a compound entity. The discussion is a continuation of the work of Archimedes, and Khayyam begins by explaining what a scale is and what some of its intricacies are. He continues by providing us with specific instructions as to how the process of weighing different elements could be conducted.

A translation of the treatise on Avicenna's Lucid Discourse (Khuṭbah al-ghurra' Ibn Sīnā)[40]

This treatise by Avicenna, which has also been called *Discourse on Unity (Khutbah al-Tawḥīd)* among other titles, was originally written in Arabic. Khayyam made an interpretive translation of it, which is why we can include this among his works. As usual, he begins by praising God, and, in describing His attributes, Khayyam questions whether they are accidental or substantial. Khayyam describes difficulties in assuming each one to be the case and then offers a discussion regarding the relationships among time, motion and God. This treatise ends with an Avicennian discussion on incorporeal substances, celestial spheres and their relationship to angels.

On being and necessity (Risālah fī'l-kawn wa'l-takl īf)[41]

'Abd al-Raḥīm Nasawī, the Imām and Qāḍī of the Fārs province in 473/1082, wrote a letter to Khayyam questioning the mystery of Divine wisdom for the creation of man and religious obligations. Nasawī specifically asks for clarification of certain philosophical issues, and presents them poetically to Khayyam:

> O, wind of Ṣabā, oblige me and when you blow, take my greetings to 'Allamāh Khayyam and humbly kiss the dirt of his door with a humility that is worthy of the great *ḥakīm* ... and ask him of the wisdom of "being" and what is incumbent [upon us], seek their proofs and read them to me.[42]

Referring to these complex issues, Khayyam replies to Qāḍī Nasawī[43] and composes this treatise in which he states at the beginning that the question of "being" and "necessity" are among the most perplexing philosophical questions. He argues that the fundamental questions in philosophy are of three types. First, ontological questions which are concerned with "what is." Second, the question concerning "what is it?" which pertains to the substance or essence of a thing; though Aristotle considers substance and essence to be two separate things, Khayyam seems to equate them as one. Third, "why is it?" This last question, he states, seeks to determine the cause of a thing. Many of the philosophical problems, Khayyam tells us, are due to the fact that philosophers do not properly differentiate among these three categories. He defines "being" (*kawn*) as the existence of contingent beings and "necessity" (*taklīf*) as having to do with the "whatness of existent beings." This treatise becomes somewhat less philosophical towards the end when he discusses the necessity of observing the religious laws and eschatological rewards.

The necessity of contradiction in the world, determinism and subsistence (Ḍarurat al-taḍād fi'l-'ālam wa'l-jabr wa'l-baqā')[44]

In the opinion of some Khayyamian scholars such as Sulaymān Nadawī, this treatise, too, is written in response to questions posed by Qāḍī Nasawī and contains elaboration with respect to three questions. The first question deals with the nature of contradiction and its relationship to God, which Khayyam, in his subsequent discussions, applies to the problem of evil (theodicy) and of how evil comes to be. On the one hand, Khayyam tells us that God cannot be the source of evil; on the other hand, there cannot be other necessary beings besides God. Therefore, the question remains: from whence has evil come? The second question treated here concerns free will and determinism. In order to approach the problem of evil, Khayyam explores the ontological foundation of why evil exists. The third question concerns substance and whether it is an accidental attribute or essential attribute. If it is the former, it cannot be applied to the Necessary Being, and if the latter, it causes other theological and philosophical problems such as multiplicity within unity.

The light of the intellect on the subject of universal knowledge
(Risālah al-ḍiyā' al-'aqlī fī mawḍū' al-'ilm al-kullī)[45]

This treatise, which has also been called *The Treatise on Transcendence in Existence* (*Al-Risālah al-ulā fi'l-wujūd*), investigates a number of issues such as the relationship between existent beings and existence, the accidental relationship between them and whether either of them exist by their own necessity. Finally, the relationship between essence (*māhiyyah*) and existence (*wujūd*), which is the salient feature of Islamic philosophical thought, is also treated here.

On the knowledge of the universal principles of existence
(Risālah dar 'ilm kulliyāt-i wujūd)[46]

Written in Persian, this treatise appears to have been written at the request of Niẓām al-Mulk's son since in the beginning he states, "This exalted man [Mu'ayyad al-Mulk] asked me to write on the universals of knowledge, so this treatise was written due to his request so the men of knowledge and *ḥikmah* come to realize that this brief [treatise] is more useful than volumes."[47]

Khayyam begins this work with a discussion on such Aristotelian concepts as substance and universals and their divisions into simple and compound. He goes on to discuss a variety of standard philosophical topics such as the relationship between generation and corruption, an infinite succession of contingent dependent beings, the Aristotelian categories and the difference between the necessary and contingent beings. The book comes to an end with a classification of the seekers of knowledge into theologians, philosophers, Ismā'īlīs and Sufis. It is here that Khayyam unequivocally supports Sufism by saying, "This tradition is the best of all, for the seeker knows that no perfection is better than His majesty, God, and that state is one in which there is no obstacle and veil."[48]

The *Treatise on the Universal Principles of Existence* has a special place in Khayyam's philosophical thought in that it was his last philosophical treatise and was written long after he had completed his other works.[49] Therefore, it provides us with a better picture on the nature of Khayyamian philosophical thought, which on one hand relies on discursive philosophy as a way of pursuing knowledge, and on the other hand, demonstrates a tendency towards intuitive knowledge whereby reason is incapable of understanding the truth. His mystical tendencies are most apparent at the end of this work and are in line with many other Persian philosophers including Avicenna, who developed mystical views in his mature years.

On existence (Risālah fi'l-wujūd)

Written in Arabic, this treatise begins with a discussion of different types of accidents and how the intellect is able to comprehend the essence of things. Khayyam discusses topics such as existence, the meaning of existence and non-existence, the necessary and contingent beings and in what way God can be regarded as the cause of creation so that motion is not introduced into Divine nature. In addition, he introduces examples to support the theory of emanation, such as how fire produces light without intending to do so.

Response to three philosophical problems
(Risālah jawābān thulāth masā'il)[50]

Over four decades ago, M. Minovī wrote a major article announcing the discovery of this treatise by Khayyam.[51] In this unpublished work of Khayyam, we learn for the first time that he went to the province of Fārs where he met the grand jurist, a man by the name of Abū Ṭāhir, with whom he had an intellectual exchange of ideas. In the beginning of his response to the second question in this work, Khayyam says, "In 473/1082, when I was staying in Fārs, I wrote a treatise on this subject matter for the grand judge (Qāḍī al-Quḍḍāt) of Fārs, Abū Ṭāhir. A copy of it is in Fārs, Iṣfahān and Baghdād, but I do not have a copy."[52]

This work, written in Arabic, primarily treats three topics. The first is whether a rational soul survives the death of the body in such a way that its individuality remains specific to it. Secondly, is it possible for contingent events to have a single cause? In this context, he discusses the problem of succession of contingent, dependent beings. The third discussion covers the subject of time and of how it is intertwined with the notion of motion, in particular, the extent of celestial movements and how this motion does not exist by its own necessity.

At the end of this treatise, there is a one and one-half page addendum; it is not clear if it belongs to Khayyam, but the style and the theme is consistent with the rest of the treatise and discusses existence and essence.

On discovering the truth of Norūz (Risālah dar kashf ḥaqiqat Norūz)[53]

By all accounts the treatise known as *Norūz nāmah*, which traditionally has been attributed to Khayyam, is an apocryphal text; and, in this regard, I have adopted Mālik's modified name,[54] *Treatise on Discovering the Truth of Norūz*, to refer to a particular part of *Norūz nāmah*. There are three parts to this work, only one of which was likely to have been written by Khayyam himself. This treatise is very different from other works of Khayyam, both stylistically and substantively. The work is entirely on the ancient Persian new year known as "Norūz," literally meaning, "the new day," which occurs in the beginning of the spring equinox. Khayyam provides a brief history of Norūz according to Persian mythology and then offers a detailed account of the etymological analysis of the Persian names of the twelve months of the year which are in Pahlavī language. This work ends with an historical account of the reign of different Persian emperors.

I find it highly improbable that this part of *Norūz nāmah* may have been written by Khayyam; neither its style or content remotely resemble other writings of Khayyam. It is unlikely that Khayyam would have made such grave mistakes in describing the etymological roots of the names of months such as "Isfand," which in Pahlavi language means "pure, sacred," but Khayyam says it means "fruit!" Khayyam's thoroughness is evident in his philosophical and scientific works as well as his debates with other scholars concerning etymological and morphological connotations of certain Qur'anic terms. Would a man who pays so much attention to details be so careless? Reference to this treatise here was deemed necessary since historically a number of scholars have regarded Khayyam's authorship as a possibility.

Quatrains and other poems (Ruba'iyyat wa ash'ār)

Perhaps the most difficult and controversial aspect of Khayyamian studies are his *Ruba'iyyat*, most of which are in Persian and a few in Arabic. The number of these poems varies greatly from twelve to several hundred, and even up to 1,200 poems attributed to him in various versions and editions. Despite a long history of heated debates, articles, books and conferences regarding the number of authentic poems, Khayyam's authentic *Ruba'iyyat* remains a mystery. Suffice it to say that most of these quatrains are written in simple but exquisite Persian.

A thorough analysis of Khayyam's Persian *Ruba'iyyat* is offered in Chapter Four of this work, but something must be said about his Arabic poems. It is noteworthy that even though it is the Persian *Ruba'iyyat* for which Khayyam has gained such a legendary fame, twenty-five Arabic poems each consisting of two hemistiches are also attributed to him. These poems, also subject to the question of authenticity are virtually omitted from traditional scholarship on Khayyam. 'Imād al-Dīn Kātib in his *Kharidat al-qaṣr*[55] is the earliest source where four of these poems are mentioned, Shahrazurī in his *Nuzhat al-arwāḥ* mentions these poems and cites an additional three poems. In a different part of *Nuzhat al-arwāḥ*, Shahrazurī includes another three poems.[56] Among others who have quoted Khayyam's Arabic poems are Qifṭī who mentions four poems in his *Tārikh al-ḥukamā'*,[57] and in *Itmām al-tatimmah*[58] we find eleven poems that are not mentioned by others. In his Arabic poems, similar to his quatrains in Persian, Khayyam expresses his deep disappointment with betrayal and the beastly nature of humans. In one poem he remarks:

> I spent my life looking for a brother I can trust,
> One who will stand by me if others betrayed me,
> I befriended many but found how unworthy they are,
> Changed companions but failed to find true friends
> I said to myself "cease your search for in this life,
> You shall not find a true human you can trust."[59]

2

Reconstructing a Tarnished Image: Omar Khayyam According to his Contemporaries and Biographers

Eternal Cause when first my being wrought,
A course in Love from very start He taught;
Then of the filings of my loving heart,
A key He made for treasure-house of thought.[1]

Few people in the annals of Islamic literature are more controversial and misunderstood than Omar Khayyam. The ideas of this multidimensional figure lend themselves to different interpretations. An atheist, an agnostic and a hedonist can each easily find evidence in Khayyam's thought to claim him as one of their own; and Sufis,[2] too, can offer a spiritual interpretation of the imagery contained in the *Ruba'iyyat* to argue that Khayyam perhaps belonged to an antinomian Sufi tradition such as *Malāmatiyyah*.[3] However, there is the other extreme that views him as a man of faith by simply negating the attribution of these *Ruba'iyyat* to him.[4]

In what follows, I will attempt to reconstruct the image of Khayyam's complex personality based on authoritative sources; some were his contemporaries who had met him and others lived not too long after him. These sources, some of them translated into English for the first time, provide us with a more complete perspective of Khayyam's personality, intellectual orientation and personal views on faith and heresy. As will be seen, Khayyam was a controversial figure even in his own time, and there were ambiguities regarding his faith. But he also seemed to enjoy a high degree of respect in his community, which would not have been possible had he been branded as a heretic.

The oldest source in which Omar Khayyam is mentioned is a letter which Abū'l Majd Majdud ibn Ādam, also known as Sanā'ī Ghaznavī,[5] wrote to Khayyam from Herat asking for his intervention regarding a misunderstanding. An account of the story has been included in the previous chapter, and the letter itself is among the most beautiful examples of Persian literature. While the letter is too long to include here in its entirety, the most relevant section where Khayyam is mentioned is as follows:

> The purpose of this letter is to attest that since Omar is attentive to guard the substance of the honor of prophecy, then he is not impervious to care for the pearl of wisdom either, for the Book [Qur'an] and wisdom are two jewels in a shell as the holy Qur'an says.[6] For [the understanding of] a book such as that [Qur'an] requires an Omar such as you and wisdom too needs an Omar with your stature; so using prosperity, these two domains can become prosperous. ... Cleansing of these two domains requires the authoritativeness of a man such as you Omar, may your life be one with that of a mountain [in its endurance] ... The expectation of this sincere lover [of wisdom] is that when this letter reaches the leader of *ḥakīms*, at once like 'Alī with the Zulfaqār[7] of tongue, run to them and with an Omarian awesomeness, tear their intentions to pieces.[8]

Perhaps the most important feature of this quotation is that it is written by Sanā'ī, a literary genius and a man of considerable fame. In his letter, Sanā'ī praises Khayyam on a number of issues which reveals much about Khayyam's personality as well as his standing in the society. In the entire letter, there is no mention or reference to Khayyam's poetry, and that strengthens the case of those who have argued that Khayyam was not a poet. If Khayyam had written poems, it is reasonable to expect that the issue of poetry would have come up in conversation between the two poets. However, there is no evidence of such discussions, adding credence to the theory that perhaps Khayyam is not the author of the *Ruba'iyyat.* To give him the benefit of the doubt one may argue that he was not a poet like Sanā'ī, Ḥāfīẓ, Rūmī and many others. Khayyam may have been a poet of a different kind who composed his *Ruba'iyyat* for himself or perhaps his close students and can not be classified as a "professional poet." Traditional masters in the Islamic world often began a scholarly session by reciting a few poems, or they referred to poems during their lectures. This long-standing tradition continues today. It is likely that Khayyam composed some poems in this context or, as we will see later, used poetry as a means of avoiding the thorny religious issues which he did not want to directly address. It is also quite possible that, due to the controversial nature of his poetry, Khayyam did not want to share it with Sanā'ī.

Another conclusion that can be drawn from this quotation bears witness to Khayyam's faith. Sanā'ī tells us that Khayyam is the guardian of "the substance of prophecy," a description which must have matched Khayyam's reputation. Had he been the skeptic whose faith was under question, Sanā'ī would not have sought Khayyam's assistance or would have used a different language. Sanā'ī's second reference to Khayyam as an "authoritative man" provides us with yet more evidence of how Khayyam was perceived by the scholarly circles. The traditional Islamic worldview holds a theocentric perspective which asserts that, in order to be recognized in any field of human endeavor, one has to be a person of faith. Khayyam could not have been a man whose authority was recognized and respected by the local powers if his faith was under scrutiny. Finally, there is the reference to him as "the leader of *ḥakīms*," a highly respected title which bears religious connotations worthy of an eminent scholar such as Khayyam. The word *ḥikmah*, which can roughly be translated as "wisdom," is inclusive of philosophy, but is not limited to it. In fact, *ḥakīm* is a title that refers to an erudite scholar whose breadth and depth of knowledge encompasses a wide array of subjects, especially the religious sciences. What can be deduced from the passage under discussion is that Khayyam was known to have been a man of faith, a learned scholar in religious subjects and one who was respected by the locals as well as by scholars such as Sanā'ī, who knew him personally.

The second oldest source in which Khayyam is mentioned, though briefly, is said to have been written around 515 AH/1124 CE by ʻAbd al-Raḥmān Khāzenī titled *Mizān al-ḥikmah*. While the date of this treatise is subject to debate, the author mentions that Khayyam had written a treatise on water scales.

> During the period of the victorious government, may God keep it safe, Abū Ḥafṣ Omar al-Khayyamī examined it [the water scale] and confirmed what had been stated about it and proved the correctness of what he had seen and what was relevant to a specific amount of water without the use of a known scale.[9]

What is missing from the above is any allusion to Khayyam's poetry. We know for certain that Khayyam was respected for being a mathematician-astronomer, but clearly he was not known for his poetry otherwise a reference, however brief, would have been made to it. It is also entirely possible that Khayyam composed his poems but read them to a select group of friends and associates whom he knew had the capacity to understand and not condemn him. This point, as I will demonstrate in the forthcoming chapters, is more plausible given the religious and political milieu of the time in which Khayyam lived. It is no wonder that few of his biographers have made references to his poetry, and others such as Sanā'ī and Khāzenī, his contemporaries, remained silent with regard to it.

One of the most interesting accounts of Omar Khayyam is by Abu'l-Qāsim Maḥmud ibn Omar ibn Muḥammad Zamakhsharī, a contemporary of Khayyam, in his *Al-Zājer lilṣighār ʻan muʻāriḍāt al-kibār*.[10] Zamakhsharī, who composed this work prior to 516 AH/1125 CE, remembers that one day he was with his teacher, Abū Manṣūr Iṣfahānī, in the city of Marv where they met Khayyam, whom Zamakhsharī refers to as "Shaykh al-Imām al-Khayyāmī." A disagreement concerning the proper pronunciation of two words that describe the "sword" ensued. On another occasion, Khayyam met the same two figures and another discussion regarding the etymology of an Arabic word followed. These accounts of Khayyam indicate his mastery of Arabic grammar and his concern for detailed grammatical issues, as well as his sense of thoroughness and erudition in different fields of Islamic scholarship.

The next account of Khayyam, dedicated to Prince Hishām al-Dīn Ghurrī sometime between 550–552 AH/1159–1162 CE, is offered by ʻAruḍī Samarqandī in his *Chahār maqālah*, also known as *Mujmaʻ al-navādir*. Samarqandī's description of Khayyam's will and grave has already been given in the last chapter, but a full translation of his comments about Khayyam sheds some light on him:

> In the year 500 AH in the quarter of slave traders of Amīr Bū Saʻīd, I saw Imām Omar Khayyāmī and Imām Muẓaffar Isfizārī and I heard from *ḥujjat al-ḥaqq* (the evidence of truth) Omar who said, "every Spring, the north wind will spread flowers upon my grave." When in 533 (1142), I arrived in Nayshābūr, that noble soul was buried and the corporeal world had become an orphan due to his absence. Since he was my teacher, one Friday, I and a companion went to visit his grave in the cemetery of Ḥayrah. I turned left and in the bottom of the walls of the garden saw a grave with pears and apricot trees whose blossoms had covered Khayyam's grave just as he had predicted. This reminded me of the conversation I had heard from him in the city of Balkh. I wept since in the four corners of the world, I had seen no one like him, May God, the Sacred and Most High, place him in heaven with honor and generosity.
>
> ... Even though, I had seen verdicts of *ḥujjat al-ḥaqq* Omar, but he did not have much faith in the principles of meteorology nor did I see or hear from the learned anyone who believed in the principles. In the winter of 508, Ṣadr al-Dīn Muḥammad ibn al-Muẓaffar, peace be upon him, said "Khāwjah, call upon Imām Omar to determine when we should go hunting so it will not snow or rain in those days"; and Khāwjah Imām Omar was a companion of Khāwjah and lived in his residence. Khāwjah sent someone to call him [Khayyam] and told me the story. Khayyam contemplated for two days, made a sound decision and went to tell the Sulṭān. When the Sulṭān came [to hunt], at once the weather became turbulent, clouds came, wind blew and snow began. They laughed and the Sulṭān wanted to go back. Khāwjah Imām [Khayyam] said, "O Sulṭān, do not worry, for this very hour clouds will move and in the next five days there will be no rain." The Sulṭān rode, the clouds opened and in those five days there was no rain and no one saw clouds.[11]

Despite this detailed account of Khayyam, which points to his acumen as an astronomer and meteorologist, he did not believe that predicting the weather was a science. What this passage does allude to is his fame as an astronomer and his closeness to the Sulṭān. There are other inferences that can be made from this significant quotation. Reference to Khayyam as an "Imām" once again indicates Khayyam was at least outwardly a man of faith. The Sulṭāns have traditionally been defenders of the faith. Even though they themselves have not necessarily been pious, the orthodox jurists close to the royal court made sure that the Sulṭāns were surrounded by men of faith. A clear example is that of Shihāb al-Dīn Suhrawardī, who was at the court of Malik Ẓāhir Shāh, the son of the famous Ṣalāḥ al-Dīn Ayyūbī. He was perceived by the orthodox to have been corrupting the king and so the Muslim jurists, who traditionally had little tolerance for what they perceive to be heretical ideas, issued a religious edict (*fatwā*) at the order of Ṣalāḥ al-Dīn Ayyūbī, resulting in the execution of Suhrawardī.

According to some of his biographers, Khayyam was close to a number of the Sulṭāns and he was invited to "sit on the throne with Sulṭān Sanjar." He must have had a reputation for being a pious man otherwise his presence would not have been tolerated by the Sulṭān and his courtiers. Furthermore, referring to him as "the proof of truth" (*ḥujjat al-ḥaqq*) by his contemporaries,[12] a title typically reserved for religious authorities, is yet another clear indication that Khayyam was held in great esteem as a scholar of religious sciences.

The picture that once again emerges from Samarqandī's comments regarding Khayyam is that of a devout and faithful Muslim, respected by religious scholars, the royal court and the orthodox jurists in the court. This picture is certainly different from the agnostic Khayyam of the West and the popular image of him in the East.

Perhaps the most extensive reference to Khayyam is by Muḥammad ibn al-Ḥusayīn al-Bayhaqī in *Tatimmah ṣiwān al-ḥikmah*, written sometime between 548–565/1159–1171. In these comments, we can see various aspects of Khayyam's personality as well as his intellectual acumen. Bayhaqī describes him as:

> Philosopher, *ḥujjat al-ḥaqq* (the evidence of truth), Omar ibn Ibrāhīm al-Khayyāmī: the origin, birth and his forefathers and ancestors were from Nayshābūr. He was a follower of Abū 'Alī [Sīnā] in certain parts of the science of *ḥikmah* (philosophy) but in temperament he was unpleasant and narrow-minded.
>
> While in Iṣfahān, he read a book (*Mutawwal*) seven times and upon his return to Nayshābūr, he dictated it and we compared it with [the original] manuscript and there was not much difference.
>
> His ascendant was Gemini, the Sun and Mercury were on the degree of ascendant in the third degree of Gemini, Mercury was Samimi and Jupiter were looking on both from triangulation.[13]
>
> In teaching and writing he was not prolific and did not write except in some natural sciences and a treatise on existence and a treatise on being and necessity; and in morphology, jurisprudence and history he was learned. It is said that Imām 'Omar Khayyāmī one day came to Shihāb al-Islam 'Abdallah ibn 'Alī, the nephew of Niẓām al-Mulk and the Imām of the reciters, Abu'l Ḥasan Ghazzāl[14] was present and discussion began concerning differences among the masters of recitation concerning a certain verse. [When Khayyam came], Shihāb al-Islam said "an expert came" and so he was asked on an independent version from different versions. He elaborated upon various versions of the recitations, explained the justification for each one and explained the reason for the superiority of each one. So the Imām of reciters said "May God increase such learned ones as you; consider me as one of your followers and be amicable with me. I did not think that any of the reciters in the world can explain these versions and their differences much less a *ḥakīm*.
>
> He, Omar ibn Ibrāhīm Khayyāmī, possesses knowledge of different sciences in *ḥikmah*, mathematics and its different branches. One day Imām Ḥujjat al-Islam Muḥammad Ghazzālī came to him and asked "if all the points in a celestial sphere are similar, what distinguishes two points in a celestial sphere that determines a diameter? I have mentioned this in my book, *'Arāys al-nafāys*. Then Imām Omar Khayyāmī began a lengthy elaboration by discussing motion and stated various opinions and this was a habit of that great scholar until it became noon and the call for prayer was uttered.

> Imām Ghazzālī said "truth came and falsehood vanished" and then left.
>
> One day Imām Omar Khayyāmī came to the great Sulṭān Sanjar who at that time was a young man suffering from measles. Upon his departure, his vizier, Fakhr al-Dawlah said "how did you see him and how would you cure him?" Imām Omar Khayyāmī replied "the life of this young man is fearsome." A Sudanese slave heard this and told the Sulṭān, following his recovery, due to his enmity with Imām Omar Khayyāmī, he [Sulṭān] did not like him much.
>
> Sulṭān Malik Shāh treated him [Omar Khayyāmī] as he did his companions, and the sovereign, Shams al-Mulūk in Bukharā respected him more than anyone and sat with him on the same throne.
>
> One day, Imām Omar Khayyāmī was telling my father the following story: Once I was sitting with Sulṭān Malik Shāh, face to face, and a young man who was the son of a noble family came in and showed great politeness. I was astonished by his mature mannerism despite his youth; and the Sulṭān said, "do not be surprised for a chicken that is hatched without having been taught picks out seeds but, without guidance, one can not find his nest ..." After these words from the Sulṭān, I was astonished and said to myself, 'great people are [deservedly] heroic.'
>
> With my father, peace be upon him, I went to Imām Omar Khayyāmī in 507 (1113) and he asked me the meaning of a verse of epic poetry which is as follows ... and then told my father "where is a son who bears no sign of his father." [15]

Bayhaqī's account of Khayyam ends with the story of the last day of his life which has been mentioned in the previous chapter. Once again, we have evidence from another source to conclude that Khayyam was held in high esteem both as a scholar and as a religious authority. Receiving the title of "*ḥujjat al-ḥaqq*" is a clear indication that Khayyam was known to his contemporaries as a man of religious stature. Bayhaqī provides us with another source to conclude that Khayyam, philosophically was a staunch Peripatetic (*mashshā'ī*) as evidenced by the fact that on the last day of his life he allegedly was reading Avicenna's *Ishārāt*. In addition, Bayhaqī emphasizes Khayyam's temper and his reluctance to teach others. It is entirely possible that he did not tolerate the dogmatism of his peers and students, which led him to irritation and a fear of being exposed. Or perhaps the realization that his rightful listeners and readers were not present was the reason for his reluctance to teach or write extensively. In a quatrain that is revealing of why Khayyam preferred to remain aloof, he says:

> The secrets which my book of love has bred,
> Cannot be told for fear of loss of head;
> Since none is fit to learn, or cares to know,
> 'Tis better all my thoughts remain unsaid.[16]

Khayyam realized that it was safer for him to write on science and mathematics than philosophy. After all, even Avicenna did not escape the wrath of the jurists who accused him of heretical thought.[17] We have to bear in mind that Khayyam lived under the watchful eyes of Ghazzālī who listed twenty philosophical issues which he considered to be heretical and condemned those philosophers who embraced them.[18]

Bayhaqī, similar to other biographers of Khayyam, emphasizes his knowledge of the Qur'an by alluding to Khayyam's mastery of different and rare versions of the art of Qur'anic recitations. The fact that Bayhaqī chose the above point and Ghazzālī endorsed Khayyam as a religious scholar should remove any suspicion that Khayyam had propagated "heretical ideas." Throughout the quotation, there is nothing but praise for Khayyam's breadth and depth of knowledge. Based on such religious titles as "Imām," "*ḥakīm*" and "*ḥujjat al-ḥaqq*," one can conclude with certainty that Khayyam's faith must not have been questioned.

It is interesting to observe that those biographers who remark about his *Ruba'iyyat* tend not to praise his religious character, and those who refrain from making reference to the *Ruba'iyyat* tend to focus on his religiosity. The recognition of the irreconcilability of Khayyam the poet and Khayyam the man of faith must have begun early on. This perceived tension, which is a by-product of an either/or approach to Khayyam's thought, is a fallacious view that sacrifices the complexity of the human condition to the convenience of an either/or dichotomy. This subtle but profound point has led to a misunderstanding of Khayyam throughout history by developing two diametrically opposed perspectives of who he "really was," a point which will be elaborated.

Another biographer of Khayyam, 'Imād al-Dīn Kātib Iṣfahānī, in his work, *Kharidat al-qaṣr*,[19] written in 572/1181 describes him:

> Omar al-Khayyam, there is none like him in his era and he was unparalleled in the science of astronomy and *ḥikmah* and he is revered. He composed this [Arabic] poem in Iṣfahān [and said]:
>
> If I satisfy myself by a game of chance through a language
> Painstakingly, my hand and my arm have attained;
> I am safe for the vicissitudes of all accidents.
> So O time, be my hand or my helper.
> Is it not the fate of the heavens in their rotations
> To turn all good fortune into misfortune?

Iṣfahānī's reference to Khayyam confirms that not only was he the leading scientist of his time, but he also was a poet and had a reputation of being a *ḥakīm*, which once again denotes his mastery of philosophy and theology.

In the latter part of the sixth/twelfth century, Khāqānī Shervānī, one of the major literary figures of his time makes a reference to Khayyam. In a poem that he composed for his uncle, Omar Uthmān, Khāqānī uses the similarity of his uncle's name and that of Omar Khayyam to compare their virtues. The poem concludes:

> Thy intellect telling Omar Uthmān,
> [You are both] Omar Khayyāmī and Omar Khaṭṭāb.[20]

Khāqānī Shervānī, in one of his letters written during the reign of Malik Shāh, recalls a story regarding a conversation between Khayyam and a high-ranking administrator indicating Khayyam's quick mind and sense of humor, which are reflected in much of his poetry:

> The story of the great Khāwjah Kāshānī during the rule of Malik Shāh and *ḥujjat al-ḥaqq* Omar Khayyam occurred as such: one day Khāwjah was at the office, Omar Khayyam came and said "O noble of the world, my ten-thousand Dinārs annual stipend has dwindled and not much is left. The aids to the office need to be directed so they

> may bring it." Khāwjah said "what service do you perform for the Sulṭān of the world that every year ten-thousand Dinārs should be given to you?" Omar Khayyam replied "What a wonder, what service do I perform? It takes a thousand years for the sky and heavenly bodies to rotate in ups and downs so from this mill a seed like Omar Khayyami may arise and from the seven cities in the high grounds and the seven villages in the low grounds, a caravan leader such as I is produced. But if you want, from every village from around Kāshān, I will bring out tens and tens of people such as Khāwjah and place them in your position who can do what Khāwjah does."
>
> Khāwjah stood up with his head down for he had met a firm response. An account of this encounter was told to Sulṭān Malik Shāh who said, "In God [I swear] Omar Khayyam spoke the truth."[21]

The religious title "*ḥujjat al-ḥaqq*" which once again is used to refer to Khayyam by Kāshānī, himself a courtier, clearly indicates that he was also known to the court as a religious scholar. This is further confirmation that his interest and expertise in religious matters must have been serious enough to have gained him the reputation of a scholar well versed in religious subjects among the locals, the scholarly community and the court. Even though he had not written extensively, his reputation must have been obtained through teaching and scholarly debate. Finally, there is the arrogance which is implied in Khayyam's conversation with Kāshānī, but Khayyam was a man who knew his own worth and did not play the game of false humility. He is not an exception in this regard, for we see similar statements regarding the assertion of self-worth by philosophers such as Avicenna and Suhrawardī, as well as others.

The next biographer of Khayyam, Fakhr al-Dīn Muḥammad ibn Omar al-Rāzī, in *Tafsīr mafātiḥ al-ghayb*, describes him:

> The first part in the elaboration of a statement, for each one of them, is as follows: the first type of proofs are to reason regarding the celestial states and we have mentioned our interpretation of what the Most High has said "He made the earth your couch and heaven your canopy."[22] We mentioned that as another type of discourse related to Omar ibn Khayyam. He read the book *Almagest* (al-*Majisṭā*) with Omar al-Nabīrī so some of the jurists said, one day when he read it,

> he explained the verse from the Qur'an that was "Do they not look at the sky above them to see how they are built?"[23] So he explained its foundations.[24]

Fakhr al-Dīn Rāzī, in a different treatise entitled *Risālat fi'l-tanbih 'alā ba'ḍ al-asrār al-maw'dah fī ba'ḍ al-surah al-Qur'an al-'azīm*,[25] refers to Khayyam and states:

> If we said God has no care for the properness of [elements], then how did He create them? Omar Khayyam conveyed this meaning in Persian in a poem and said:
>
> Since mortal compositions are cast by Hand Divine,
> Why then the flaws that throw them out of line
> If formed sublime, why must He shatter them?
> If not, to whom would we the fault assign?[26]

This poem has been the subject of great controversy, and most of his critics who have accused him of heretical ideas have relied on this quatrain. Here, Khayyam questions several issues that are of a philosophical nature. To begin with, it is traditionally assumed that our world is the best of all possible worlds, but Khayyam challenges this notion. How do we reconcile the claim in the Qur'an "Surely We created man of the best constitution,"[27] with the presence of so much evil both natural and man-made? The problem lying at the heart of Khayyam's message is theodicy, a theme that reverberates throughout his *Ruba'iyyat*; this philosophical riddle was put to rest in the early period of Islamic intellectual thought, since raising the issue of why there is evil in the world is inconsistent with the spirit of Islam which demands submission to the Divine will.

Attempts to understand and resolve the problem of theodicy, however, were indirectly continued by Muslim philosophers as they devised philosophical schemes which explained evil as a constituent of the corporeal world. Philosophers such as Avicenna as well as others offered an ontological analysis of the problem of evil by considering it to be a natural consequence of a corporeal world.[28]

Khayyam appears to be breaking away from the "sacred silence" regarding the question of theodicy, not by addressing it directly in a treatise which would not have been an acceptable form of expression, but by choosing poetry as an alternative vehicle. Poetic imagery, as developed by Khayyam, does not negate the integrity of the more "serious" form of inquiry that is a discursive method, and yet it offers what some Western scholars have called a "theology of Protest" and others, "post-death of God" theology.[29]

Indirectly, Khayyam alludes to the conclusion of the discussion on theodicy, namely that imperfections in the created order can only be attributed to creation, when he asks in his poem, "To whom should the fault be assigned?" Perhaps the scene from his last day of life when he was reading the *Ishārāt* is directly related to Khayyam's obsession on the theme of suffering and evil. It is said that when he arrived at the chapter on "Unity and Multiplicity," he stopped reading; and a few hours later he passed away. Is it a coincidence that the problem of unity and multiplicity happens to be the fundamental problem from which comes the thorny issue of theodicy? If God is all-good but from Him come all things, then evil must have come from Him. Since in the beginning there was only one God and nothing else, it then follows that evil must have been part of God. Is Khayyam merely alluding to the problem, or accepting the unacceptable?

Muḥammad Shahrazūrī, the well-known biographer, in his *Nuzhat al-arwāḥ*[30] has restated what Bayhaqī has said almost word for word, and therefore, we will not include it here. In a different text, however, titled, *Madinat al-ḥukamā'*, which is attributed to Shahrazūrī, he makes a reference to Khayyam:

> The philosopher Omar ibn Ibrāhīm al-Khayyāmī is one of the *ḥakims* of Khūrāsān, an overflowing sea, may his status be elevated and his life be lengthened, excelled in mathematical calculations. Qāḍī al-Imām 'Abd al-Rashīd ibn Naṣr said that once they gathered in a bath in Marv and asked about the meaning of the two incantations (*al-mu'azzatayīn*)[31] and the reason for the repetition of some of the letters. He enumerated in a masterly fashion upon every rare view and brought examples such that if it were to be put together, it would have become a volume. This was his praised status in short and in [the science of Qur'anic] interpretation he did not quit

> [learning] even when he was away and he did not shun any effort to dispense with the knowledge of the unknown in his life even when he was very far away. He has beautiful and stunning poems.[32]

Contrary to some comments which cast doubt on the religiosity of Khayyam, the above authenticates that he was a man of faith with an amazing knowledge of Qur'anic exegesis. He is called by the notable historian, Shahrazūrī "a distinguished *ḥakīm* of Khurāsān," and his knowledge of the intricacies of the Qur'an is praised even by a religious judge such as Qāḍī Naṣr. Even though the term *ḥakīm* is not exclusive to religious authorities, it is inclusive of them. This quotation also bears testament to the powerful and supposedly photographic memory of Khayyam.

In a late seventh/thirteenth-century commentary on *Tatimmah ṣiwān al-ḥikmah*, Shaykh Najm al-Dīn Abū Bakr Rāzī, known as "*dāyyah*," in his work *Mirṣād al-ibād min al-mabda' ila'l-ma'ād*[33] (620/1229), refers to Khayyam and philosophers in a pejorative way:

> ... wisdom is to see the exalted and luminous spirit [wrapped] in the form of dark corporeality. In contrast with the cutting of the attachment of spirit from the form, and destruction of the form, yet the form is brought back from what spirit is created and issued forth. So man may not be among "those beasts who are lost"[34] and can reach the status of a human being and to free himself from the veil of ignorance. [This is so he may] set foot on the spiritual path; what he envisions and brings forward, is due to the eye of the faith and the fruit of gnosis (*'irfān*).
>
> Pity on the philosophers, materialists and naturalists who are deprived from these two states [faith and vision] and are bewildered and perplexed. One of the learned ones known to them for his virtuosity, wisdom and political acumen and knowledge is Omar Khayyam who in the extremity of wonder and ignorance composed these odes and expressed his blindness.
>
> In the circle where we come and go,
> There is no beginning or an end to go.
> None speaks the truth in this journey,
> From whence we come and to where we go.[35]

Rāzī also indicates, "in response to the wisdom of emulating death after life and bringing to life after death, the perplexed lost man [Khayyam] says":

> Since mortal compositions are cast by Hand Divine,
> Why then the flaws that throw them out of line?
> If formed sublime, why must He shatter them?
> If not, to whom would we the fault assign?[36]

It is clearly evident that less than a century after his death, Khayyam had come to be known, at least by some, as being affiliated with heretical ideas since he is referred to by al-Razi as "philosopher, materialist and naturalist." The allegation is part of a complex philosophical discussion on the relationship between the soul and the body. This issue will be discussed later, but to put Rāzī's comments in context, a brief explanation is necessary. Rāzī is advocating the Avicennian view on the relationship between the soul and the body often referred to as "dualism." Accordingly, the body and the soul interact with each other, yet each is independent of the other such that if the connection is cut off by the absence of one side, the other survives. Khayyam's adherence to this view is being questioned here. In being identified as a "philosopher, materialist and naturalist," Khayyam is suspected of being an epiphenomenologist, that is, one who believes there is an essential relationship between the soul and the body such that when the body disintegrates, the soul or consciousness, to use a modern term, cannot survive.

Rāzī is somehow associating the epiphenomenological position with being a "philosopher, materialist and naturalist" who rejects the notion that the soul can survive after physical death. This philosophical perspective was perceived by some Muslim philosophers to be of Greek origin, and clearly undermines the concept of life after death. Khayyam's numerous poems in which he either questions life after death or makes sarcastic remarks about those who believe in it provide his critics with ammunition.

Rāzī also refers to the concept of *'irfān* (gnosis), which in its epistemological sense is the product of later Islamic philosophical developments, but is nevertheless used here in the same context. *'Irfān,* which tends to be a synthesis of discursive philosophy, intellectual intuition and practical wisdom, is claimed by its adherents to provide the knower with a complete mode of knowledge with which an object of inquiry can be understood. Khayyam is reported by Rāzī to have lacked this mystical knowledge which Rāzī identifies as a lack of faith. Since the "philosopher, materialist and naturalist" are deprived of this knowledge, they are "bewildered and perplexed."

The two poems quoted by Rāzī are clearly chosen from among many to show Khayyam's quandary, but it is not clear in what sense they show that Khayyam broke away from the traditional Avicennian position and accepted a purely naturalistic stance.

Al-Qifṭī is a historian and biographer of the seventh/thirteenth century whose work, *Tārikh al-ḥukamā'*, written in 646/1255, is regarded to be one of the authoritative sources for the study of major figures of the Islamic intellectual tradition. He places Khayyam well within the Greek intellectual tradition but not in the same sense as Rāzī. He explains:

> Omar al-Khayyam, the Imām of Khūrāsān and the 'Allāmah (learned master) of his time who knows Greek sciences, discusses and seeks the one religion and attempts to cleanse his bodily movements and his human soul and in matters pertaining to civic politics, he followed the Greek principles. Later Sufis understood his poems outwardly and considered them to be part of their [mystical] tradition. In their sessions and gatherings, [Khayyam's poems] became subject of conversation and discussion. They [his poems] however, are inwardly like snakes who bite the *shari'ah* [Islamic law] and are chains and handcuffs [placed on religion].
>
> Once the people of his time had a taste of his faith, his secrets were revealed. [Khayyam] was frightened for his life, withdrew from writing, speaking and such like and traveled to Mecca. Once he arrived in Baghdād, members of [a Sufi] tradition and believers in primary sciences came to him and courted him. He did not accept them and after performing the pilgrimage returned to his native land, kept his secrets [to himself] and propagated worshiping and following the people of faith. In the science of *ḥikmah* and astronomy he was unique and became an exemplar.[37]

A thorough reading of al-Qifṭī's account of Khayyam reveals that Khayyam's thought was perceived by some living a century after his death as somehow devious and by others as pious. Al-Qifṭī's account is contradictory; the first part is complimentary, and the second section is a diatribe in which Khayyam's character and thought are deprecated. Khayyam is referred to as an "Imām" and "*'Allāmah*" both of which clearly place him in the category of being a faithful, learned Muslim. Likewise, his mastery of Greek sciences and philosophy puts him in the category of a serious philosopher and a follower of Avicenna, a Peripatetic whose adherents generally did not have Sufi tendencies. So far, the picture al-Qifṭī provides us with is that of a devout Muslim who is well-versed in Islamic religious intricacies as well as Greek wisdom, an image ranking him with the likes of Fārābī, Avicenna and even Ghazzālī. Furthermore, there is the claim that Khayyam "cleansed his bodily movements and his human soul," a strong reference to Khayyam's asceticism and an indication that he may have belonged to a secret Sufi order in Nayshābūr.

The tone of the writing, however, changes suddenly when al-Qifṭī suggests that Khayyam's poems are cryptic, and that while their outward, apparent and exoteric meaning is Sufi-oriented; inwardly, Khayyam has an anti-religious agenda. The Khayyamian agenda against faith, a profane attempt to commit sacrilege against Islam, was somehow revealed and his true purpose was exposed leading to the disclosure of his aversion toward faith. What al-Qifṭī fails to explain is how "the Imām of Khurāsān," "the *'Allāmah* of his time" can also be a duplicitous heathen at the same time? It is true that the intellectual elites have often kept their views from the public eye, but this is not al-Qifṭī's point. Furthermore, there is a second ambiguity here, and that is the conflicting sense in which Sufism is portrayed. In the first paragraph, Sufis are presented in a positive context in which they understood Khayyam's *Ruba'iyyat* in its exoteric sense as opposed to the inwardly "devious nature" of the *Ruba'iyyat*. In the second part, Sufis are referred to pejoratively as they become a group that Khayyam shuns and from which he publicly disassociates himself in order to prove his commitment to religion, implying that Sufis are somehow beyond the pale of faith.

Even before Ghazzālī embraced Sufism, mainstream Sufis were tolerated and respected by some, and yet there were the antinomian Sufis among whom *Malāmatiyyah*[38] became known as the embodiment of heresy. Al-Qifṭī' in his account of Khayyam is not consistent; if we are to preserve the integrity of this report, we have to assume that Khayyam was an antinomian Sufi, as some of his modern biographers such as A. Dashtī, in *Damī bā Khayyam*, mention.[39]

Was Khayyam in so much trouble with the orthodox elements that he had to perform the pilgrimage to Mecca as a way of defending his faith? And yet, at the end of the quotation, al-Qifṭī once again acknowledges Khayyam's learnedness in philosophy and religious sciences when he says, "in the science of *ḥikmah* ... he was unique." The question is, how can a man who is referred to as "the Imām of Khūrāsān," "the *'Allāmah* of his time" and "*ḥakīm*" be regarded as an apostate? These titles, as well as those by his own contemporaries, reveal much about who Khayyam was and how he was perceived; the picture that emerges helps us to reconstruct his image.

Al-Qifṭī was a historian whose views on Khayyam were based solely on what he had read and collected from other sources, and there appears to have been two different schools of thought with regard to Khayyam from the very beginning. The first school saw him as an Imām, *'Allāmah*, *ḥakīm*, and a man of faith. Al-Qifṭī has presented this perspective rather faithfully. The second school viewed him as an outright apostate, an antinomian Sufi. Assuming al-Qifṭī's account of the diverse views of Khayyam at the time are accurate, it follows that Khayyam may have been an apostate Imām, an agnostic *'Allāmah* and a bewildered *ḥakīm*, contradictions which have come together in the very being of the legendary Khayyam. He can therefore be called, *Imām al-shakkākīn* (The Imām of doubters!), as his predecessor, Zakariyyā' Rāzi was called.

Al-Qifṭī's account of Khayyam becomes problematic if we use an either/or model to understand these contradictory accounts. The contradictions, however, are placed in their proper context and made sense of if we see Khayyam as a complex figure who acknowledges that to exist is to suffer, to question, to doubt, and to wonder, and yet he acknowledges the religious dimension of humans by being a practicing Muslim. The human condition and the vast galaxy within which we are *thrown* is too complex for a serious thinker such as Khayyam to exchange the restlessness of uncertainty for the peace that comes with "certitude." Khayyam is too "sober", to use a Sufi terminology, to give in to easy answers, and too "drunk" to heed to the orthodox party line. Intellectual honesty demands one to resist the transcendental temptation of the traditional scenarios predestined to end in a happy rapprochement between faith and doubt.

"A philosopher I am," opponents erroneously say
God knows, I am not who they say
While I am in this sorrow-laden nest,
I know not who and why I am nor why I should stay.[40]

During 642–645/1251–1254, when the famous Shams Tabrīzī, the spiritual guide of Rūmī, was in Konya, one of his close disciples, Shaykh Ibrāhīm, asked him a question regarding one of Khayyam's *Ruba'iyyat*. Shams elaborates on the poem, and part of this dialogue which appears in Shams' *Maqālāt* is as follows:

> Khayyam in a poem has said that no one understands the secrets of love and he who has arrived at it is bewildered.
>
> Shaykh Ibrāhīm raised an objection to Khayyam's words, and asked [Shams] "Once arrived [at Truth], why be bewildered and why be bewildered if never arrived [at Truth?]"
>
> I [Shams] said, "He was describing himself for he was perplexed. Once, he accuses the heavens or life and another time destiny, [he] rejects God almighty and yet praises Him, his words are convoluted and dark. A man of faith is not bewildered; faithful is he for whom His Eminence has dropped the mask and lifted the veil, sees his purpose, is obedient, certainty within certainty and there in certainty lies spiritual pleasure.[41]

In the same work, Shams also refers to the story of Khayyam and Ghazzālī with a slight variation:

> Muḥammad Ghazzālī, peace be upon him, was studying the *Ishārāt* of Abū Alī [Sīnā] with Omar Khayyam. He [Khayyam] was learned and for that reason he [Ghazzālī] refers to [Khayyam] in the

> *Iḥyā' al-'ulūm* pejoratively. [Khayyam] commanded [Ghazzālī], to read it a second time, "have you not understood it yet?" Read it [*Ishārāt*] a third time, [Khayyam commanded Ghazzālī]. Musicians and drummers had been told to play once Ghazzālī left so it became apparent that [Ghazzālī] was studying with him [Khayyam] so he [Ghazzālī] may benefit from it.
>
> He who falsely claims "I am the truth,"
> Suffice it to say he is flipping in suspense.[42]

This account of Khayyam is one of the most unfortunate cases, since it is not entirely clear what the basis of Shams' criticism is other than a negative reputation which had survived or been attributed to Khayyam by way of his *Ruba'iyyat*. One may expect that Shams Tabrīzī, the eminent teacher and giant figure of the Sufi tradition, had at least interpreted the *Ruba'iyyat* from a Sufi point of view. Like so many others who have acknowledged Khayyam's scholarly merit, Shams does mention his philosophical acumen but chastises him for being perplexed. Clearly, Shams Tabrīzī's view was based on the popular heresy, but what it also indicates is that the school of thought that considered Khayyam to be an apostate only a century after his death had spread far beyond Nayshābūr even as far as the North-Western part of Persia, in today's Āzarbāyjān, where Shams came from.[43] The irony of Shams' view with regard to Khayyam is that Shams himself made so many antinomian statements parallel to Khayyam's heretical views.[44] In addition, why a person, himself the center of so much controversy, would criticize Khayyam so severely remains a mystery.

The only plausible explanation is that Shams' view is based on a vague reputation of Khayyam and a general understanding of him rather than a thorough reading and comprehension of what Khayyam had actually written. This conclusion is plausible because Shams makes the same kind of careless and negative comments with regard to other eminent figures such as Fakhr al-Dīn Rāzī, Shihāb al-Dīn Suhrawardī, 'Ayn al-Qoḍāt Hamadānī and even Ibn 'Arabī. Shams was not a scholar; and just as it is highly unlikely that he had a thorough familiarity with these figures, it is equally unlikely that he had studied any of Khayyam's works.

The other biographer of Khayyam is Zakariyā' Muḥammad ibn Maḥmūd Qazwīnī. In his *Athār al-bilād wa akhbār al-'ibād*, written in 674/1283, he refers to Khayyam's role in Sulṭān Malik Shāh's observatory and restates Shams Tabrīzī's account of Ghazzālī and Khayyam:

> It is said that every day a jurist before the sunrise went to Khayyam and studied the complexities of the science of *ḥikmah*. Once he left, in peoples' presence, he criticized Khayyam. Omar Khayyam asked the drummers and trumpet players to hide in his own house and when that jurist in accordance with his habit came for his studies, Khayyam asked the drummers to beat on their drums and blow on their trumpets. People came from every corner and Omar Khayyam said "O citizens of Nayshābūr, this is the same master who every day at this time comes to study with me and praises me for what I teach him. Is it not shameful to praise the teacher in his presence and say evil things about him in his absence?"[45]

It is highly unlikely that an eminent personality such as Khayyam would humiliate Ghazzālī who was both learned and influential. The notable part of this story is the unwritten underlying conflict that had come to fruition between philosophers and theologians at the time. The above story symbolically emphasizes the sort of animosity that existed between the rising dogmatism of the Ash'arite theology represented by Ghazzālī and the more rationalistic philosophy of the Peripatetics (*Mashshā'is*) represented by Khayyam.

Often, the desire of the popular culture or even the scholarly community is demonstrated by allegorical stories such as the encounter between Ibn Rushd, the rationalist philosopher, and Ibn 'Arabī, the supreme gnostic of the Islamic world. The dichotomy of the "heart" and the "mind" is often expressed through metaphor and allegorical stories. An entire literary genre is devoted to such didactic literature in Islam, among which we can name Aṭṭār's *Tadhkirat al-'uliyā'*.[46]

The part of the story that refers to Ghazzālī's love-hate relationship with Khayyam may reveal more about his difficult relationship with philosophers in general than Ghazzālī in particular. We know that Ghazzālī experienced his famous doubt with regard to religious truth, generally believed to have occurred in the later phase of his life, when he was teaching in Baghdād. His doubt may well have begun much earlier and his denunciation of Khayyam's philosophical thought may have been partially an attempt to maintain his own image and prestige as an orthodox Ash'arite theologian. Deep within, however, Ghazzālī may have been trying to deal with his own doubts, which he himself must have disliked but could not evade or escape by studying philosophy.

In the later part of the seventh/thirteenth century, in a treatise entitled *Mukhtaṣar fī dhikr ḥukamā' al-yunāniyyīn wa'l-mallīyyīn*, a work based on *Tatimmah ṣiwān al-ḥikmah* of Bayhaqī, we find additional evidence with regard to Khayyam's intellectual orientation:

> The master philosopher, *ḥujjat al-ḥaqq* (The Evidence of Truth), Omar ibn Ibrāhīm al-Khayyāmī, is originally from Nayshābūr and he is a successor to Abū Alī [Sīnā] in *ḥikmah* except that he has a shortcoming in temperament. It is said that he read a book in Iṣfahān seven times and memorized it. He was learned in jurisprudence, history and the science of recitation however with regard to parts of *ḥikmah*, he was reluctant to teach it.[47]

By now, we can conclude that Khayyam, once again referred to as "*ḥujjat al-ḥaqq*" and "*ḥakīm*," was a philosopher whose views were not completely divorced from religious thought. The above source also confirms Khayyam's knowledge of Islamic law and the science of reciting the Qur'an. None of these descriptions are befitting of an agnostic hedonist whose heretical ideas constituted the salient feature of his *Ruba'iyyat*.

We encounter the same paradigmatic obstacle that we encountered before: the conflict between recognizing him as a religious authority and the skeptic of his *Ruba'iyyat*. If there is going to be a solution, it would dismiss neither his faith nor his disbelief, but argue that a rapprochement between the faith and infidelity exists. Otherwise, we have to embrace the idea that either there are two Khayyams, as has been suggested: Khayyam the agnostic-poet and Khayyam the scientist and faithful Muslim; or we have to allow for the assumption that Khayyam was a hypocrite, a duplicitous character with some form of split personality who fooled everyone. Neither of these explanations, I argue, is acceptable. A third explanation possibly accounts for both Khayyam's belief and infidelity; but this alternative defies the traditional Persian-Islamic way of thinking, a bipolar perspective in which one is either within the domain of faith or heresy. This third explanation will be central to our understanding and analysis of the *Ruba'iyyat* and will be elaborated throughout this work.

In another reference to Khayyam, Naṣr Mustawfī Qazwīnī, in his work *Tārikh Gozideh* (730/1339), observes:

> He is Omar ibn Ibrāhīm who in most sciences especially in astronomy was the leading [scientist] of his time and was a companion of Sulṭān Malik Shāh Seljuqī. He has [written] profound treatises and wonderful poems.[48]

There is also the very brief reference to Khayyam's treatise *Concerning Algebra* by Sanjarī al-Ansārī who, in his *Irshād al-maqāṣid ilā isn al-maqāṣid*, said, "He [Khayyam] offers proofs for problems concerning algebra and geometrical proofs."[49]

One also has to take note of the pejorative comments the great literary genius, Farīd al-Dīn Aṭṭār (513–627/1117–1231) makes in his *Manẓumah-yi ilāhī nāmāh*.[50] Aṭṭār, who refers to Khayyam as a learned but "incomplete" man, writes poetically:

> There was a famed visionary for whom
> The soul of the dead were accessible
> Once he arrived at a grave
> Saw therein the corpus in the grave
> A wise man tested his vision and
> Took him to the grave of Omar Khayyam
> "What do you see below this earth?" said the wise man
> "Tell us O pure hearted man of vision"
> Replied the noble man pointing [to the grave]
> "Here lies a man [Khayyam] who is *incomplete* (*nā tamām*)
> The [spiritual] state where he had journeyed
> He only claimed to have known it
> When his [Khayyam's] ignorance became apparent
> The sweat from anxiety stuck between embarrassment and fear
> From embarrassment, he is in dire need [of salvation]."

There are a few other sources, though not very reliable, in which brief references are made to Khayyam; and even though they do not reveal new information, they do confirm similar accounts offered by other biographers. In *Ātashkadeh* of A. Bigdelī, we read the following account, "Khayyam who is called Omar sat with Sulṭān Sanjar on the same throne and was a schoolmate with [Niẓām al-Mulk] and Ḥasan Ṣabbāh. [Khayyam] decreed and donated several places where wells were dug and composed fine *Ruba'iyyat*."[51] Riḍā Qolikhān Hidāyat in *Riyāḍ al-'ārifīn* describes Khayyam as one of the geniuses of his time who was close to Sulṭān Sanjar, and refers to the friendship between Ḥasan Ṣabbāh, Niẓām al-Mulk and Khayyam. Ḥidāyat refers to Khayyam's ascetic practices and abstinence, but the interesting point no one else has alluded to is the claim that he was affiliated with the antinomian Sufis (*Malāmatiyyah*). He says, "He is a brilliant and high-minded *ḥakīm* whose *Ruba'iyyat* are profound."[52]

Finally, there is the short account in the *Majma' al-fuṣaḥā*[53] that once again refers to his close relationship with Sulṭān Sanjar, his friendship with Ḥasan Ṣabbāh and Niẓām al-Mulk, and his fine poems, but acknowledges that Khayyam did not enjoy a good reputation with the public.

The above references and quotations are by and large exhaustive of the available sources where Khayyam is mentioned by either his contemporaries or those within a century or so after his death. A reconstruction of Khayyam's "true" character to the extent possible will have to be inevitably based on these sources. There are a number of other sources where Khayyam is mentioned which have not been included here, since they are mainly references to the intricacies of the style of his poetry and do not add to our knowledge of him as a person or his intellectual orientation. These sources, however, will be discussed in the chapter on his *Ruba'iyyat*.

Before the present chapter can be brought to an end, Omar Khayyam's introductory and concluding remarks to his various treatises should be addressed. These assertions are clear indications of how Khayyam feels about the Islamic faith and where he stands with respect to it. In this regard, these statements are particularly significant for the reconstruction of Khayyam's character and his tarnished image as an agnostic-hedonist, since they consist of Khayyam's own words as opposed to other secondary accounts. These statements clearly indicate where Khayyam stands with regard to theism, and therefore only their translations are included here without an extensive commentary.

On proofs for Problems Concerning Algebra[54]

Khayyam begins this work by saying, "Praise be upon the Lord of the universe and peace be upon all His messengers ... and Allah is needed at all times and in Him I take refuge ... I grasp onto the chain of grace that is bestowed by God, hoping for success." He ends this book by saying, "Allah makes the difficulties of the path easy through his goodness and generosity."

On the elaboration of the problems concerning the book of Euclid (Risālah fī Sharḥmā ashkāl min muṣādarāt kitāb uqlidus)[55]

In the introduction, he states,

> Praise be upon Allah the possessor of compassion and goodness and peace be upon those selected obedient faithful, especially the master of prophets, Muḥammad and his pure companions. Research upon sciences and their attainment through proofs is incumbent upon every seeker of eternal deliverance. Happiness, especially those universal principles of life after death and proof of the soul and its survival, and the attainment of the attributes of the Necessary Being, Most High are obtained, in as much as is possible for man to obtain.[56]

At the end of this book, he reaffirms the above differently and again praises God and the Prophet Muḥammad.

On Being and Necessity (Kawn wa-'l taklīf)[57]

In a revealing section toward the end of this treatise, Khayyam considers obedience to religion to have three major benefits: it increases the power of rational thinking, brings about certainty with regard to religious matters and ameliorates social injustice. He summarizes:

> Thus, in Divine and prophetic command and prohibition, there are three benefits: First, through obedience, the soul is so cleansed

> through asceticism; bodily desires are reduced and the power that causes intellectual powers from darkening is prevented. Second, to make reflection upon Divine and eschatological matters habitual so through it, one may observe prayers, prevent vanity so he may contemplate upon the incorporeal domain. This is so Divine names are glorified within him, meaning, He who has brought all the existents into existence, glory be upon Him, and sacred are His names, and to know that there is no deity except God. Existents through an orderly succession have emanated from Him and His wisdom has been verified through analogies that are not illusory and sophistry. Thirdly, through verses, He reprimands and promises what is necessary for the implementation of religious laws. He who is to implement the *Shari'ah* should inform the people so the principle of justice and coexistence may well be put in place. This is so the order of the universe as the wisdom of God, most high has deemed necessary may remain so.[58]

Among some of the other references of Khayyam to God in this work is this, "I grab onto the virtue of that success which comes from God Most High for He is the source of good and emanator of all justice." Khayyam brings this treatise to an end by saying, "God Most High knows the best and praise be upon Him in the beginning and the end, outwardly and inwardly."

On existence (Fi'l-wujūd)

In the introduction, he says,

> In the name of God, most compassionate, most merciful, praise be upon Him whose majesty is exalted and His name sacred. He has created all things, then guides them in their proper way and counts every one of them. Blessings be upon His Prophet Muṣtafā Muḥammad and his pure companions.[59]

The book ends with a discussion concerning existence and essence:

> God is most exalted and is superior to what the perplexed and heretics have said, there is no change and no power except what comes from Him. He is watchful of my acts and determines goodness, so praise be upon Him who is the origin of the beginning; and the blessing of God be upon our master, Muḥammad, and his pure and exalted companions.

On the knowledge of the universal principles of existence
(Fī kulliyāt al-wujūd)

In the beginning, Khayyam divides the seekers of Divine knowledge into four groups: theologians, philosophers, Ismā'īlīs and Sufis. He criticizes the first three and supports the Sufis as the only possible path to come to know the reality of God. He ends the treatise by saying, "There is no perfection better than His majesty and that [spiritual] state is not forbidden or veiled to anyone. What there is [to know by way of abstraction] is due to the impurity of [human] nature, if the veil is lifted and what obstructs is removed, realities as they are become apparent."[60]

The above is sufficient to establish beyond any reasonable doubt that Omar Khayyam lived and breathed within the Islamic religious universe and that his faith and commitment to religious thought was unquestionable. So how Khayyam, who began and ended his works by paying homage to God and the Prophet Muḥammad, could have become the prophet of agnostics and hedonists is a seemingly insoluble oxymoron. And yet, against the overwhelming evidence of Khayyam's faith, like so many other great figures in the history of Islam, he is accused of having been a heretic. A Khayyamian quatrain remarks:

> These two or three fools who think they know
> Ignorant are they and oh, how it shows
> Striving to be a donkey, for they are less than an ass
> Every cow that is not a donkey, is deemed a heretic foe.[61]

3

Khayyam within the Intellectual Context of his Time

O Preacher, harder at work we are than you,
Though drunken, we are more sober than you;
The blood of grapes we drink, you that of men,
Be fair, who is more blood-thirsty, we or you?[1]

One of the major centers of intellectual and religious thought in the Islamic world has always been a vast region in the eastern part of Persia, known as Khūrāsān. This region, whose name etymologically means "the place where the sun rises in ease," has been the meeting place between the East and the West by virtue of the "Silk Road." When traveling the Silk Road from China, India, Pakistan and Afghanistan – the cradle of some of the most ancient civilizations – caravans were forced to go through Khūrāsān. This unique geographical situation produced one of the richest cultural milieux of the ancient and medieval era resulting in some of the greatest scholars of the Islamic world.

THE PHYSICAL AND INTELLECTUAL GEOGRAPHY OF NAYSHĀBŪR

One of the most important cities of Khūrāsān was Nayshābūr, the birthplace of Khayyam, a major and prosperous metropolitan area which was known for its many centers of learning and the great many scholars who have hailed from there. The modern pronunciation of Nayshābūr comes from "Nayshāpūr" which etymologically consists of three parts – *nisht*, *sha* and *pur*. *Nisht* in the Pahlavī language means "the throne," *sha* denotes "a king" or "a sovereign," and *pur* stands for "son." Nayshābūr was built in honor of Shāpūr, the first son of Ardeshīr Bābakān of the Sāsānīd empire, as the place for the throne of the king's son.[2]

The geographical position of Nayshābūr provided an immensely rich intellectual milieu for Khayyam. Religiously, Nayshābūr was a major center of Zoroastrians with Barzin Mehr, one of the major fire temples located in the vicinity of Nayshābūr. It is entirely plausible that Khayyam had come to know of the Zoroastrian faith and met some of its learned masters. After all, Bahmanyār, the student of Avicenna whom Khayyam was likely to have met, was either a first generation Muslim or a convert who was born into a Zoroastrian family.

While Nayshābūr's location has been a blessing, it has also been a curse. Its prosperity made it attractive to various armies such as the Ghuz tribes who looted the city and burned it to the ground several times. In *Tārikh Bayhaqī*, 'A. Bayhaqī tells us of a famine in Nayshābūr: "Such a famine in Nayshābūr was not remembered and most people died."[3] The city is said to have had forty-seven neighborhoods which would have ranked it among the major metropolitan cities of the world at the time. Nayshābūr is also on a seismic fault-line and has been devastated several times, including the major earthquakes of around 431 AH/1040 CE. Khayyam as a young boy must have been affected by the memories of such a major tragedy, one that may have reverberated in his poems concerning suffering and the painful fate that befalls humankind.

Politically, Nayshābūr had been the scene of the bloody wars between various dynasties such as the Seljuqs and Ghaznavīds, as well as the relentless assassination campaign of the Ismā'īlīs and the gradual eradication of the Zoroastrian culture. These bloody wars, too, may appear in Khayyam's *Ruba'iyyat* where he belittles political ambition. He sarcastically writes:

> Yon palace[4] that once vied with heaven blue
> To pay their tributes, kings there stood in queue
> We saw a dove high on its battlement
> Repeating mournfully, "Coo, coo-coo, coo"[5]

INTELLECTUAL TRENDS AND THEIR TRANSITIONS

One of the most intensely debated issues among historians and philosophers of history has been whether it is an individual who creates history and that history is "His-story," as Nietzsche said; or whether history creates the individuals, as some of the modern continental philosophers would argue. Without trying to minimize the power of the individual intellects who have shaped our human environment or to maximize the power of historical forces upon what Hans Gadamer calls, "the horizon of vision," we have to examine Khayyam and the historical context in which he lived, if we are to understand certain strands of his intellectual thought.

Khayyam, like many other thinkers, was influenced by the intellectual trends of his time and reacted to them in a variety of ways. An understanding of the intellectual milieu allows us not only better to understand his philosophical and theological writings but also his *Rubaʿiyyat*, his personality and his habits, such as his reservation and his lack of interest in teaching. I will argue that Khayyam's *Rubaʿiyyat* are not just the existential bemoanings of a thinker similar to Schopenhauer and Goethe, but also an intellectual response to the rise of religious dogmatism, an endeavor to question and deconstruct a faith-based dogmatic theology that stifled rationalism and creativity.

To understand Khayyam, it is imperative that we first survey the intellectual landscape of the Islamic civilization in the first few centuries of its inception. We shall then look for those elements which brought about one of the most outstanding civilizations of human history and then briefly glance at its demise. Even a cursory review of the history of the first four centuries of Islamic intellectual thought provides us with clues that are helpful in understanding Khayyam's thought as expressed in his prose and poetry and in determining his place on the colorful spectrum of intellectual thought at the time.

The early expansion of the Islamic civilization to the north and east led to the discovery of major civilizations such as the Zoroastrian civilization of the Persians and the wealth of their libraries as well as the school of Alexandria in Egypt, perhaps the richest center of intellectual and scientific thought in the ancient world. Despite such an encounter, the Islamic civilization did not come away philosophically enriched even though, in certain fields, such as mathematics and medicine, Muslims did gain a great deal from their encounters and translated a large number of books into Arabic and Syriac.[6] From the middle of the second/eighth century when Manṣūr became the Caliph, a massive effort began to promote science, in particular mathematics and astrology. It was at this time that Muslims came to know of the Greek intellectual heritage[7] and their use of reason and rationalism. This methodology enabled the Islamic civilization to begin the development of intellectual thought and led to the flourishing of rationalism.

After Manṣūr, Mahdī became the Caliph, but his concern was more to fight heresy and anthropomorphic interpretations of Islam which inadvertently encouraged the development of theological debate as a means to counter heresy. The scientific thinking and the translation movement that had begun during Manṣūr's and Mahdī's reigns reached a new high when Ma'mūn became the Caliph. Ma'mūn, whose mother was Persian and who had spent some time among Persians in Khūrāsān, was keenly interested in the newly formed rationalistic theology of Mu'tazilīte. Ma'mūn even propagated some of their views such as the created nature of the Qur'an as opposed to its eternal nature. His boundless interest in promoting science and rationalistic theology went so far as to ask the Sicilian king to send him part of his science library, which contained translations of major texts of Greek thought. In addition, there arose the formation of *Bayt al-ḥikmah* (the house of wisdom) whose scientists, scholars and literary figures gathered to produce and translate texts from Greek, Pahlavī and Sanskrit into Arabic.

By the beginning of the third/ninth century, rationalism had become the *modus operandi*, and many of the philosophical and theological works on logic, medicine and other branches of knowledge had been translated into Arabic. The number of scientists who conducted "cutting-edge" research in every field of human endeavor is far too great to mention here, but even a cursory review indicates the extent to which scholarship, scientific research, and the spirit of rationalism was celebrated in the Islamic world.[8] In this context, Greek thought should be given credit for the blossoming of sciences in the Islamic world; figures such as Plato, Aristotle and, to a lesser extent, Plotinus, had become the heroes of Muslims and such titles as "Divine Sages" (*al-ḥakimayīn al-ilāhī*) were bestowed upon them.[9]

Some have called the fourth/tenth century "The Golden Era" of Islamic civilization. As Gutas states in his work, *Greek Thought, Arabic Culture*, "By the end of the fourth/tenth century, almost all the Greek scientific and secular philosophical works that were available in late antiquity, including diverse topics like astrology, alchemy, physics, mathematics, medicine and philosophy, had been translated into Arabic."[10]

As the spirit of rationalism was withering away in the fifth/eleventh century, the outstanding achievements of Muslim scientists, which brought about one of the most exquisite civilizations in the human history, also began to decline. The voices of the literalists, which arose with such figures as Caliph Al-Mutiwakkil (232–247 AH) who opposed intellectual debate with regard to religious matters, gained strength. However, it took about a century for this trend to come to fruition and allow jurists such as Aḥmad ibn Ḥanbal to formally charge philosophers and theologians, particularly the Mu'tazilītes, with heresy. With freedom of expression substantially curtailed, the spirit of rationalism began to be replaced by the Ash'arites' orthodox theology, who emphasized faith as distinguished from reason as the sole criterion for discourse.[11]

In the fifth–sixth/eleventh–twelfth centuries when Khayyam lived, the glorious days of intellectual debate and creativity had come to an end; and jurists began to issue *fatwā*s (religious decrees) against rationalists, particularly philosophers. Islamic law (*Shari'ah*) had become the supreme truth, and formalism was identified with faith; orthodox jurists of the time had established their hegemony and the era of free thinking had effectively come to an end. Figures such as Fārābī, Avicenna, Zakariyā Rāzī and Bīrūnī, all of whom were once venerated figures, became symbols of apostasy and heresy. In schools that were established in Khūrāsān, even teaching intellectual sciences became forbidden. Libraries were disenfranchised and poets took pride in criticizing the philosophers in a derogatory manner.[12] Few philosophers in the fifth–sixth/eleventh–twelfth centuries were not branded as heretics, and some had to save themselves by calling others heretics. For example, Muḥammad ibn Nijā' al-Arabālī was forced to make a public confession, saying, "God most exalted is the Truth and Avicenna was wrong."[13]

The circle of the permissible sciences was shrinking as indicated by the Shi'ite theologian, Mūsā al-Nobakhtī, who, in his work on the refutation of logic wrote, "He who practices logic is a heretic."[14] First, philosophy was denounced, and then logic was said to lead to the rejection of faith and thus viewed as an instrument of the devil. Whereas a jurist may learn some arithmetic which enables him to perform the necessary dictums of the *shari'ah,* geometry was pronounced to be heretical, as seen by the following statement of Aḥmad ibn Thawābah: "God, I take refuge in you from geometry, protect me from its evils."[15] Ghazzālī, in *The Beginning of Sciences* (*Fatiḥat al-'ulūm*), rejects mathematics all together and offers a detailed list of all the evils that arise from studying mathematics.[16] Neither did astronomy escape the wrath of the dogmatic jurists. Mūsā al-Nobakhtī, whose family was known to have been among the notable astronomers, wrote a book entitled *Treatise on the Rejection of Astronomers* (*Kitāb al-rad 'ala'l-munajjimīn*). Even the opinions of the eminent jurist Imām Shāfi'ī, who had lived earlier (150–205/767–820), himself a practicing astronomer who abandoned and condemned its use, was used by jurists as a source of condemnation. Finally, even the science of medicine was not spared from the wrath of the orthodoxy. Jāḥiẓ, the famous theologian, wrote a book rejecting the use of medicine, regarding it as an interference with God's will.

Perhaps the spirit of the time is best described in an apocryphal Ḥadith, clearly made up to justify the dogmatic position of the jurists. It is reported that the Prophet Muḥammad has said, "There is no benefit in the science of medicine, and no truth lies in the science of geometry, the science of logic and natural sciences are heretical and those practicing them are heathens."[17]

Khayyam lived at the end of an era when free thinking was coming to an end and theological stricture was on the rise. His lack of interest in teaching publicly as well as his lack of patience for scholarly debate must be understood in light of his fear of condemnation by the orthodox elements. Khayyam may have said:

> The secrets of the world, our book defined
> For fear of malice could not be outlined
> Since none here worthy is amongst the dolts
> We can't reveal the thoughts that crowd our mind.[18]

His short treatises, which were clear and concise indications of his support for the rationalism of the Peripatetics, are a loud affirmation of the past, the "good old days" when rational thinking was revered. His use of poetic expression to criticize the formal orthodoxy is better understood as a reaction against the rise of dogmatism. Even though Khayyam was not a product of his time, he was not completely divorced from the emerging forces among the intellectual elite either. He was engaged with the intellectual debates of his time as any scholar of Khayyam's caliber would be. The real question is whether Khayyam took refuge in poetic license to fight theological dogmatism?

Khayyam was reluctant to enter into theological debates of the type in which the Mu'tazilītes and Ash'arites were engaged. These debates, politicized with different politicians taking sides, often led to violent clashes between their supporters. Khayyam considered such theological debates as futile and idle speculations since certitude with regard to such matters is ultimately unattainable. While he does not provide a systematic theological response to these theological issues, he does offer a rebuttal in poetic form; and it is in this context that the *Ruba'iyyat* can be regarded as an intellectual response to the theological debates of his time. It was Khayyam's way to be engaged in these issues without being recognized as party to the conflict. He advocated freedom of thought and, as the following quatrain suggests, "free from truth and quest, from path and goal" his poems may have shielded him from possibly being harmed.

I saw a mystic, strange! he did not heed
For caste or creed, for faith or worldly greed;
And free from truth and quest, from path and goal,
He sat at ease, from earth and heaven freed.[19]

THE MU'TAZILITE-ASH'ARITE DEBATE AND KHAYYAM'S POETIC RESPONSE

Let us briefly consider the specific points of contention between the rationalist Mu'tazilītes and the orthodox theologians of the Ash'arite school and Khayyam's response to them. Khayyam's response consistently relies on the insufficiency of evidence as a way of reminding us of the futility of theological debates.

For instance, the Ash'arites emphasize the notion of certainty with regard to religious matters; and, as their chief exponent, Ghazzālī asserts, "Certainty is the essence of religion and from ascertaining it, there is no relief."[20] Khayyam could not possibly reject Ghazzālī's call for certainty in religious matters in a prose form but he could have responded in a quatrain such as:

Ye do not grasp the truth but still ye grope
Why waste then life and sit in doubtful hope
Beware! And hold forever Holy Name
From torpor sane or sot in death will slope.[21]

The heart of the issues around which the Mu'tazilite-Ash'arite debate centers can be reduced to the following five principles:

1. Unity (*Tawḥīd*)
2. Justice (*'Adl*)
3. The promise of reward and punishment in the hereafter (*Wa'd wa waīd*)
4. The state between the two states (*Manzil bayn al-manzilatayn*)
5. Commanding to do good and prohibiting from doing evil (*Amr bi'l-ma'rūf wa nahy 'an al-munkir*)

Unity (Tawḥīd)

For Muslim theologians (*mutikallimīn*), unity (*tawḥīd*) means to bear witness that there is only one God. On this question, both

Mu'tazilītes and Ash'arites are in agreement; the problem, however, comes when the relationship between God and His attributes is considered. God is eternal, but what about an attribute like "justice"? Is justice an accidental attribute or an essential one? If accidental, then it is in a sense added to God but since God has always been just, the attribute of justice must have always existed. What follows from this argument is the problem of the co-eternity of God and His attributes. If the attributes, however, are essential, meaning they are part of God, then God must be a compound entity in order to have all the names and attributes that constitute Him. Between Mu'tazilites and Ash'arites, the relationship between God and His attributes was one of the major points of contention, one that Khayyam must have thought was not a fruitful endeavor, since we can neither figure out the ultimate answer nor does the discussion help to alleviate the suffering and agony of the human condition. A Khayyamian quatrain explains:

> Some strung the pearls of thought by searching deep,
> And told some tales about Him, – sold them cheap;
> But none has caught a clue to secret realms,
> They cast a horoscope and fall in sleep.[22]

Justice ('Adl)

According to Mu'tazilites, *'adl* implies that God is all-just, and from an all-just God only justice may emanate. Therefore, all of his actions by necessity must be just even though some of them may appear as unjust. Qāḍī 'Abd al-Jabbār, one of the most eminent figures of the Mu'tazilite school, describes divine justice as follows: "From the knowledge and what is related to *'adl*, the person should know that God's acts are all good and he does not do what is bad and does not refrain to do what is necessary for Him. In informing us, [He] does not lie and in judging does not do injustice."[23]

Therefore, it is plausible to conclude that all that occurs is just and the seemingly unjust events are, from a Divine perspective, just, even though they appear to us to be unjust. The very nature of justice and whether God can be unjust and other such matters were the subjects of great controversy, and Khayyam once again takes issue with the notion of a just world. In fact, the most salient feature of Khayyam's *Ruba'iyyat* seems to be his response to the question of justice, which is the subject of much of his ridicule. Khayyam considers the world to be fundamentally unjust; and if there were any reason for the presence of so much apparent evil, men of knowledge should have some insight into it. Khayyam comments:

> Had I but over the heavens control
> I'd remove this bullish ball beyond the goal
> And forthwith furnish better worlds and times
> Where love will cling to every freeman's soul.[24]

> I wonder if Lord could change the world
> Just so that I may see his plans unfurled
> Would he remove my name from roll of call?
> Or would my dish with larger sops be hurled?[25]

Khayyam's objection is not merely to be viewed as a poet's play with words, nor should it be given any less weight than a well-formulated philosophical argument. At a time when the injustices and corruption of the court, and of the king, and when death, destruction and famine throughout the land stood as obvious examples of injustice, the debate between Mu'tazilites and Ash'arites concerning the intricacies of how God's justice can best be explained seemed hardly relevant. Khayyam reacts against this intellectual debate not only by questioning the whereabouts of this justice, but also by going further in pointing a finger at God as the possible source of evil and injustice. He says:

> Since mortal compositions are cast by a Hand Divine,
> Why then the flaws that throw them out of line?
> If formed sublime, why must He shatter them?
> If not, to whom would we the fault assign?[26]

The promise of reward and punishment in the hereafter (Wa'd wa wa'īd)

The second theme of great significance and a salient feature of Khayyam's *Ruba'iyyat* involves the thorny debate concerning eschatology. Khayyam treats few issues more extensively than the promise of reward and punishment and the question of bodily resurrection. He argues that the whole subject matter derails one's attention, diverting it from the here and now, where one should be focused.

The discussion concerning reward and punishment and bodily resurrection in the Qur'an is a theologically complex one in that it is intertwined with notions such as the freedom of will and moral responsibility, God's knowledge of future events and predestination, which inevitably follows from omniscience. When God promises reward and punishment, does He know from the beginning whether one's actions are such that they will be rewarded or punished? If He does know, then determinism follows; and if He does not, then God is not omniscient. To this contentious debate is added further complexity by the fact that change cannot be introduced into the Divine essence and that God cannot learn or come to know of something new, since this would imply a change. Qāḍī 'Abd al-Jabbār summarizes this when he states, "Regarding God, since intention and decision making is impossible for Him, assumption of the violation of intention to Him [is impossible] for He is power and more exalted than such allegations."[27]

Khayyam's response to this debate is what can be called "satirical deconstructionism," or a version of *reductio ad absurdum*, a method he seems to have adopted and used consistently in responding to intellectual debates of his era. Khayyam's response and methodology will be elaborated in the forthcoming chapters, but a few examples will be sufficient to clarify his position. If bodily resurrection is possible, Khayyam argues, then however we die, we should be resurrected as such. It is entirely possible that he composed the following quatrain in response to the orthodox Ash'arite theologians who argued for the bodily resurrection. Playing on this theme, he asserts:

> Anon! The pious people would advise,
> That as we die, we rise up fools or wise
> 'Tis for this cause we keep with lover and wine
> For in the end with same we hope to rise.[28]
>
> In Paradise are angels, as men trow
> And fountains with pure wine and honey flow

If these be lawful in the world to come
May I not love the like down here below?[29]

As always, Khayyam begins by questioning the epistemological foundation of certitude and thereby undermines the very foundation of orthodoxy's authoritative claim to truth. In this case, he asks, "How do you know there is even life after death much less can you discuss the intricacies of what is in the other world when even Prophet Muḥammad said, " 'After death, you shall join the mysterious caravan of death?' "

Ye go from soul asunder this ye know,
And that ye creep, behind his curtain low;
Hence sing His Name, ye know not whence ye came
And live sedate, ye know not where to go.[30]

Following the above quatrain which undermines the Mu'tazilite-Ash'arite debate by questioning the epistemological foundation of their eschatological views, Khayyam brings our attention to where he thinks we ought to be focusing it – here and now. This quatrain, which does lend itself to hedonism, is in actuality anything but. He makes the following claim:

They tell "In Heaven angels come to greet!"
I say "The juice of Vine, in truth, is sweet."
Take the cash, let go of future promises,
We bear with drums when further far they beat.[31]

Khayyam's satirical deconstructionist project, which begins by casting doubt upon eschatological debate and continues by putting the emphasis on the here and now, takes a radical turn undermining the entire discussion on the subject, when he says:

From thee, O *sāqī*![32] Those who went away,
They fall, of course, to dreaming pride, a prey,
Drink the chalice of wine and hear this Truth
"Just empty air is every word they say."[33]

The state between the two states (Manzil bayn al-manzilatayn)

The fourth major point of contention between the Mu'tazilites and Ash'arites is actually the debate which split the Mu'tazilites. One of the theological debates in the early period of Islamic history was over the eschatological state of a Muslim who sins. Clearly, a Muslim who sins must have a different state before the eyes of God than an infidel; and, therefore, an extensive discussion took place to determine the relationship between the sinner and the sin. Theological schools such as Khawarij maintained that anyone who sins is a heretic. The well-known theologian, Ḥasan Baṣrī, and his famous student, 'Amir ibn 'Ubayd, however, argued that a Muslim who sins is neither faithful nor a heretic but a hypocrite (*munāfiq*). Waṣīl ibn 'Aṭā, supporter of Ḥasan Baṣrī, argued that such a person is neither a heretic nor faithful nor a hypocrite but has simply acted sinfully (*fāsiq*).

Legend has it that a debate took place between Waṣīl ibn 'Aṭā and 'Amr ibn 'Ubayd concerning the state of a Muslim who sins. When 'Ubayd stated his view and left the circle, he was called "the withdrawn one" (*mu'tazilī*). This incident has been recounted in different versions, but they all agree that the central point of contention was whether there can be an intermediary state between being a Muslim and being a heretic. Mu'tazilites, with regard to their fourth principle, take an uncharacteristically non-rational approach to this topic, as evidenced by the words of Qāḍī 'Abd al-Jabbār: "The problem is a religious question and there is no room for the intellect [to judge] since within the context of this problem, there is discussion regarding the extent of punishment and reward, this is something that the intellect does not know."[34]

The gradations of sin and the question of reward and punishment are an extension of eschatology and a continuation of the promise of reward and punishment. Omar Khayyam's satirical deconstructionism goes through three layers of casting doubt on the whole discussion. First, there is the insufficiency of evidence; second, there is the fixing of one's attention on the present; and finally, the deliverance of the final punch. He mentions:

O unenlightened race of human kind
Ye are a nothing, built on empty wind
Ye a mere nothing, hovering in the abyss
A void before you, and a void behind.[35]

For Khayyam, whether or not there is a state between the two states is a diversionary issue, which takes us from the real existential problem; for all we know we come from the abyss of nothingness to which we return.

Commanding to do good and prohibiting from doing evil
(Amr bi'l-ma'rūf wa nahy 'an al-munkir)

This injunction originally comes from a Qur'anic verse in which the Prophet Muḥammad is addressed, "You are the best of the community who have come for people, command them to do what is right and forbid them from doing wrong."[36]

This controversial topic, which is a seemingly simple religious injunction, quickly became an epistemological issue, in that one has to be certain with regard to what is good before one can command someone else. The epistemological aspect of knowing good and evil leads to a discussion concerning normative ethics and metaethics. As Qāḍī 'Abd al-Jabbār argues, sometimes good becomes bad, and one does not always know what is good.

> If one knows or suspects that one's drinking wine or burning of a neighborhood may lead to the death of a group of Muslims, forbidding him is not necessary, in fact it is not good or desirable.[37]

The Mu'tazilite-Ash'arite controversy also addresses the nature of ethical values and their classification, such as those values which are practiced by Imāms as distinct from those practiced by the masses. Naturally, there were those who argued that good and evil are subject to rational discourse, as in 'Abd al-Jabbār's example above; and whereas God ultimately knows what is good, we can only speculate. One can clearly see how a consequentialist position clashes with the more faith-based approach or deontological ethics in which Qur'anic injunctions for right and wrong must be followed "out of respect and reverence for the moral law," to echo a concept from Immanuel Kant.

Khayyam's approach to this problem is to argue that good and bad are intrinsically embedded within us; therefore, in a sense one does not need an external source of instruction, i.e. religion. He conveys this:

> The good and evil in the mold of man
> The joy and grief in fate and fortune's plan
> Leave not to the wheel of fortune, for in reason
> A thousand times more helpless than in man.[38]

The five issues that have been treated here are not exhaustive of the points of contention between the Mu'tazilites and Ash'arites. Among others, we can name Divine attributes and their contingency upon Divine essence, God's omniscience and one's ability to act freely, and finally, the complex issue of whether we can have a vision of God either in this world or the other one as the Qur'an promises.

THE RISE OF THE INDEPENDENT THINKERS AND THE PERIPATETICS

Along with the extensive theological debate, there arose in the third/ninth century, a parallel movement to treat a wide range of intellectual problems systematically. This movement was led by the philosophers who, by this time, had mastered Greek thought. The first notable figure of what can be regarded as a transition from theology to philosophy is al-Kindī. His ideas were more closely associated with the Mu'tazilites, as the names of several of his treatises suggest: *First Philosophy*, *Prostration of the Outermost Heavenly Body and its Submission to God*, *Proximate Cause of Generation and Corruption*, and *Refutation of the Arguments of Atheists.*[39] Al-Kindī supports the concept of the creation of the world *ex nihilo* (out of nothing) and its philosophical implications, the origination and destruction of the world by God, as well as the resurrection of the body, the possibility of miracles and the validity of prophetic revelation. As it can be seen, these topics are more in line with the Mu'tazilites, but his treatment is more systematic, and he uses Greek philosophy to vindicate the tenets of Islam rather than opposing Hellenic thought.

Through al-Kindī, we see the development of metaphysics, or "First Philosophy," which he defines as "knowledge of the First

Reality which is the cause of every reality."[40] Perhaps the most important contribution of al-Kindī was opening the channel of ration-alization as a path that is "more akin to the nature of things," and to open the pursuit of knowledge to other avenues, particularly Greek and Indian thought.

Following al-Kindī, we see an even bolder and freer use of reason and intellect by figures such as al-Naẓẓām[41] and Ibn al-Rāwandī,[42] both of whom questioned the fundamentals of the Islamic faith and the validity of scriptures advocating some form of naturalism based on pure faith and deism. Was Khayyam part of this trend? Certainly his criticism of faith and emphasis on the futility of a theological debate is most apparent throughout his *Ruba'iyyat.*

Systematic freethinking reaches its zenith in Zakariyā' Rāzī in 240/854 when he was reported to have written the following works: *Trickery of the Prophets* (*Makhāriq al-anbiyā'*), *The Stratagems of Those Claiming to be Prophets* (*Ḥiyāl al-mutanabbiyīn*) and *A Critique of Religions* (*Fī naqd al-adyān*).[43] In this remarkable figure and the little that has survived of his works, not only do we find learned arguments, but also the kind of spirit that Khayyam had inherited, a spirit whose demise he was witnessing during his time and for whose revival he no doubt yearned. One needs only to compare Rāzī's critique of religion and narrow mindedness of people to that of Khayyam in order to see the striking similarities. Rāzī tells us:

> If the people of this religion are asked about the proof for the soundness of their religion, they flare up, get angry and spill the blood of whoever confronts them with this question. They forbid rational speculation and strive to kill their adversaries. This is why truth became thoroughly silenced and concealed.[44]

And Khayyam is reported to have said:

> The secrets which my book of love has bred,
> Cannot be told for fear of loss of head;
> Since none is fit to learn, or cares to know,
> 'Tis better all my thoughts remain unsaid.[45]

This is not to say that orthodoxy did not exist at the time of Rāzī or that the Islamic world enjoyed an abundance of freethinkers who relied on reason as the *modus operandi*, but it is an indication of the presence of the kind of ambiance which allowed Rāzī to speak freely, an ambiance that had disappeared by the time of Khayyam. Was this the reason Khayyam was forced to adopt a different mode of expression, that is, poetry?

The same spirit is found in Ibn Rāwandī, Fārābī, Avicenna, Suhrawardī and many others who wrestled with Islamic intellectual thought in their own ways. Perhaps Ibn Rāwandī summarized it best when he said that either revelation is reasonable or it is not. If it is reasonable, then we need to follow reason and do not need revelation; and if it is unreasonable, then one should not follow what is unreasonable. Ibn Rāwandī died of natural causes, but Muslims from Khayyam's era up to the present with similar views would not have survived, and that illustrates the spirit of independent thinking in the first four centuries of Islam and its demise thereafter.

As evidenced by the title of Fārābī's work, *The Reconciliation between the Opinions of the Two Divine Sages, Plato and Aristotle*,[46] Fārābī, along with Avicenna and other Peripatetics, began a grand synthesis of Plotinus' system of emanation and certain themes of Plato and Aristotle. No other civilization was more successful in transmitting and interpreting Greek thought than the Islamic civilization, so much so that Plato's political thought became the basis for Islamic political philosophy, in particular Shi'ism. By the time Fārābī (257–339/870–950), Avicenna (370–429/980–1037) and other Peripatetics came on the scene, "free-thinking" had become so intertwined with thinking intellectually that it was seen as the hallmark of being a philosopher rather than as a deviant trait. In fact, there appears to have been three categories of thinkers: those who were perceived to have been well within the tradition and whose ideas originated from the Qur'an, those who were outright heretics and who were outside the pale of religion and thus not tolerated, and those who made use of what Shahrastānī, in his book *Nations and Sects* (*al-milal wa'l-nihal*), calls "authoritative use of personal opinion" (*al-istibdād bi'l-ra'y*). Philosophers fall into the third category,

Shahrastānī tells us. He discusses seventy-three sects in Islam. To do so, he divides his book into two parts: in the first part, he discusses what he calls "religion of sects"(*al-diyānat wa'l-milal*); and in the second part, he treats those religions he considered to hold "arbitrary notions" (*al-ahwa' wa'l-nihal*) including religions of India, Sabeans and the pre-Islamic *Jāhiliyyah* (age of ignorance). The philosophers are also discussed in this section.[47] Such a classification is more symbolic of the *zeitgeist* of how philosophers and independent thinkers were perceived, not as orthodox Muslims and certainly not as heretics either, but rather, as independent thinkers who were allowed to remain so.[48]

DEMISE OF RATIONALISM AND THE RISE OF THEOLOGICAL STRICTURE

The period in the history of Islamic civilization when the domain of intellectual activity was much wider began to come to an end. As S. Strouma, in her work, *Free Thinkers of Medieval Islam*, argues, "Historically, indeed, Islamic orthodoxy had the final word. One cannot ignore the fact that this typical freethinking of Islam appears in its full-fledged, outspoken form, only on a very limited scale, and for a relatively short period: the ninth and tenth centuries."[49] By the fifth–sixth/eleventh–twelfth centuries during which Khayyam lived, the intellectual scene was very different, free and independent thinking within the context of Islam was a legacy of the past. The spirit of rationalism had not died, but was shifted from Persian dominated circles to the Western part of the Islamic world where it flourished until its climax in the seventh/thirteenth century when the Arab-Spanish Andalusia produced such great masters as Ibn 'Arabī, Ibn Masarrah, Al-Majritī, Ibn Bājjah, Ibn Ṭufayl and, finally, the great master of rationalism, Ibn Rushd himself. Despite the revival of Peripateticism in Andalusia, dogmatism on one hand and Sufism (thanks to Ghazzālī's conversion) on the other hand, were on the rise and closing in on the philosophers' camp. It was not too long, however, before rationalism died among the Muslim philosophers of the Western regions of the Islamic world.

The demise of rationalism, which had begun with Caliph Al-Mutiwakkl Billāh (232–247), a staunch Sunni who forbade discourse on religious matters and encouraged following the Qur'an, Hadith and Sunnah alone, led to the harassment of the Mu'tazilites, forcing many to move north where they survived on a much smaller scale. Such orthodox jurists as Aḥmad ibn Ḥanbal found an opportunity to include even mathematicians among heretics. The Ḥadith scholars who had long emphasized absolute obedience to the Prophet's statements and tradition, used this opportunity to implement their views forcefully, giving rise to the importance of "Transmitted sciences" (*'ulūm al-naqlī*) at the expense of the decline of "intellectual sciences" (*'ulūm al-'aqlī*). Such a closure of intellectual activities reached a new high when Caliph Alqādir Billāh (381–422), issued a decree on "forceful belief" in which he not only embraced the position of orthodoxy but legally enforced it.

In Persia, with the conquest of the Ghaznavīd and Seljuq dynasties, we see a shift from patronage of rational thought by the Royal court to an embracing of orthodoxy. Maḥmud ibn Saboktakin, who invaded the city of Ray, wrote to Sulṭan Alqādir Billāh saying that the Daylamites, who gave refuge to the Mu'tazilites, were heretics and atheists, not people of faith.[50] In schools (*madrasah*s), the teaching of intellectual sciences became forbidden and was replaced by religious sciences; and many eminent poets such as Khāqānī, who lived a bit after Khayyam and Sanā'ī,[51] contributed to the anti-rationalist tendency which had come to permeate the intellectual life of the Islamic world, by composing poems criticizing rational thinking.

In light of the foregoing discussion, let us visit Khayyam's position in the context of his time and draw some conclusions. Thoroughly familiar with the scientific and intellectual achievements of the previous four centuries of Muslims, Khayyam saw it all take a nosedive as the nexus of the Islamic civilization shifted from free intellectual inquiry, which produced the alchemy of Jābir, the mathematics of Khwārazmī, and the philosophy of Avicenna, to a strict legalistic interpretation of Islam. He must have been angry, saddened and rebellious but could do so little about it. The following Khayyamesque *Ruba'iyyat* are clear indications of the radical encounter with and strong reaction to orthodoxy:

> Serve only the wise if and when you find
> Let fast and prayer blast, you need not mind
> But listen to truth from what Omar Khayyam says
> Drink wine, steal if you should but be ever kind.[52]
>
> If ye would love, be sober, wise and cool
> And keep your mind and senses under rule
> If ye desire your drinking be loved by God
> Injure no person, never act a fool.[53]

Khayyam knew that writing directly to question orthodoxy would only lead to being branded as a heretic; and, even if he did write, his writings would not have survived, just as those of Rāzī and Ibn Rāwandī did not. Many other figures such as Ibn Ṭufayl and Avicenna had relied on parables like *Ḥayy ibn yaqẓān*,[54] to elucidate philosophical problems, a tradition that was continued both by Sufis and philosophers such as Shihāb al-Dīn Suhrawardī who did not survive the wrath of orthodoxy.[55] At times when freedom of expression becomes limited, thinkers find ways to be creative. For example, in the arts, one can see the development of the Persian miniature, outwardly illustrations of stories which, inwardly, represent esoteric and Sufi concepts. Under these circumstances, no other mode of expression can be more useful than the poetic. Stroumsa indicates:

> It appears that after the tenth century, blunt prose expression of free-thinking was no longer possible. The preoccupation of intellectuals with prophecy then found very different expressions. Philosophical parables like Avicenna's, or poetry like al-Ma'arrī's and Jalāl al-Dīn al-Rumī's, offered ways for discussing this preoccupation that were deemed safer for the writers, and perhaps also intellectually more rewarding. For, rather than forcing these thinkers into a head-long collision with the notion of prophetic religion, these new ways made it possible to integrate transformed echoes of freethinking into the Islamic legacy.[56]

Following the triumph of dogmatism and orthodoxy, Khayyam, whose views are no less controversial than Rāzī's and Ibn Rāwandī's, and are similar to those of Abu'l 'Alā' Ma'arrī, also resorted to poetry as the only available "safe" avenue of expression. It is, therefore, imperative that we see Khayyam's *Ruba'iyyat* not only as isolated poems in which he expresses his quandary with the riddles of life, but also as the response of a profound thinker who is challenging the formal opinions of orthodoxy and is able to get away with it precisely because of the poetic mode of expression he has adopted. This explains how Khayyam could have been respected by the orthodox elements in various royal courts and yet remained critical of them.

Finally, something has to be said about the possible influence on Khayyam by the Arab poet, Abu'l-'Alā' Ma'arrī. There are those who have maintained that even though the two poets never met, Khayyam may have been influenced by this Arab poet, whose perspective on life bears striking resemblance to Khayyam's. The relationship is partially due to the fact that Khayyam frequently quoted Ma'arrī. An account of this is reported by Zamakhsharī, who witnessed Omar Khayyam reading the following poem by Ma'arrī:

> A prophet of the Arabs said "they do not follow the laws"
> We were told that the people are despairing[57]

Ma'arrī, who was born in 363/973 in Ma'ar, became blind when he was only four. This blindness resulted in a bitter and unhappy life, which was reflected in his poetry. Like Khayyam, early on Ma'arrī was also accused of heresy and of having anti-Islamic views. Nāṣir Khusraw tells us that Ma'arrī was accused of imitating the Qur'an and questioned some of its principles such as "Verily, we have created the heavens and the earth on the basis of justice."[58] Javādī[59] offers a number of instances where the two figures hold the same position: neither see a purpose or meaning in life, nor do they believe in life after death. Ma'arrī states, "There is no evidence before me or others that indicates there is life after death."[60] Khayyam, too, in numerous quatrains alludes to this very notion and states:

> The sphere upon which mortals come and go,
> Has no end or beginning that we know
> And none there is to tell us in plain truth
> Whence do we come and wither do we go[61]

Khayyam's sarcasm with regard to heaven and hell also resembles the aphorisms of Ma'arrī, who even wrote a satire entitled *Risālah al-ghufrān* in which an imaginary poet by the name of Ibn Qarih goes to heaven and hell and writes about his observations. Ma'arrī argues, "Life, death and resurrection is a tale, my friend."[62] In some cases, Khayyam's quatrains are almost direct translations of Ma'arrī's; the following example is exactly why some scholars have argued that Khayyam was influenced by Ma'arrī:

Ma'arrī: Has there been a dead man who has come
To tell us of what he has been promised
Should we abandon the wine at hand
For the promise of milk and wine in the heaven.[63]

Khayyam: Of Paradise, they talk of angels sweet
The juice of grape I hold as better treat;
Ah, take the cash and let the credit go
Sweet sounds the drum when distant is the beat.[64]

In addition to specific common themes such as pre-destination, pessimism and harsh criticism of religious hypocrisy, Khayyam and Ma'arrī even use specific imagery such as jug, dust, grass growing from our dust, etc.

Despite the similarities of issues, themes and topics among the two figures under discussion,[65] it is difficult to argue conclusively that Khayyam was influenced by Ma'arrī so much so that he was transformed by him or merely copied him. There are no references or documentation made by historians or people close to Khayyam of such an influence. In fact, Khayyam was so learned and independent minded that it is highly improbable that he was influenced to this extent by a less-educated poet. Ja'farī, a contemporary scholar asks, "What can Khayyam, who is next to Avicenna in stature and is himself a mathematician and philosopher of the highest ranking, learn from Abu'l-'Alā' Ma'arrī, who was only a poet?", adding "Abu'l-'Alā' was not a philosopher or a *ḥakīm* and was not even learned in philosophy."[66]

What is clear is that Khayyam was familiar with Ma'arrī, and he may have been inspired by him and his use of certain images, but there simply is not sufficient evidence to conclude that Khayyam was profoundly influenced by Ma'arrī, or that he became his follower. Khayyam was erudite and familiar with a wide range of subjects and figures; and while it is plausible to conclude that, like any other intellectual giant, he was cognizant of other perspectives and may have even been influenced by Ma'arrī, it would be hasty to conclude, as some have argued, that Khayyam had gone through a metamorphosis as a result of his encounter with Abu'l-'Alā' Ma'arrī.[67]

4

The Ruba'iyyat

The compend of the Book of Truth is Love,
The leading line of Ode of Youth is Love;
O Witless Man, to World of Love so blind!
Bear this in mind, *the core of life is love.*[1]

The word *Ruba'i* (*Ruba'iyyat* – plural), meaning "quatrain," comes from the word *al-Rabi'*, the number four in Arabic. It refers to a four-lined stanza that became popular in Persian poetry for the simplicity of its style and its short length which allows an aphorism to be delivered effectively. A *Ruba'i* consists of two hemistiches for a total of four parts. This type of poem has also been called "*tarāneh*" (snatch) or "*dobaītī*" (two-liner). Whereas in the early period of Persian literary tradition the four parts often rhymed, by the time of Khayyam, only the first, second and fourth lines rhymed, providing the poet with a greater degree of freedom.

The first problem in discussing Khayyam's *Ruba'iyyat* is the monumental task of determining the authentic *Ruba'iyyat* from the inauthentic ones. Scholars of Khayyam have relied on a variety of means and methods to discover the "real" *Ruba'iyyat*. While some have focused on the style,[2] others have considered the content, language and character of the *Ruba'iyyat* to be the criterion for determining their authenticity. Using this method, some have even divided the *Ruba'iyyat* into early and late works of Khayyam, arguing that the agnostic Khayyam of the early years had matured into a Sufi master.[3]

In his book, *Khayyam shināsī*,[4] contemporary Khayyam scholar, M. Foulādvāndī, establishes five criteria for determining the authenticity of the *Ruba'iyyat*, and they are as follows:

1. Every *Ruba'i* follows a theme from four different approaches.
2. The logical and coherent structure of each *Ruba'i*.
3. The dominance of the message over form.
4. All the *Ruba'iyyat* pose one of the following themes: quandary concerning the riddles of life, doubt, protest, confrontation and sarcasm.
5. Poetic elegy.

While the above conditions may not be extended to every single *Ruba'i*, Foulādvāndī argues that they provide us with the necessary criteria to decipher those that are likely to be authentic. Such scholars as A. Dashtī[5] argue certain words and phrases are essentially "Khayyamian," and they provide us with clues for the authentic *Ruba'iyyat*. Dashtī's method is somewhat speculative: he begins by reporting that, based on all the authentic accounts, Khayyam was humble, learned and a man of integrity who loved a simple life. He had a mild temperament, a contemplative personality whose ideas may have been a reflection of his character. Having painted a detailed picture of his character, Dashtī uses it as a criterion for judging which of the *Ruba'iyyat* fits within this character.[6] Needless to say that, while this method may be of some use, it remains quite subjective, the outward character of a person not always corresponding to one's most private thoughts.

Despite insurmountable problems concerning the question of authenticity with regard to the *Ruba'iyyat*, a brief survey of a few attempts to establish the more reliable quatrains might serve us well. If Khayyam is to be known, it would have to be on the basis of such allegedly authentic *Ruba'iyyat*.

There appears to be a consensus among a number of the scholars of Khayyam that the *Ruba'iyyat* which appeared in the earliest sources are likely to be authentic. These sources are: one *Ruba'i* quoted by Imām Fakhr al-Dīn Rāzī some ninety years after Khayyam's death in his *Al-tanbih 'alā ba'd asrār al-maw'ḍat fi'l-Qur'an*,[7] two *Ruba'iyyat* quoted by Shaykh Najm al-Dīn Dāyyah in *Mirṣād al-'ibād* one of which is the same as the one Rāzī had quoted;[8] this work is written about a century after Khayyam's death. Among the earliest sources we also find one quatrain is in *Jahān goshā-yi juwaynī*, another one in *Tārikh-i gozidah* and thirteen *Ruba'iyyat* in *Munis al-aḥrār.* Below, the literal translations of the first lines of the stanzas of thirteen reliable *Ruba'iyyat* in the above mentioned sources with their original Persian are included. They are:[9]

1. The Composer who mixed the elements so sublime. (*Al-tanbih* and *Mirṣād*).

   دارنده چو ترکیب چنین خوب آراست

2. The cycle wherein we come and go. (*Munis al- aḥrār* and *Mirṣād*)

   دوری که در آن آمدن و رفتن ماست

3. Once parts of the goblet are intertwined. (*Jahān-goshā-yi Juwaynī* and *Tarikh-i waṣṣāf*)

   اجزای پیاله ای که در هم پیوست

4. Every particle belonging to a piece of earth. (*Tārikh-i gozidah, Firdaws al-tawārikh, Nuzhat al-majālis*)

   هر ذره که بر روی زمینی بوده است

5. Once the clouds in the Spring wash the face of the tulips. (*Munis al-aḥrār)*

   جون ابر به نوروز رخ لاله بشست

6. This sea of existence that has emerged from the hidden. (*Munis al-aḥrār*)

   این بحر وجود آمده بیرون ز نهفت

7. Though it is for your eyes that the world is ornate. (*Munis al-aḥrār)*

   بر جشم تو عالم ارچه می آرایند

8. Since neither our fate nor life can be lessened or extended. (*Munis al-aḥrār*)

چون روزی و عمر بیش و کم نتوان کرد

9. It was a drop of water, it became united with the sea. (*Munis al-aḥrār*)

یك قطره آب بود و با دریا شد

10. It is dawn; rise o dear beloved. (*Munis al-aḥrār*)

وقت سحرست خیز ای مایه ناز

11. O the old wise man, rise earlier in dawn. (*Munis al-aḥrār*)

ای پیر خردمند پگه تر برخیز

12. Permanently, I do not dwell in this world. (*Munis al-aḥrār*)

جاوید نیم چو اندرین دهر مقیم

13. Days of life are dishonored of the one. (*Munis al-aḥrār*)

ایام زمانه از کسی دارد ننگ

14. Drink wine for heaven is bent on killing you and I. (*Munis al-aḥrār*)

می خور که فلك بهر هلاك من و تو

15. Last night, I smashed a jug made of clay. (*Munis al-aḥrār*)

برسنگ زدم دوش سبوی کاشی

16. Behold for you are the result of four and seven. (*Munis al-aḥrār*)

ای آنکه نتیجه چهار و هفتی

A secondary and less reliable set of sources consists of four works. The first of these is *Nuzhat al-majālis* [10] in which we find thirty-one *Ruba'iyyat*. The book was composed some 200 years after Khayyam's death and contains several thousand verses of poetry, among which we find sixteen scattered quatrains and fifteen in a chapter designated to Khayyam. What casts doubt on the authenticity of these quatrains is the fact that a number of them have been found in other works of poetry such as the *Diwān* of Kamāl al-Dīn Ismā'īl to give an example.

Whereas some scholars have considered these thirty-one to be authentic because of their form, Dashtī applied his method of measuring a *Ruba'ī* against Khayyam's character and judged otherwise. He argued that references to "wine" and "Sufism" and the implied pessimism in these quatrains are too incompatible with Khayyam's character. Exercising extreme caution, Dashtī omitted nineteen *Ruba'iyyat* he considered to be more dubious; this leaves us with twelve quatrains, but such eminent scholars of Khayyam as 'Alī Furūghī accepted all the thirty-one *Ruba'iyyat* as authentic, primarily based on their rhyming and poetic quality.[11] Numbering them sequentially to follow the other acceptable *Ruba'iyyat* in *Nuzhat al-majālis*, the first lines of these quatrains literally translated are:[12]

17. Given the riddle will never be understood by you.
گیرم تو بادراك معما نرسی

18. Do not heed to the words of the complacent.
مشنو سخن زمانه ساز آمدگان

19. He who has been driven to the world of causes.
آنرا که به صحرای علل تاخته اند

20. Once the synthesis of the elements work in your favor.
ترکیب طبایع چو بکام تو دمی است

21. I visited the potter's shop at dusk.
در کارگه کوزه گری رفتم دوش

22. Take the goblet and the jug, O dear one.
بر گیر پیاله و سبو ای دلجوی

23. For every secret that is hidden in the heart of the wise.
هر راز که اندر دل دانا باشد

24. Every now and then, one comes claiming "I".
هر یك چندی یکی بر آید که منم

25. The sun will not shine on the hidden clay.
خورشید بگل نهفت می نتوانم

26. I bought a jug from a potter once.

از کوزه گری کوزه خریدم باری

27. When nature calls for flowers to bloom.

در دهر چو آواز گل تازه دهند

28. Mention not, the day that is past.

از دی که گذشت هیچ ازاو یاد مکن

Both Furūghī and Dashtī have also used two unpublished manuscripts [13] written 230 years after Khayyam's death as reliable sources for the *Ruba'iyyat*. In the first one, there are eleven *Ruba'iyyat* and in the second five. Furūghī accepts thirteen of them but Dashtī is more cautious and accepts only five; the first lines of the stanzas of these *Ruba'i yyat* are:[14]

29. From those who have walked on this long path.

از جمله رفتگان این راه دراز

30. If given two weighty jugs of wine.

گر زانکه بدست آیدت از می دومنی

31. O One who needs neither food nor sleep.

آنی که نبودت بخور و خواب نیاز

32. From the world, what you eat and wear.

آن مایه ز دنیا که خوری یا پوشی

33. Those who have aged and those still young.

آنها که کهن شدند و آنها که نوند

The third source which traditionally has been highly regarded is *Sand-bād-nāmah*.[15] This work is particularly significant because it was composed in the second half of the sixth/twelfth century, effectively making it one of the oldest sources where we find five *Ruba'iyyat*. Whereas Khayyam is not mentioned as the author of these five *Ruba'iyyat* in this source, four of them are attributed to Khayyam in other sources we have already mentioned. We can therefore conclude that they are reliable since they are cross-referenced. The first lines of the stanza of the remaining *Ruba'i* is:[16]

34. The celestial wheel about which we are bewildered.
این چرخ فلك كه ما، در او حیرانیم

In an unpublished manuscript written by Yāquti Aharī in the seventh/thirteenth century we find two other *Ruba'iyyat*. Dashtī, Foulādvāndī, Furūghī and many others consider them to be authentic based on their content, style and rhyming characteristics. The first lines of these *Ruba'iyyat* are:[17]

35. In search of the *Jam-i Jam,*[18] I journeyed the world.
در جستن جام جم جهان پیمودم

36. Abandoned in this old dome.
مائیم در این گنبد دیرینه اساس

Ironically, in the sixth/twelfth century there is not a single quatrain that is attributed to Khayyam: the *Ruba'iyyat* appears for the first time in various sources in the seventh/thirteenth century. While the number of the *Ruba'iyyat* grows for centuries to come, if we are to take any of them seriously as belonging to Khayyam, we have to accept those mentioned in early sources between the beginnings of the seventh/thirteenth to the end of the eighth/fourteenth centuries. The number of such *Ruba'iyyat* by the middle of the eighth/fourteenth century when *Munis al-aḥrār* was composed had reached sixty. Such conservative scholars as Dashtī accept thirty-six of them, which have been included here and yet Furūghī, an eminent scholar of Khayyam, puts the number of the authentic *Ruba'iyyat* at one hundred and seventy-eight.

The project of deciphering the authentic *Ruba'iyyat* in the West goes back to the nineteenth century, since when various Western scholars of Khayyam have attempted to devise a method to determine the authenticity of the *Ruba'iyyat*. Zhukovski,[19] in his book, *'Umar Khayyam and the Wandering Quatrains,* and Christensen,[20] in *Recherches sur les Ruba'iyyat d' 'Omar Khayyam*, as well as Rozen and Ross, came up with four different criteria to establish the authenticity of the *Ruba'iyyat.*

1. All the poems found in the early poetry prior to Khayyam should be eliminated.
2. All the *Ruba'iyyat* that are attributed to others should be recognized as suspicious and eliminated.
3. Only those *Ruba'iyyat* attributed to Khayyam by his contemporaries should be accepted.
4. The style and composition of the words, content, worldview and panegyrical aspects should be taken into consideration.

The concept of "Wandering Quatrains" first used by Zhukovski has been used as a method of casting doubt on a number of *Ruba'iyyat*. On one hand, the wandering *Ruba'iyyat*, the number of which are about eighty-two, do not appear in literary works prior to the eighth/fourteenth century. On the other hand, they appear in the works of such figures as Ḥāfiz, Ṭusī, Ansārī and Rūmī among others. E.G. Brown offers a table[21] of the so called "Wandering Quatrains" clearly demonstrating how widely these quatrains had been used by other poets.

Christensen, the Danish scholar of Khayyam, in a treatise he gave as a birthday gift to Rozen, a Khayyam scholar of great significance, argues that within 350 years after Khayyam's death, the authentic and inauthentic *Ruba'iyyat* were so intertwined that distinguishing them remains impossible.[22]

The discussion concerning the *Ruba'iyyat* of Khayyam has been a major preoccupation of scholars, and numerous volumes and conferences have been devoted to an endeavor that inevitably fails. The lack of concrete evidence and reliance on second- and third-hand accounts concerning the authenticity of the *Ruba'iyyat* are facts recognized by most scholars.

Based on the diversity of views regarding the number of authentic *Ruba'iyyat*, they range from 1,200 to 1,400! Whereas one can clearly identify some as inauthentic based on the style and the use of language, deciphering the authentic ones remains ultimately an impossible task. It is for this reason that, rather than trying to find the "messenger", the search should be directed towards the message that runs through most of these *Ruba'iyyat*. In addition, we should speak not of the historical Khayyam, but rather of a "Khayyamian school of thought." This school of thought has been the voice of the bewildered thinkers who preferred to maintain their state of quandary and not settle for cheap and pre-fabricated answers. For them the tension between faith and reason is too real and troubling to be relinquished. The Khayyamian School represents the voices of those thinkers who for centuries have spoken through a proxy without being lynched by the orthodox. It is a perennial voice which ultimately represents the eternal conflict between reason and faith, a voice which Khayyam portrays in an exquisite and eloquent manner as a philosopher and a poet.

Such endless discussions regarding the question of authenticity which are of interest among literary circles are beyond the scope of this work, and the intricacies of scholarship in this regard do not contribute to a better understanding of Khayyamian thought. As I have indicated in the introduction, I find the discussion concerning Khayyam's authentic *Ruba'iyyat* somewhat diversionary and irrelevant to his message, and whereas such a discussion is necessary for academic and scholarly purposes, it does not shed new light on the intellectual content of Khayyam's thought. For these reasons, such discussions are omitted here while we proceed directly to examine a representative sample of Khayyam's *Ruba'iyyat* regarded to be among his most authentic poems. The poems selected here cover a wide array of topics and themes which constitute the salient features of the *Ruba'iyyat*. Before the *Ruba'iyyat* can be analyzed and interpreted, let us briefly consider some of the major themes of Khayyam's *Weltanschauung* to provide an overview of Khayyam's apothegms.

The central and salient features of Khayyam's *Ruba'iyyat* can be divided into seven categories that are treated and elucidated upon by him in a variety of ways. While the message is simple, repetitious, and similar to so many of the great literary and intellectual figures before and after him, it is not what he says that makes him unique but how he says it. It is in Khayyam's approach where we see the unleashing of his poetic genius in the treatment of the enduring questions that constitute the fabric of our existential condition. These themes are:

1. Impermanence and the meaning of life
2. Theodicy and justice

3. The here and now
4. Doubt and bewilderment
5. Death and afterlife
6. Determinism and predestination
7. *In vino veritas* (In wine there is truth)

Before a discussion concerning each of the above themes, let me provide an overview of how they all form a unified system of belief. What lies at the heart of the Khayyamian message is the notion of impermanence. Life is in a state of flux; it is changing like the sands of the desert and clouds in the sky, and only a fool can take this game seriously. Khayyam's central thesis bears great resemblance to Buddhism and Epicurianism.[23] He tells us that life is not only impermanent, but also fundamentally unjust. To begin with, it is a mystery why a good God would allow so much suffering to be inflicted upon us in the continuous cycle of suffering from birth to death, leaving us with little choice but to see this world as the promised hell of the scriptures.

In light of the impermanence of life and of an existence deeply steeped in suffering, the wise have no choice but to focus on the here and now, which constitutes the third principle of Khayyam's thought. Emphasis on the here and now lends itself to numerous interpretations from a Buddhist path of moderation, to the Epicurean sense of hedonism, to the Sufi emphasis on spiritual presence as indicated by the saying "the Sufi is the child of the moment."

The fourth theme is a peculiarly Khayyamian doubt, a mode of being which realizes that major riddles of life and questions of an ultimate nature are ultimately insoluble. The wise should transcend faith and infidelity since there is not sufficient reason to support either one.

> Since neither truth nor certitude is at hand
> Do not waste your life in doubt for a fairyland
> O let us not refuse the goblet of wine
> For, sober or drunk, in ignorance we stand.[24]

The other focal point of Khayyam's thought is death, not so much in and of itself, but more as a symbol of impermanence. It is by focusing on death that one can live in the here and now, and this theme is echoed by Socrates who regards philosophy as preparation for death. The reality of death renders certain philosophical questions irrelevant to the human condition and makes investing in them a vacuous intellectual endeavor. Death might not be a finality, but it is a mystery, and diving into mysteries, says Khayyam, is futile, "for neither you nor I know the Divine mysteries." So look around and see that you are here, thrown into a place where the only realities are generation and corruption. We are neither asked to come into this life, nor are we asked when we would like to leave; and in this "eternal recurrence of the same," as Nietzsche says, we are pounced upon by the merciless forces of nature while our cries for help are to no avail.

Determinism is the seventh theme in Khayyam's *Ruba'iyyat*. It is imperative to understand that he did not believe in philosophical determinism nor did he support predestination as it is generally understood; otherwise, he would not have relied on aphorism and apothegms, both of which invite us to pursue a contemplative lifestyle. Khayyam realizes that there is an existential determinism embedded in our very presence; we are here and suffer not by choice, such is the human condition. We find ourselves in the midst of this peculiar predicament. The wise are those who can play this game well without taking it seriously.

And then, there is the wine of wisdom, that which enables the "wise fool" to play the chess game of existence without taking it seriously. Wine is one of the central themes of Khayyam's poetry and runs throughout his entire *Ruba'iyyat*, whether he is specifically addressing life after death or admonishing the faithful for believing in it. Wine is the symbol of the type of wisdom whose effect brings about the detachment one needs in order to live life to the fullest extent possible. Like a drunken man who is oblivious to the fact that the ship he is sailing on is on fire, humans, too, should sail worry-free through the turbulent waters of life in a ship that we know is slowly sinking.

In light of the foregoing discussion, we can now proceed to analyze and interpret a representative sample of Khayyam's *Ruba'iyyat* in order to shed further light on the eight themes of his intellectual paradigm.

IMPERMANENCE AND THE MEANING OF LIFE

Throughout his *Ruba'iyyat*, Khayyam creatively uses the imagery of a "jug" (*kuzeh*) and earth to denote the principle of generation and corruption. The Qur'an tells us that God created men from clay, and then He blew unto him from his own breath. The transient nature of the clay that constitutes our worldly existence should be a constant reminder of the fragility and worthlessness of worldly endeavors.

> I saw the potter in the market yesterday
> Pounding and pounding upon a fresh piece of clay
> "Behold," said the clay to the potter
> Treat me gently for once like you, now I am clay.[25]

And in a different *Ruba'i* he says:

> I once bought a jug from a potter's hand
> The jug revealed secrets from every strand
> "I was a king with a golden chalice" said the jug
> Now look, I am a jug in every drunken hand.[26]

Khayyam is continuously engaged in a dialogue between the past, the present and the future, and earth and clay provide him with powerful symbols alluding to the impermanence of life. The potter is sometimes the universe, and often God. The jug represents humans, and the bazaar is life, where the potter makes the jugs that are bought and sold as they get old, crack and vanish. For the wise, however, the transient nature of life and the lesson of *carpe diem* can be learned even from a simple jug.

> O friend, let us not fret tomorrow's fears
> Seize the moment and enjoy life with cheers
> For when we depart away from this old mill
> We are companions to those dead seven-thousand years.[27]

The past, present and future come to an end in death where all concerns, fears and hopes vanish into the abyss of nothingness. It is Khayyam's emphasis on this very point that has led to nihilistic interpretations of his views in addition to regarding him as an advocate of hedonism and pessimism. While it is true that one possible interpretation of Khayyam's concept of impermanence could lead to nihilism, the more accurate understanding is reflected in the Qur'anic verse, "All things shall perish except His face" and "We come from Him and to Him we return,"[28] which refers to the impermanence of all except the reality of God. Qaraguzlū, in his work *Omar Khayyam*,[29] asserts that Khayyam's emphasis on the impermanence of the world is a testament of the reality of the only permanent Being, God. One may argue that, whereas this interpretation might put too much emphasis on the theistic understanding of the *Ruba'iyyat*, Khayyam is trying is to turn the reader's attention from what is unstable and perishable to what is important in life. What is important in life, in addition to God, in whom Khayyam seems to have believed, are love and joy. *Carpe diem* echoes in the quatrain, when he claims "seize the moment and appreciate life in cheers."

> Few in number, days of our lives have passed away
> Like water in a creek and wind in the valley; they sway
> The sorrow of two days have never haunted me
> The day that hasn't come and the one that has gone away.[30]

The experience of the here and now, a natural by-product of the impermanence of life which is most evident in the above *Ruba'i*, may lead one to conclude that we should "live it up" or "give it up." A cursory and selective reading of Khayyam's *Ruba'iyyat* has traditionally led to the first thesis, while a more inclusive reading of Khayyam, including his philosophical treatise, supports the second conclusion. Khayyam does not call for hedonism but rather advocates renunciation of the world; for who could take events in life seriously in light of their fleeting nature? The prescription for "living it up" is clearly not one that Khayyam himself pursued. By all accounts, he observed the religious laws (*Shari'ah*), and few of his contemporaries ever mention his "heretical ideas." At worst, his faith, similar to so many other poets, was called into question for simply having been a poet. Traditionally, poets have not been regarded as orthodox, perhaps because of the Qur'an's condemnation of the poets as such.[31] The question that remains to be explored is, if the quatrains we have discussed thus far do belong to Khayyam, how could he have reconciled his religious side with his cynical views on religion?

The apparent conflict is obvious, reconciliation of them however requires much discussion. It is necessary to delve deeper into the "live it up/give it up" dichotomy of Khayyamian thought if we are to make sense of this paradox. Let us assume, for the sake of argument, that Khayyam was convinced of the meaninglessness of life and the absence of a *telos*, a purpose. After all, what else can a rational person conclude when one fails to solve the existential puzzles of life and to make sense of it all? Even those who thought they had mastered the game, realized their failure in the end:

> The desire for knowledge, I could not forego
> Few secrets remained that I did not know
> For seventy-two years, I thought night and day
> Until I came to know, I had nothing to show.[32]

Even if one became the master of the chess game of existence, he too would be checkmated by the fleeting nature of it. Death always wins.

> While still a child, mastery I achieved
> Joyous I became with the grand mastery I perceived
> Listen to my tale for what came at the end
> Like clouds I came and wind I went, deceived.[33]

In a scenario that echoes the experience of Satori in Zen Buddhism, one must look deeper for Khayyam's message, which is that an authentic spiritual experience is possible and open to the contemplative person who has chosen "the life of the mind," to borrow a term from St. Augustine. The human condition is steeped in ignorance, suffering, and amidst this peculiar mode of being, speculation with regard to metaphysical issues is nothing but a superficial attempt to deal with the anxiety related to life's temporality. Khayyam's message is clear, resist the temptation and avoid trying to make sense of it all. It is only then that you can free yourself from the transcendental temptation for and obsession with explaining our existence. One may then live in the here and now.

In light of the foregoing discussion of Khayyam's concept of impermanence, three possible interpretations emerge:

a. Hedonism

Given the impermanence of life, one might argue, the only plausible and rational life is that of hedonism, especially in the absence of certitude with regard to life after death. Even though this is a plausible interpretation supported by some of the *Ruba'iyyat*, Khayyam's own lifestyle and the majority of his writings decisively rule out this reading. To see Khayyam as a hedonist is to understand his *Ruba'iyyat* in their literal and shallow sense. Excluding the deeper existential dilemma he is facing, and ignoring the corpus of his philosophical writings traditionally missing from Western scholarship, permits many to regard him as a hedonist.

b. The Sufi interpretation

Seeing Khayyam as a Sufi is a long-standing tradition within the Persian scholarly circles and with some of his Western admirers. If you approach most Iranians who grew up learning a few *Ruba'iyyat* and ask how they see Khayyam, the majority of them, even the illiterate peasant, will tell you that he was a great Sufi like Ḥāfiẓ or Rumī. The cultural understanding of him is not based on historical evidence but on a popular view that the "real" message of his *Ruba'iyyat* lies below the surface.

Let us briefly consider the presence of Sufi elements in Khayyam's thought and see if a bridge can be made from his *Ruba'iyyat* to Sufi doctrine. Even though gnosticism (*'irfān*) in Iran is regarded as a later development and does not reach its peak until the tenth/sixteenth century, the central underlying principle of gnosticism, which regards God as the True Reality and all else as impermanent and therefore unreal, dates back to the Qur'an itself. The Neoplatonic perspective which asserts that from the One emanates other realities, or gradations of beings, each of whom is less real and ontologically inferior to the one above it, became an integral part of Sufi thought. Early on in the history of the Islamic intellectual tradition, a division was made between real and unreal. That which is not unchangeable, eternal and immutable is unreal and, therefore, not worthy to be taken seriously. In the annals of Islamic history, there are ample examples of philosophers, theologians, and poets who have denounced everyday life in order to delineate their great deference for the only Reality. This may well have been Khayyam's project, to belittle life and all that we hold so sacred in order to transcend the form and see the formless.

Whereas this interpretation of Khayyam is more plausible than the hedonistic perspective, it is still difficult to establish whether or not Khayyam was a Sufi. Since I will discuss this thesis in greater length in the forthcoming chapter, I will not elaborate any further here. Suffice it to say that, except for a few brief remarks about his Sufi affiliation[34] and possible membership in the antinomian Sufi order, *Malāmatiyyah*, the majority of his contemporary biographers have not referred to him as a Sufi. Just as an inclusive approach to the entire corpus of his writings rejects his supposed hedonism, it also reveals that a Sufi interpretation is not appropriate to Khayyam's overall worldview. There are no references to the key elements of the Sufi path such as the master (*Shaykh*), invocation (*dhikr*), states (*ḥāl*) and stations (*maqām*) or to the ultimate Sufi goal, annihilation of the self in God (*fanā*). If Khayyam was a Sufi, he must have been a Sufi *at heart* since there is no concrete evidence of his Sufi tendency.

c. *The Middle Path*

"One has to be intellectually honest to the point of harshness," Nietzsche said, and Khayyam epitomized this sort of intellectual courage. He realized that, in the absence of certitude, formulating theories and making truth claims, even if convincing only a few, is a self-deceptive process and an intellectually dishonest and vacuous enterprise.

> Since neither truth nor certitude is at hand
> Do not waste your life in doubt for a fairyland
> O let us not refuse the goblet of wine
> For, sober or drunk, in ignorance we stand.[35]

Khayyam's numerous references to the Creator and the mystery of creation move him out of the modern existential camp and bring him closer perhaps to a Zen position whereby emphasis on the here and now and even silence replaces theological speculation. Khayyam proposes a middle path, one that is between dogma, doctrine, and metaphysical speculations on one side, and faith on the other. He navigates through the troubled sea of uncertainty and sees the shores of life with clarity; he shares with us his vision, that is, the experience of the here and now can be profound and fulfilling while one lives amidst uncertainty. The mystery of the universe and creation, the awesome nature of this "*mysterium tremendum*," demands awed silence. Khayyam has transcended faith and reason; for the former is based on belief on an insufficient ground, and the latter is an idle speculation. They both represent a futile attempt to crack the mystery of creation, a mystery that is not meant to be cracked but to be lived and cherished. Khayyam's position should not be mistaken with the modern existentialist philosophy, for he is not questioning the existence of God but the purpose for which this God created the world. Khayyam encourages suspension of metaphysical doctrines and speculations one cannot prove. He argues that focusing on the experience of the here and now can be profound and fulfilling. "Take the cash and let the credit go," he tells us.

THEODICY AND JUSTICE

Khayyam asks several questions pertaining to this theme. Why is there suffering? How and why would a creator allow so much suffering? Can we overcome and transcend suffering? The *Ruba'iyyat* show an incredible interplay and concern for the problem of suffering, in general, and theodicy, in particular; the extent to which these issues are intertwined with his concern for cosmic justice is striking. Khayyam's approach is fundamentally a Buddhist one, and what he advocates as a way of coming to terms with and "solving" the problem of suffering is strikingly similar to the Buddhist path. In fact, it can be argued that Khayyam's view in this regard is nearly identical with the Four Noble Truths of Buddhism with the exception that, while Khayyam does not leave the theistic world-view, he tries to solve the problem of suffering independent of God. His four axioms, recalling Buddhism's Four Noble Truths, are as follows:

1. To exist is to suffer
2. Suffering is caused by greed and attachment
3. Suffering is soluble
4. The solution is to extinguish the flame of desires.

In what follows, I will attempt to reconstruct Khayyam's perspective on the question of suffering based on the above motifs. Suffering is an integral part of the very constitution of the world and, therefore, an inescapable condition. We are reminded of this repeatedly throughout the *Ruba'iyyat*, in a quatrain that might be Khayyam's and is reminiscent of Ma'rrī, we read:

> In what life yields in this Two-door monastery
> Your share in the pain of heart and death will tarry
> The one who does not bear a child is happy
> And he not born of a mother, merry[36]

By a "Two-door monastery" he is referring to the world where one comes through the door of birth and leaves from the gate of death. The world here is analogized to a monastery where monks live an austere and ascetic life and tolerate suffering. There are those who would characterize this poem as pessimistic in essence, but Khayyam would regard it as self-evident and realistic, for nothing is more apparent than the continuous and perpetual cycle of suffering. The mystery, however, is not the presence of suffering in our lives but the role of God with regard to it. In a Khayyamian poem, it is sarcastically remarked:

> Life is dark and maze-like, it is
> Suffering cast upon us and comfort in abyss
> Praise the Lord for all the means of evil
> Ask none other than He for malice.[37]

God, who in Islam is all-good, merciful and compassionate, in a twist of fate has decreed for us all that is evil and painful, so much so that we need not look elsewhere for a source of suffering. God seems to be there to ensure and sustain a continuous supply of suffering,

Khayyam remarks. Furthermore, the question of theodicy is not one that can be resolved through rationalization, certainly not in a theistic world-view. In a Khayyamesque quatrain we hear the voice of an existentially frustrated poet who tells us he has tried to solve this riddle, but it has led nowhere.

> You wish to be wise, yes even you!
> Perplexed you are and know not what to do;
> So Time, your teacher, flogs you and strikes
> Until out of pain, you pray to Him too.[38]

Failure to understand the presence of suffering in general, and theodicy in particular, did not hamper Khayyam's effort to argue that while the problem cannot be resolved, one can come to terms with it. Contrary to Avicenna's ontological explanations and some of the other Peripatetics and gnostics, Khayyam gave up fancy philosophical explanations for the presence of evil. The religious answer, "Submit and do not ask the question," is equally unacceptable to Khayyam. Instead, he tried to solve the problem independent of God, faith, and reason, in a solution that has its own logic. His alternative perspective, which is both Sufi and Buddhist, is to renounce the world, not in an extreme ascetic sense, but in a rational and Epicurean sense, arguing that much suffering is self-caused and driven by greed, possessiveness, and a desire to have more. The fundamental cause of evil is attachment, a condition that coerces us to fluctuate between the fear of not having and the desire for more. The solution is detachment, and Khayyam asks, given the impermanence of the world and the transient nature of life, how can one not see the wisdom of detachment from worldly affairs? It is as if the natural by-product of impermanence is the renunciation of world.

> O friend, do not indulge in this world's sorrow
> From the world of vain grief and sadness, don't borrow
> The past is gone and the future is not yet here,
> Be happy and fear not the sorrow of tomorrow.[39]

Clearly, attachment brings suffering, Khayyam says, and this is most evident in the lives of those who have surrounded themselves with wealth.

These Noble lords who lead the worldly van,
Are sick of life, their hides alone they tan
But strange! *I* shun the yoke of greed *they* bear –
The beasts! They call me "beast" and not a man.[40]

The real question at this point is, "How does one become detached; and what is the mechanism by which one renounces the world, for it is easier said than done." Khayyam in his *Ruba'iyyat* is a spiritual pragmatist who eschews metaphysics, rituals, and doctrine as he realizes that the desire for and attachment to worldly pleasures, whose inevitable results are pain and suffering, is so great that one cannot simply will to renounce them. On the other hand, there is the massive and complex Sufi prescription based on ascetic practices, moral instructions, supervision by the Sufi master and initiation in an order.

Khayyam's solution circumvents all these, which he sees as unnecessary, since the impermanence of life and all the events in it lead to a rational conclusion: in order to live wisely and see "the good in life," one has to dispose of goods in life. In two *Ruba'iyyat* which might be Khayyam's we read:

Whoever has a loaf of bread to eat,
A lowly hut wherein to rest his feet,
Who neither is the lord nor slave of one
Tell him to live happy, for his world is sweet.[41]

Nor good for mosque, nor fit for Church I am
Ah, God alone knows type of clay I am
Nor faith, nor wealth, nor hope for paradise
Like homely whore and pagan tramp I am.[42]

The way to Khayyamian enlightenment is the Sufi way of *qinā'at* (refraining from excessiveness) without the metaphysical baggage. In this regard, Khayyam's way is much closer to the early Buddhism of Theravada and later of Zen Buddhism. What is this wisdom (Sophia) which allows one to be observant of life in such a meticulous and thorough manner and not to get lost in the everydayness of it? Khayyam analogizes this Sophia to wine and drunkenness, a traditional Sufi imagery. But this is not the *Sophia perennis* or perennial wisdom, as some of the contemporary scholars of Sufism have supposed. Khayyam's wine imagery represents a perceptive, profound, and simple understanding that allows change and influx. It would be foolish to become attached to the changeable, while it is wise to sit back and appreciate the aesthetic value of living in the present. This perception, understanding, insight or vision, is the result of living a contemplative life, a life dedicated entirely to the pursuit of knowledge and inquiry into what matters. And what matters is not *telos* (the end) in life, but *prokope*, your moral progress, which consists in learning how to be free from passion (*aeatheia*) and attachment; in Avicennian terminology, it is not the length of life that matters but the depth of it. Several *Ruba'iyyat* belonging to the Khayyamian school of thought claim:

> Desire no gain from the world, with bliss you trade;
> In good or bad times you need not wade;
> Remain sedate, so that the whirling Wheel
> Would snap itself and blow us days it made.[43]
>
> Why wear our blissful heart in woeful ways?
> And crush with stones of toils our blissful days?
> Who knows what crops up from the hidden stores?
> Hence we should love Him, sing our happy lays.[44]
>
> When Yesterday is vanished in the past
> And Morrow lingers in the future vast
> To neither give a thought but prize the hour
> For that is all you have and time flies fast.[45]
>
> O Khayyam, the world is shamed by those who moan
> They frown of Fate, and greet distress with groan
> Ah, drink the chalice of wine and tune the harp
> Before life's crystal breaks upon the stone.[46]

Khayyam was an Epicurean in one sense and a stoic in another, with regard to the question of suffering and pleasure, a delicate matter which will be discussed in Chapter Six on his philosophical thought. For now, however, it can be concluded that Khayyam believed that at least much of the self-caused suffering in the world can be reduced if we extinguish our flame of desire (Nirvana, literally means "to extinguish") and live a contemplative life focused on what matters to the human condition here and now. This wisdom for Khayyam is symbolically represented in drinking wine since drunkenness leaves one forgetful of what is mundane.

THE HERE AND NOW

Now that impermanence has been recognized and acknowledged by the wise, it has to be applied in such a way that it can reconcile us with suffering that results from the unstoppable results of aging. Khayyam reminds us that a necessary condition for reflecting upon the present is to do away with the unnecessary desires in life and be mindful of what has an immediate impact upon us.

> To seek and fetch what just you eat and wear,
> Though not essential, may be thought as fair;
> The rest is trash and needless, hence beware
> You sell no life's assets to buy despair.[47]

What is particularly interesting here is the fact that Khayyam's apothegm is placed outside a theological-mystical package, and it is this non-contextual message which separates him from traditional Sufis. Realizing that the source of much of our pain and suffering comes from attachment, greed, and a desire for possessions, Khayyam wisely advocates the attainment of the type of wisdom which allows us to think "properly." The dichotomy between a "contemplative mode of thought" and a "calculative mode of thought," as Heidegger maintains, breaks down in Khayyam; for when it comes to the art of living, a rational approach reveals that the contemplative mode is the way.

> What matters if I feast, or have to fast?
> What if my days in joy or grief are cast?
> Fill me with Thee, O Guide! I cannot ken
> If breath I draw returns or fails at last.[48]

Khayyam was well acquainted with the consequences of focusing on the here and now and the two possibilities that this type of reflection may bring forth. Some may decide to take refuge in God and seek meaning therein, while others might choose the path of hedonism and seek pleasure. The following quatrain, which may be Khayyam's, addresses this very point:

> The man who has in him a grain of wit
> With folded hands is never wont to sit
> He either plies to gain the grace of God
> Or keeps his heart in bliss, and thus is quit.[49]

Khayyam's way is not idle speculation but a rational contentment with our given reality, a realization of the human condition and of the precarious position in which we find ourselves. Let us assume the worst-case scenario: Khayyam maintains that materialism is true; we are nothing but dust and dirt thrown in a godless universe. What then would be the right way of living, the "proper mode of being" as Kierkegaard would ask? The outcome, as Nietzsche has so skillfully argued, lends itself to both a negative and positive nihilism. Evidence for the negative one, a pessimistic and passive nihilism, can be found in a number of Khayyam's *Ruba'iyyat*, but a deeper reading of him clearly shows that this is not an option he endorses. The positive nihilism in the Khayyamian context is not to jump on the bandwagon of the religio-theological doctrine, but to resist the transcendental temptation. Khayyam rejects both options, the former because it is unwise and the latter because of lack of certitude. Be content with the beauties of life and have a profound spiritual experience of the moments when happiness is there, for reason leads to no other conclusion.

> The nature's knit by breath or fancies
> Be happy if imposed on you, that is ail
> Sit thou with wise and see that "I" and "thou"
> Is grain of dust, a spark, a drop and gale.[50]

For Khayyam, the right conclusion to draw, given the impermanence of life, is to drink the wine of wisdom which results in a profound appreciation for the here and now before life comes to an end.

Today is thine to spend, but not to-morrow,
Counting on morrow breedeth naught but sorrow;
Oh! Squander not this breath that heaven hath lent thee,
Nor make too sure another breath to borrow.[51]

Khayyam's existential prescription does not advocate a willful decision to relinquish the desire to possess and not to fear the future, but rather a gradual understanding that once one does shed the petty concerns of life, a greater reality emerges. Those who have been diagnosed with an incurable disease certainly experience this mode of being to which Khayyam refers: "a disappearance of all the petty concerns" and an instant focus on what matters in the here and now. Life is an incurable disease with many ups and downs, trials and tribulations; so throw away the mundane worries and allow the feeling of appreciation and exuberance for being here to emerge – this is Khayyam's sense of intoxication.

Khayyam's perceptive mind does not forget the eschatological consequences of a path that is not theologically grounded. In an immensely rich quatrain, he criticizes a theology-based solution whereby asceticism, piety, hell, heaven and all the arsenal of religion are employed to solve the problem:

To drain the cup, to hover round the fair
Can hypocrite's art with these compare?
If all who love and drink are bound for hell
There is many a Wight of heaven may well dear.[52]

Examples from which one can draw further evidence to support the view that I have attributed to Khayyam are numerous among his *Ruba'iyyat*, but the foregoing discussion offers a perspective which is consistent and coherent with Khayyam's overall approach to the enduring questions of life.

DOUBT AND BEWILDERMENT

Existential doubt and bewilderment come in many forms and are the result of many modes of thinking. Bewilderment is often the result of being perplexed, puzzled, in a state of quandary; and this may be either due to knowing or not knowing. In his introduction to *The Sufi Path of Knowledge*, W. Chittick defines bewilderment in the Sufi context as follows:

> To find God is to fall into bewilderment (*ḥayra*), not the bewilderment of being lost and unable to find one's way, but the bewilderment of finding and knowing God and not-finding and not-knowing Him at the same time. Every existent thing other than God dwells in a never-never land of affirmation and negation, finding and losing, knowing and not-knowing. The difference between the finders and the rest of us is that they are fully aware of their own ambiguous situation.[53]

Chittick argues that from all of the comprehensive names of Allah, "three properties stand out from the rest: declaration of incomparability, worship and bewilderment (*ḥayra*)."[54] It is this sense of bewilderment that is echoed by Rudolph Otto in his classic work, *The Idea of the Holy.* Otto describes elements of bewilderment, "awfulness," "majestas," "energy," "fascination," "Wholly Other," and a *mysterium tremendum.*[55]

Khayyam's doubt and bewilderment is peculiarly difficult to analyze since it does not exclude the type of perplexity that results from knowing God. Nor is Khayyam's bewilderment of a mystical nature like the type Otto discusses, whereby an encounter with an unspeakable reality he calls "numinous"[56] brings about this mode of being. If Khayyam's bewilderment on the most profound level was of a mystical nature, he certainly, in the tradition of great mystics, did not reveal it. Khayyam's quandary is not the result of his engagement with specific mystico-theological issues; rather it is life as such which he sees as a tremendous mystery, a reality which should not have been but is.

To begin with, he is puzzled by the contradiction between the seemingly perfect world of nature and all its shortcomings. Who is to be blamed for it?

> Since mortal shapes are cast by Hand Divine
> Widen the flaws that throw them out of line?
> If forms are aright, why must He shatter them?
> If not, to whom should we the fault assign?[57]

Khayyam's bewilderment, therefore, begins not with a mystical encounter with God but by questioning the very purpose of creation, the riddles, puzzles, and the apparent senselessness of it. God, being all-intelligent, must have created the world and us for a purpose, but Khayyam is bewildered by the lack of evidence for such a purpose:

> The sphere upon which mortals come and go,
> Has no end nor beginning that we know;
> And none there is to tell us in plain truth:
> Whence do we come and whither do we go.[58]

In the above quatrain, which brings to mind Nietzsche's thesis of the "eternal recurrence of the same," Khayyam describes life as cyclical or walking on a circle, the symbol of an idle deed for which there is no beginning or end. In angry and defiant language, he refutes the arguments of those who claim to show the way and solve the puzzle. In his bewilderment, which began with questions concerning theodicy, Khayyam proceeds by calling into question the very purpose of existence and moves on to express a sense of wonder which permeates every facet of his life and thought. It is not always clear to whom Khayyam is addressing these issues. Sometimes he uses the third person singular and often a plural pronoun, which almost gives the impression that he is admonishing God. Sometimes, in more ambiguous terms, it appears that he is referring to the universe as a whole for being responsible for this travesty we call "life":

> That earthen bowl of such exquisite make,
> Not even drunkards would attempt to break;
> So many lovely heads and dainty hands –
> For whom He makes, for spite of whom does break?[59]

As is evident, Khayyam is bewildered by the mysterious ways of the world more than the mystery that may be behind the world, a mystery which he regards as fundamentally insoluble. Speculation on the mystery removes us from focusing on the here and now.

Eternity! – for it we find no key;
Nor any of us past the Veil can see.
Of Thee and me they talk behind the Veil,
But when that parts, no more of Thee and me.[60]

As a mathematician and astronomer, Khayyam delved deep into the mystery of creation, realizing the complexities of the cosmos and the precious moments of unique consciousness that stem from finding oneself before a tremendous reality. He must have experienced the anxiety, fear, and dread of this momentous and blissful circumstance along with the profound realization that this delicate and harmonic symphony of the cosmos cannot be the result of chance and randomness. Khayyam, this master of intellectual honesty, who despised "holy lies" and "its protectors," acknowledges two conclusions that one arrives at in light of such an observation. First, we do not understand fully what life is about. When the intellect fails to grasp, to understand and make sense of it all, the result is perplexity and bewilderment. The second observation, which we can make and be certain about, is our own helpless condition. Our presence in and absence from the corporeal world, the pain we endure and the fury and wrath of nature that befall us, do not seem to be of any consequence to the universe. These are the only types of certitude we can have in life, which creates a different sense of bewilderment. This divine comedy, this apparently senseless cycle of pain, agony, disease and death, and the never-ending cycle of betrayal by those one comes to trust, are sources of continuous wonder for him.

We halt on earth a while in our course
And lo! We gather naught but plague and sores
Alas! Not one in hundred doubts resolved
We go with heavy hearts and deep remorse.[61]

Khayyam's sense of doubt, wonder, and bewilderment is neither a reflection of his vision nor an encounter with an Ultimate Reality such as that of traditional Sufi masters like Ḥallāj, Bayazīd, or Rumī; nor is it the ignorance of *how* things are. Rather, his concern is with *why* things are the way they are. For, in opposition to the rationalization of the inconceivable drama of human life amidst impermanence, suffering and evil, and the apparent purposelessness of life, Khayyam throws his hands up and does what an honest, responsible thinker should do. Khayyam proclaims that he is bewildered and he does not know the answer, a concept that is echoed in Socrates when he said he is truly wise because he knows that he does not know.

> My hue is pearly, words with fragrance flow
> With beaming face and lofty gait I go
> He made this dusty house and decked me so
> But why? – I cannot ken, nor cared to know.[62]

DEATH AND AFTERLIFE

Whether we rely on the so called "authentic quatrains" or accept the larger corpus of the *Ruba'iyyat* that is attributed to Khayyam, the perspective on eschatological matters appears to be consistent. Our Khayyam who represents a particular world-view is a thinker who finds an appropriate mode of expression in poetry and, therefore, he should not be mistaken for a poet who is merely uttering his feelings and deep sentiments. His views on death and afterlife are consistent with other themes treated by him, and he rather skillfully applies his epistemology of not making a truth claim in light of the insufficiency of evidence in this domain as well.

Death, for Khayyam, is not only a symbol of impermanence but an impulse for adopting the religious consciousness and the fall into the never-ending cycle of religious interpretation of the human condition. Khayyam is a rationalist, a pragmatic thinker who is not fooled by what *might* be there. Intellectually, he is too courageous and honest to accept Pascal's "wager" and opt for the religious answer because it is "safer," and he is too honest to adopt Kierkegaard's view that although there is a "risk" of being wrong in embracing faith, one must take the risk. Perhaps it is Khayyam's independence which has placed him in a unique position in the annals of Islamic intellectual history. He refused to accept cheap and prefabricated answers, be they idle philosophical and theological speculations or religious and mystical options.

Some bring us here, while others lead away
But why they make the show they never say
O Lord! Impart to me but this much grace
My heart which is Thy gift with Thee I lay.[63]

For Khayyam, the reality of death casts doubt on the reality of life, turning it into *māyā*, an illusion not to be taken seriously. But he also acknowledges that humans cannot live and not take life events seriously either; the death of a loved one cannot be brushed aside easily. Furthermore, because we are inclined to take life seriously, we attach an eschatological doctrine to it in order to give meaning to an otherwise senseless series of events we call life. Khayyam warns us against this instinctual gravitation towards doctrinal justification, an attempt to make sense of an existence for which there are no apparent reasons.

Behind the curtain none has found his way
None came to know the secret as we could say
And each repeats the dirge his fancy taught
Which has no sense – but never ends the lay.[64]

Khayyam uses the imagery of a jug over and over to expound upon the phenomenon of death, perhaps because the clay from which a jug is made symbolizes recycled bodies of our ancestors. Yet the primary function of a jug is to contain water, which itself is the symbol of life:

A lover like me was this jug, in snare
Of Beauty's tousled tresses long and fair;
The handle 'round its neck you see was once
The hand that fondly twined her lovely hair.[65]

Khayyam's observation of death is followed by pointing his finger at the powers that throw us amidst a senseless existence, followed by suffering and an inevitable death.

We come and go, but for the gain, where is it?
And spin life's woof, but for the wrap, where is it?
And many a righteous man has burned to dust
In heaven's blue rondure, but their smoke, where is it?[66]

His observation of the reality of death and the coming to an end of all things good poses a question concerning the rationalization of suicide, a theme appropriate to the twentieth-century existentialist movement, which nevertheless finds a home in the thought of our fifth/eleventh century thinker.

Khayyam finds a purposeless existence to be a daunting and depressing condition from which he wants to free himself. What is also notable in the *Rubaʿiyyat* is Khayyam's reference to his failure to find a companion who understands him. One finds Nietzsche's similar outcry in his *The Anti-Christ*: "This book belongs to the very few, perhaps none of them is even living yet ... These are my readers, my predestined readers: what do the rest matter?"[67] One can imagine that Khayyam would have echoed these thoughts if he had decided to write a treatise questioning central themes of the faith. Undoubtedly, he would have found himself in the same position as Ibn Rāwandī and Zakariyā' Rāzī, if not Suhrawardī and Ḥallāj; for they all were branded as heretics, and the latter two were put to death.

The reality of death gives rise to the myth of the hereafter, Khayyam says, even though there is not a shred of evidence to indicate the existence of life after death. He neither rejects that the self survives physical death, nor confirms it. He takes an agnostic position. Khayyam, in a scattered but systematic way, destroys the basis for believing firmly in the hereafter. His argument consists of three parts:

1. For all we know, everything perishes; therefore, there is insufficient evidence for believing that we survive death.
2. No one has ever come back from the other world to tell us about it.
3. When in doubt, focus on what is certain, and that is the here and now. After all, descriptions of heaven can be emulated here and now as well.

The first argument is an inductive one in which one observes that all things perish. Therefore, it is reasonable to conclude that death is the end, because particularly, that which constitutes us seems to be of a corporeal nature.

O you, the child of Seven and the Four,
In fray with *Four* and *Seven* evermore;
Drink wine! I warned a thousand times before,
Once gone, you shall return Here nevermore![68]

In the above *Ruba'i*, Khayyam sees men as the result of the coming together of four substances, water, fire, earth and wind and the seven heavens, which are Moon, Mercury, Venus, Sun, Mars, Jupiter, and Saturn. Khayyam, however, uses them in a context that implies the randomness of our existence, meaning that we are the accidental by-product of the rotation of heavens and the mixing of corporeal substances. On this basis Khayyam, in direct and pointed language, says, "Once gone you shall return Here nevermore." Only a fool can see a grave and the transient world that rises and falls and takes with it all things to the abyss of nothingness, and yet remain firm in the resolve that there is life after death. Two of his *Ruba'iyyat* in this regard are as follows:

Each particle of dust on ground you see
A beauty proud like Venus once was she
Ah, gently wipe the dust from Loving's face
That, too, was once a beauty fair and free.[69]

I saw at the potter's shop one dust of day
Two thousand voiced but silent pots of clay
One vessel then on sudden cried aloud
"Where are they – potter, seller, buyer – pray?"[70]

Khayyam's second motif bears resemblance to David Hume's argument against supernatural phenomena, in particular, miracles: such accounts are always based on second-hand information. If we base the validity of a claim on the verifiability of it, then life after death cannot be believed for no one has returned to tell us about it. The fundamental basis upon which people believe in life after death is the authority of the scripture. In most of his prose and poetry, Khayyam directly challenges the authority of the scripture, while at no time does he reject the existence of God. "Who has come from the other world to assure us of its existence?" Khayyam cries aloud.

Of those who trod the long, long road before,
Who's come to help us Mystery explore?
Lo, in this double way of wish and dream,
Leave naught undone; you shall return no more.[71]

They say that heaven has golden ruby parks
And nectar streams with ever singing larks
No thanks – just fill a jug of wine for me
A groat is more than thousand Paper Marks.[72]

Here too, Khayyam remains consistent by advocating the same message, that is, in the wake of uncertainty, leave no desire unfulfilled, for life is a path of no return. Lack of evidence for the existence of life after death for Khayyam is not only a philosophical problem but is also a reason to transcend the whole issue in order to be able to deal with the more immediate existential matters that are staring us in the face. Khayyam's repeated claim that the solution lies in becoming "intoxicated" is one which shall be treated extensively; but in summary, he argues, there is enough here – within the corporeal domain – that can bring about a spiritually fulfilling experience. Let us then depart from our concern with hell and heaven and focus on what is at hand. A Khayyamian quatrain replies:

I asked my heart "what heavens should I seek?"
The heart replied "The wise thus never speak"
I said "But all affirm that there's a heaven!"
Replied "Of course they all will eat the leek."[73]

In the third part of Khayyam's eschatological perspective, here and now becomes a replacement for hereafter. Once again, this thesis is not to be taken in its strict theological sense, since a wider reading of Khayyam, which includes his philosophical writings, reveals that in some sense he did believe in life after death. In his poetic mode of thought, however, where Khayyam is wrestling with death and surely with his own old age and impermanence, he has no patience for a flight of fantasy or philosophical arguments, nor does he have respect for faith as an alternative.

Some ponder over faith and cult and creed
Some seek the doubtful from the sure to weed
Of sudden then a voice from void proclaims
"Nor this nor that. O Fools, the path you need."[74]

Epistemology of ignorance and Khayyam's refusal to give in to prefabricated answers, logically lead to the abandonment of speculation, and an acceptance of our given reality with all its limitations. What is the relevance of this hell and heaven to the human condition in the here and now, and in what ways can their traditional descriptions be brought forth here on earth? If heaven, as the Qur'an describes it, provides us with the companionship of angels and rivers of milk and wine,[75] they are all accessible in our world as well! Is not a bird in hand better than two in the bush?

As one reads the *Ruba'iyyat* for content, style and its direct and no nonsense approach to metaphysical issues, it becomes clear that Khayyam sees the traditional descriptions of heaven and hell as metaphors which are reflections of our moments of joy and pain in this world. When one is in a state of bliss and happiness, is that not a paradisal state? Similarly, can pain, sorrow and unhappiness not be regarded as dwelling amidst an inward hell? The only way that Khayyam says the ideas of heaven and hell could make sense, is by seeing them within the context of the here and now and by relating them to the joy and delights, and trials and tribulations of this life.

The world is but a belt of fading years
The Oxus but the trace of running tears
And Hell is but the spark of futile toil
And Paradise a flash of fleeting cheers.[76]

Of Paradise they talk and *hooris*[77] sweet
The juice of grape I hold as better treat;
Ah, take the cash and let the credit go
Sweet sounds the drum when distant is the beat.[78]

DETERMINISM AND PREDESTINATION

One of the myths that has surrounded the misunderstood Khayyam of the popular culture is that he believed in determinism (*jabr*) and predestination. As always, there are a few poems that, if taken literally without respect or regard for the overall Khayyamian *Weltanschauung*, could lead one to conclude that he was a determinist. If determinism and predestination imply that one could not have done otherwise, Khayyam clearly did not believe in it. Repeatedly, he tells us in an imperative manner to be happy, live in the here and now and shed the worries of the temporal life; and this stands in opposition to the very notion of determinism.

Khayyam's notion of predestination is a much more profound and existentially-based idea than a causally connected one. In fact, one can argue that Khayyam believed in free will amidst a form of cosmic determinism. There are specific conditions imposed upon us, Khayyam argues, with regard to which we have no choice but to submit. They are as follows:

1. We are born and we die by necessity.
2. To exist is to suffer.
3. All creation, animate and inanimate, is subject to the laws of nature.

A Khayyamian quatrain echoes this:

> You never make your weal, but it is sent
> Perchance they kill you, not by your intent
> Resign in him, and ever be content
> For good or bad in world you can't invent.[79]

Khayyam's existential determinism, therefore, is not to be mistaken for what is generally understood by the term "determinism," which implies that every act is causally determined and we cannot do otherwise. Khayyam's determinism, however, implies that our presence in the world is determined and the ruthless forces of nature make us nothing but pawns in the chess game of life. There are those who have accused him of pessimism, arguing that his sense of determinism leads to a sense of nihilism and bewilderment. Dashtī[80] argues that Khayyam did believe in determinism, had become perplexed and developed a negative attitude towards life; but there is no indication that he had lost his faith in God.

One can quote a number of contemporary scholars of Khayyam who have misinterpreted his determinism to mean a causal determinism whereby each and every action is causally determined. Khayyam's determinism, however, must be understood in its existential sense as an ontological oxymoron in which we are born without having willed it, and are dragged out of existence without our will, while we remain bewildered and puzzled with respect to the whole purpose of this game while we are here.

> The world will long be, without you and me
> No sign, no trace for anyone to see;
> The world lacked not a thing before we came,
> Nor will it miss us when we cease to be.[81]

> At first they brought me perplexed in this way
> Amazement still enhances day by day
> We all alike are tasked to go but Oh!
> Why are we brought and sent? This none can say.[82]

The existential determinism of Khayyam brings with it some freedom, that is, we have the freedom to live our given reality to its fullest extent and to reflect upon the more profound aspects of life. In a beautiful metaphor, Khayyam uses the established rotation of heavens to argue that humans can determine their own destiny and "rotate as they wish" in order to liberate themselves from perplexity.

> The Wheel now whispers in my ear "I know
> What fate decreed – just ask and I will show
> Could I but check the push which whirls me round
> I should have saved myself from reeling so."[83]

The human condition steeped in suffering brings about a feeling of helplessness and despair; but one must resist *thanatos*, the dark and depressing tendency of the human psyche to give in to the cruel fate that befalls us. Instead, Khayyam, like a great Sufi master who has reached the state of contentment (*riḍā*), states that we should accept our existential abandonment; for our fate has been sealed from the beginning. Khayyam may have responded:

Why should you vainly count on coming grief?
Foreknower gathers thorns alone in sheaf;
Be calm, the heart's too small to hold the world
By moaning, Fate will not rewrite your leaf.[84]

What is done is done; be content and do not fight the human odyssey whose boundaries are determined by forces far greater than ourselves. It is only by accepting our destiny that we can begin to change what can and should be changed; and to do so requires an abandonment of the quest to know *why* there is suffering, impermanence, and death. Khayyam's position, similar to early Buddhism where suffering and impermanence were taken for granted as an integral part of life, holds that the challenge is not to figure them out but to come to terms with them. One way to accept our fate is through a process of "existential therapy", that is, to come to a rational understanding of the destiny of humankind, its constraints, limits, and fundamental constitutions. A Khayyamian quatrain explains:

The Fate will not correct what once she writes
And more than what is doled no grain alights;
Beware of bleeding heart with sordid cares
For cares will cast thy heart in wretched plights.[85]

The above *Ruba'i* is a clear example of the Khayyamian view on free will and determinism, and one can call it a "celestial determinism" in which everyone is on the same journey but not treated the same way. Even though birth, suffering, and death are all part of the inescapable human condition, as fate has it, some receive more than their share of suffering. It is in the third hemistich of the above quatrain that Khayyam tells us to be content, there will not be another chance for one's re-entry into existence.

The following two *Ruba'iyyat* summarize Khayyam's position with regard to determinism and predestination, namely that he believed in a kind of cosmic and existential determinism whose nature and purpose remain a mystery. What is known is that death wins; and, in the process, we have a choice among living a meaningful life, falling into the abyss of sorrow and pessimism, or developing fancy theological systems. Khayyam favors the first option.

> We come and go, but bring in no return,
> When thread of life may break we can't discern
> How many saintly hearts have melted here
> And turned for us to ashes – who would learn?[86]
>
> Time brought me here: what profit did it gain?
> It takes me hence, but conquers no domain
> My Master knows, but none can ever guess
> Why Time thus brings and carries me again.[87]

IN VINO VERITAS (IN WINE THERE IS TRUTH)

Khayyam's concept and usage of wine is undoubtedly both the most significant and the most misunderstood aspect of his thought. Intoxication and wine bring together various aspects of Khayyamian thought and offer a coherent and existential theory as to how one can encounter temporality and death and still live a spiritually fulfilled life. Whereas the possible mystical connotations and interpretations of the place of wine, according to Khayyam, will be discussed in the forthcoming chapter, his "real intent" in employing this imagery is the subject of our discussion here.

Before diving into this key concept, let us briefly remark on the three possible interpretations of the use of wine by Khayyam:

1. The intoxicating wine (popular)
2. The wine of love (mystical)
3. The wine of wisdom (philosophical)

There are those who have taken Khayyam's use of the concept of wine in its literal sense and, ironically, have adhered to two contradictory understandings of it. The first interpretation has two extremes. There are those such as Nāṣir Khusraw who in his *Safar nāmah* argues that drinking wine is necessary to forget the pain of the world and even prescribes it for the *ḥakīms*.[88] The other extreme is exemplified by the orthodox such as S. Nakhjavānī, who, in his puritanical study of Khayyam entitled *Khayyam pendārī*,[89] rejects the notion that Khayyam could have ever prescribed drinking wine, for he was a devout and sincere Muslim. Instead, the references to wine in his *Ruba'iyyat* are false attributions to him by heretics. Ṭabāṭabā'ī, in his work *Khayyam yā khayyāmī*,[90] which is a more serious study of Khayyam than the previous work, argues that there are two different Khayyams; a scientist who was too serious to write about wine and intoxication and a poet who is the true author of the *Ruba'iyyat*. In referring to wine, Khayyam the poet meant the wine in its literal sense which brings intoxication. Finally, there is the view of those such as Khūrāsānī,[91] who argues that Khayyam had Sufi tendencies, but, being a skeptic and a pessimist, he prescribed drinking wine as a solution to his own unhappiness.

A more inclusive reading of Khayyam clearly rules out this interpretation, for a man of Khayyam's caliber who was wrestling with existential questions, alcoholic intoxication hardly seems to be a solution. Repeatedly, Khayyam prescribes drinking wine as a response to major riddles of life, such as questions of being and nothingness, impermanence, etc. In what way would drunkenness solve these problems?

> Wine strengthens my body and life sustains
> Unveils the hidden secrets therein where it remains
> I cease searching for this world and the next
> A sip of wine is better than all the hidden domains.[92]

> Drink wine, worries of unity and multiplicity fade
> From excess or decrease and feud of creed
> And do not shun this mead, a drop thereof
> Will cure ten thousand banes. 'Tis what you need![93]

Since Khayyam is operating on an intellectual level and not the level of everyday problems of life, the type of temporary forgetfulness that wine might bring about is clearly not a solution to the enduring questions of an ultimate nature. A careful reading of the above *Ruba'iyyat* reveals that such intellectually-loaded concepts like "multiplicity" and "unity" refer to the creation of the world of multiplicity from the one God, and "seventy-two nations" refers to debate among sects. Khayyam's use of wine as a metaphor is too complex by far to see it as simply drinking ordinary wine as a solution to the fundamental questions of human existence.

The other interpretation of the place of wine in Khayyamian thought is that of an esoteric and Sufi nature, in which a rich tradition of the use of this imagery puts wine within a sacred domain. From Ibn Al-Fārid's "Wine Ode" (*al-Khamriyyah*) to Ḥāfiz, the Persian wine-poet, the notion of wine has been used by most, if not all, Sufi poets in the Islamic esoteric tradition which symbolically represents wine as Divine ecstasy.

> Drinking wine and the love of a rosy face
> Better than the hypocrisy of the ascetic, that is base
> When the lover and a drunk are doomed to hell
> Who is left to see the heaven to embrace?[94]

Criticizing religious hypocrisy and the false ascetics and using the term "drunken-lover" are hallmarks of Sufism. There is a long-standing tradition of interpreting Khayyam's poetry within a Sufi context; figures such as Qazwīnī, Nasr, and Omar Alī Shāh, and some of the Western scholars of Khayyam such as Robert Graves, Anthony Burgess, and Henry Massé can be mentioned. An esoteric interpretation of his overall views will be offered in the forthcoming chapter, where I will demonstrate that Khayyam was not a Sufi in the traditional sense of the word. Neither in practice nor intellectually did he adhere to Sufism, and a Sufi interpretation of him is possible only by reading it into his *Ruba'iyyat* and by stretching the content to fit the classical Sufi doctrine.

The third interpretation of Khayyam's use of the concept of wine is as the "wine of wisdom," a philosophical image which enables one to come to terms with the merciless forces of nature through an all-too-human wisdom. Khayyam uses the imagery of wine as a "mode of being" and not a "mode of knowledge"; it is a way of being in the world which offers existential therapy for the perplexed. This reading of Khayyam is first and foremost consistent with the salient features of his thought, one that supports his middle path, rejecting the nihilism of the first interpretation and avoiding the theological and esoteric complications of the second.

> The mystery is great and the answers are rare
> Wise men have searched but you should not care
> Make thy own heaven here with this moment and wine
> For their heaven is a fairy tale, nothing but Air. [95]

To begin with, Khayyam lays down his now familiar premise, that of the epistemology of relativity and ignorance, and argues that the mystery is too deep and prodigious to make sense of it. The task at hand is to base your life on what is certain and can be understood at present. This type of wisdom is neither achieved nor obtained through drinking wine nor through a discursive mode of thought; it is a type of wisdom that is acquired from years of contemplation and reflection upon the more significant questions of life; it is the wisdom of living well. To do so, one has to relinquish the discursive path of inquiry, for this only leads to intellectual slavery.

> Those imprisoned by the intellect's need to decipher
> Humbled; knowing being from non-being, they proffer
> Seek ignorance and drink the juice of the grape
> Those fools acting as wise, scoffer [96]

In an apparent reference to the philosopher's concern for epistemological issues and the role of the five senses, four substances, six directions (N, S, E, W, above and below) and the seven heavens, Khayyam reiterates that an intellectual endeavor to solve such issues is futile; the question of temporality can only be solved by drinking the wine of wisdom.

> How long shall you repeat the story of five[97] and four[98] O *Sāqī*[99]
> Riddles, be at one or hundred thousand O *Sāqī*
> We are but dust, take the harp and play, O *Sāqī*
> We are but wind, fetch the goblet, O *Sāqī*. [100]

> O one departed from the warmth of the spiritual domain
> By four, five, six,[101] and seven,[102] bewildered and constrain
> Drink wine for you know not where you came from
> Be joyous for you know not where you go again. [103]

Khayyam's remarkable ability to remain focused on his intellectual deconstructionist project and on what matters here and now leads him to resist engagement in speculative matters which do not yield any result. He extends this to other philosophical problems for which he prescribes drinking wine, such as eternity and the createdness of the world.

Since our stay is impermanent in this Inn,
To be without wine and beloved is a sin;
O *Ḥakīm*,[104] why worry if the world is created or eternal,
Once dead, what if created or eternal the inn.[105]

What distinguishes this mode of being from a mode of knowledge is precisely the admission that amidst uncertainty, ignorance, and impermanence, it is not *what* you know that matters but *how* you live that matters, and this *howness,* to the dismay of metaphysicians, requires a wisdom that is fundamentally human.

I know not whether he who mixed my clay
Decreed heaven or hell for me, array
A goblet, an idol, and a harp by a meadow
Let these three be mine and you take heaven, pray.[106]

In Hinduism, the problem of being (*sat*), knowledge (*chit*), and bliss (*anandā*) is solved by becoming liberated (*jivān muktī*), through gaining the consciousness that your body (*prakirtī*) and soul (*prussia*) are separated. For Khayyam, too, liberation is the answer to the problem of suffering. His liberation, however, involves gaining the wisdom which allows him to see the sublime and the beautiful in what the world has to offer. Wine, lover, beloved, spring, river, flowers and nightingale are all beautiful symbols of the world; and existence can be seen as a gift if one can drink the wine of wisdom and dwell properly amidst what Suhrawardī calls a "prosperous-ruinous"[107] domain, a place we call home.

As Spring and Fall make their appointed turn,
The leaves of life one aft another turn;
Drink wine and brood not – as the Sage has said:
"Life's cares are poison, wine the cure in turn."[108]

Khayyam, if drunk with wine you be, rejoice,
If next to lovely face you sit, rejoice
And since the world in nothing ends, suppose
Your life be flown – while it is not, rejoice.[109]

CONCLUDING REMARKS

In the foregoing discussion, I attempted to clarify the intricacies and complexities of one of the most misunderstood thinkers of the Islamic world. Omar Khayyam's *Ruba'iyyat* were divided into seven themes which together constitute the intellectual paradigm of the "Khayyamian school of thought." To what extent the ideas of the historical Khayyam correspond with the foregoing characterizations remains ultimately a mystery; but even if a fraction of the *Ruba'iyyat* which are attributed to him are truly his, our analysis and interpretation remain valid. Let us briefly review the salient features of Khayyam's thought in light of our foregoing discussion.

Khayyam's long life and arduous scholarly activities did not lead to a solution concerning the major riddles of life and human existence. His *Ruba'iyyat*, I argue, may lead one to one of the following three perspectives:

1. Nihilism
2. Sufism
3. Rationalism

Khayyam could have taken the existential dive into the abyss of nothingness, rejected faith altogether and advocated a type of hedonism, perhaps a stoic-epicurianism. This is not what Khayyam advocated either in his personal life and conduct or in his philosophical and scientific treatises, as discussed in Chapter Two. Nihilism, as Nietzsche declared, may be negative or positive.[110] The negative sense of Nihilism, whose natural consequences are despair, depression and suicide, is clearly inconsistent with Khayyam's repeated call to "live and be happy." The positive sense of it, however, which requires an active engagement with and an appreciation of life despite the fact that we are swimming amidst an existential sea of uncertainty, doubt, and suffering, is what Khayyam advocates.

Khayyam, on one hand, realizes that many of the principles upon which religion is based are unverifiable, and therefore, it would be intellectually dishonest to embrace it as if they were certain. On the other hand, he never rejected religion outright since the mystery is bigger than us all; therefore, he can be characterized as an agnostic who rejected the negative sense of Nihilism and, embracing the possibility of a profound human experience of the world, he is almost a Zen master.

Khayyam's relationship with Sufism is difficult to characterize. Perhaps it would not be too far from the truth to describe it as a love-hate relationship. What is appealing about Sufism to Khayyam is what Kierkegaard defines as "an objective uncertainty held fast in the appropriation-process of the most passionate inwardness."[111] The Sufis are in love with the world, for the beauties of the world are a reminder of the Beloved's face. It is this enchantment with the world in combination with an understanding of its impermanence which resonate deeply with Khayyam.

What distinguishes him from Sufis, however, is the absence of a "Sufi doctrine," an intellectual framework within which Sufi tenets can be understood. Even though one can find traces of Neo-Platonism in Khayyam's philosophical writings, they are not strong enough to substantiate the claim that Khayyam was a gnostic (*'ārif*) or a Sufi. In fact, a Sufi solution might be conceived of as an easy way out, a sell-out to the epistemology of ignorance and a surrender to the temptation of fabricating holy lies, however sublime, beautiful, and profound they might be, to justify what one does not understand. The Sufi way is the way of contentment (*riḍā*); and yet, Khayyam was like Job: he questioned, rebelled, protested, and shook his fist at the heavens for all the suffering they impose upon us. This is not the Sufi way.

The Khayyam who emerges from the *Ruba'iyyat* is a figure similar to Socrates for whom intellection was the end-all rather than a means to an end. In his deep appreciation for a good life and the *good* in life, as well as in intellectual temperament with zero tolerance for nonsense, he was an Aristotelian. Philosophically, he is fundamentally a rationalist, a Peripatetic who valued reason and what is verifiable. In lieu of all the metaphysical and philosophical speculation of philosophers and the amorphous emotionalism of the Sufis, he chose to remain centered. A Khayyamian quatrain addresses this concept:

> The world's a sketch our fancy draws on skies
> This real truth is seen thro' wisdom's eyes
> So stay sedate entranced with Master's Grace
> Aloof from fantasies and all their lies.[112]

Khayyam could have adopted Kierkegaard's scheme and opted for risk taking, for the attainment of the jewel that lies at the heart of faith necessitates taking a risk. Khayyam also could have taken the easy way out and accepted Pascal's wager, a "divine cost-benefit analysis" whereby, despite the insufficiency of reason, it is more prudent to accept the existence of God and the tenets of the faith just in case there is a God. Khayyam, however, is too honest, intellectually speaking, and takes an uncharacteristically non-Islamic stance in his *Ruba'iyyat* that is reflective of his pragmatic-agnosticism. There is a part of him which remains an agnostic all the way to the end, a part that is inconsistent and incongruent with the Khayyam of his philosophical and scientific work in which he expresses his faith and devotion in an unqualified manner. The challenge has been and is to reconcile these two diametrically opposed sides of Khayyam and to account for his clear sense of agnosticism and expressed belief in Islam, a challenge which will be addressed in forthcoming chapters.

> Ye go from soul asunder this ye know
> And that ye creep, behind His curtain low
> Hence sing His Name, ye know not whence ye came
> And live sedate, ye know not where to go.[113]

5

Khayyam and Sufism

O pure Sufi! that saunter in His quest
He has no place, would you go East or West?
If thou knowest Him, why thou seekest Him?
If not, at whose feet would you like to rest?[1]

Most contemporary Iranians see Khayyam as a *rind*, a spiritual cynic, and wise poet whose *Ruba'iyyat* are to be understood as the esoteric utterances of a spiritual master. To think otherwise would be a cultural oxymoron: an agnostic poet has become the cultural hero of Persians! Seeing some of the *Ruba'iyyat* as examples of Sufi poetry, however, is not entirely unfounded, and a large number of them do lend themselves, with a bit of stretch, to Sufi interpretation. After all, Khayyam employs much of the same Sufi symbolism and poetic imagery of the Sufi poets before and after him, such as Ḥāfiẓ and Rūmī. There is no reason why Khayyam could not have used this symbolism within the Sufi context.

The view that Khayyam was the master of esoteric Islam, an accomplished Sufi and a gnostic (*'ārif*), is supported by a number of Persian and Western scholars of Khayyam. An esoteric interpretation of the *Ruba'iyyat* puts him well within the Sufi tradition and regards him as a major figure in the tradition of Persian Sufi poetry. Aḥmad

Ghazzālī[2] was among the major contemporaries of Khayyam, who saw him as a Sufi; he mentions some of Khayyam's *Ruba'iyyat* and comments on them. This point is particularly significant since it reveals that as early as Khayyam's own time, there must have been a tradition of understanding his *Ruba'iyyat* within a Sufi context. Also, Aḥmad Ghazzālī is a renowned Sufi master whose more famous brother, Abū Ḥāmid Ghazzālī knew Khayyam and engaged him in intellectual debates. Whether Aḥmad Ghazzālī had met Khayyam or knew of him, the fact that Ghazzālī quoted Khayyam and offered an esoteric interpretation of several of his *Ruba'iyyat* is a strong and clear indication of Khayyam's reputation as a Sufi.

Figures such as Seyyed Hossein Nasr,[3] Robert Graves, Anthony Burgess, Henri Massé,[4] Zhukovski,[5] and Christensen[6] have also offered an esoteric reading of Khayyam. Even the eminent thirteenth/nineteenth-century scholar, Abbās Kayvān Qazwīnī, wrote two esoteric commentaries on the *Ruba'iyyat* of Khayyam. In a story that reminds one of Suhrawardī's dream-vision of Aristotle and his conversation with him, Qazwīnī had a similar spiritual experience of Khayyam. Upon completion of his second commentary, Qazwīnī claimed that the spirit of Khayyam visited him and assured him that he agreed with the content of Qazwīnī's commentary. Qazwīnī supposedly asked the spirit of Khayyam about the dubious poems that are attributed to him, and Khayyam told him which of the *Ruba'iyyat* were actually authentic.[7] Qazwīnī's commentary remains the most lucid and scholarly work to date to offer an esoteric verse by verse interpretation of Khayyam's *Ruba'iyyat*.

Despite the above authoritative views, the best evidence for Khayyam's views on Sufism comes from Khayyam himself. In his *On the Knowledge of the Universal Principles of Existence*, he classifies the types of the seekers of truth:[8]

1. First are theologians (*mutikallimūn*) who are content with theological arguments and consider "this much knowledge of God, exalted is His name" to be sufficient.
2. Philosophers and sages who have relied on discursive reasoning to know the principles of logic as a way of knowing and have not

been content with what is satisfying to oneself. They too, however, have not remained faithful to the conditions of logic and have become helpless with it.

3. The Ismā'īlīs and instructionalists (*ta'limiyūn*) who questioned how one can seek knowledge other than through authentic instruction, for in proofs concerning knowledge of the Creator, His essence and His attributes, there are many difficulties. The reasoning of the opponents [are too weak] and intellects are bewildered and helpless [to understand the truth], and therefore, it is better to seek the truth from the one who knows.
4. The Sufis who do not seek knowledge intellectually or discursively but, by the cleansing of their inner self and purgation of their morals, have cleansed their rational soul from the impurities of nature and incorporeal bodies. When that substance [soul] is purified and becomes a reflection of the spiritual world, the forms in that status are truly unveiled without any doubt or ambiguity. *This path is the best of them all.* It is known to the servant of God that there is no perfection better than the presence of God, and in that state, there are no obstacles or veils. For all that man lacks is due to the impurity of nature, and if the veil [of ignorance] is lifted and the screen, [which is] an obstacle, is removed, the truth of things as they really are becomes apparent. The master of the created beings, [Prophet Muḥammad] upon him be peace and praise, has alluded to this and said, "During the days of your existence, Divine grace comes from God. Do you not want to follow them?"

If we go by the above classification of Khayyam, clearly the discussion ends here, for he endorses Sufism and puts it above all the other available ways of knowing. While Khayyam never claims to be a Sufi – and technically, endorsing the Sufi way does not make him a Sufi – certainly the implication is there. It is not a coincidence that his contemporary Ghazzālī, in his *Deliverance From Error*,[9] and Suhrawardī, who lived not too long after Khayyam, in his *The Philosophy of Illumination*,[10] make the exact same classification putting the Sufi way above all other ways of knowing.

In what follows, I will offer a Sufi interpretation of Khayyam's *Ruba'iyyat* with emphasis on the elucidation and elaboration of the symbolism of the imagery used in his poetry. It is my intention to argue that while Khayyam's Sufi tendencies and possible Sufi affiliation cannot be rejected outright, it can be said with some degree of certitude that he was not a Sufi in the traditional sense of the word.

Once again, the question of the authenticity of the *Ruba'iyyat* is one which is not a primary concern here. Instead, what is being investigated is the spirit of the "Khayyamian school of thought." In this regard we shall cast the net wider and include a larger number of *Ruba'iyyat*, that figures such as Govinda Tirtha and P. Yogananda among others consider to be authentic while others cast doubt on them.[11]

Let us approach Khayyam's Sufism systematically and treat those central themes in his *Ruba'iyyat* which constitute the heart and soul of Sufism. They include:

1. The transcendental nature of God
2. The major and minor intellect
3. Love and Beloved
4. Asceticism and the Sufi order
5. Initiation and the master
6. The spiritual journey
7. Unity

THE TRANSCENDENTAL NATURE OF GOD

Sufism begins with bewilderment and awe rather than with doubt and skepticism, a fine line that one may argue Khayyam never crossed. Despite his cynical views with regard to just about every aspect of religion, Khayyam never questions the existence of God in any of the quatrains. In a poem which might not be authentic but is nevertheless representative of Khayyam's view on God, he refers to his heart and vision as having been illuminated, both of which are the traditional Sufi concepts.

HE IS, and nought but Him exists, I know,
This truth is what creation's book will show;
When heart acquired perception with His Light,
Atheistic darkness changed to faithly glow.[12]

In another Khayyamian quatrain, the author elaborates on the unspeakable reality and mystery of God. In an image that reminds us of what Lao-Tzu describes in his *Tao Te Ching* as "the Lord of the ten thousand shadows," the quatrain unfolds:

The Chief of Being's secrets that Thou art,
Thy traits depict to view the Being's chart;
Veiled in Thy Greatness from the creatures here
Presidest Being Thou in open Mart.[13]

Khayyam's confession that, despite his mastery of the exoteric and esoteric sciences, he is still bewildered by the mystery of it all is evident in the following quatrain. Using drunkenness as the symbol of being base and low, he says:

I know existence and non-existence, outwardly though
I know all that is high and what is below
Despite my mastery, shamefully, I am ignorant
For I know not a degree higher than darkness to go.[14]

This poem is consistent with the account that his son-in-law gave of the final hours of Khayyam and his prayer shortly before he died.[15]

The major and minor intellect ('aql-i kullī wa 'aql-i juz'ī*)*

Having placed God in a transcendental domain beyond the reach of reason, the stage is now set to belittle reason and rationality, also a favorite theme of Sufis. Traditionally, rationalization and discursive reasoning have been denounced by Sufis as an inferior faculty (*'aql-i juz'ī*), which is incapable of understanding Divine reality.

The use and abuse of the intellect in its rational sense has been a point of contention between Sufis and philosophers. Assuming the authenticity of the above *Ruba'iyyat*, Khayyam seems to be siding with Sufis when he supports the traditional Sufi perspective that reason fails when it comes to understanding God. The following *Ruba'iyyat* best represents the Khayyamian school of thought on this subject:

No understanding reached Thy height sublime,
For thought can only move in space or time;
No soul can grasp Thy perfections, O Lord!
And Thou alone could gauge Thy height, O prime![16]

My soaring mind cannot approach Thy throne.
I kiss this ground and thus for sins atone.
O wondrous Charmer! Who can know Thy Being?
Perchance, Thy knower may be Thou alone.[17]

With the minor intellect suppressed, the major intellect – or what the illuminationist (*ishrāqī*) philosophers have called "intellectual intuition" (*dhawq*) – is then open to apprehend the mysteries of the Divine realm. Yogananda[18] offers a translation of and commentary on the *Ruba'iyyat* with strict emphasis on their esoteric connotations. He offers an impressive glossary, which presents the "inner meanings" of the *Ruba'iyyat*, and also indicates the extent to which one has to read into them the traditional Sufi concepts in order to "Suficize" them. In a quatrain attributed to Khayyam we read:

Dreaming when Dawn's Left Hand was in the sky
I heard a voice within the Tavern cry
Awake, my little one, and fill the cup
Before Life's liquor in its cup be dry.[19]

In his work, *Wine of the Mystic: The Ruba'iyyat of Omar Khayyam – A Spiritual Interpretation*, Yogananda tells us that Khayyam is a Sufi poet and offers a spiritual hermeneutics whereby most concepts in the *Ruba'iyyat* have a hidden meaning not apparent to those who are not initiated into the mystical, spiritual universe. Yogananda defines "Dawn's left hand" as the perennial wisdom and the first yearning to solve the riddles of life. "A voice" stands for *dhawq* and "tavern" is the "sanction of inner silence." "Fill the cup" is the consciousness of the mystic, and the "cup" is the corporeal body which needs to be filled with the new intellect.

Khayyam embraces the *sophia perennis* and tastes the sapiential wisdom that lies at the heart of all the divinely revealed religions. To do so, in the tradition of great Sufi masters, he has to denounce reason and intellect in its rational sense as well as the formalism of the religious law (*shar'iah*). Wine, this powerful symbol of Divine intoxication and of dissolving and annihilating oneself in Divine love, is used by Khayyam exactly as traditional Sufis do.

> You know my friends, with what a brave Carouse
> I will enrich myself with two goblets of wine in my house
> Divorced old barren of reason and faith thrice
> And took the daughter of the vine to spouse.[20]

LOVE AND BELOVED

With intellect, reason and rationalization out of the picture, the path of experiential wisdom is thus paved. Sufism is the path of love, which is both a mode of being and a mode of knowledge; the Sufi knows through love what love is, and, ultimately, his very being is consumed by love just as a butterfly is burned by the flame of the candle around which he rotates. The paradox of love is that a love that does not kill is not love. On this point Khayyam may have remarked:

> Without Love and Guide the world's a restless round,
> When heart will tune to flute then He is found;
> I scanned the world around, at last I find
> That bliss is truth – the rest is hollow sound.[21]

If a case can be made for Khayyam's Sufism, it is precisely his treatment of the concept of love, which constitutes the heart and soul of Sufism. It is here where his Sufi tendency is not only most apparent, but also resembles the traditional Sufi perspective. A Khayyamian quatrain states:

> May lovers in the ruin consult and meet,
> May ascetics burn in their own pious heat;
> And may the motley-coats and azure-robes
> To crave a lover's blessings, kiss his feet.[22]

The word for "ruin" in Persian is " *kharābāt*," a favorite term of Sufis with many connotations. Sufis were known to have withdrawn themselves from people and cities, the places of sin, and preferred solitude. A Sufi is often referred to as a " *rind*," meaning a wise-fool, a spiritually astute person who chooses the solitude of ruins over the crowds and association with people. Wise also is he who accepts the world as it really is, a ruin compared to the incorporeal and angelic world. Khayyam criticizes asceticism and the hypocrisy of the seemingly pious for their Sufi appearance, those who worship the form will not transcend to see the formless. It is love that must be embraced, a point that is so eloquently implied here.

There are two key concepts in the *Ruba'iyyat*, which, depending on how they are interpreted, may leave us with a different Khayyam; they are the notions of wine and Beloved. These two key concepts that are repeated in the overwhelming majority of the *Ruba'iyyat* play a crucial role in understanding Khayyam esoterically. Clearly, it can be argued, as many have, that by "Beloved" Khayyam means none other than the only Being worthy to be loved. This long-standing tradition and interpretation of Khayyam, reiterated by scholars such as Qazwīnī, Daftary[23] and Nasr, only highlights the Sufi usage of the concept of beloved (*ma'shuq*). If taken literally, one ends up with the Khayyam of Victorian England, an agnostic hedonist who prescribes worldly pleasures as a remedy for the meaninglessness of life. However, if wine and the Beloved are understood in their traditional Sufi connotations, then we have a different Khayyam, a Sufi master who belittles all that is transient and thus unreal. Amidst the ever-changing river of life, it is the awareness of an awakening to the Reality of the Beloved, which like wine intoxicates the soul with Divine radiance; it is only God who is real. So the Qur'an says, "All things perish except His face."

For Khayyam, love is not an abstract idea, but an ideal which constitutes the heart and soul of life. The world is an expression of love which emanates from Love. Khayyam may have commented:

The compendium of the book of truth is love
The leading line of Ode of Youth is love
O witless Man, the world of love so blind!
Bear this in mind: The core of life is love.[24]

ASCETICISM AND THE SUFI ORDER

With love comes pain, the existential pain of remembering our original abode and the taste of oneness with God; this is where asceticism, an integral part of Sufism, comes into the picture. Despite several quatrains, such as the following, in which Khayyam alludes to his endeavors to cleanse his soul, there is no evidence that Khayyam practiced asceticism. If he did, none of his biographers mention it, nor is it reflected in his *Ruba'iyyat*. A quatrain composed in the Khyyamian style explains:

> I am embattled with my ego which I cannot tame
> I am ashamed of my deeds but they fan the flame
> The mercy will forgive, but then, alas
> Thou saw me sin, can I forget the shame?[25]

In fact, Khayyam seems to have been opposed to ascetic practices and repeatedly equated them with some type of hypocrisy, for what matters is what lies in the heart of the lover and not the outward façade.

> To lovers true what matters, dark or fair
> In hell or heaven, love mates would not care
> Nor if a brick or bolster rest their heads
> Nor whether silk or serge Beloved does wear.[26]

Despite his apparent opposition to asceticism, one does find brief references to ascetic practices. In a revealing passage in his *Risālah fi'l-wujūd*, Khayyam clearly demonstrates that asceticism helps to open up the intellect to the possibilities of higher realities:

> In my opinion, it is appropriate of the status of the wise that intelligibles do not remain veiled from them. Thus, those who find their souls incapable of understanding such meanings should know that their souls have erred due to hallucination. These men should practice *austere forms of asceticism* and seek guidance from God alone for He is to be trusted for answers.[27]

Sufism is generally divided into three phases: asceticism (*zuhd*), love (*'ishq*), and gnosticism (*'irfān*). One finds representatives of these three types of Sufism throughout the history of Islam. The ascetic period is generally identified with the early period which preceded Khayyam; and gnosticism, which is a synthesis of philosophy and practical wisdom, is a product of the later period. Khayyam, one may argue, belongs to the Sufism of love. Antinomian statements and behavior, belittling of religious law and putting emphasis on the truth (*ḥaqiqah*) as opposed to law (*Shari'ah*), is the salient feature of this school of Sufism. Khayyam fits well within this esoteric paradigm, for his emphasis on love constitutes the existential core of the human condition; nothing else matters, not the story behind creation or our final destiny. What is at stake here is one's mode of being in the world, the nature of the relationship between the lover and the beloved, *the way* we are, one might say. Khayyam expresses this in terms of classical Sufi language:

> Entranced and drunk, in love we are today
> In Magian Lane[28] we worship wine today
> Completely rapt, we are beyond ourselves
> Attached forever to thy Lord[29] today.[30]

Similar to the absence of evidence concerning Khayyam's ascetic practices, there does not seem to be any mention of him belonging to a Sufi order. We know that when he went to Baghdad, a group of Sufis approached him; but Khayyam refused them and stayed aloof. The only reference to this is by al-Qifṭī in his *Tārikh al-ḥukamā'*:

> Omar al-Khayyam, the Imam of Khurāsān and the 'Allāmah (learned master) of his time who knows Greek sciences, discusses and seeks the one religion and attempts to cleanse his bodily movements and his soul and in matters pertaining to civic politics, he followed the Greek principles. Later Sufis understood his poems outwardly and considered them to be part of their tradition and in their sessions and gatherings [his poems] became matters for conversation and discussion. They [his poems], however, are inwardly like snakes who bite the *shari'ah* [Islamic law] and are many chains and handcuffs [upon religion].
>
> Once the people of the time had a taste of his faith and his secrets were revealed, he [Khayyam] was frightened for his life,

> withdrew from writing, speaking and such like and wayfared to Mecca. Once he arrived in Baghdad, members of [a Sufi] tradition and believers in primary sciences came to him and began to socialize with him. He did not accept them and after performing the pilgrimage returned to his native land, kept his secrets and preached worshiping and following the people of faith. In the science of *ḥikmah* and astronomy he was unique such that he became an exemplar.[31]

Even in the above, there is no mention of a specific Sufi order with whom Khayyam was affiliated. The lack of such a reference, one might argue, does not definitively rule out the possibility that he belonged to a Sufi order. To begin with, he may have belonged to the Uwaysīs,[32] a Sufi order whose members ultimately are initiated through the hidden master, *Khiḍr* (also known as *Idris* and *Enoch*). Also, Sufi orders were far less organized in the medieval period than they are today, and belonging to an order was not "required" as is prevalent now. Also, Khayyam may have been an independent Sufi who disliked institutionalized Sufism, as is apparent in his numerous comments about the hypocrisy of the Sufis. In either case, while there is no evidence that Khayyam practiced asceticism or belonged to any established Sufi order, he may have considered himself as a kind of Sufi without formally having been initiated into an order or ascribing to the whole Sufi doctrine.

INITIATION AND THE MASTER

The role of a Sufi master is indispensable to Sufism. Initiation into an order through a Sufi master is the gate by which one enters the Sufi tradition. We can speculate, as we have above, that Khayyam may have been an Uwaysī, but once again we are faced with a lack of concrete information whether Khayyam had a master or had been someone's spiritual master. In none of his writings does Khayyam mention his spiritual master, nor is it even implied in his *Ruba'iyyat* that he had one. If anything, he considers himself to be a follower of Avicenna, the peripatetic master of Greek philosophy. Since we are giving Khayyam the benefit of the doubt that he may have been a Sufi, let us see if the master/disciple relationship can be found in his *Ruba'iyyat* in some fashion.

As it has been argued, evidence of Khayyam's initiation into a Sufi order is nonexistent; yet one can argue that this absence is consistent with Khayyam having been an independent Sufi, a member of the Uwaysī Sufi order, or perhaps an adherent of an antinomian Sufi order such as the *Malāmatiyyah*. As Nasr in his *Sufi Essays* states:

> To be sure, there are those rare people such as the Uwaysis who are initiated into the way by *Khaḍir* or *Khiḍr*, the prophet possessing an unusually long life who can initiate men into the Divine Mysteries and who corresponds in many ways to Enoch in the Judeo-Christian tradition, or by the 'men of the invisible hierarchy' (*rijāl al-ghayb*), or, in the case of Shi'ism, by the Hidden Imam who is the spiritual pole (*Quṭb*) of the Universe.[33]

Khayyam, therefore, could have transcended the intermediary between himself and God and established a direct relationship with the Beloved. Consumed by Divine love, Khayyam may have said:

> In tavern rather I in Thee confide
> Than pray without Thee at the Pulpit-side
> O Thou, who art creation's First and Last
> Now burn or bless me as Thou may'st decide.[34]

Once again, we encounter the same problem; namely, if Khayyam was a Sufi, he could not have been a traditional one; and if he had a spiritual master, he kept it a secret. One could argue that Khayyam's master was not a person but rather all the manifestations of the Beloved, whose ethereal presence permeates every facet of life. If the role of the master is to show the way (*ṭariqah*) and to lead one from the corporeal to the incorporeal, for Khayyam, a flower, a nightingale, a river, as well as the beauty of the face of a woman could do precisely that. What need does the soul of a spiritual giant like Khayyam have to awaken his spiritual acumen, since his perceptive mind sees the master in all things? Khayyam did not seek an external master, but saw the Master within himself; he might have expressed this concept in the following quatrain:

> O You who seek your Lord at night and day
> with purblind eyes you seek Him far away
> The Lord reveals Himself and ever says
> See me from head to foot with thee – and stay.[35]

Khayyam may have seen the Prophets as the gates of initiation and their revealed doctrines as a sufficient source of spiritual instruction:

> Now the new year revives old desires
> The thoughtful soul the solitude retires
> Where the White Hand of Moses on the Bough
> In every breath, there is Jesus who from the ground suspires.[36]

THE SPIRITUAL JOURNEY (*ṬARIQAH*)

The traditional Sufi concept of *ṭariqah* means a spiritual journey from the outward (*ẓāhir*) to the inward (*bāṭin*), from the exoteric to the esoteric, by means of ascetic practices and cleansing of the soul. Sufi literature provides us with a rich and copious set of aphorisms pertaining to how the journey must be followed. These instructions range from how fasting should be observed to abstinence and invocation of divine names. In this regard, the richness of classical Sufi literature is too extensive to treat here.[37]

There is, however, not a single apothegm or aphorism in the *Ruba'iyyat* where Khayyam offers specific instructions of how the spiritual journey should be followed, nor is there any reference to the notion of the *ṭariqah* in the corpus of his writing. And yet, despite the lack of evidence in this regard, we know that Khayyam has placed Sufism above all other modes of knowledge; and this implies that either he was a practicing Sufi or that he had an insight into the spiritual journey. Since this is the case, we can now ask the following question: if Khayyam was on a spiritual journey, what path would that have been? Certainly, it was not the path of traditional Sufi orders; but then this, too, is in line with Khayyam's overall orientation in which he eschews the formalism of the traditional Sufi orders and goes to the heart of the Sufi message: by reflecting upon the temporary and transient nature of events, one is naturally led to see the permanent reality that lies at the heart of all that exists. Whereas this method might seem too general, Khayyam is somewhat systematic in his methodology of satirical deconstructionism by belittling all that veils the seeker of truth from reality. The following quatrain is a perfect example of Khayyam's perspective on the human condition and our journey:

> We came as purest gold, but changed to dross
> We came sedate, but griefs have made us cross
> We loved with cheerful eyes and flaming hearts
> But cast our lives to winds, in dust we toss.[38]

The spiritual journey begins by the realization that we live in an "unreal" domain. If *ṭariqah*, as Nasr defines it, is "a means whereby man can return to the origin of the Islamic revelation itself,"[39] then Khayyam's powerful message that only the Beloved is worth remembering addresses the heart and soul of the Sufi message. The spiritual journey is a process which begins with reflection, contemplation, and recognition that to exist is to be on a journey, the direction of which is determined by the spiritual goal of the seeker. One could become attached to what is temporary and transient and spend a lifetime looking for happiness in possessing objects, or one could realize his/her own place in the universe and focus on a genuine spiritual journey.

> We are no other than a moving row
> Of magic shadow-shapes that come and go
> Round with the sun-illumined lantern held
> In midnight by the Master of the show.[40]

Khayyam's spiritual journey may not fulfill the criterion set by traditional Sufism, but it is a journey of immense depth whereby he peels layers and layers of deceptive aspects of life which allure and tempt by reminding us constantly how temporary life is. The mind then naturally gravitates towards the Unchangeable, Immutable, and Eternal Truth, the Reality whose existence makes other things less real. This journey is a form of "existential therapy," "philosophical therapy," or the philosopher's way to transcend the form and to see the formless, a journey which is both compatible with the Sufi way and has the intellectual integrity that is worthy of a powerful intellect like Khayyam.

UNITY (*FANĀ*)

The final goal of a Sufi and ultimate destination of the spiritual journey for Sufism is union with God or, as Sufis say, "annihilation of the self in God" (*fanā*). *Fanā* occurs while one is a prisoner of the corporeal body and not when the soul has departed and achieved unity with the incorporeal world. For the Sufis, the Prophet Muḥammad's saying, "Die before your death," refers to a spiritual death and rebirth, a rebirth whose ultimate aim is to achieve unity with God. The annals of Sufi literature are full of examples of Sufis implicitly or explicitly reporting their experience of unity and the arrival at the station of *fanā*. Bāyazīd, the Sufi of the third/ninth century, referring to himself, said, "in this cloak there is nothing but God;" and Ḥallāj, the famous Sufi martyr, was crucified for saying, "I am the truth" (*ana'l-ḥaqq*). These two are among the more explicit examples of those Sufis who have achieved *fanā*.

There are of course those few *Ruba'iyyat* which make a more traditional reading of *fanā* possible; a typical Khayyamian quatrain purports:

> In danger who allureth? I or thou
> And who with tigers playeth? I or thou
> I cannot speak myself if I be thine
> If I am thou, who speaketh? I or thou.[41]

By "danger" Khayyam refers to the perils of the spiritual path that await a Sufi. It takes the strength of a lion to pursue the path of love and to get through all the pitfalls along the way. When the unity occurs, Khayyam asks, who is speaking, I or thou?

If *fanā* is to be understood only in the traditional Sufi context, Khayyam did not adhere to it; for neither in his *Ruba'iyyat* nor in his philosophical writings is there any reference to this concept. If anything, there is ample evidence, one may argue, that Khayyam thought that the end of life is the final destination, and one should not seek anything above and beyond it. As Khayyam states:

> Tomorrow, when we depart from this perishing domain
> (*dayr-i fanā*)
> We are equal with those who are seven thousand years old.

One could, however, argue that the concept of *fanā* is a loaded term which lends itself to different connotations and interpretations and that Khayyam may have embraced a notion different from the traditional understanding. There is an abundance of verses whereby Khayyam expresses his awe of the beauty of the Beloved, the power of love, and the mystery of it all. Can one not conclude that a union or absorption, in an experiential sense, into a mystery we call human existence is a case of *fanā*?

Ḥallāj's claim, "I am the truth," seems to appear in Khayyam's *Ruba'iyyat* in a different context; that is, the unity is not of a transcendental nature with God but is with the experience and the ecstasy that is derived from an acute observation of the human condition and its surroundings in a mysterious place we call the world. It is the awe of the "thereness" (*Dasein*) of man in the wilderness of human existence.

In a reinterpretation of the concept of "annihilation and subsistence" (*fanā* and *baqā*), Khayyam alludes to the inner unity that exists between the knower and the known, the seeker and God, and mentions that the unity already is there, but one needs to have the eyes to see it. Those who seek unity externally in the celestial domain or on an abstract metaphysical plain, miss the unity that exists between the lover and his Beloved within the very self. A quatrain attributed to Khayyam conveys:

> Oh thou that seek to find eternal light
> When evoking His name, you gain celestial height

The Lord's with thee, His highest seat thy heart
If not with thee, where could thou find Him right?[42]

CONCLUDING REMARKS

As we have noted before, despite the presence of several *Ruba'iyyat* which can be interpreted in terms of traditional Sufi doctrine, Khayyam's world-view fundamentally lacks traditional Sufi elements. One can perhaps read these into the *Ruba'iyyat*, as I have in the foregoing discussion; but even then one cannot see Khayyam in the tradition of Sufi masters such as Rūmī, Ḥallāj, Bāyazīd, Abū Sa'īd Abu'l- Khayr or Rabi'ah. For all we know, Khayyam neither had a Sufi master nor was he initiated into a Sufi tradition. None of his biographers have alluded to his Sufi affiliation, and the one exception I have mentioned previously asserts that Sufis misunderstood his *Ruba'iyyat* and interpreted them as they wished. Furthermore, just as one can find those *Ruba'iyyat* which lend themselves to traditional Sufi notions, it is possible to find numerous *Ruba'iyyat* in which those very traditional concepts are criticized severely. Ascetics, for example, are called hypocrites; the discovery of the inner truth of Islam, which is the goal of Sufis, is belittled and is the subject of Khayyam's sarcasm.

There are primarily two reasons why Khayyam, at least among his fellow Persians, has come to be identified as a Sufi-like poet. First, he is culturally identified with Sufism; and second, there is the possibility that he may have adopted certain strands of Sufi thought. Since, in an Islamic religious universe, Khayyam cannot be an agnostic-hedonist – and there are few indications that he was, at least in terms of the life he lived – how are we going to explain this "embarrassment" called the *Ruba'iyyat*? We have one chance to save our cultural hero from the charges of heresy and doubt, and that is to investigate what Khayyam "really had in mind," to cultivate and speculate upon the inner meaning of the *Ruba'iyyat* and to understand the esoteric dimensions of his thought. After all, the symbolism of wine, women, lovemaking, impermanence of life, etc. is widely used among most of the Persian Sufi poets.

In this way, therefore, the cultural forces and the powerful presence of Islam in Iran have been influential in the sense that they predetermined the limits of who Khayyam was or could have been, and Sufism in this context was his saving grace. Sufis have had a "mystical license", and when a "poetic license" is added to it, a Sufi-poet can assume less responsibility than a philosopher or a theologian can. Khayyam had to be rescued from the charges of atheism, agnosticism, and hedonism; and the only possible way to do so was to see him as a Sufi whose utterances really mean other than what they seem. This can only be done by reading this into his quatrains. The fact that so many *Ruba'iyyat* have been attributed to him only allows greater latitude in conducting a spiritual hermeneutics and reading Sufism into the *Ruba'iyyat*.

The second alternative is to ask: if Khayyam were to be a Sufi, what type of Sufi would he be? Among the modern scholars of Khayyam who have entertained his Sufi affiliation is Furūghī. One of the forerunners among scholars who has made a major endeavor to classify and introduce the authentic *Ruba'iyyat*, Furūghī believes "it is possible that Khayyam may have liked the principles of Sufism and his ideas may have been consistent with that of Sufis at times ... but there is no evidence that he was formally a Sufi."[43]

We can, however, speculate about the type and nature of Khayyam's possible Sufi tendencies. If he was a Sufi, as it has been argued before, he either belonged to the *Uwaysī* Sufi tradition or the antinomian *Malāmatiyyah* tradition – or perhaps was an independent Sufi. There are good reasons to assume that if Khayyam was a Sufi, he belonged to the *Malāmatiyyah*. First and foremost, this movement originated in Khurāsān and particularly in the city of Nayshābūr in the latter part of the third/ninth century. *Malāmatiyyah* was a movement that came about through a group of very pious Sufis who protested the puritanical façade of orthodoxy. Afīfī, in his work *Malāmatiyyah, Ṣufiyyah wa futuwwat*, describes the *Malāmatiyyah* as a "relentless struggle with any Sufi formalism and a return to the piety of early Islam." [44] Afīfī continues to say that the *Malāmatiyyah*'s unhappiness with the government and politicians, the stifling formalism of the jurists and the hypocrisy of some

Sufis, brought about a negative attitude among the members of this movement which was expressed in prose and poetry:

> *Malāmatiyyah* are an order distinct from other pious and ascetics. Muslim, they have their own ethical and spiritual specifications ... Perhaps, through this he wanted to distinguish between *Malāmatiyyah* and Sufis.[45]

There are several references by figures such as Abū Ḥafs Suhrawardī, who lived just a few years after Khayyam and wrote *'Awārif al-ma'ārif*, and Sulāmī, author of *Risālah Malāmatiyyah*. Both scholars refer to the presence of a large number of *Malāmatiyyah* in Khurāsān and around Nayshābūr. It would be inconceivable to imagine that Khayyam did not come into contact with the antinomian Sufis of Nayshābūr and was not affected by them.

Khayyam's possible affiliation with the *Malāmatiyyah* is also advocated by a number of contemporary scholars. I'timād devotes a chapter of his book, *Sha'r-i falsafi-yi Khayyam*, to an analysis of the *Malāmatiyyah* and the central features of their thought, and finds a perfect match with Khayyam's lifestyle and ideas.[46] Independence of thought, eschewing the formalism of religious life, distancing themselves from the centers of power, criticizing orthodoxy severely, and resisting the rise of dogmatic theology are among the salient features of the *Malāmatiyyah*; Khayyam represents them all. The eminent contemporary scholar Dinānī alludes to this possible affiliation, arguing that Khayyam's antinomian statements are more in line with the *Malāmatiyyah* Sufi order than with mere hedonism.[47] The following quatrain is an example of the antinomian tendencies of the Khayyamian school of thought:

> Till mosques and religious schools ruins will not roll,
> The path of Sufis does not become our goal
> Till faith's unfaith, and then unfaith is faith,
> None truly sees that God is God as Sole.[48]

While Khayyam did not live a lavish lifestyle and refrained from becoming a statesman, he certainly was not an ascetic. He asked his friend Niẓām al-Mulk for a stipend of 10,000 Dinārs and an estate in Nayshābūr, and certainly neither of these requests are in line with the concept of *qinā'ah* (to be content in poverty), which also implies "simplicity" and some degree of "poverty." The concept of taking a vow of poverty is based on the Sufi understanding of the Prophet's saying, "My poverty is my pride."

Khayyam lived a comfortable life without a spiritual master or an affiliation with a Sufi order or ascetic practices. Despite this, some of the central themes of Sufism, such as acknowledgment of the impermanence of the world, the attainment of a particular type of joy, and the wisdom that is the result of drinking the wine of wisdom, remains the focus of Khayyam's message. His adherence to Sufism was consistent with the spirit of his anti-formalism that permeates every facet of the Khayyamian school of thought. Khayyam celebrated the beauty of the world as a manifestation of a beautiful mystery, and he lived in the here and now since the Beauty, mystery, and a sense of wonder are open to be experienced in the present only. It is said that a Sufi is the child of time – *sufi ibn al-waqt ast*.

To Khayyam, the above is the heart and soul of Sufism and the rest is what he calls "fake tales," a charade and façade that a man of his caliber does not need. Khayyam had embraced and immersed himself in the Sufi message that Ruzbihān Baqlī describes: "the love of a human being is the ladder towards the love of the Beloved." The eloquence of the *Ruba'iyyat* and the glittering symbolism closely interwoven in every hemistich is intended to "reveal and conceal," one may argue. If Khayyam was a Sufi poet, it would be futile to attempt to offer a purely profane or mystical interpretation of the *Ruba'iyyat*. As Anne Marie Schimmel states:

> Ambiguity is intended, the oscillation between the two levels of being is consciously maintained and the texture and flavor of the meaning of the word may change at any moment, much as the color of the tiles in a Persian mosque varies in depth according to the hour of the day.[49]

Khayyam's Sufism, therefore, is not an innate and integral part of his *Ruba'iyyat*, and, depending on his state of being, he may have slipped in and out of a Sufi mode of thought. Certainly, there are aspects of the Sufi doctrine that resonate deeply within him; and yet, his skeptical and rational sobriety prevents him from falling into the kind of irrational emotionalism which opens Pandora's box for flights of fantasy and never-ending cycles of unverifiable claims.

Despite the fact that a thorough reading of Khayyam's *Ruba'iyyat* in conjunction with his other writings indicates that they do not lend themselves to a purely Sufi interpretation, some have found the transcendental temptation to Suficize him to be irresistible. One such case is Robert Graves and Omar 'Alī-Shāh who support the thesis that Khayyam was a Sufi master. Their uncanny claim was based on the hoax that they have found the "original *Ruba'iyyat*," one which provided the much needed evidence to establish the Sufi nature of the *Ruba'iyyat*. In their work, *The Original Ruba'iyyat of Omar Khayyam*, Graves' and 'Alī-Shāh's near obsession to see the *Ruba'iyyat* as nothing less than the utterances of a Sufi master, began a process of esoteric hermeneutics. As a result, Khayyam's use of "wine" in his *Ruba'iyyat* became representative of divine wisdom, "beloved" denoted God, drunkenness a state of ecstasy, intoxication as being filled with divine wisdom and lovemaking as the state of unity with the Beloved.

The source of such an authoritative interpretation was a report by Idris Shah, a proponent of Sufism, that his great-great-grandfather, a nineteenth-century Sufi master of an unknown order in HindūKush by the name Jān-Fishān Khān, had access to the original *Ruba'iyyat*. These *Ruba'iyyat* were not only known by the Sufis but were used to test the spiritual acumen of the would-be Sufis. Khan reports:

> It is recorded that three new students once came to the Khan who, having received them kindly, told them to go away, read the *Rubaiyyat* with care and presently report on him. They came back on his next Day of Audience. The first disciple reported that he had been made to think as he had never thought before; the second, that Khayaam appeared to be a heretic; the third, that the poem contained a deep mystery which he hoped one day to understand. The first was kept as a disciple; the second was passed on to another Sheikh; the third was sent back to study Khayaam for another week.[50]

In a detailed analysis of the *Ruba'iyyat*, Graves makes a scathing attack on FitzGerald's translation for forcing the *Ruba'iyyat* into his own hedonistic world-view in order to create a picture of Khayyam which was conducive to the Victorian audience. Comparing Khayyam to Jesus, Graves writes: "Khayyam may well have privately mocked at the 'painted' or false Sufis, very much as Jesus denounced the 'painted' Pharisees while enjoining his disciples."[51]

Omar 'Alī-Shāh who takes the Sufi reading of the *Ruba'iyyat* to a different level not only appears to have an esoteric agenda but also a nationalistic one. He asserts that Khayyam "was born in Nishapur in A.D. 1015 of Afghan parents from the Sufi community of Balkh"[52] and his teacher Muwaffaq al-Dīn was a member of the Qadarī Sufi order. 'Alī-Shāh even argued that Khayyam, meaning "tent-maker" in Persian, is a misnomer; using the "science of letters" (*'ilm al-jafr*), Khayyam "reveals the Sufic name *'al-Ghaqī'* or squanderer of good."[53]

There is absolutely no shred of evidence to support the above claims and until now they remain unsubstantiated. Despite the lack of evidence, 'Alī-Shāh lays a barrage of criticism on all those who cannot see the Sufi Khayyam. He explains:

> Though the *Rubaiyyat* was clearly written for readers with a grounding in the Sufi lore to which it traditionally belongs, a stubborn rear-guard of Oriental and Occidental scholars will doubtless continue to cite alleged instances of Khayaam's anti-Sufic verses. This will be simply because the poem's technical terms, semantic nuances and argumentative *judo* – obvious enough to readers trained in the Sufic way of thinking – baffle and provoke natural resentment in non-initiates.[54]

The hoax that came to be known as the "Jān-Fishān Khān's manuscript" was fully disclosed by Elwell-Sutton in his article "The Omar Khayyam Puzzle,"[55] and was put to rest for good by Bowen in his article "The Rubaiyat of Omar Khayyam: A Critical Assesment of Robert Graves' and Omar Ali Shah's 'translation'."[56] Bowen reveals how this non-existent manuscript from Afghanistan that had become the basis for Robert Graves's translation was actually based on FitzGerald's translation.

While the manuscript that Robert Graves and Omar 'Alī-Shāh claim to have existed was never found, the myth of the real meaning of the *Ruba'iyyat* bears testament to the strong historical inclination to bring him within the pale of religion. As I have argued before, much of this desire is a symptom of Persian-Islamic culture according to which one is either a heretic or *somewhere* within the pale of religion. Khayyam could not have been the former, and therefore he had to be the latter.

6

Khayyam's Philosophical Thought

"A philosopher I am," the critics falsely say,
But God knows I am not what they say;
While in this sorrow-laden nook, I reside
Need to know who I am, and why Here stay.[1]

Unlike his *Ruba'iyyat* whose authenticity and authorship have been the subject of contentious debate, Khayyam's philosophical treatises despite a few claims to the contrary are decisively his own. These short but dense philosophical writings provide us with insight into the philosophical world of Khayyam and open yet another door to the personality and genius of this multifaceted figure.

Khayyam has left us with the following six philosophical treatises:

1. *On Being and Necessity*
2. *The Necessity of Contradiction in the World, Determinism and Subsistence*
3. *The Light of the Intellect on the Subject of Universal Knowledge*
4. *On the Knowledge of the Universal Principles of Existence*
5. *On Existence*
6. *Response to Three Philosophical Problems*

There is considerable discussion with regard to the order of these writings and even their number. For instance, *The light of the*

Intellect on the Subject of Universal Knowledge and *On Existence* appear to contain contradictory materials, and only a few biographers have mentioned the former as a work of Khayyam. Some scholars, such as Iṣfahānī,[2] have considered *Response to Three Problems* and *The Necessity of Contradiction in the World, Determinism and Subsistence* to be one and the same, whereas Malik[3] considers them to be separate.

For reasons that go beyond the scope of this work and which primarily have to do with the readership for which this volume is being prepared, I have omitted such discussions and have included the six authoritative editions as representative of Khayyam's philosophical thought.

While the above treatises represent Khayyam's philosophical thought in the strictest sense of the word "philosophy," his philosophical perspective is not limited to these treatises and is spread throughout his *Ruba'iyyat* as well. What the above writings do clarify is Khayyam's position on the central themes of Peripatetic (*mashshā'ī*) philosophy.

Khayyam's philosophical treatises, written in the peripatetic tradition, are not only clear representations of the philosophical thought of Omar Khayyam himself, but also are indicative of the philosophical issues which were of prime concern to the scholarly circles of the time. Our discussion will be limited to a brief exposition of the salient features of these themes; for those who desire a more in-depth reading of Khayyam's philosophy, a complete translation of his philosophical treatises is included in the Appendices.

Before we embark upon an analysis and interpretation of the salient features of Khayyam's philosophical thought, let us review his overall intellectual framework. We know that Khayyam was well-grounded in Greek philosophy and an avid follower of Avicenna, whom he calls "his teacher." We also know that Ghazzālī may have studied Greek philosophy with Khayyam; and if Rashidī Tabrīzī's account of the story in *Tarabkhāneh* is accurate, and there are reasons to doubt this, Khayyam was the most learned philosopher of his time.

> Once it became known to the Imam Muḥammad ibn Muḥammad al-Ghazzālī that he wanted to study a treatise in philosophy with a master who can clarify the reasons and proofs of the philosophers, and to show the contradictions of their elaborate web of ideas and to bring religious laws to fruition, at the time there was no one superior in philosophy to Khayyam.[4]

The relationship between Ghazzālī and Khayyam appears to have been that of love-hate, with Ghazzālī representing the emerging orthodoxy of the Ash'arite and Khayyam who was resisting as an independent thinker the rise of dogmatism and theological stricture to the point that the contemporary scholar M. I'timād says, "It appears that the works of Muḥammad Ghazzālī, with all the dogmatism he shows in his *Deliverance From Error* and *Reconstruction of Religious Sciences*, was the reason why Khayyam composed some of his philosophical *Rubai'yyat*."[5] Dinānī, in his scholarly article on Khayyam, goes so far as to raise the possibility that Ghazzālī's famous doubt and skepticism may have been due to his associations with Khayyam.[6]

Even though there have been other figures who are in some ways similar to Khayyam, Khayyam appears to have been a unique intellectual figure for his time. He is not a typical Peripatetic philosopher like Fārābī and Avicenna, even though he is quite learned in Aristotelian philosophy and has composed several treatises in that tradition. In addition, he is not a theologian, since his style of writing and the issues he discusses are purely philosophical. He is not a gnostic *ḥakīm ('ārif)* such as Ibn 'Arabī and Mullā Ṣadrā, who brought about a synthesis of philosophy and Sufism, nor is he a Sufi in the tradition of Ḥāfiẓ, Rūmī and Hallāj. The challenge is, therefore, to understand the place of Peripatetic philosophy in the overall scheme of his thought as well as his place within the history of the Islamic intellectual tradition.

If an answer to this complex question is to be offered, Khayyam's philosophical thought first has to be understood. Khayyam discusses his intellectual perspectives both in his alleged *Ruba'iyyat* and in his philosophical treatises. The former has been treated previously in Chapter Four. We concern ourselves here with the more

Peripatetic writings of Khayyam and offer analysis and interpretation of their salient features. The central questions which Khayyam discusses throughout his treatises can be categorized as follows:

1. The Existence of God, His Attributes and Knowledge
2. Gradation of Being and the Problem of Multiplicity
3. Existence and Essence
4. Theodicy (the Problem of Evil)
5. Determinism and Free Will
6. Subjects and Predicates, and Attributes
7. Eschatology

THE EXISTENCE OF GOD, HIS ATTRIBUTES AND KNOWLEDGE

In the tradition of Peripatetics, Khayyam refers to God as the Necessary Being. While throughout his writings the existence of the Necessary Being is implied and one does not see an in-depth discussion or endeavor to prove the existence of God, there are numerous references to and brief treatments of the subject matter. Khayyam's argument for the existence of God is what is traditionally referred to as the cosmological argument. According to this argument, since every event must have at least one cause and the cause itself is an event in need of another cause, we end up either with a Necessary Being who has no cause or an infinite succession of contingent, dependent beings which goes on *progression ad infinitum*.

The notion of *ad infinitum* poses numerous philosophical problems, one which Khayyam, similar to many medieval philosophers, rejects. We are left with the existence of a Necessary Being whose existence is not caused by any other. Khayyam reflects:

> We say, it is not possible that the essence of any contingent being, ever be the cause of necessity; for it is either an intermediary or something else which is the same as the contingent being. [We say] A is possible and A must be the efficient cause of the existence of B and thus it is known that B is a contingent being. No contingent being comes to existence unless its existence had become necessary and therefore B had become a necessary existence even though A is not a

> necessary being and therefore, B is contingent from one aspect and necessary from another, except that the possibility of being comes to it from another being which brings about the necessity of existence for it [this matter can not be understood]. A is the cause of the existence of B and not something else while A is a contingent being and therefore the essence of a contingent being has become the efficient cause of the necessity of an existence and this is impossible. Therefore, it is not possible for the essence of any contingent being to be the cause of any necessity.[7]

The rest of Khayyam's cosmological argument is implied here. That is, a Necessary Being can be the efficient cause of a contingent being; and since the world is a contingent being, there must be a Necessary Being who is the efficient cause of the world. What is further implied here is that the world is contingent in that it can or cannot be but is necessary since, given the right cause, the particular effect will necessarily follow a chain of causality which ends with the Necessary Being.

In his other work, *On Being and Necessity*, Khayyam reiterates the cosmological argument:

> If you look upon all existents and their "what-ness" reflectively, you would conclude that "what-ness" of all things leads to a "why-ness," a Cause or Means for which there is no "why-ness," cause or means. The proof for this problem is as follows: if they say why is there A, we say because of B, and if they say why B, we say because of C, and if they say why C, we say because of D ... inevitably a discussion concerning causality leads to a Cause for which there is no cause, otherwise an [infinite] succession or circularity will emerge and that is impossible.
>
> Thus, it is true that the cause of all existents leads to a cause which has no cause. And it is clarified in theology that there is a cause without having been caused and that is He who is the Necessary Being in essence and unified in all aspects and is without any deficiency and all things lead to Him and become existent because of Him.[8]

Whereas Muslim philosophers were prolific concerning the question of essence and existence, the existence of God, considered to be self-evident, has generally received cursory treatment.

With regard to the cosmological argument, Khayyam offers different versions which are Aristotelian in nature and almost identical with Avicennian arguments. In addition to several places,[9] he makes a brief reference in his work, *On Existence*, where we see the "ontological argument" for the existence of God. This argument puts emphasis on the idea of God as an innate or *a priori* concept rather than on the causal connection and claims that humans are born with a concept of God. The perfect nature of this concept and the fact that perfection can only come from perfection necessitates that our concept of God could have come only from God Himself. Khayyam's condensed version of the ontological argument is as follows:

> The Necessary Being, may He be exalted, is an essence that is not possible to be conceived except by an existent. Therefore, the attribute of existence before the intellect is due to His essence and *not because one has placed it there.*[10]

Following a discussion concerning the existence of God, Khayyam comes to the subject of attribution and the complexities that are affiliated with it. In the long-standing tradition of Islamic philosophy, Khayyam first focuses his attention on the preservation of Divine unity and attempts to bring about a rapprochement between God and his attributes.

> The essence of the Necessary Being is one in all aspects and in no case can there be multiplicity except in abstraction in which case its number can reach infinity. The essence for which multiplicity in abstraction is conceived does not become multiple. Generally, all of the attributes of the Necessary Being are essentially abstract and none of them contains any existence.[11]

Khayyam's view that attributes are devoid of existence is perhaps partially a response to theological discussions between the Mu'tazilites, the Ash'arites and some of the earlier anthropomorphic groups, around which much controversy concerning the relationship between Divine essence and attributes revolves. Whereas for most theologians Divine attributes are in some sense real, Khayyam seems to argue to the contrary, bringing him closer to the position of a Sufi, a deist or some of the Peripatetic philosophers who see God as pure Being.

In *The Necessity of Contradiction in the World, Determinism and Subsistence* Khayyam explores the problem of necessity in order to argue that, even though there are different types of necessities and things whose attributes are necessary, these senses of necessity are different than the sense in which God is Necessary.

Having offered a discussion concerning different attributes, their classification into primary and secondary types, and how all attributes necessarily lead to their source, which is necessary, Khayyam divides different attributes of the Necessary Being into three divisions:

1. Some of the attributes, due to the priority of the description of what is described, imply necessity[12] (e.g. all bachelors are unmarried males).
2. Some of the attributes, due to the priority of some of the other attributes are not necessary, rather they are essential attachments of what is being attributed, and thus are necessary beings.[13] Khayyam gives the example of how "singularity" is a necessary attribute for "three-ness," but this necessity is only an intellectual one and does not exist in the external world.
3. Some of the attributes, due to the intermediary of a different cause are not necessary. Their necessity is from [a different] essence, and, therefore, they are necessary beings.[14]

These senses of necessity, Khayyam observes, are not necessity in the real sense since they can only exist in abstraction and have no external existence. "Therefore, these mentioned attributes ... are present in the intellect and absent in the external world, and thus the existence of these attributes are due to a man's reflection upon his soul and intellect and not in the world."[15] There is an implied premise here in Khayyam's argument, which he does not mention but which is essential for a full understanding of his argument: in order for a sense of necessity to be truly real, it must exist both abstractly and externally.

Having criticized other forms of necessity and the sense in which their existence is necessary, Khayyam turns to God and argues that

His necessity is the only real necessity since it exists both in the abstract sense (*i'tibārī*) and the real sense of the word:

> Thus it has been argued that the Necessary Being in the external [world] is unified from all aspects and is the cause of all external existent beings ... Therefore, God most Exalted is the Cause of all the objects realized in the intellect and externally.[16]

Khayyam has established that all God's attributes are secondary and not real except necessity, which is an inseparable part of Divine essence.

Finally, there is the problem of God's knowledge of the universals and particulars, which has traditionally been a subject of great contention among theologians and philosophers. Whereas Khayyam's contemporary, Ghazzālī, writes extensively about the subject matter and admonishes the philosophers for arguing that God does not know the particulars,[17] Khayyam's treatment of the issue is cursory at best:

> Thus, His knowledge is existential (*wujūdī*) meaning through the apprehension of the forms of the intelligibles in his essence, except that they all are contingent beings and necessary for it. The discourse in this regard has been extensively brought forth elsewhere and so it should be sought therein.[18]

It is not entirely clear what Khayyam means by "elsewhere." Possibly, there was a treatise now lost, in which he elaborated on the subject. Despite the brevity of his comments, "the apprehension of the forms of the intelligibles" bears the signature of Avicenna and other Peripatetic philosophers and indicates that Khayyam's view with regard to God's knowledge, similar to the rest of his philosophical thought, was very much in line with the Peripatetic view.

GRADATION OF BEING AND THE PROBLEM OF MULTIPLICITY

According to Khayyam himself, the most important philosophical question is how to account for and differentiate among the multiplicity of existent beings. Furthermore, how these differences account for the superiority of a being over another is a bewildering question worthy of extensive exploration according to Khayyam. In his most important philosophical work, *On Being and Necessity*, Khayyam describes:

> What remains from among the most important and difficult problems [to solve] is the difference among the order of existents. Their order of nobility is a problem that most people are perplexed by, to the point that one cannot find anyone who is rational and wise and not bewildered in this regard. Perhaps I, and my teacher, the master of all who have proceeded before him, Avicenna, have thoughtfully reflected upon this problem and to the extent that it is satisfactory to our intellects, we have understood it. What has satisfied us is either inwardly reprehensible and outwardly foolish, or is inherently stable and (true). It is in this aspect which we have come to accept it.[19]

The reason Khayyam finds this philosophical problem to be "the most important and different problem" is not only its inherent significance but also the wide implications of this major philosophical riddle upon a variety of other issues. When the problem of multiplicity is discussed, naturally in a theistic world-view, the concept of unity must be addressed. With multiplicity coming from unity, the mechanism through which this happens, namely emanation or creation *ex nihilo*, becomes of central importance. A discussion concerning the full range of the philosophical consequences of the above is beyond the scope of our work here.

In his work, *On Being and Necessity*, Khayyam begins by offering an Aristotelian account of what philosophy is: "The essential and real issues that are discussed in philosophy are three, [first] ... 'is it?' ... second 'what is it?' ... third 'why is it?'."[20] While Khayyam's analysis and the interpretation of these categories reflect the standard Aristotelian model, his application of them is somewhat original. Being interested in the question of the gradation of being, he argues that the question of "what is it?" is a particularly significant issue, since it implies the reality of a thing. That which is real is higher or superior to that which is not. What is ultimately unreal is non-existing, and the most real is none other than Being itself, which is why Khayyam says, "Because a group of logicians have not understood the difference between these two types, they have fallen into fallacy and become perplexed."[21]

The question of the gradation of being for Khayyam is used to solve a different problem as well, and that is the existence of a Necessary Being. In all of his philosophical treatises, the proof for the existence of God remains central, leaving little room to doubt that despite his skeptical views, as expressed in his poetry, Khayyam must have been at least a deist. In arguing for the existence of God he relies on the impossibility of a succession of contingent, dependent beings leading to *ad infinitum*, a proof that is at least mentioned if not discussed in most of his treatises.

The existence of God as pure Being is the backbone of Khayyam's philosophical views. The centrality of the Necessary Being is evident for Khayyam: "If you reflect upon all beings and consider their 'why' thoroughly you will realize that the 'why' of all beings leads to another 'why' and therefore the succession of these events should lead to a Cause which has no cause."[22]

With regard to this Aristotelian Uncaused Cause, Khayyam concludes that "contingent beings emanate from the Sacred Existence in sequence and order and then wear the cloth of existents."[23] Like many other Muslim philosophers, Khayyam has adopted the Neoplatonic scheme of emanation, providing him with a perfect context in which to explain what he considers to be the most important philosophical question: "how to account for the distinction among the existent beings in their degree of nobility."[24] To account for a distinction among beings and their degree of nobility, Khayyam proposes in *On Being and Necessity*:

> The true and certain proof establishes that God has not created all existents together, rather he has created them from his own presence sequentially and therefore the first thing God created was pure intellect. Since the first origin (intellect) has the highest proximity to God, it is the noblest of all existents and this order of nobility descends to the less noble, this is the way creation of the existents has taken place until the least [noble] gives rise to the lesser [noble], the lowest of all existents which is the nature of corruptible corporeals. [God] then

> has begun an ascending curve towards nobility until man, who is the noblest of all compound existents and who is the last to reach the world of generation and corruption. Therefore, among creatures, whatever is closer to the first origin is more noble, and in the nature of compounds whatever is further its nobility increases[25] and God the Blessed and Most High has determined that compounds be created at different times, for the sum of objects that are contradictory and contrary is not possible.[26]

In his other treatise, *On the Knowledge of the Universal Principles of Existence*,[27] Khayyam adopts an Avicennian scheme of emanation and explains how the ten intellects emanate from each other and their corresponding heavens with their souls. However, despite the similarities between Fārābī, Avicenna and Khayyam's notion of the theory of emanation, towards the end of his treatise *On the Knowledge of the Universal Principles of Existence*, Khayyam deviates from his predecessors and offers his version of emanation. According to Avicenna, every intellect creates a soul who in turn creates a heavenly order, and the last intellect, the active intellect (*wāhib al-ṣuwar*), creates the world of generation and corruption. Khayyam's version is that intellects and souls *together* are in charge of the governance of the heavenly order. Contrary to Avicenna's view that the active intellect is the effect of the ninth intellect, Khayyam views it as the first intellect and thus a direct emanation from the Necessary Being and the closest one to it.

The above view, placing the active intellect in the first order of emanation, is actually closer to that of Ikhwān al-Ṣafā, whose Neoplatonic tendencies outweighed their peripatetic views.[28] There are those who have alluded to possible affiliation of Khayyam with Ikhwān al-Ṣafā, citing similarities such as Khayyam's use of numbers to explain the gradation of beings.

There is no major deviation in the above from the mainstream peripatetic position and, in particular, the Avicennian view. It becomes clear that Khayyam thus far has made an attempt to solve three problems. First, he establishes the existence of God. Second, he embraces the Neoplatonic scheme of emanation. Finally, through emanation and its by-product, he explains the gradation of beings.

Through this philosophical framework, Khayyam preserves the unity of God, while he accounts for the multiplicity of the created order.

Now that the framework and the ontological structure of his philosophical views are in place, Khayyam proceeds to treat some of the other issues within the context of emanation. Few have been the subject of greater contention than the relationship between essence (*māhiyyah*) and existence (*wujūd*).

EXISTENCE (*WUJŪD*) AND ESSENCE (*MĀHIYYAH*)

With regard to the relationship between essence and existence in general and to Khayyam's ontological views in particular, three theories have traditionally been offered in Islamic philosophy:[29]

1. The existence of an existent being is the same as its essence. This view is attributed to Abu'l-Ḥasan Ash'arī, Abu'l-Ḥasan Baṣrī and some of the other Ash'arite theologians.
2. Commonly known as the principality of essence (*iṣālat al-māhiyyah*), this view maintains that essence is primary and existence is added to it. Many philosophers such as Abū Hāshim Jubā'ī and later on Suhrawardī and Mīr Dāmād have come to advocate this view.
3. Commonly known as the principality of existence (*iṣālat al-wujūd*), this view maintains that existence is primary and essence is then added.

Before we embark upon an exposition of Khayyam's view on essence and existence, we must first understand where he stands on this issue. There are indeed a few references to the principality of essence, the most notable being what Khayyam says in *Risālah fi'l-wujūd:* "Existence is abstract by way of emanation." In addition, in section 17 of this treatise entitled "Existence is an added concept to essence," he observes, "The traces of existence can be found in all things such as accidents and there is no doubt that existence is a concept added to essence, that is intelligible. There is no evidence that our discussion here is concerning existence in reality."[30]

Is Khayyam putting forward his own views on the matter or is he being an interpreter and commentator of Avicenna? A close textual reading of Khayyam's philosophical writings reveals that he actually supports both views. This may be because the distinction between the principality of existence and essence is a discussion that appeared in a later period of Islamic philosophical tradition, particularly with the advent of the School of Iṣfahān,[31] which brought forth two outstanding figures, Mīr Dāmād and his celebrated student, Mullā Ṣadrā. Applying the development of a later philosophical period to an earlier one creates some misunderstanding, namely, the one we are facing. Khayyam, who was not aware of the two intellectual camps, commented on the subject matter without recognizing that being a follower of Avicenna (as he claimed) and advocating the principality of essence were incompatible. In the corpus of his writings, one may find evidence that supports both views even though Khayyam's references and treatment of the principality of essence is more lucid.

Nasr, in his article, "The Poet-Scientist Khayyam as Philosopher," makes the same point and argues that placing Khayyam in either of these two schools would be inappropriate since the distinction essentially appeared in the fifteenth century:

> Although the distinction between the principality of *wujūd* (*aṣālat al-wujūd*) and the principality of *māhiyyah* (*aṣālat al-māhiyyah*) goes back to the School of Iṣfahān and especially Mullā Ṣadrā, later students of Islamic philosophy have tended to look upon the whole earlier tradition from this point of view and sought to determine who belonged to which school. If we apply this later distinction with its own particular terminology to Khayyam, then we could say that Khayyam, like Suhrawardī, Naṣīr al-Din Ṭusī, Ghiyāth al-Dīn Manṣūr Dashtakī and Mir Dāmād belongs to the school of principality of quiddity, although he does not use the term *aṣālat al-māhiyyah* as was done by Mullā Ṣadrā and many other later philosophers.[32]

There are several contemporary scholars who have argued that Khayyam believed in the primacy of essence over existence. Nizhād Awwal, in his brief commentary on Khayyam's treatise, *On Existence*,[33] argues that Khayyam, in order to comment on the theory of emanation, in keeping with his predecessors such as Fārābī and Avicenna, has made a logical and metaphysical distinction between essence and existence. So far we are in agreement, but then he makes the claim that Khayyam regards "essence to be the principle and existence to be an abstract predicate of it."[34]

Despite the above, one cannot conclusively state that Khayyam supports the principality of essence since the textual evidence in this regard is mixed, if not contradictory. Furthermore, Khayyam has clearly stated that he considers himself to be a follower of Avicenna who by all accounts adhered to the principality of existence. Supporting the principality of essence would go against the very grain of Peripatetic philosophical thought, and it would be inconceivable for one to say, "My teacher is Avicenna, but I support the principality of essence." In the Western philosophical context, it would be like saying, "I am a rationalist in the Descartian sense, but I am an avid follower of David Hume, the empiricist!"

In *On Existence*, Khayyam also considers existence to be an added element within the domain of mental existence, such as the existence which is added to triangularity to make it a triangle; but in the external cases of existence this is not necessarily the case. In a section entitled, "How Does the Intellect Know the Essence and Existence of Man," Khayyam contends:

> Once the intellect realizes the essence which is called man, it knows that animality and rationality are intrinsic to his essence and not because someone has placed them [from outside] and existence for it comes from other [than itself] ... therefore the necessity of an adjective of existing from the aspect of attribution comes to them extrinsically.[35]

Clearly, Khayyam presents the principality of essence rather than existence. However, in his other work, *The Light of the Intellect on the Subject of Universal Knowledge*,[36] Khayyam offers three reasons why existence is not added to essence and therefore is primary:

1. Existence cannot be added to the essence, otherwise a succession could follow *ad infinitum*. The proof for this claim will be considered shortly.

2. Existence is not added to the essence. Otherwise essence should have existed prior to existence, and this, too, will lead to *ad infinitum*.
3. With regard to the Necessary Being, existence clearly is not added to the essence, for dualism would follow.

To refute the primacy of essence over existence, Khayyam offers an argument based on the relationship between the subject and predicate. He argues that, "Existence exists and does not need another existence."[37] But Khayyam, who is cognizant of the counter argument, states that one may object by saying that the same argument holds true with regard to essence, and one can say, "A man is a man through man-ness and man-ness does not need another man-ness to be man-ness."[38]

Khayyam calls this objection a form of sophistry and offers a rebuttal that places him squarely in the camp of the advocates of the principality of existence. He argues that the essence is fundamentally non-existent, and then it becomes existent. Furthermore, in order for it to become existent, it requires existence. Khayyam asks, "How can something that requires something prior to itself to exist have been existent?"[39] Essence, therefore, in Khayyamian thought, appears to be secondary to existence and a contingent being, which nevertheless is significant in that it helps a being to distinguish itself from others; "that which is not distinct from other than itself is non-existent."[40]

In a brief but dense discussion on the division of existence, in his *In Response to Three Philosophical Problems*, Khayyam tells us of the two meanings of existence: the external and that which is within the soul. Existence in its first meaning is what most philosophers have in mind when they refer to this concept; and the second sense of existence as internal, Khayyam argues, is a mental construct. For example, if it is said that "the attribute of animality to a man or the sum of the angles of a triangle is equivalent to two right angles, our reference to this existence is a mental existence and not external."[41]

With the hierarchy of existence having been established, Khayyam traces the source of all beings to God whom, using

Aristotelian terminology, he calls the "Final Cause" of beings. Discussion concerning existence, according to Khayyam, is possible not in the ultimate sense of the word "existence" but in so far as it pertains to contingent beings, since assuming them as non-existent does not imply or entail a contradiction. By inference, the existence of God, not in the sense of whether God exists but in the sense of what some call the "is" of copula, is not subject to inquiry since His existence is necessary and self-evident. Whereas the non-existence of Existence entails a contradiction, the non-existence of mental entities does not, and this is another argument that the only Necessary Existence is that of God, who exists by necessity both in abstraction and in reality.

THEODICY (THE PROBLEM OF EVIL)

The problem of evil or theodicy which permeates every facet of Khayyam's thought is explored in both his *Ruba'iyyat* and his philosophical works. What is interesting and ironic is that in his philosophical treatises Khayyam offers a perfectly rational explanation for the existence of evil; and yet in his *Ruba'iyyat*, as if he has forgotten his own ontological analysis, questioning and bemoaning the presence of evil becomes a prevalent theme. One may argue that such an inconsistency bears witness to the fact that the philosophical treatises and the *Ruba'iyyat* are not authored by the same person. While this remains a strong possibility, the more important question is: if these diametrically contradictory works had been written by Khayyam, how would we explain this inconsistency? Perhaps this discrepancy speaks more to the human condition that, despite our rationalization of the problem of evil and logically held beliefs, we remain fundamentally forgetful and emotional beings.

Scholarship concerning Khayyam's view on the problem of evil has traditionally been limited to his *Ruba'iyyat*, and his philosophical treatises where theodicy is one of the central issues both explicitly or implicitly have been ignored. Khayyam treats the problem of evil in a number of his treatises, but in *The Necessity of Contradiction in the World, Determinism and Subsistence*, he responds to the following question put to him by Qāḍī Abū Naṣr: "It is therefore necessary that the Necessary Being be the cause of the emergence of evil and contradiction and corruption in the world. This is not worthy of Divine status. So how can we resolve this problem and the conflict so evil will not be attributed to the Necessary Being?"[42]

Let us proceed with Khayyam's response to the problem of theodicy. In his work, *On the Necessity of Contradiction in the World, Determinism and Subsistence*, he offers three arguments to account for the presence of evil:

1. Ontologically, creation of anything necessitates the creation of its opposite, and therefore, the presence of so much good in the world also necessitates the creation of some evil.
2. The amount of good in the universe far exceeds the amount of evil in the world.
3. Evil is an accidental category and therefore cannot be attributed to the essence of the creator.

Khayyam begins by offering an analysis of the fundamental ontological ground from which evil is born:

> All contingent beings from the existence of the Necessary Being have emanated in a particular order. Among these existents some of them are necessarily contradictory not because someone has placed them as such. Now, if this existent is created in the external world, contradiction is created by necessity, and if contradiction comes to be necessarily, non-existence is created necessarily, and if non-existence is created necessarily, evil is created necessarily.[43]

From the above, it is clear that Khayyam identifies evil with non-existence or absence. As pain is the absence of pleasure, melancholy is the absence of happiness and disease is the absence of health. Needless to say, by creating a positive category, A, its negation –A is necessarily created, and therefore, ontologically it is impossible to create something without creating its opposite. Good, therefore, cannot be created unless bad is born along with it. When evil is conceived abstractly, it remains as evil in *potentia*, but when it is actualized in the realm of reality, the evil gains a real existence.

God, Khayyam argues, has created the essence of all the contingent beings, and they are good in and of themselves since any being is ontologically a positive presence. God, therefore, has created what is present and is not responsible for what is absent. Khayyam gives the example of the colors of white and black. God intended to create one color, but its opposite was also created by necessity. Khayyam concludes that the presence of evil is not to be attributed to God, who intended to create only good, but it appears that evil is part of the ontological structure and an inherent necessity of creation. Khayyam states:

> The intention of the First Actor even though He is devoid of intention,[44] through the grace of Eternal Master of Truth, gravitates towards good. Good however is not devoid and empty from evil and nonexistence and therefore evil is attributed to the accidental qualities of the Necessary Being, whereas the objective of [the perplexed] is to attribute evil to the essence of the Necessary Being and not its accident. I recommend to all the philosophers I know to exonerate the Necessary Being from oppression and evil.[45]

Khayyam's treatment of the problem of evil, though it is not extensive, is systematic. He has established an ontological necessity for the presence of evil which resembles Leibniz's notion of the problem of the possible worlds. Contrary to Leibniz, however, the question for Khayyam is not whether God could have created a world in which there is no evil; he has already demonstrated that it is an inherent and necessary part of any creation where there is good to have evil. The more fundamental and complex question for Khayyam is neither why evil exists nor whether God could have created a world without evil but, "Why did God create something which necessitates non-existence and evil?"[46] To begin with, the question of why there is something rather than nothing is a much more complex and daunting question than that of theodicy, the ultimate question with which so many philosophers have wrestled in vain.

Khayyam poses the above question and tries to respond to it. The question, however, lends itself to the following two diverse interpretations, one of which is Khayyam's question:

1. Why did God create a world whose existence requires non-existence or evil?
2. Why did God create something rather than nothing knowing that creating something would bring about evil?

It is my contention that Khayyam is asking the second question, a question that is closer to Leibniz's view of the possible worlds, since the first one has been answered in his ontological analysis of the very structure of creation. Khayyam's answer to the first question contains a subtle and profound point. The basic supposition upon which his response is based is that if one were to conduct a good versus evil "cost-benefit analysis," the good far exceeds the evil that is present in the universe. Khayyam states that "the ratio between the goodness that darkness [brings] to the evil it causes exceeds that of one to a million ... and in accordance with divine wisdom in the world, there is very little evil that is qualitatively or quantitatively comparable with good."[47]

As to the second question, which many philosophers have considered to be the ultimate and enduring philosophical riddle, "Why is there something rather than nothing?" Khayyam's implied answer is that "being" is better than "non-being," the very gift of existence is ontologically good and the world has been created by a God for a good purpose. In his major philosophical work, *On Being and Necessity*, Khayyam reiterates the same argument, saying that, "avoiding a great amount of good due to the necessity of having little evil is itself a great deal of evil."[48]

What is interesting here is that Khayyam discusses this point in the middle of offering an analysis concerning the gradation of being and the nature of existence. For him, the question of theodicy is fundamentally an ontological problem and not an epistemological one. It is almost as if in his philosophical works he treats the problem of evil from an ontological perspective; but his poetic treatment of theodicy is left for his *Ruba'iyyat* where he focuses on the existential aspects of the problem.

DETERMINISM AND FREE WILL

In both the East and the West, Khayyam is famed for being a determinist (*jabri*), and some of his poems certainly lend credence to this view. His existential protest concerning the predestined nature of the human condition, however, does have a philosophical basis and is not limited to mere poetic sentimentalism. In his treatise, *On Being and Necessity*, Khayyam briefly treats the concept of necessity (*taklīf*) and ironically avoids the traditional use of the term *jabr* to denote determinism or predestination.

Contrary to the popular view, which once again is based on his *Ruba'iyyat*, Khayyam was not a determinist in the strictest sense of the word nor did he believe in free will as such. He was too learned a philosopher not to realize the philosophical consequences of either position. Determinism is incompatible with individual moral responsibility, which, if taken seriously, renders useless the concepts of heaven and hell. If all my actions are determined, then I cannot do otherwise and thus am not responsible for the moral outcome of my actions. The concept of free will, however, is incompatible with Divine omniscience and God's knowledge of future events as well as the inherent opposition of free choice to the law of causality.

Let us further analyze Khayyam's stance with regard to this thorny subject which has been the cause of so much contention and debate and even violent clashes among the followers of these schools of thought. The word *taklīf* literally means "commandment, duty, what is incumbent upon you," and Khayyam's use of it is somewhat equivalent to what modern metaphysicians call "soft determinism," a position that is a rapprochement between a strict sense of determinism and free will.

There is some textual evidence for this perspective as well. In his treatise, *On the Necessity of Contradiction in the World, Determinism and Subsistence*, Khayyam clearly proposes that determinism is more in keeping with his position provided it is not taken to its extreme:

> As to the question of his Highness[49] concerning which of the two groups (determinism or free will) are closer to truth I say initially and

> in the first sight, perhaps the determinists are closer to truth provided we do not enter into their nonsensical and absurd [claims] for those are far from truth.[50]

Having accepted determinism in general while rejecting it in the strictest sense, Khayyam's view on necessity or determinism can be divided into three parts:

1. Universal-Cosmic Determinism
2. Socio-Economic Determinism
3. Ontological Determinism

Universal-Cosmic Determinism

Khayyam begins his treatise *On Being and Necessity* by offering an analysis of the concept of being (*kawn*) and then proceeds to treat the concept of necessity. This is significant in that any version of determinism can be discussed only within a particular ontological framework, and much of Khayyam's view on determinism is to be extracted and inferred from his ontological perspective. We will treat this shortly, but let us first focus on his particular argument on necessity and determinism. Khayyam explains: "Necessity is a command which is issued from God Most High, so *people may attain* those perfections that lead them to happiness."[51] This, of course, is essentially a Platonic concept elaborated by many, and Khayyam seems to have adopted Fārābī's definition: "For every being is made to achieve the ultimate perfection it is susceptible of achieving according to its specific place in the order of being."[52]

From the above, it is obvious that necessity in the Khayyamian sense does not deprive the person from choosing and does not apply to the individual action. The phrase, "people may attain perfection," implies free will, an intentional and willful act. Whereas the overall movement of history and the order of the universe might be determined by the will of the creator directly or perhaps in a Hegelian sense through divine providence, our ability to will and to choose, appears to be at least partially intact.

For Hegel, determinism is a type of necessity that through divine providence (*Geist*) guides humans toward higher states of consciousness. Khayyam echoes the same by stating that divine providence "prevents them from committing oppression, evil and the attainment of imperfection."[53] Khayyam is explicit about the presence of a willful and intentional process of decision making, which can hardly be called determinism. The overall determined or predestined scenario of the human condition, however, does not prevent us from "being able to resist our bodily desires which prevent us from following our intellectual power."[54]

Socio-Economic Determinism

Certainly, this version of Khayyam's view of determinism is rarely noticed or treated by Muslim philosopher, who have shown little if any interest in social disparities. It is refreshing to see that this aspect of determinism has not skipped Khayyam's attention. In all likelihood, Khayyam's interest in the subject matter is the result of having come from a deprived family and his intimate knowledge of how high-minded metaphysical speculations take a back seat when extreme poverty takes over and determines the material conditions of life. In an attempt to reconcile heaven and earth, Khayyam argues that "the whatness of things depends on their I-ness."[55] But in order for something to be determined, first it has to *be*, which necessitates that the thing in question have an identity. Khayyam quickly turns this argument from a metaphysical discourse to an ethical and moral one stating that "God created the human species such that it is not possible for it to survive and reach perfection unless it is through reciprocity, assistance, and help. As long as food, clothes, and a home that are the essentials of life are not prepared, the possibility of the attainment of perfection does not exist."[56]

Here Khayyam is referring to the necessities of mundane existence which occupy the life of most humans and effectively trap us, determining and limiting our choices. Few cases of determinism are more tangible and painful than socio-economic ones, and few philosophers have even addressed the issue, much less considered it a form of determinism. Khayyam advises us to assist one another in matters of life, bringing about a form of liberation from socio-economic determinism: "Every human can release and liberate his fellow man from shouldering all the burdens of life by himself."[57]

As can clearly be seen, neither Khayyam's cosmic and universal sense of determinism nor the more socially oriented determinism implies the kind of hard determinism that has been attributed to him. One can hardly draw anything but a sense of soft determinism from Khayyam's perspective of having been thrown into a condition whereby liberating oneself remains at least theoretically possible.

Ontological Determinism

This sense of determinism represents the Peripatetic and Neoplatonic perspective of Khayyamian thought and rests upon the notion that in the long chain of being and the scheme of emanation, every existent being is endowed with a particular ontological status. This status then determines, to a great extent, the choices and decisions that one may select. A frog can only be a frog and may not decide to engage in the sort of activities that are possible for a dog; a rose can only be a rose by virtue of the ontological status that is bestowed upon it.

Khayyam does not treat ontological determinism as a separate category in his writings, as he does the previous two types of determinism. Perhaps this is so because it is regarded as self-evident and a natural consequence of the theory of emanation. Throughout his writings, however, there are numerous references that bear testament to this implied sense of determinism.

In *On Existence* he says, "Once intellect realizes the essence which is called 'man-ness,' it knows that animality and rationality are part of this essence and not because one has placed them there."[58] Since what constitutes the identity of an existent being is its essence and because these essences are intrinsically what they are, it follows that things in the world come into existence with a fixed essence. This implies determinism, not in the strictest sense of the word, but in a limited way, in that the higher one is on the ontological hierarchy, the more freedom one has, and, by definition, God is the only one who is absolutely free.

Khayyam's ontological determinism is most evident where he discusses the intricacies of emanation, namely in his *On Being and Necessity*. It is here that he tells us that the "what-ness" of all beings is determined in accordance to their latitudinal arrangements. How and why this differentiation is made, Khayyam tells us, "is among the most significant and complex of all questions," but the relationship between the place of a thing in this hierarchy and determinism is evident. In describing the relationship between determinism and hierarchy, Khayyam maintains, "What-ness is the providence on the basis of which all things are arranged in their descending succession both latitudinally and horizontally, and they come from the First Origin."[59] Following a discussion concerning levels of being, which is along the lines of standard Avicennian classification, Khayyam describes, "The order of the world is in accordance to how the wisdom of God decreed it."[60]

Ironically, Khayyam's soft determinism theory remains valid regardless of whether we see him as supporting the primacy of essence over existence or vice versa. If existence was added to the essence, then essence, which constitutes the identity of a thing, must have existed before the thing came into existence. This means that the possibilities for different ways of being of a thing in question are predetermined, and that the predetermined essence of a rose in the overall scheme of creation leaves little room for a rose to be anything but a rose. The same follows for humans, whose essence of "man-ness" predetermines the extent and possibilities of different ways of being in the world. Yet, humans appear to be able to defy much of what compels humans to choose, not only by choosing to be or not to be but also by choosing to act other than what the necessary conditions dictate; this is indicative of some sort of a free will.

If, however, the primary of existence over essence is true and essence is added to existence, the picture is not very different. This model, which is closer to the modern existentialist movement, provides much more room for free will; but, by virtue of having an essence, limitations on the ways one can be are nevertheless imposed upon all existents. The notion of essence brings with it the concept of determinism and limitation, and Khayyam's ontological determinism is no doubt intricately related to the notion of essence as viewed by the Peripatetics.

SUBJECTS, PREDICATES, AND ATTRIBUTES

One of the most difficult aspects of Khayyam's philosophical thought is his analysis concerning the relationship between the subject, predicate and attributes. While his analysis is Aristotelian in nature, there are a few instances where Khayyam's own original views and insight are asserted as well. He begins by dividing the attributes into two parts, essential and accidental. Some of the accidental attributes, Khayyam tells us, are necessary for the subject and some are contingent. Furthermore, both essential and accidental attributes are of two types, those that are abstract (*i'tibārī*) and those that are existential (*wujūdī*).[61] Khayyam gives the example of something that is described by "blackness" since "blackness" is added to the concept of existence, arguing that there exists an X such that this X has the property of "blackness." Khayyam considers this analysis to be self-evident, and therefore, there is no need to offer a proof for it.

However, the abstract sense of accident, Khayyam says, is like the description of two as being half of four, and in a similar fashion, one may find infinite ways of describing something which is obviously incompatible with an essential attribute. As for a case of what is an abstract sense of an essential attribute, Khayyam tells us it is like the relationship between "blackness" and a generic substratum we can call "colorlessness," since colorlessness is essential in order for "blackness" to be an attribute of it. The above is illustrated by the following chart:

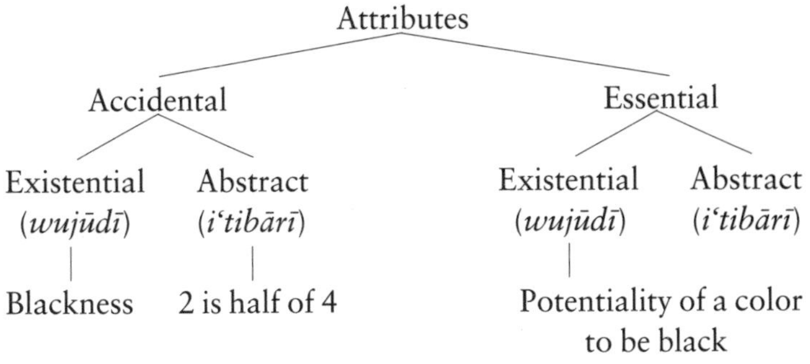

The reason "colorlessness" is not an added attribute to the essence of "blackness" in reality is that if it were, it would be an accident, while blackness, too, is an accident, and we know that an accident cannot be the accident of another accident. Khayyam goes on to offer other arguments in this regard to clarify the complex relationships among subjects, predicates and attributes, but an examination of all of them is beyond the scope of this work.

Khayyam then deviates from the standard Peripatetic perspective and makes a scathing attack on those whom he says "are perplexed" and "have not found the path" because they have not paid attention to the abstract sense of attribution:

> The meaning of our saying is that an abstract (*i'tibārī*) attribute is that which when the intellect considers a concept which it analyzes, through intellectual dissemination it abstracts its various components [from one another]. If that concept be simple and indivisible for all the existing accidents in reality, then one knows that those attributes exist in abstraction and not in reality for it is not possible for a simple entity to exist as an existent in the real sense.[62]

Khayyam considers the above to be one of the principles of metaphysics about which one may be certain, but even though for philosophers these principles are axiomatic, there are those among them who have ignored this self-evident truth. The reason why some philosophers have become perplexed, Khayyam tells us, is that "with regard to the first principles (axioms) there is no middle ground for positive and negative propositions."[63] Even though it is not obvious how the above follows or is related to the previous discussion, for Khayyam "this is so clear that there is no need to treat it or refute it, for that would be foolish."[64]

In either case, the notion of abstract attributes plays an important part in Khayyam's philosophical thought, not only because he thinks lack of emphasis on the subject matter has epistemological ramifications, but also because he uses it to offer an ontological analysis and respond to the question of "why some have become perplexed with regard to the concept of existence."

Khayyam continues the argument in *The Necessity of Contradiction in the World, Determinism and Subsistence*[65] and once again tries to clarify his views by offering numerous examples. He proposes that essential attributes are those which are not possible to conceive of without the preconception of these *a priori* (*badawī*) attributes, such as "animality which is an essential attribute of man." The other salient feature of these essential attributes is the essential priority of their subject, such as the priority of animality and rationality to man.

Regarding accidental attributes, conceiving of what is being described without conceiving of these attributes is possible; priority and posterity are of no consequence here. Accidental attributes are of two types. First are those that, while they are essential to the subject, are nevertheless potential, such as rationality, laughter, and sadness, all of which may be actualized but not necessarily so. The other type of accidental attributes is mental abstractions. Khayyam gives the example of a black crow in which blackness and crow are separate in the mind but not in the body.

ESCHATOLOGY

There are those scholars both in the medieval period and the modern era who have argued that Khayyam believed in the transmigration of the soul (*tanāsukh*) and even corporeal resurrection in this world. Most of these accounts are based on his *Ruba'iyyat* in which Khayyam tells us repeatedly that we shall return to this life as grass and earth from which other bodies will be crafted. If these poetic references are taken metaphorically, along with Khayyam's philosophical writings, it positively confirms that Khayyam did not believe in any form of transmigration.

Despite the above, there have been several accounts regarding Khayyam's belief in transmigration of the soul, the most important of which is reported by Aḥmad N. Taṭavī, the author of *Tārikh-i alfī*. The account of this highly inaccurate story, which has been reiterated by modern orientalists such as Zhukovski and repeated by a number of other scholars, allegedly took place in an old school in

Nayshābūr. The school was under construction and the crew was carrying bricks loaded on the back of a donkey. One day, when Khayyam and his students in the tradition of the Peripatetics were walking in the courtyard having a discourse, a donkey loaded with bricks stopped by the door and refused to enter. Khayyam allegedly approached the donkey and recited the following poem:

> O you who went and now return as stale
> To men you seem a sorry fairy tale
> Your nails have rolled around in single hoof
> Your beard is sweeping ground a shaggy tail.[66]

To the amazement of everyone present, once the donkey heard the quatrain, he entered the school. Students asked Khayyam how this was made possible, to which he replied, "The soul of this donkey belongs to a master who taught at this school but was too embarrassed to enter as a donkey, but once he realized that his friends knew him, he abided by it."[67]

The story is unfounded and not true. A thorough reading of the *Ruba'iyyat* clearly contradicts the possibility of a return in any sense of the word as the following indicates:

> Ye go from soul asunder this ye know
> And that ye creep, behind His curtain low
> Hence sing His Name, ye know not whence ye came
> And live sedate, ye know not where to go.[68]

> When soul would cease to play with me and thee
> Two bricks in pit will stay with me and thee
> And then to lay the bricks for other graves
> In moulds they cast the clay with me and thee.[69]

Furthermore, if this story is true, Khayyam may have been speaking sarcastically with regard to the whole idea of resurrection, transmigration and life after death so intensely debated among the theologians at the time. It is also possible that Khayyam's source of inspiration may have been a similar story in which Pythagoras admonished a man who was beating a dog because the barking of the dog was actually the voice of his dead friend.[70] Ironically, there is not an extensive treatment of eschatology in any of the philosophical writings of Khayyam, but there are enough references to the concept of the soul that make it plausible to conclude that despite the fact that his *Ruba'iyyat* may indicate otherwise, Khayyam may have believed in life after death. Perhaps it is not the very existence of life after death that he opposed so much as the theological speculations concerning the intricacies of the hereafter, which appear to have annoyed him.

CONCLUDING REMARKS

Iṣfahānī concludes his learned article[71] on Khayyam's ontological views by identifying twenty-four principles which constitute the salient features of Khayyam's philosophical views. Some of them are discussed by Khayyam himself and others are merely alluded to in his various treatises. Due to the significance of their classification, which brings various aspects of Khayyam's philosophical views to light, a rendition of these principles are included here in order to provide the reader with a synopsis of his philosophical thought.[72]

1. The world is knowable through conventional epistemological methods, that is, sense perception is the primary medium through which knowledge of the external world is made possible.
2. The law of non-contradiction is an axiom that underlies sound philosophical thinking.[73]
3. The concept of existence is present to the intellect in an immediate, axiomatic and unmediated manner.[74]
4. Mental existence and external existence correspond with each other, but the former exists in the primary sense of the word and the latter in the secondary sense.[75]
5. The soul and the cognitive faculty in addition to its ability to understand the external world through correspondence is able to understand the non-existents in the external world.[76]
6. The best mode of cognition is the path of Sufis. Khayyam tells us at some length that among the four groups of the seekers of truth, the Sufi's knowledge of God is the most clear and distinct.[77]

7. The subject of philosophy is existence and not existent.[78]
8. The truth of existence, both external and abstract, is an indication of the truth of the gradations of beings (*tashkik*) and their separation and not of their intertwinedness and a mixture.[79] Iṣfahānī notes that this is more in line with Plato's teachings than Aristotle's since, according to the above, mental existence is an aspect of external existence.
9. Existence in both senses, external and abstract, is abstract[80] and therefore, not principle or primary.[81]
10. Particulars are subject to generation and corruption, and this is the reason why the ancient philosophers have not commented upon them.[82]
11. What counts for the inherent poverty of existents is that from a certain [ontological] perspective they are non-existing.[83]
12. Divine knowledge descends upon those forms that are receptive to it.[84]
13. The true cause of all things is the Necessary Being and to conceive of any other cause for existence is fallacious.[85]
14. The Necessary Being is devoid of whatness.[86]
15. There can be no multiplicity of God even in its abstract sense.[87]
16. The Necessary Being is a unity in all its aspects.[88]
17. The Necessary Being is devoid of essence and I-ness.[89]
18. Emanation of the world from God is due to the existence of the Necessary Being and not a divine will that is added to His essence.[90]
19. Emanation of existents from God is gradual and is in a descending order from the highest to the lowest.[91]
20. Except for the Necessary Being, existents are substances, either corporeal or simple. Corporeal substances are divisible, while incorporeal substances, such as the soul, are indivisible.[92]
21. Understanding the emanation of evil from God lies in understanding their gradual descending order and how it is not possible to avoid issuing a great deal of good to avoid some evil.[93]
22. Evil belongs to the corporeal world of compound entities.[94]

23. With regard to the problem of determinism and free will, neither determinism nor free will is true in the absolute sense of the word.[95]
24. The reason for having prophets in the world is to balance the order of good and evil, which results from human actions. The principles advocated by prophets have three benefits: 1) avoidance of base virtues and evil; 2) making of noble virtues to become habitual and permanent in the soul; 3) declaration of the promise of reward [in the hereafter] and promotion of virtuous traditions in the society.[96]

Khayyam's Peripatetic writings and commentaries should be regarded as a mode of thought which represents his rational side. It is imperative to realize that without the inclusion of his *Ruba'iyyat* into an overall picture, the Khayyamian world-view remains a fundamentally distorted one.

7

Khayyam the Scientist

The heavenly spheres which in this domain reside,
Have bewildered the wise, thinking far and wide;
Behold and don't lose the trail of wisdom,
For the price of wisdom is to reel to every side.[1]

One, if not the most important, aspect of our multi-dimensional Khayyam is his mathematical genius and original contributions to fields such as algebra, geometry, arithmetic, physics, music theory, astronomy and meteorology. Khayyam wrote very little in these fields even though sciences and, in particular, mathematics, remained his primary preoccupation. What he did write, however, was dense and ground-breaking. While a detailed discussion concerning Khayyam's mathematical perspectives would be too technical to include here, a comprehensive work such as this would not be complete without at least a cursory survey on the subject matter.

Despite the fact that much attention has been paid to Khayyam's view on mathematics in the last century, Khayyam's philosophy of mathematics remains a neglected area of scholarship. Nasr in his work on Khayyam[2] discusses the three basic mathematical ideas which Khayyam treats philosophically. First is the question of mathematical order, namely "where does this order issue from and why does it correspond to the order dominant in the world of nature?"[3] Khayyam's answer, Nasr argues, can be found ironically in his philosophical treatises, especially those in which he treats the subject of existence. According to Khayyam, not only does all existence emanate from God but "also the source of order which is inseparable from the very act of existence. To speak of *wujūd* is also to speak of order which the science of mathematics studies."[4]

The second mathematico-philosophical problem is that of the significance of philosophical speculation in solving the problem of postulates and principles. As it will be demonstrated shortly, Khayyam showed that Euclid's fifth postulate, called the "parallel postulate", cannot be proven simply on the basis of the other Euclidean axioms. He used the geometry of converging lines to argue for replacing this postulate. Nasr argues that "the fact that he did not envisage a non-Euclidean geometry, however, was primarily philosophical rather than mathematical. Moreover, in his study of the fifth postulate, Khayyam discussed concepts of space and geometric order which are of much importance to the philosophy of mathematics."[5] Khayyam even refused to introduce the notion of motion as some mathematicians like al-Haytham had done. Motion is a by-product of matter, and Khayyam wanted to avoid using corporeality to solve mathematics, which he thought belonged to the realm of pure intelligibles.

Finally, there is the third principle of Khayyam's philosophy of mathematics, which is the distinction he made between natural body (*al-jism al-ṭabi'ī*) and mathematical body (*al-jism al-ta'limī*). While the first type, also called "volume" (*ḥajm*), is defined as an entity that belongs to the category of accidental attributes and cannot stand on its own independently, the latter belongs to the category of substance and has no external existence in the world. Nasr explains, "The first is the body with which the natural sciences deal and the second is the concern of mathematicians. The distinction made by Khayyam and others between the two types of body in question is ... of great significance for the philosophy of mathematics and the relation between mathematics and physics envisaged from a philosophical point of view."[6]

In what follows, a brief discussion concerning five areas of Khayyam's scientific views and their significance are brought forth. They are as follows:

1. Mathematics
   a. Algebra
   b. Geometry
   c. Arithmetic
2. Physics
3. Music Theory
4. Astronomy
5. Meteorology

MATHEMATICS

a. Algebra

In his *On Proofs for Problems Concerning Algebra*, Khayyam treated the subject of cubic orders and demonstrated the relationship between mathematics and the metaphysical significance of Euclidean geometry. Khayyam in a sense improved upon Khwārazmī's treatment of the quadratic equations by solving all types of cubic equations having a positive root by the use of intersecting conic sections. Khayyam, who did not recognize negative numbers as coefficients, offered a geometric demonstration of the solution by considering fourteen types of cubics that cannot be reduced to linear or quadratic equations when dividing by x or x^2. David M. Burton in his *The History of Mathematics*[7] illustrates Khayyam's method as follows:

> "Let us illustrate Khayyam's procedure for the equation $x^3 + qx = r$, which he chooses to write as $x^3 + b^2x = b^2c$.
>
> Referring to the figure, Khayyam takes the line segment AB to have length b. A perpendicular BC of length c is then drawn to AB. Next he constructs a parabola with vertex B, axis BF, and

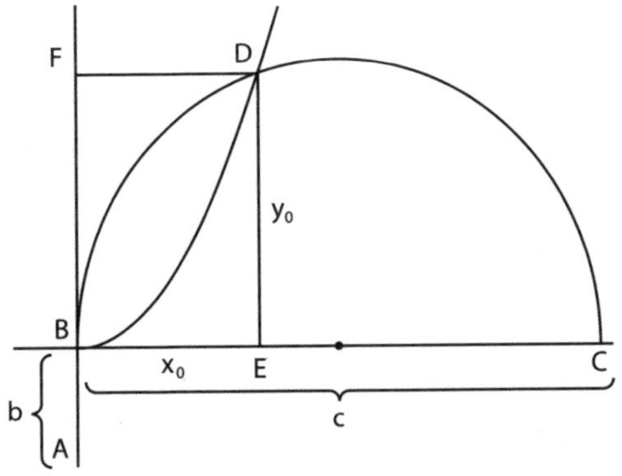

parameter b. In modern notation, the parabola has equation $x^2 = by$. Now, on BC as diameter, a semicircle is described. Its equation is

$$\left(x - \frac{c}{2}\right)^2 + y^2 = \left(\frac{c}{2}\right)^2$$

or

$$x(x-c) + y^2 = 0.$$

The semicircle will meet the parabola at a point D whose abscissa, or x-coordinate, provides a root of the given cubic. Geometrically the root is represented by the line segment BE, with E determined by dropping a perpendicular from D to BC.

To see this algebraically, let (x_0, y_0) be the coordinates of the point D. Since D lies on the parabola, we have $x_0^2 = by_0$, which implies that $x_0^4 = b^2y_0^2$. But D is also on the semicircle, whence $y_0^2 = x_0(c - x_0)$. Combining these equations yields

$$x_0^4 = b^2 y_0^2 = b^2x_0(c - x_0)$$

or $x_0^3 = b^2(c - x_0)$. Thus x_0 satisfies the cubic equation $x^3 + b^2x = b^2c$.

In treating each of his 14 cases, Khayyam was aware that a cubic might possess two positive roots, depending on how the conics involved intersect. Bold as he was, he ignored negative and repeated roots. He also failed to discover the possibility of three roots occurring, as with an equation of the type $x^3 + qx = px^2 + r$ (one concrete example being $x^3 + 11x = 6x^2 + 6$). Khayyam also erroneously concluded that it is not possible to find an algebraic solution of the general cubic. But this should not detract from his mastery of the geometrical theory of third-degree equations, which may be regarded as the most successful accomplishment of an Arabic mathematician."[8]

Based on Khayyam's own references to figures and concepts, it is clear that he was intimately familiar with the works of mathematicians before him. From his comments, we know that he must have read Ibn al-Haytham's treatise on how to find four line segments between two given segments such that all six remain proportional. He mentioned and briefly alluded to the central themes of such major mathematicians as al-Māhānī, al-Būzjānī, Ibn Irāqī, al-Khāzin, al-Wafā', al-Saghānī and Abū al-Jud ibn al-Layth.

Khayyam referred to rudimentaries of algebraic geometry twice, once in *On the Division of a Quadrant of a Circle*. The other time was in *On Proofs for Problems Concerning Algebra* where Khayyam mentions the name of some of his predecessors, in particular al-Layth, a third/ninth-century figure who had gone so far as to devise a classification of cubic equations prior to calculating conic curves for each one. Khayyam wrote, "And I always aspired intensely – and I still do – to investigate all their species [i.e. of equations of the first three degrees], and to distinguish by means of demonstration what is possible from what is impossible with respect to the forms of every species."[9]

Khwārazmī, the other Persian mathematician of the third/ninth century, had solved equations of the first two degrees using radicals; and Thābit ibn Qurrā', also from the third/ninth century, had provided a geometrical justification for them. A cubic equation such as $X^3+100X=10X^2+1000$ requires that X be found so that when it is placed in the equation the two sides are numerically equal. Since the use of radicals was yet unknown, in order to solve this problem, Khayyam had to devise a model based on Khwārazmī's. He stated:

> We have written a book to demonstrate the correctness of these methods and the fact that they fulfill the requirements; and we have spoken abundantly about the kinds thereof, I mean about the determination of the sides of the square-square of the squared, of the cubed-cube, whatever degree it may reach. No one has done it before us.[10]

By the time of Khayyam, mathematical concepts and definitions had been developed by major mathematicians, in particular Khwārazmī, and Khayyam did not add to terms such as "unknown," "its square," "polynomial expressions," and "higher powers," just to mention a few. The genius of Khayyam was the application of geometry to these concepts, either in two or three dimensions. The application of geometry to algebra, though not entirely new, was advanced by Khayyam extensively, as he wrote:

> When the algebraist uses the word squared-square in measurements, it is metaphorical, not properly speaking, as it is impossible for the squared-square to fall within magnitudes as what has one dimension, that is the root (or the side, if it be related to its square) and then, what has two dimensions, that is the surface. (And the square falls within magnitudes: it is the square surface). Then what has three dimensions, that is solid (and the cube falls within magnitudes) it is the solid which is contained by six squares.[11]

Khayyam embarked upon a classification of twenty-five equations using a combination of four terms: number, unknown, its square, and its cube, and he goes on to elaborate on the specifications of each classification. His achievements were further developed by his successors, namely Sharīf al-Dīn Ṭusī.[12]

Rashed and Vahabzadeh, in *Omar Khayyam the Mathematician*, offer a detailed comparison of Khayyam and Descartes with respect to their views on geometry, concluding that Descartes' theory of algebraic equations is the completion of Khayyam's project. They write, "Descartes is repeating al-Khayyam's method: he does actually refine it, generalize it, take it to its feasible logical limit, in short he completes it, but really without reaching the essence of it or redefining its meaning."[13]

b. Geometry

Khayyam had a short treatise called *On the Elaboration of the Problems Concerning the Book of Euclid*,[14] where he presented his own views on geometry, and for which he has come to be regarded as a major figure in the non-Euclidean geometry. The treatise is based on definitions and postulates. In the first part of this treatise, Khayyam discusses the fifth postulate of Euclid regarding the parallel line theorem. Considering Euclid's as inadequate, he proposes eight axioms of his own. In the subsequent two sections, he redefines Eudoxus' concept of a number by the use of a continuous fraction as a way of formulating a ratio. Osman Baker, in his work *Tawḥīd and Science*,[15] tells us "Khayyam shows us irrational ratios, those with non-terminating continuous fraction developments, and true numbers can be placed on the same operational scale, on that account almost admits the irrational to the status of a number."[16] Khayyam, contrary to the Greeks, applied arithmetic to ratios in order to comment on the quality of ratios. He explained that given magnitude *g* is commensurable with a unit, it belongs to the realm of numbers. He mentions that this method is used by those who rely on divisible numbers, such as land surveyors. Rosenfeld and Youschkevitch, in their article "Al-Khayyami," consider that Khayyam "by placing irrational quantities and numbers on the same operational scale, began a true revolution in the doctrine of number."[17]

Khayyam argued that Euclid's fifth postulate, also known as "the Principle of Parallelism," is not as self-evident as the other four. He accepted the first 28 propositions of Euclid but replaced the 29th with one of his own. The 29th proposition states:

> A straight line falling on parallel straight lines makes the alternate angles equal to one another, the exterior angle equal to the interior and opposite angle, and the interior angles on the same side to two right angles.[18]

Khayyam, having argued that two perpendiculars to the same straight line neither diverge nor converge, moved to offer an analysis of a quadrilateral, such as the figure below, in which two sides AD and BC are equal and both are perpendicular to the side AB. In this analysis, which in modern mathematical terminology is called "Saccheri's quadrilateral," Khayyam demonstrated without using the fifth postulate that angles ADC and BCD are equal.

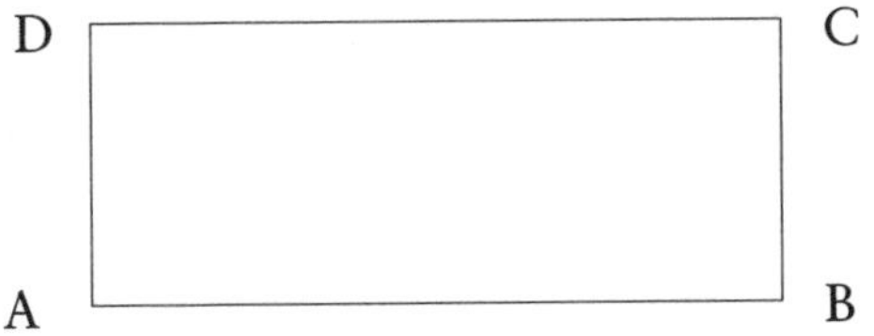

David Smith in his article "Euclid, Omar Khayyam and Saccheri"[19] shows that the first of Saccheri's theorems are essentially the same as Khayyam's; even the way figures are lettered are the same.

A number of Muslim mathematicians who based their views on Greek mathematicians made a vain attempt to revise and improve the fifth postulate. Khayyam in the beginning of several of his mathematical works shows his familiarity with the commentaries of his predecessors on Euclid's fifth postulate. Among such figures he mentions Abu'l-Abbās al-Fāḍl ibn Ḥātim al-Nayzirī, the Latin Anaritius (d. about 922) and Ibn Haytham (354AH/965CE), Abu Ja'far al-Khāzin and finally Jawharī and Shannī. Khayyam argued that his predecessors either accepted the fifth postulate without proof or on fallacious proof. Some of them, such as Ibn Haytham, even went so far as to introduce motion into the discussion with Khayyam saying that "geometry has no relation with motion."[20]

Khayyam criticized Euclid for not having set the fundamentals of geometry first and postulated on some of the more trivial aspects of geometry, arguing that Euclid should have added the following principles:

1. Every quantity is indivisible *ad infinitum*. To prove this, geometricians have tried to offer geometrical proofs, whereas the real solution lies in the application of philosophy and logic to geometry. Khayyam argued that the solution can be understood through *Burhān innī* (*a posteriori*) and not *Burhān lammī* (*a priori*).

2. Regarding two straight lines that intersect and move beyond the point of intersection, their distance grows further.
3. Two straight lines whose distance lessens will intersect.

Using the above principles, which Khayyam argued can be proven *a posteriori*, he moved on to solve the Euclidean problems by substituting "Euclid's fifth principle using a quadrilateral with two equal sides and right angles."[21] Khayyam's method of investigation, which distinguishes him from other mathematicians of his time, was his extensive use of logic. As Chāvoshī, one of Khayyam's modern commentators, remarks, "There is a strong connection between logic and mathematics for Khayyam. That explains the postulate of parallels differently which Khayyam sees as more logical than the method of Euclid."[22]

Khayyam's other major contribution to geometry was to extend the possibility of discussing geometrical objects in more than three dimensions. In classical Euclidean geometry, geometrical objects could only be discussed in three dimensions in space, but Khayyam, whose philosophical background allowed him to think of intelligible and possible worlds, argued that it is possible for spatial dimensions to be more than three. A discussion concerning multi-dimensional aspects of space and geometry remains one of Khayyam's invaluable contributions to the field.[23]

Khayyam's contribution to the field of mathematics went beyond the field of algebra and geometry and extended to other branches of mathematics such as arithmetic. A discussion concerning all his contributions is beyond the scope of our work here, but a brief treatment of his views on arithmetic clearly indicates Khayyam's mastery of the subject matter.

c. Arithmetic

In arithmetic there is the field of calculus, of probability and the concept of the arithmetical triangle, or the so-called "Pascal's triangle." Chāvoshī, in his article "Omar Khayyam and the Arithmetical Triangle,"[24] indicates that, whereas this type of triangle had been discussed in European, Indian and Chinese literature, the particular application of it was first made by al-Karajī in the tenth century and improved upon by Khayyam. Chāvoshī states, "Considering that Khayyam was completely familiar with the 'arithmetical triangle' and used it for the extraction of roots – the same method which became common in Europe after Khayyam – it is reasonable for this triangle to be called "al-Kharajī-Khayyam's triangle."[25]

Allegedly, Khayyam had written a treatise titled *Difficulties of Arithmetic* (*Mushkilāt al-ḥisāb*) which has not survived, but in his other work *On Proofs for Problems Concerning Algebra* (*Fi'l Barāhīn 'ala'l-masā'īl al-jabr wa'l-muqābilah*) he explained:

> The Hindus have their methods for extracting the sides of squares and cubes based on the investigation of a small number of cases, which is through the knowledge of the squares of nine integers, that is, the squares of 1, 2, 3, and so on, and of their products into each other, that is, the product of 2 with 3, and so on. I have written a book to prove the validity of those methods ...[26]

It is not entirely clear how Khayyam knew of the Hindu method but he may have known it through some of the earlier works such as *On the Principles of Hindu Arithmetics* (*Fī uṣūl ḥisāb al-hind*) by Qushayr ibn Labbāb al-Jilī (971–1029) or the other major work titled *Things Sufficient to Understanding Hindu Arithmetic* (*Al-muqni' fi'l-ḥisāb al-hindī*) by 'Alī ibn Aḥmad al-Nasawī. Both of these figures who have offered methods of extracting cubic roots show their familiarity with the Hindu tradition but their method is actually closer to the Chinese method.

PHYSICS

Khayyam has a small treatise entitled *On the Deception of Knowing the Two Quantities of Gold and Silver in a Compound Made of the Two*, which is an elaboration on the Archimedes' principle of hydrostatics. This principle maintains that a body submerged in a liquid loses weight equal to the weight of the liquid that is displaced by it.

Two of Khayyam's contemporary physicists, Abd'l-Raḥmān Khāzenī, who wrote *Mizān al-ḥikmah*, and Abū Manṣūr Nayrīzī, have elaborated upon this problem. E. Wiedemann, the German scholar, analyzed this treatise extensively and concluded that Khayyam's solution is the most precise and complex of them all. Khayyam in the above treatise remarked:

> If you want to know how much gold and silver there is in a compound entity, first, you have to calculate the weight in air and water and then equivalent to its weight choose gold and silver and determine their weight in air and water. Then calculate the ratio of the weight of the pure gold and silver in air and water separately and compare these three ratios; if the ratio of the compound is equal with gold, then it becomes apparent that all of the compound is gold.
>
> If the ratio of the compound is equal to the ratio of the silver, it becomes known that the compound is all silver. If (the ratio) does not become equivalent to either of them, it becomes clear that the compound is made of gold and in comparing the ratio of the compound with gold and silver and their differences, one can calculate how much of the compound is gold and how much silver.[27]

The rest of this short treatise is devoted to a detailed discussion concerning how a scale works and the mathematical underpinnings of the divisions of a scale.

MUSIC THEORY

Khayyam had composed a short treatise on music theory, which is said to have been a commentary upon Euclid's work on music. While the original no longer exists, there have been two translations of this work into Persian.[28] Khayyam's major contribution was a reclassification of musical scales, as S. Sepanta in his article explains, "At the time of Khayyam, musical scales were based on tetrachordal patterns. A tetrachord was divided into four intervals; Khayyam classified twenty-one tetrachords with a series of mathematical figures."[29]

In this short treatise consisting of only a few pages, Khayyam discussed the 21 tetrachords and described the sonoral effects of each one with adjectives such as "sonorally pleasant," "sonorally unpleasant," "strong," and "aesthetically pleasing." In discussing the tetrachords, Khayyam tells us there are three of them: strong, soft and colorful; he went on to elaborate on the space between the notes numerically and said that traditionally musicians would connect two or several tetrachords conjunctively or disjunctively – what Fārābī would call "genus." A genus having one of its dimensions not bigger than the ratio of the sum of their two values is called a "strong genus." A genus that has one of its dimensions bigger than the sum of the other two dimensions is called a "colorful genus," and a soft genus is one whose space is bigger than the square of the sum of the other two spaces. Using modern terminology, a strong genus is called major and a colorful genus, minor.

Khayyam uses the theory of commensurable ratios in his work *On the Proposition that Asserts Genera Are of Four Types* (*Al-qawl 'alā ajnās alladhī bi'l-arba'ah*) to elaborate on what Euclid had commented on earlier in his *Sectio Canonis*, that is, dividing a fourth into three intervals which correspond to chromatic, diatonic and enharmonic tonalities. Khayyam mentions twenty-two examples of the section of the fourth, of which three are his original contribution. As to the rest, Khayyam seems to have adopted eight from Ptolemy's "Theory of Harmony," thirteen from Fārābī's *Great Book on Music* (*Kitāb al-musiqī al-kabīr*) and fourteen from Avicenna's *The Book of Healing* (*Kitāb al-shifā'*).

ASTRONOMY

As has been discussed in Chapter One, it was during the reign of Sulṭān Jalāl al-Dīn Malik Shāh (fifth/eleventh century) that a group of astronomers, such as Abu'l-Muẓaffar Isfazārī, Maymoūn ibn Najib Wāsiṭī and Abd'l-Raḥmān Khāzenī under the direction of Khayyam himself, was invited to the royal observatory. Whereas the actual location of the observatory is subject to debate, in all likelihood it was in Iṣfahān. Khayyam's mission was clear: improve upon the existing calendar and correct its shortcomings.

The Sulṭān wanted the first day of Spring, which traditionally has marked the beginning of the new year for Persians (Norūz) to remain unchanged, and therefore he asked Khayyam to find a way to make this possible. Khayyam studied the problem of the existing calendar known as "*yazd gerdī*," that consisted of twelve 30-day months and five extra days, which would be added to the eighth month (Ābān). Since the year is 365¼ days, every four years, one day is needed and every 120 years we end up with a year that is thirteen months.

Khayyam thoroughly analyzed the problem and devised a new calendar known as "*taqwīm-i Jalālī*." He insisted on keeping the names of the pre-Islamic months of the Persian calendar as opposed to adopting the Arabic names for them. His motive has been interpreted in a variety of ways; for some, it is proof of his membership in the Persian nationalist movement (*Shu'ubiyyah*) against the Arabs, and for others, it denotes his respect for the wisdom of his forefathers and the Persian scientific heritage. Yet, there are those who see this as indicative of his knowledge of Pahlavi language; the latter is highly improbable.

Without going through the details of Khayyam's mathematical and astronomical calculations, in summary, Khayyam took the extra five days and spread them over a long period of time, and by adding an additional 15 days every 62 years, the length of a year would be 365.241935 days, and thereby for every 5000 years, the calendar has to be adjusted by one day. The new calendar, called "Malikī calendar" (*taqwīm-i malikī*) or "Jalālī calendar" (*taqwīm-i jalālī*), is based on thirty-three years. The years 4, 8, 12, 16, 20, 24, 28, and 33 became leap years of 366 days with the average year being 365.2424 days. This new calendar was inaugurated on the 10th of Ramaḍān, 471 AH/15th of March 1079 CE.

It is noteworthy that in the Gregorian calendar commissioned by Pope Gregory XIII in the tenth/sixteenth century, now widely used in the West, the average year is 365.2425 days. This is less accurate than Khayyam's, since for every 3330 years, the Gregorian calendar has to account for one day, where as Khayyam's calendar has to adjust the one day every 5000 years.[30]

METEOROLOGY

Predicting the weather has been of particular interest to kings and farmers alike, to the former for its military application and to the latter for agricultural reasons. It is not entirely clear whether Khayyam, despite his mastery in the field of astronomy, believed in predicting the weather. The dubious nature of his belief concerning predicting the weather has already been shown in the first chapter. The Sulṭān decided to go hunting in winter and Khayyam was asked to determine a suitable date for hunting and he reluctantly did so. Niẓāmī ʻAruḍī offers the following account of the story:

> ... Even though, I had seen verdicts of *ḥujjat al-ḥaqq* Omar, but did not see his faith in the principles of astronomy[31] nor did I see or hear from the learned anyone who believed in the principles. In the Winter of 508 AH, Ṣadr al-Dīn Muḥammad ibn al-Muẓaffar, peace be upon him, said "Khāwjah, call upon Imām Omar to determine when we should go hunting so it will not snow or rain in those days" and Khāwjah Imām Omar was a companion of Khāwjah and lived in his residence. Khāwjah sent someone to call him [Khayyam] and told me the story; Khayyam contemplated for two days, made a wise decision and went to tell the Sulṭān. When the Sulṭān came [to hunt], at once the weather became turbulent, clouds came, wind blew and snow began. They laughed and the Sulṭān wanted to come back. Khāwjah Imām [Khayyam] said, "O Sulṭān, do not worry for this very hour, clouds will move and in the next five days there will be no rain." The Sulṭān rode, the clouds opened and in those five days there was no rain and no one saw clouds.[32]

By carefully analyzing the story, one may also argue that Khayyam did believe in the science of meteorology. It appears that from the time that the messenger informed Khayyam, he deliberated for two days and then informed the Sulṭān that he could begin his hunting. Farīd,[33] an Egyptian meteorologist, explains that based on five successive sunny days, one can conclude that Khayyam was working with weather patterns. In mild climates such as Nayshābūr, Farīd adds, when the temperature drops suddenly and is followed by a certain amount of fog, it is indicative that sunny days follow.

Khayyam's delay in deciding may have been because of his knowledge of the weather patterns.

If Khayyam did take the science of meteorology seriously, he would have composed something about it. But if he did not think that weather could be predicted, it is expected that a man of his stature would have shared that with the Sulṭān and saved himself possible embarrassment. In either case, Khayyam's firm insistence that he should proceed leads one to conclude that while meteorology is not an exact science, patterns can be established on the basis of which some degree of prediction is possible. Among other works by Russian scholars on Khayyam's mathematics, one can name B.A. Rosenfeld and A.P. Youschkevitch's *Omar Khayyam*. This work contains detailed biographical essays and analyses of Khayyam's mathematical works.

While Khayyam was not an architect, some of his theories played a major role in the designing of some of the great monuments, such as the dome of the Shāh Mosque of Iṣfahān. It is said that in a dispute between mathematicians and masons concerning structural problems, Khayyam offered a solution using cubic equations. It is said that he wrote an untitled treatise[34] in which he says, "If it was for the elevated status of this convocation ... and if I did not owe so much to the one who posed the question ... I would have been very far from commenting on this field."[35] Khayyam then offers a solution by elaborating on a special right triangle the hypotenuse of which is equal to the sum of the perpendicular and the short side. We know of this work through the work of another unknown author titled *On the Intertwinedness of the Analogous and Identical Patterns.*[36] A. Özdurad, in his article "Omar Khayyam and Architecture,"[37] argues that by the term "field" (*wādī*), Khayyam is really referring to a school of architecture in which he had reluctantly become involved.

Khayyam's lasting legacy among Muslim scientists became the basis of numerous commentaries by such notable figures as Nāṣir al-Dīn Ṭusī who criticized Khayyam and developed an improved version of his theory of postulates. There were also mathematicians such as Ibn 'Umar Abharī and Shams al-Dīn al-Samarqandī,[38] both of whom were Ṭusī's contemporaries, and Qāḍī-zādeh al-Rumī.[39]

While Khayyam's most important work on algebra is entitled *On Proofs for Problems Concerning Algebra*, his views on mathematics in the modern world came to the forefront of attention through his formulation of a geometrical theory of equations. Whereas we see interest in Khayyam's mathematical views as early as the late seventeenth century by figures such as Golius, Wallis, and Saccheri, it is not until 1850 that the French orientalist F. Woepcke, encouraged by the work of others such as the German scholar A. Von Humboldt and M. Chasles, offered translations of Khayyam's works on algebra. Woepcke's translation was the first high-quality work that introduced the western readers to this aspect of Khayyam's thought.

Khayyam's mathematical genius and his legacy have been duly noted by Western mathematicians both in Europe and America. The specialized nature of the subject matter, however, prevents us from offering a more extensive discussion that examines the technical aspects of it.

8

Khayyam in the West

> It is good for America that it has men who find the time, amid the hurly-burly of modern life, to study these philosophers of long ago, and keep burning in the world the lamp of their wit and wisdom kindled in earlier ages. Worcestrians may be proud of the part that citizens of this town have had in the pleasant works of culture.
>
> (From a Lecture at the Omar Khayyam Club of America, 1922)

ORIENTALISM AND THE EUROPEAN KHAYYAM

In the present discussion, we are not so much concerned with the accuracy of the "European Khayyam" as we are with the transmission of his *Ruba'iyyat* to the West and its impact upon certain literary circles.

The earliest and first translation ever made of the *Ruba'iyyat* was by Thomas Hyde in the 1700s, when he translated one quatrain into Latin, which appeared in Hyde's *Veterum Persarum et Parthorum et Medorum Religionis*. Despite this encounter in the 1700s, the introduction of Omar Khayyam in Europe is primarily a nineteenth-century phenomenon, one that spread like wild fire. In England and America, Khayyamian studies were conducted in a more organized manner, and in France and Germany, in a less institutional and more scholarly way. Discovery of Khayyam by Europeans first and then Americans was, as we shall see, partially a coincidence and partially indicative of the readiness of the West for Khayyam's message.

European Romanticism which had turned eastward seeking spiritual wealth and the marvels of the Orient, found in our Persian poet-philosopher a message which matched the *Zeitgeist* of Europe and America. How the first session of the Omar Khayyam Club of America is described by Charles Dana Burrage, one of the founders of the Club, bears testimony to a romantic notion of the East: "from the Persian vase in the table's center with its one rose of Kashmir to the various items of the menu from Chilo to Shirāzī wine and Persian rose leaves, the session was decidedly Omarian."[1]

The eighteenth–nineteenth-century view of the Eastern world based on the eyewitness accounts of missionaries, military personnel and some scholars, was, and still is to some extent, of a strange, exotic, mysterious and mystical world where one may have access to profundities not available in the West. Oriental wisdom, therefore, had to represent the opposite of what the West had become. In comparison with Western materialism, the East was considered to be spiritual. Western desire to be the masters of the universe was ridiculed by an Eastern sense of determinism. Against the well-planned, future-oriented Western perspective, was the Eastern view that life is too impermanent and fragile to plan.

Khayyam became the embodiment of the so-called "oriental wisdom"; while he embraced the world, his message was not worldly. Whereas determinism and predestination resonate deeply with Khayyam, one may still choose to live one's given reality to its fullest. Hence comes the message of living in the present, here and now, which reverberates throughout the *Ruba'iyyat*. It is almost as if Khayyamian thought, as perceived by Europeans, complements the Western perspective, saying, "You can have both," materialism and spirituality, determinism and individual choices, planning for the future and living our lives in the here and now.

The Western love for the *Ruba'iyyat* and admiration for Khayyam is precisely because he did not advocate this perceived message, certainly not in its superficial and shallow sense as understood by so many. As Burrage states, "The present day vogue of FitzGerald's Omar then may justly be attributed to the fact that he has caught and in pleasing fashion brought home to many the true spirit of Epicurean sybaritism."[2] Khayyam's profound existential philosophy became the victim of this stereotypical exotic, esoteric, oriental philosophy, which is not to be found in the East any more than it can be found in the West.

While the present discussion is about the transition of Khayyam to the West and not about the accuracy of European understanding of him, one has to attribute Khayyam's immense popularity in the West to this *perceived* message. Indeed, there were many other eminent Persian poets such as Rūmī, Ḥāfiz, and Ferdawsī, who were far more prolific, poetically speaking, than Khayyam; and yet they were only known by the scholarly community and were hardly as popular as Khayyam who had become a household name in America. Let us now proceed and discuss Khayyam's journey from the East to the West in some detail.

The voyage of Khayyam to Europe began in 1810 when King George III commissioned his cousin, Sir Gore Ouseley, and assigned him to be the British Ambassador to Persia. In a letter which is decorated by arabesque and bears the seal of the British Crown, King George III praises the King of Persia, informing him of his nomin-ation. Due to the historic nature of this commission, which led to the discovery of Khayyam by Europeans, we include the letter:

> Sir, My cousin: I have received Your Royal Highness's kind letter from Tabriz on the subject of Captain Paisley's arrival at Abushhest, and the possible injury both States might sustain from the supercession of Sir Harford Jones by an Envoy from the Governor General of India. I derive great satisfaction from this demonstration of Your Royal Highness's Friendship and regard for my welfare, – Mirzā Abul Ḥassan has no doubt long since informed Your Royal Highness how truly I lament the unfortunate circumstances which have occurred with respect to Our Royal Mission to the Court of Teheran. These Events have originated in error and misapprehension: I have employed every effort to prevent the recurrence of such Misfortunes. Accordingly, I have appointed an Ambassador Extraordinary and Plenipotentiary directly from Myself to the King of Persia. My Ambassador will be responsible to this Government for his conduct and although directed to co-operate with the

Executive Government of India so far as His Own judgment and His instructions from My Ministers will warrant he will not however be in any manner under the control of the Indian Government. – I have selected for the situation of Ambassador at the Court of Teheran My trusty and well beloved Sir Gore Ouseley, Baronet, a Gentleman whose Knowledge of your Language, Customs and Manners peculiarly qualify Him for that appointment and whose Conduct and Character entitle Him to general respect and consideration.— Having the fullest confidence in My Ambassador's Judgment and Discretion, I trust that the first Intelligence I shall have the pleasure of receiving from Your Royal Highness after the arrival of My Ambassador at Persia, will apprise Me of the renewal of that Harmony which I hope will subsist for Ever between the States of Persia and Great Britain. – I pray God to take Your Royal Highness into His best Care and Protection. I am with every Sentiment of Affection and Esteem,

Sir, My Cousin,

Your Good Cousin,

George R.

At My Royal Castle
at Windsor, 11th July, 1810.[3]

Based on the letter, it appears that Sir Gore Ouseley was an expert in Persian language and culture, and during his years of service, he collected a number of objects and manuscripts from different libraries in Iran and even composed a book titled *Persian Literature*.[4] Upon his return to England, Ouseley presented his collection to Oxford University where it became part of the Bodleian Library. It must have been sometime in the 1840s that Professor Edward Byles Cowell of Oxford University was browsing through Ouseley's collection at the Bodleian Library and was attracted to the illumination of a manuscript which contained the *Ruba'iyyat* of Khayyam. Cowell translated several of the *Ruba'iyyat* and, realizing the splendor and depth of them, he shared them with his learned literary friend, Edward FitzGerald, who took an immediate interest in the subject matter. Cowell went to Calcutta from 1857 to 1858 and found other *Ruba'iyyat*,[5] but before these could be used by

FitzGerald, he had published the first edition of his translation in 1859, and thus began Khayyam's entry into Europe. As Charles Rockwell Lanman states, "But for the commission,[6] it is true, the *Ruba'iyyat* would never have found their way in this available shape to Europe, and the FitzGerald translation might never have been made."[7] Since FitzGerald was the gateway through which much of the West became exposed to Omar Khayyam and his *Ruba'iyyat*, it is appropriate to begin Khayyam's journey to the West with a review of FitzGerald's life and his ingenious translation, which remains an integral part of any serious study of Khayyam.

EDWARD FITZGERALD: THE MAKER OF A REAL MYTH

> "I doubt I have given but a very one-sided version of Omar; but what I do only comes up as a Bubble to the surface and breaks."[8]

For the better part of the nineteenth and twentieth centuries, the name of Omar Khayyam was closely associated with the name of the British poet and man of letters, Edward FitzGerald. It was he who introduced Khayyam to the English-speaking world with so much eloquence and exquisite poetic style that his rather free translation-interpretation, or, as Edward FitzGerald himself called it, "a rendition" of Khayyam, stands on its own as an ingenious work of English poetry. FitzGerald brilliantly introduced Khayyam to the West while managing to do the impossible, that is, conveying the spirit of Khayyam's *Ruba'iyyat* in a way that even some of the more accurate translators of Khayyam after him failed to achieve. Having reviewed most, if not all the available English translations of Khayyam, many of whom are more accurate than FitzGerald's, I would still refer non-Persian readers to FitzGerald's translation, which simply captures the heart and soul of Khayyam's poetry.

FitzGerald, who was competent in reading Persian though had not mastered the language, made a spiritual connection with Khayyam, for as Persians say, "to be of one heart is better than to be

A composite drawing by Albert W. Ellis from photographs of several of the principal members of the Club. From menu of 1918.

of one tongue." It is perhaps for this reason that FitzGerald remained existentially engaged with Khayyam, literally until the last days of his life. Not only was he the gateway through which Khayyam entered the West, but he was the nineteenth-century "*reincarnation*" of Omar Khayyam, a tormented and bewildered man whom one of his biographers, Thomas Wright, described as:

> The *Ruba'iyyat* of FitzGerald is the mournful yet exquisite song of a thoughtful and lonely man, who again and again had questioned his soul about the great things of life and death but could get no satisfactory answer.[9]

In 1861, 250 pamphlets were placed in a second-hand bookstore in London and sold on clearance for the price of one penny. The title of this brown paper covered pamphlet was *Ruba'iyyat of Omar Khayyam, the Astronomer/Poet of Persia translated into English Verse*, published anonymously by none other than Edward FitzGerald. The book had been reduced from five shillings to one and finally placed on the penny shelf destined to be turned into waste paper.

Perhaps it was at the hands of destiny that two famous poets, Dante Gabriel Rossetti and Algernon Charles Swinburne, bought copies of the book and enthusiastically recommended it to their literary circle of friends in London. This literary circle, about which I have much to say, is what later came to be known as the Pre-Raphaelites. The publisher, Quaritch Press, brought out a second edition of the *Ruba'iyyat* and offered FitzGerald ten pounds, which he donated to the Persian famine fund.[10] In 1929, a single copy of this pamphlet was sold for $8,000.

Edward FitzGerald was born on March 31, 1809 in Woodbridge, Suffolk, into a wealthy British family. His father, John Purcell, was an Irish doctor whose ancestry had been traced to Oliver Cromwell. His mother was Mary Francis FitzGerald Purcell, the daughter of another wealthy gentleman, who was also the first cousin of John. Her parents, too, were first cousins, and in reference to this, FitzGerald commented, "We FitzGeralds are all mad."

Edward, who was the seventh of eight children and the most talented of them, grew up in wealth. His family had numerous estates including the famous battlefield of Naseby, and one in Paris where he spent several months every year. The young Edward, who showed great interest in literature and languages, attended the prestigious King Edward's School, and at seventeen entered Trinity College at Cambridge University. Despite his talent, Edward did not take his studies seriously. He was known for his lack of passion for his program; his sloppy appearance; a room filled with books, pipes, pictures; and his love for playing the piano and socializing. FitzGerald had a particular love and admiration for his brilliant circle of friends, and in 1830, when he graduated from Cambridge, he indicated

FitzGerald's cottage at Boulge. (From an original water color by Edward FitzGerald.)

that his circle of friends was the most important thing to him. His friends became scattered near and far,[11] leaving him with a deep sense of loneliness and melancholy, something which may have echoed in FitzGerald's choice of the *Ruba'iyyat*, for the theme of temporality is common among his translations.

In contrast to his love of Epicureanism, FitzGerald almost lived the life of an ascetic. He was a vegetarian and only ate meat in social gatherings in order to blend in. When he decided to settle down in a farmhouse near Woodbridge, he lived simply in a single room with little furniture, while the rest of the house was properly furnished for guests.

FitzGerald loved nature, enjoyed walking and sailing his little yacht, which he had named Shamrock, but later renamed The Scandal. This change of name may have been due to how FitzGerald saw the direction of his own life. It was through sailing that he had befriended many sailors. When one of them died, FitzGerald sold his yacht and never sailed again.

Despite the wealth of his family and numerous residences available to him, he preferred to live in a rented room in a farmer's cottage, or on the second floor of a shop in the market-place. Edward enjoyed being aloof at times; he was an indecisive character who did not like to travel and had no ambition to know about the rest of the world except by an occasional reading of literature. His life was rather aimless; he lived as a perplexed man who moved around only to see his friends, almost like a wandering dervish.

Among his friends in Woodbridge was a bank clerk by the name of Barton, who dabbled in poetry and introduced Edward to Charles Lamb and others who were interested in poetry. When Barton suffered a serious illness, Edward promised to take care of his daughter, Lucy. This was understood by Charles and Mrs. Barton to amount to a promise of marriage. Edward dwelled on this, like so many other things, for years until he decided to marry her out of a sense of duty, believing that it was the right thing. Despite the insistence of his friends not to proceed with a marriage that had catastrophe written all over it, Edward insisted and the wedding took place on November 4, 1856.

Predictably, the result was an unhappy marriage. Neither Lucy's sense of loyalty, nor Edward's duty-bound sense of morality was able to keep the marriage together and the two separated amicably. FitzGerald left Lucy with a generous allowance but never saw her again. The unhappy marriage and divorce remained a constant source of suffering and guilt, as is evident in his letter to a friend:

> You know well enough that I am very much to blame both on the score of stupidity on taking so wrong a step, and want of courageous principle in not making the best of it when taken. She has little to blame herself for, except in fancying that she knew both me and herself better than I had over and over again told her was the truth before marriage.[12]

It appears that by the time he was married, FitzGerald knew some Persian since it was in 1856 that he published a translation of Jamī's *Salamān and Absāl*. A copy of this work had been given to him in 1853, by his friend E.B. Cowell, who was a professor of Sanskrit at Cambridge University. FitzGerald considered *Salamān and Absāl* to be one of the most beautiful works of Persian literature by a Sufi author who had used metaphor as a way of saying what he did not dare to say otherwise. The translation, though it was done in an exquisite style, did not generate much interest, either during his life or after it, but perhaps that is due to the long and tiresome nature of this moral and intellectual allegory. The other major work of Persian literature that attracted FitzGerald's attention was Aṭṭār's *Conference of the Birds* (*Manṭiq al-ṭayr*), even though he never made a full translation of it.[13]

FitzGerald's interest in translating the *Ruba'iyyat* began after his divorce during a period of soul searching and utter loneliness. FitzGerald had written and translated other works among which was a book entitled *Euphranor* (1851). Written in the Socratic style and based on his experiences at Cambridge, this work critiqued the British educational system. In addition, he wrote an anthology of aphorisms called *Polonius* (1852) and made translations of a number of Greek tragedies, the most important of which were *Agamemnon* and Sophocle's *Oedipus Rex* (1880). Finally, from Spanish, he translated several dramas that were all published under the title *Six Dramas of Calderon*. It was at this juncture that Cowell, encouraged by FitzGerald's enthusiasm for his other translation projects, sent him a copy of the *Ruba'iyyat* from the Bodleian Library. FitzGerald developed an obsession with this manuscript written on a yellow paper "with purple-black ink profusely powdered with gold."[14] He carried the manuscript everywhere with him, often wandering in the streets muttering and mumbling vaguely to himself. The old master of Nayshābūr had captured FitzGerald's imagination like an eagle landing upon a pigeon. FitzGerald's arduous work paid off, and in 1858, FitzGerald translated thirty-five quatrains, which he considered to be "less wicked," and sent them to *Fraser's Magazine* for publication. The quatrains from a little-known poet did not seem to interest the editor. One year later, an unhappy FitzGerald withdrew the manuscript and published it in a pamphlet of 20 pages with Quaritch Press entitled, *The Astronomer-Poet of Persia*. Regarding his labor, FitzGerald said, "I suppose very few people have ever taken such pains in translation as I have," but the task of revising the *Ruba'iyyat* never ceased.

Rose leaves from the grave of Omar Khayyam. Brought from Persia by Professor A. V. W. Jackson.

Four versions were published during his lifetime and a fifth one was discovered after he had died. After the first translation, when he realized the free nature of his work, he chose the word *rendered* to appear on the title page instead of "translation." The first edition, which came out in 1859, contained 75 *Ruba'iyyat*. The second one, in 1868, contained 110. FitzGerald reduced the number in the third edition in 1872 and the fourth in 1879 to 101. It was not until his death in 1883 that his friends found, in a thin box, a printed copy of the fourth edition in which a number of changes had been marked. The fifth and final version, which included the changes, became part of a work that his friend, William Aldis Wright, published in 1889 entitled *Letters and Literary Remains of Edward FitzGerald.*[15]

What is immensely interesting is that all of these editions appeared anonymously, and for years even some of his closest friends, such as Carlyle, did not know FitzGerald was the author. It is not clear why he chose to remain anonymous. Perhaps he did intend to publish the final draft under his own name, and saw the first four editions only as works in progress. It is also possible that he was uncomfortable with revealing his lack of mastery of the intricacies of the Persian language even though he had captured the essence of the *Ruba'iyyat* in the most superb and exquisite manner. The other two possible explanations are that he was somewhat embarrassed by what his family had come to be known for; finally there was also a notorious criminal at the time by the same name and perhaps Edward wanted to avoid that.

FitzGerald seems to have selected only those *Ruba'iyyat* which addressed his emotional and existential condition and not all the quatrains available to him at the time. His unhappy marriage and his loneliness as he searched for something he never found, may be among the other reasons for his choice of *Ruba'iyyat*. Among the *Ruba'iyyat* FitzGerald selected for translation are themes expressing pleasure, temporality of relationships, betrayal, and drunkenness.

FitzGerald immersed himself in the fantasy world of poetry. Brigham wrote, "At the time, he sought relief in Epicurean philosophy and in that mood, he found in Omar's glorification of the juice of grape a degree of relief and even exhilaration."[16] His selection, though not exhaustive, did produce a coherent and unified set of quatrains, which he refined until the end of his life. A brief look at the minor changes he made, despite the many years that had passed from when he had first translated the poem, reveals his diligence, perfectionist attitude and the seriousness with which he treated the *Ruba'iyyat*. In 1859, he wrote:

> Awake! For Morning in the Bowl of Night
> Has flung the Stone that puts the Stars to Flight:
> And Lo! the Hunter of the East has caught
> The Sultan's Turret in a Noose of Light.

And after nine years, in 1868, he modified it to:

> Wake! For the Sun behind yon Eastern height
> Has chased the Session of the Stars from Night,
> And, to the field of Heav'n ascending, Strikes
> The Sultan's Turret with a Shaft of Light.

There is no evidence that FitzGerlad was religious or had any affinity towards religion. In fact, it appears that FitzGerald had a cynical view about religion. His older brother, John, was somewhat of a preacher who went from village to village preaching the Gospel. FitzGerald once said, "FitzGerald's are all mad, but John is the maddest of us all." One of the reasons why he moved away to Woodbridge is said to have been in order to distance himself from his brother.

It is, therefore, understandable why FitzGerald ignored one of the most important aspects of Khayyam, his religious side. Not only was FitzGerald frustrated with the religious fanaticism of his preacher brother, but he found the religious quest irrelevant to his condition.

FitzGerald's lack of interest in the many-sidedness of Khayyam is rather peculiar,[17] and while we are indebted to his translation which introduced Khayyam to the literary community, he is also responsible for the misconceptions he created precisely due to the selective nature of his translations. As Brigham recognizes "Great as is the Omar interpreted by FitzGerald, there lay concealed until our own time a greater Omar whose vision of Divine Immanence soared far beyond the mist and clouds in which FitzGerald almost blindly groped."[18]

It is not entirely clear who found whom. Was it Fitzgerald, "the hunter of the East," as Thompson, one of his admirers, called him, who found Khayyam?; or was it Khayyam, whose message made the hunter hunted for the rest of his life? FitzGerald had read many literary figures of both the East and the West and yet did not fall prey to any of them, so why Khayyam?

Perhaps some psychoanalysis is called for here since FitzGerald's condition appears to have been *ready* for Khayyam's message. In order for a message to resonate deeply within the very being of a person, one must have walked in the shoes of the messenger. To begin with, FitzGerald's selection of the *Ruba'iyyat* was not solely for aesthetic purposes, but they echoed something about FitzGerald's lonely and unhappy life. Glyde, one of his biographers, remarked, "A melancholy cast of continence – a mist of despondent sadness hung

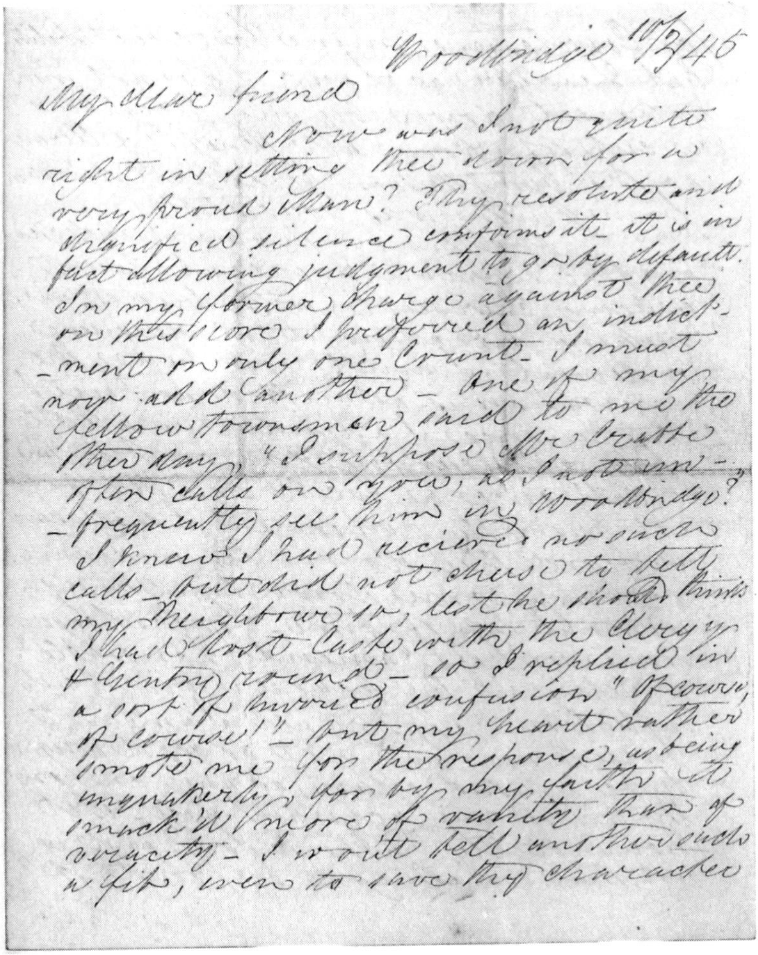

Woodbridge 10/2/46

My dear friend

Now was I not quite right in setting thee down for a very proud Man? Thy resolute and dignified silence confirms it - it is in fact allowing judgment to go by default. In my former charge against thee on this score I preferred an indict-ment on only one Count - I must now add another - One of my fellow townsmen said to me the other day, "I suppose [illegible] often calls on you, as I [illegible] -frequently see him in Woodbridge?" I knew I had received no such calls - but did not chuse to tell my Neighbour so, lest he should think I had lost Caste with the Clergy & Gentry round - so I replied in a sort of hurried confusion "Of course, of course!" - but my heart rather smote me for the response, as being unquakerly, for by my faith it smack'd more of vanity than of veracity - I wou'dn't tell another such a fib, even to save thy character

A sample of Edward FitzGerald's handwriting.

over his face."[19] It was FitzGerald's quest to deal with his profound unhappiness that turned his attention to different projects. At times, as he told his friend Cowell who discovered Khayyam's manuscript, FitzGerald saw himself "most ingeniously tessellated into a sort of Epicurean Eclogue in a Persian garden."[20]

In 1883, FitzGerald went to visit his friend, Crabbe, and it was there that he quietly died in his sleep at the age of 74. He was buried in the courtyard of Boulge by a small chapel where the fragrance of the roses that William Simpson later brought from Nayshābūr permeates FitzGerald's tomb. Swinburne, an eminent man of letters and a friend of FitzGerald, called the *Ruba'iyyat* "that most exquisite English translation, sovereignly faultless in form and color of verse."[21] FitzGerald himself, in a letter that accompanied his quatrains, which he sent to his friend, Gerald, describes the *Ruba'iyyat* as "a desperate sort of thing, unfortunately at the bottom of all thinking man's minds, but made music of."[22]

One may ask whether FitzGerald read into the *Ruba'iyyat* or from them, that is, whether he made Khayyam in his own image or he found in Khayyam the message that suited his own temperament? These two are not mutually exclusive. Clearly, he found in Khayyam something he could relate to, something that kept his attention focused for the rest of his life; the message could not have been detached from his personal and emotional condition. FitzGerald was obviously working with the *Ruba'iyyat* that were available to him at the time, but the fact that he selected some of the available *Ruba'iyyat* for translation and not others alludes to his interest and emotional state of being. The real reason behind his choice of the *Ruba'iyyat* for translation, however, may never be known.

THE IMPACT OF KHAYYAM ON WESTERN LITERARY CIRCLES AND FIGURES

Omar Khayyam and the Pre-Raphaelites

Before any elaboration on Khayyam's relationship with and possible influence upon the Pre-Raphaelites, let me first offer a brief survey of who the Pre-Raphaelites were and their influence upon the literary scene at that time.

In its literary context, the use of the term "Pre-Raphaelite" to refer to a group of people is a relatively new concept, for the term belongs to the history of painting. In September, 1848, three gifted students at Oxford University, William Holman Hunt, John Everett Millais and Dante Gabriel Rossetti, who have been called the

William Michael Rossetti

Dante Gabriel Rosetti

"young rebels," argued that British painting in the post-Raphael period was suffering from stagnation. They believed that the traditional British art of painting needed to gain originality, freshness and free itself from the overarching domination of Raphael; and "thus, they organized the Pre-Raphaelite Brotherhood and to their signature began to add the secret and therefore mysterious initials P.R.B."[23] The Pre-Raphaelite Brotherhood, under the charismatic direction of its founder, Rossetti, soon became a movement; but some of the new members such as Rossetti's own brother, William Michael Rossetti, were interested not just in art but in literature as well. Michael Rossetti described the central tenants of the Pre-Raphaelian Brotherhood as follows:

> That the Pre-Raphaelites valued moral and spiritual ideas as an important section of the ideas germane to fine art is most true, and not one of them was in the least inclined to do any work of a gross, lascivious, or sensual description, but neither did they limit the province of art to the spiritual or the moral ... the bond of union among the Members of the Brotherhood was really and simply this: 1, To have genuine ideas to express; 2, to study Nature attentively,

> so as to know how to express them; 3, to sympathize with what is direct and serious and heartfelt in previous art, to the exclusion of what is conventional and self-parading and learned by rote; and 4, and most indispensable of all, to produce thoroughly good pictures and statues.[24]

In 1857, Alfred Lord Tennyson, a friend of FitzGerald and Rossetti, who was one of the first famous poets to discover and propagate FitzGerald's translation of the *Ruba'iyyat*, was engaged in discussions concerning the application of the salient features of nature, such as leaves of a tree, forms, shapes, colors, wind, water, etc. in poetry. Any cursory reading of the *Ruba'iyyat* or a review of the P.R.B.'s magazine called, *The Gem: Thoughts Towards Nature in Poetry, Literature, and Art*, explains why the Pre-Raphaelite Brotherhood might have become interested in Omar Khayyam.

The 1850s witnessed the demise of the Pre-Raphaelite Brotherhood, as a number of members moved or converted. "The whole Round Table is dissolved," Rossetti told his sister. The Pre-Raphaelite Brotherhood at the time needed a new life and direction, one that at least some of its members found in Omar Khayyam.

One has to be careful not to make an unnecessary connection between Omar Khayyam and the Pre-Raphaelite Brotherhood and not to overemphasize the relationship which, while it was there, requires some degree of speculation. Lange, in his work, *The Pre-Raphaelites and Their Circle*, alludes to this connection:

> The connection of Algernon Charles Swinburne, George Meredith, and Edward FitzGerald with Pre-Raphaelians ranges from advantageous to fictitious. One day, in 1861 a copy of FitzGerald's *Ruba'iyyat* anonymous and still ignored, was given to Rossetti, who immediately recognized its merit and sang its praises.[25]

Lange, a contemporary scholar of the Pre-Raphaelites, went on to include the entire translation of the *Ruba'iyyat* by FitzGerald in his book, *The Pre-Raphaelites and Their Circle*, effectively recognizing them as part of the literature that belongs to the circle. It was during the second flowering of the Pre-Raphaelites under the effective leadership and dominating personality of Dante G. Rossetti,

Algernon Charles Swinburne

John Ruskin

when Rossetti and Swinburne discovered FitzGerald's translation of the *Ruba'iyyat* in 1861. FitzGerald himself by this time had become a notable figure in the literary circles in London. Whereas FitzGerald had nothing to do with the revival of the Pre-Raphaelite Brotherhood, some of the most important members such as Dante G. Rossetti, Tennyson, and Swinburne, among others seemed to have spread the Khayyamian message to the Pre-Raphaelite Brotherhood, for the *Ruba'iyyat* had all the characteristics which defined the very essence of this movement.

Rossetti is described by his brother as "a sentimentalist, a dreamer, a mystic, and an aesthete." Like FitzGerald, he had a gift for poetry and an ill-matched marriage that led to the suicide of his wife. He understood and appreciated the *Ruba'iyyat*, which spoke so elegantly to Rossetti's own condition. "Rossetti thought and felt visually and painted poetically," said Lange, and while the full impact of the *Ruba'iyyat* on the Pre-Raphaelites in general and its founder, Rossetti, in particular, remains to be further studied, there is no doubt that Edward FitzGerald had been regarded as a central figure among the Pre-Raphaelites, and the *Ruba'iyyat* as an exquisite example of the kind of literature that belonged to this literary circle.

William Morris

George Meredith

As FitzGerald's translations were beginning to have an impact in many different literary societies, a more systematic and organized attempt was underway to study and introduce Khayyam's poetry and thoughts. For years, the Royal Asiatic Society with its many branches and affiliated scholars had made the study of the Orient in all its aspects the focal point of its academic endeavor. There were, however, those both within the Society and outside of it, who felt that sufficient attention was not being paid to the more spiritual aspects of the Orient.

In 1887, Sir Richard Burton, known as the "Arabian night man," who was dining at Lord Coleridge's house, commented that, "Oriental societies had too much pedantry."[26] The discussion led to a suggestion by Eben Francis Thompson to Nathan Haskell Dole "that a club be formed of admirers of the astronomer-poet on the basis of good fellowship as well as Oriental learning."[27] What is ironic is that both gentlemen were Classicists and Dole was a Professor of Greek language, but they had become interested in Omar Khayyam for reasons unknown to us. It was the interest of these few that became the basis upon which the Omar Khayyam Club of London was created, a subject to which we now turn.

The Omar Khayyam Club of London

In October of 1893, Moncure D. Conway delivered a lecture in Alderborough entitled, "The Omar Khayyam Cult in England," in which he explained the reason for the formation of the Omar Khayyam Club of London as being the reverence so many have towards the *Ruba'iyyat* and the contribution of Edward FitzGerald. Conway added that "feelings of this kind, mingled with intellectual appreciation led to the formation, last year of the Omar Khayyam Club of London." The Club, therefore, must have been inaugurated in 1892, only five years after Sir Richard Burton had told Lord Coleridge that "Oriental Societies had too much pedantry." The Club began with "a dozen of gentlemen who with almost as many guests, have twice dined together."[28]

The Club seems to have been started by three or four people who initially discussed the idea, namely, Fredrick Hudson, secretary of the Club; Arthur Hacker, an artist who made menu cards; and Mr. Solomon and Mr. Shannon. The Club's exclusive membership was kept to fifty-nine men of letters, and while their activities do not seem to be as well documented as some of the other Omar Khayyam clubs, such as the American and the German clubs which almost simultaneously came about, it appears that the social aspect of this gathering and "good fellowship" had become the salient feature.

Among the central figures of the Club, one can name Justin Huntly McCarthy, the president of the Club, who studied Persian so he could read Khayyam in the original language. He made a few translations of the *Ruba'iyyat* which never gained notoriety. Other prominent figures included George Whale, a lawyer who was the vice-President of the Club; Shorter, editor of the *Illustrated London News*; Edwin Clodd, who was an author and a banker; Frederick Hudson, an attorney and the secretary of the Club and William Simpson, an artist and traveler. It was William Simpson who was part of the British-Afghan Boundary Commission, and when he passed through Nayshābūr, he brought back with him the roses which were planted later at FitzGerald's grave site at Boulge Chapel.

Edmund Gosse, a member of the club who attended the ceremony at Boulge, wrote the following quatrain to describe the scene:

> Reign here, Triumphant Rose from Omar's grave,
> Borne by a dervish o'er the Persian wave;
> Reign with fresh pride, since here a heart
> That double glory to your master gave.[29]

Andrew Lang, another member present at the ceremony of planting roses from Nayshābūr at FitzGerald's grave, read:

> Ah, not from learned Peace and gay content
> Shall we of England go the way *he* went
> The singer of the Red Wine and the Rose
> Nay, otherwise then his our day is spent.[30]

"An Anonymous Member" of the Club, in his article, states that "not one of the original members" whose numbers he puts at "seven or eight, had any knowledge of Persian."[31] There appears to have been a rift in the Club since "A Member," who writes anonymously, tells us that Justin Huntley McCarthy came as a guest, but "an absurd statement got abroad that he was the founder of the Omar Khayyam Club."[32] McCarthy, however, with his thorough knowledge of FitzGerald and with his own translations of Khayyam remained an integral member of the Club.

The Club decided to maintain an exclusive membership. Among the notable members of the Club, one may mention Judge Keene, who undertook a serious study of Persian, and also Edward Clodd and Edmund Gosse, both men of letters. The Club met quarterly for dinner and discussion; but whereas the meeting had a social side to it, a glance at the prestigious list of those attending at one of the early dinners reveals that the Club took its mission seriously. Among new members were J.M. Barrie, Max Pemberton, Anthony Hope Hawkins, Frederick Greenwood, Coulson Kernahan, Andrew Lang, Augustine Birrell, H. Massingham and Stephen Phillips, all of whom were known for their scholarly and literary interests. There were also two well-known journalists, Sir George Newnes and Sir William Ingram, as well as Mr. Asquith, a distinguished lawyer and politician in London, and Henry Norman, who became the president of the Club for one year. The Club had also invited G.W. Cable from America who had arrived the very day of the meeting and gave a lecture about the reception of Khayyam in America.

The discussion went on to include George Macmillan's promise that the next edition of FitzGerald's *Ruba'iyyat* would be dedicated to the Omar Khayyam Club of London; and in praise of Khayyam, Stephen Phillips recited a poem he had composed for the occasion:

> Omar, when it was time for thee to die,
> Thou saidst to those around thee, Let me lie
> Where the North wind may scatter on my grave
> Roses; and now thou hast what thou didst crave,
> Since from the Northern shore the Northern blast
> Roses each year upon thy tomb hath cast.
> Thy more familiar comrades, who have sped
> Many a health to thee, send roses red.
> We are but guests unto the tavern brought,
> And have a flower the paler for that thought;
> Yet is our love so rich that roses white
> Shall fall empurpled on thy tomb to-night.[33]

The Club adopted a design made by Arthur Hacker and by Mrs. Fredrick Hudson. The design is that of an apple tree with fifty-nine apples representing the number of members, five apples to the right for the original members and the rest to the left. Perhaps Theodore Watts, a well-known poet and literary figure, summarized the mission of the club best:

> Although I am compelled to forego the great pleasure of dining with you on Friday," writes Mr. Watts, "I must not miss the opportunity of telling you how entirely I admire, and aspire to be in sympathy with, what I am sure must be the temper of an Omar Khayyam Club. The King of the Wise was, first and foremost, a good fellow, as every line of his poems shows; so was old Fitz, the greatest man, save Nelson, that has been produced even by East Anglia, and I must say that I never came across a genuine, thoroughgoing disciple of the Master who was *not* a good fellow. ...[34]

As the Club matured, its members began to compose *Ruba'iyyat* of their own, which were recited at different Club meetings. An early example of such quatrains is composed by Owen Seaman, a Club member who wrote a long poem entitled "To Omar." A few of his quatrains are as follows:

> Master, in memory of that Verse of Thine
> And of Thy rather pretty taste in Wine
> We gather at this jaded Century's end
> Our Cheeks, if so we may to incarnadine.[35]
>
> Not so with Thee; but in Thy place of Rest
> Where East is East and never can be West,
> Thou art the enduring Theme of dining Bards;
> O make Allowances; They do their Best.[36]

And the chairman of the Club, J.H. McCarthy writes:

> Omar, dear Sultan of the Persian song;
> Familiar friend, whom I have loved so long;
> Whose volume made my pleasant hiding-place
> From his fantastic word of right and wrong.[37]

The list of British Omarian poets is too extensive to include here, but the above clearly demonstrates the depth of Omar Khayyam's presence in England. The Club went on to undertake other noteworthy activities pertaining to Khayyam. In 1897, Edmund Gosse announced that the Omar Khayyam Club of London had sent a letter to Nāṣīr al-Dīn Shāh of Persia stating the need to restore the grave of Omar Khayyam in Nayshābūr, which Simpson had reported to have been in a ruinous condition. Nāṣīr al-Dīn Shāh, not realizing the popularity of Khayyam in the West and also fearing the wrath of the orthodox Muslim clergy, who perceived Khayyam as a heretic, told the Club to take the matter into their own hands and to restore it if they wished. The Shāh responded to the Club's inquiry in 1896 shortly before he was assassinated, and the Club's wish to see a tomb worthy of the master was never materialized.

With the ever-increasing popularity of Omar Khayyam in England, a reaction to this newcomer seems to have been at work.

The meetings of the Club became the object of ridicule, and new translations were perceived as a "fad." A description of the Club's meeting in the magazine *Blackwood's* goes as follows:

> We are told how these respectable men of Letters sit with vine leaves or some other vegetable encircling their scanty locks; we have a vision of them pouring the cheap wine of Italy over the roses of Shirāz; their weak little parodies of the Master's quatrains are passed round an appreciative press, until we are forced to believe that the most coterie which never advertises believes the eye of posterity is upon it. It would all be very droll but for the careless use of FitzGerald's name (sic). A dinner is as good an excuse for advertisement as anything, and logs are easily rolled across a dining table. But why should Edward FitzGerald be thrust into this orgy of Culture? He never belonged to a modest club, he never Sat with vine leaves round his head in the very Presence of an industrious press, and the Omar Khayyam Club may not even plead the recklessness of hot youth for its unwarranted usurpation of an honored name.
>
> This strikes one as a little shrill and deliberate.[38]

Another sarcastic piece about Omar Khayyam appears as a dialogue between a child and an adult published in *The London Academy*:

> Q.—Omar. Who is this Omar, anyhow?
> A.—Omar was a Persian.
> Q.—Yes?
> A.—A philosopher, and a poet, and a tentmaker, and an astronomer.
> Q.—When?
> A.—At about the time that William II. and Henry I. were reigning here.
> Q.—And what did he write?
> A.—He wrote rubaiyat.
> Q.—Ru—?
> A.—Rubaiyat—stanzas. A "rubai" is a stanza.
> Q.—What are they about?
> A.—Oh, love and paganism, and roses and wine.
> Q.—How jolly! But isn't some of it rather steep?
> A.—Well, it's Persian you see.
> Q.—And these Omarians, as members of the Omar Club call

themselves; I suppose they go in for love and paganism, and roses and wine, too?

A.—A little; as much as their wives will let them.

Q.—Wives?

A.—Yes; they're mostly married. You see, Omar serves as an excuse for meeting more than anything else.

Q.—But they know Persian, of course?

A.—No; they use translations.

Q.—Are there many translations?

A.—Heaps. A new one every day.[39]

By 1898, Omar Khayyam had become so famous and his followers so widespread that even the man who first discovered him, Professor Cowell, had become troubled about the cultish attitude of Khayyam's followers. In a letter written on April 3, 1898, from Cambridge to the translator, editor, and scholar of Khayyam, Cowell wrote:

> I yield to no one in my admiration of Omar's poetry as literature, but I cannot join in the 'Omar cult,' and it would be wrong in me to pretend to profess it ... I admire Omar as I admire Lucretius, but I cannot take him as a *guide*. In these grave matters I prefer to go to Nazareth, not to Naishāpūr.[40]

Despite opposition, the work of the Club became a gateway through which many European countries were influenced by the *Ruba'iyyat*, even French and German discoveries of Khayyam were not independent of FitzGerald.

It appears that by the late 1800s, Omar Khayyam had become as famous in America as he was in England. William Simpson of the Omar Khayyam Club of London reports a story about his friend, Hinchcliff, which is quite telling about the popularity of Khayyam in America.

> Hinchcliff was once at sea near Panama, in a formidable storm, when some on board were expressing doubts whether they could weather it. Hinchcliff said: 'He knows about it all – He knows – He knows!' Instantly his hand was seized by an American, named Clarke, who cried, You have been reading Omar Khayyam!' The two men fairly embraced, on account of the ancient Persian, and

remained friends throughout life. Mr. Simpson could not tell me more about this Clarke, nor his first name, but Mr. Quaritch says that from the first, Omar Khayyam has been more widely read in America than in England.[41]

Omar Khayyam in America

The great journey of Omar Khayyam to America began in October of 1869, when Charles Elliott Norton published an article in the *North American Review* where he reviewed FitzGerald's translation. Norton's review was exceedingly positive, and he managed to include with his review 74 of FitzGerald's translations of the *Ruba'iyyat*. It did not take very long for the *Ruba'iyyat* to become popular among certain literary circles in the New England area. W.J. Black argues that America was ready for the Khayyamian message, since the "lofty idealism that precipitated the Civil War had given way to a sordid materialism." Was America ready to hear Khayyam saying,

Ah, take the cash, and let the credit go
Nor heed the rumble of a distant Drum!

With the rise of materialism, especially in the post-war period, a sense of hedonism and moral decay followed. Khayyam's cry for *carpe diem* must have been quite timely.

Ah, my Beloved, fill the Cup that clears
To-Day of past requests and future Fears
To-morrow? – Why, To-morrow I may be
Myself with Yesterday's Sev'n Thousand Years.[42]

The memory of hundreds of thousands of young men who had died in the war was still fresh. How beautiful and timely Khayyam's quatrain must have sounded to the wounded society of America. Facing death, emptiness, and horror calmly, he sees some beauty amidst the transient nature of life and death.

And Those who husbanded the Golden grain,
And Those who flung it to the winds like Rain,
Alike to no such aureate Earth are Turn'd
As, buried once, Men want dug up again.[43]

Finally, there is the secularization of the American society, disappearance of religious certainty, and what Black calls "struggling resentfully against a scientific hypothesis advanced by Darwin."[44] A nation founded by puritans slips into doubt.

> The Moving Finger writes; and, having writ,
> Moves on: nor all your Piety nor Wit
> Shall lure it back to cancel half a Line,
> Nor all your Tears wash out a Word of it.

THE OMAR KHAYYAM CLUB OF AMERICA

The readiness of America for the Khayyamian message, the beauty of FitzGerald's translations and the appreciation of a few who saw how FitzGerald had applied Khayyam's pessimism to the problems of the Nineteenth-Century West, led to a more organized endeavor to understand Khayyam and thus was born the Omar Khayyam Club of America.

The first session of the Club was held on the 91st birthday of Edward FitzGerald at the Young Hotel in Boston on Saturday, March 31, 1900. The meeting, which was called "the Festival of Saint Edward," consisted of a number of exclusive intellectuals each of whom could relate to an aspect of Khayyam's thought. The nine original founders of the Club included Nathan H. Dole; Thompson; Arthur Foote, who was a musician; Arthur Macy, a poet; Alfred C. Potter of Harvard Library; Sylvester Baxter and Ross Turner, both of whom were men of letters; William E. Story, a mathematician; and Colonel Thomas Wentworth Higginson.

The mission of the Club and its charter was agreed upon by the officers to be "An association of men, mostly professional, who believe in good fellowship and who are interested in the Orient in one way or another; and more particularly in that 'King of the Wise,' the astronomer, philosopher, and poet, Omar Khayyam."[45]

Following the election of the officers,[46] the Club members met several times including a major session in 1901, but the real work of the Club took place on the side. Members and their friends began to collect new versions of the *Ruba'iyyat* and amateur translations of them began to take place. Members composed poems following the style of the *Ruba'iyyat*, such as Stephan C. Houghton, whose philosophical poems *In the Path of the Persians* gained some recognition and Charles Hardy Meigs, who composed a work of miniatures capturing the spirit of the *Ruba'iyyat*. Meanwhile, through the membership of some of the non-native English speakers, Khayyam's writing began to be translated into different languages. A case in point is Carlos M. Uzzio Säenz-Pena from Argentina, who became affiliated with the Club while he was a student in Boston. Upon his return home he translated the *Ruba'iyyat* for the first time into Spanish.

By 1908, the Club had over fifty officers, most of whom were prominent literary figures and academics who were publishing and propagating the ideas of Omar Khayyam, both through various translations and also through writing odes honoring Khayyam. The work of the Omar Khayyam Club of America soon went beyond Khayyam's poetry, and attention was paid to the more scientific aspects of his thought. Perhaps one of the earliest examples of this was a major lecture by William Edward Story, a member of the Club and a professor of mathematics at Clarke University. On April 6, 1918, he delivered a paper titled, "Omar as a Mathematician." This lecture is not only significant because it elaborates upon various aspects of Khayyam's mathematical ideas but also because Story compares Khayyam's views with figures such as Kepler, Cavalier, Leibniz, and Newton. Story was so impressed by Khayyam's mathematical genius that he remarks, "All things considered, I'm inclined to think that Omar Khayyam was the most original and therefore the greatest of the Sarccheri Mathematicians."[47]

By 1919, the Omar Khayyam Club of America had made major contributions to the field of Khayyamian studies through introducing and translating the *Ruba'iyyat* and some of Khayyam's other works. The achievements of the Club are here described by its president: "The Club has as it were, stood over his monumental translation of the whole of Omar Khayyam's quatrains – a formidable volume, very much more extended, of course, than FitzGerald's very free version and very different."[48]

عمر خیام
OMAR KHAYYAM CLUB
DINNER.
MARCH 25th 1897.
EDMUND GOSSE
PRESIDENT.
MENU
Awake! for Morning
in the Bowl of Night
Hath flung the Stone
and put the Stars to flight
And Lo! the Hunter
of the East has caught
The Sultan's Turret in
a Noose of Light

THE OMARIANS OF NEW ENGLAND

With the Club having established itself as the center for literary figures concerned with Omar Khayyam, its members and affiliates began to create a literary school calling themselves "Omarians." Omarians had this to say about Khayyam and themselves: "Omar Khayyam, Persian philosopher and poet, established a cult immortally cherished by the choice souls of successive generations. Omarians are generally gentle, always genial, and when opportunity offers, joyfully congenial."[49]

Throughout the country, the Omarian literary movement soon found many contributors who were directly or indirectly influenced by Khayyam. Among the more notable members of the movement who made literary contributions of their own in the Khayyamian tradition, we can name Lawrence C. Woodworth who sent an edition of Tennyson's poems to FitzGerald; Colonel Higginson who composed poems praising "Omarians past and present;" and Nathan Dold who composed poems including the following in praise of Khayyam:

> Hail to you Omar, friendliest of the sages
> Your message cheers us, ringing through the ages.[50]

An unknown poet belonging to the Omarian literary circle, read the following poem at one of the meetings of the Club:

> On his high throne a cardinal sat,
> Cogitating on this and on that;
> "Omarkh," quoth he,
> "Has nothing on me
> For I have my own Rubyhat[51]
> Not FitzGerald nor Thompson," he said
> "Nor Dole, Whinfield nor Roe are ahead;
> As surely as they
> I am truly O.K.
> For my Rubyhat is much red!"[52]

A member of the Club, Henry Harmon Chamberlin, also from the Omarian literary circle at Worcester, inspired by Khayyam's

Twentieth Anniversary
OMAR KHAYYAM CLUB
of AMERICA
APRIL 3, 1920

emphasis on temporality and death, composed a poem called "The Price." Mourning the death of love among what he calls "The Brotherhood of Man," especially at the time of war, he read the following poem at the March 31, 1917 meeting of the Omar Khayyam Club of America:

> Brother of Death, Sin's crowned and armed birth
> How long shall this new Anarch reign on earth,
> Unsmitten of thy thunderbolt, O Lord?

The following year, Chamberlin, who was deeply touched by the horrors of World War I, read a number of *Ruba'iyyat* that are among the best examples of the impact of Khayyam on literary circles in the West. He writes:

> CHAMPAGNE SONG OR THE WINE OF VICTORY
> (Read at the annual dinner, 1918, of the Omar Khayyam Club of America)
>
> Still wine hath an intimate fire
> That gratefully tickles each vein;
> But the springtime of youth and desire
> Bubbles up in the wine of champagne.
>
> Chorus:
> Bubbles up in the glass of champagne, my boys,
> Bubbles up in the sparkling champagne, my boys,
> Bubbles high in the golden champagne, my boys,
> The sparkling, golden champagne.
>
> With shot and with shell and the terrors of Hell,
> The Germans swept over the Aisne,
> But the spirit of France broke their onward advance,
> And dashed all their hopes in Champagne.
>
> Chorus:
> Then here's the Poilus of Champagne, my boys,
> Who scattered the Boche in Champagne, my boys,
> From the Marne and the Aisne to Champagne, my boys,
> When red grew the grapes of Champagne.

They gave up their lives for their children and wives,
But they shed not their lifeblood in vain,
For the world they made free over land, over sea,
By the battles they fought in Champagne.

Chorus:
Then here's the Poilus of Champagne, my boys,
Who laid down their lives in Champagne, my boys,
To the living and dead in Champagne, my boys,
Let's drink to them all in champagne.

For the loved ones that mourn, they no more may return,
A tear for each bumper we drain;
But we at the height of this festival night,
Let our hearts be as light as champagne.

Chorus:
Then here's to the merry champagne, my boys,
And here's to the gallant champagne, my boys,
And the glory of France in Champagne, my boys,
The glorious, victorious champagne.

HENRY HARMON CHAMBERLIN

The work of another Omarian poet, William Bacon Scofield of Worcester, who writes a poem about Abraham Lincoln but does so under the influence of this literary circle, is another example of the Omarian poetry. His poem, read at the meeting of April 15, 1919, is as follows:

Somehow I think that in the near Beyond
He sits and broods O'er all this human strife
And that new furrows line his kindly face,
Full sad enough from his own weary life
While the great heart, that throbbed for others' care
Still thrills in pity for us, even there.

By 1921, the work of the Club had stimulated much interest in Khayyam, and his thought had become popular in places not known for having much interest in the Orient. An example is the letter that

Johnson Brigham, the State Librarian from Iowa, wrote upon his discovery of a copy of the book published by the Omar Khayyam Club of America.

IOWA STATE LIBRARY

Des Moines, Iowa,
May 24, 1921.

Mr. Charles Dana Burrage,
85 Ames Building,
Boston, Mass.

Dear Mr. Burrage,

Please accept and convey to the Omar Khayyam Club of America and the Rosemary Press my thanks for the beautiful volume kindly sent our State Library, entitled "Twenty Years of the Omar Khayyam Club of America."

Its interesting reading matter, combined with the perfect printing and exquisite binding, fill me with delight. I took it home with me last evening, and under its inspiration wrote a quatrain, a copy of which I enclose. I am sending a copy to the Atlantic. Though it may not be up to grade as to poetry, I am sure you will appreciate the spirit which prompted it.

Yours very truly,
(signed) JOHNSON BRIGHAM,
State Librarian.

What is interesting and distinguishing about Brigham is that he appears to have been a devout Christian and to have seen Khayyam, not in his Victorian dress, but as a mystic and a religious man. In a lecture he delivered on August 20, 1924, before the Prairie Club of Des Moines, Iowa, he said:

Omar Khayyam's nature was profoundly religious and as a pagan preacher of "righteousness, moderation, and judgment to come," he has a message to millions of our western world who profess and call themselves Christian and yet do not take their profession seriously.[53]

Having been deeply affected by the Omarian tradition of poetry, Brigham composed several quatrains of his own. One such poem called "Facing the East" begins with the subtitle " *The Rose Garden of Omar Khayyam* " and reads:

> Though far removed in spirit, time and space
> From the Rose Garden of my early dreams,
> The westering wind of summer evening seems
> To press the scent of roses 'gainst my face.

The other example of the impact of Omar Khayyam on Western literature is the poetry of George C. Stratton of Washington D.C. whose *Ruba'iyyat* closely follows Khayyam's style and content:

> When, on that Summer day at Twin Oaks, you
> First brought th' immortal Omar to my view
> I gave the deathless quatrains scarce a thought—
> Ah, 'twas but very little then I knew!
>
> But as, from time to time, I read them o'er
> Their beauty grew upon me more and more.
> And now I hope that I may be enrolled
> With the Elect who've entered in the Door.
>
> 'Tis pleasant, then, to place upon the Shelf
> With all my Omars, prized above mere pelf,
> This handsome Book of those who love the Poet;
> Which shows so much also of your own Self.[54]

Strangely enough, another poet by the name of Charles Haywood Stratton, whose relationship to the previous poet is unknown but clearly belongs to the same Omarian tradition, composed a long poem on Omar Khayyam only five days after George C. Stratton (May 27, 1921). Responding to a verse that appears in the volume entitled *Twenty Years of Omar Khayyam Club of America*, he states;

> Reserve your censure; do not criticize
> This book; 'Twas only meant for friendly eyes

Charles Haywood Stratton, in his long poem entitled "To the editor," continues

To the Editor,
Twenty Years of the Omar Khayyhm Club of America:

You ask the reader not to criticize
The Book you only meant for friendly eyes.
Ingrate, indeed, must be the one who'd brook
Aught but the kindliest words upon your Book!
But may not criticism be in friendly view?
And serve to call your inspiration forth again?
Wise Omar said it well for all to read –
'Tis Fellowship that lets our Life proceed.
Your happy Book now adds another link
To his strong chain of evidence, I think.
And since 'tis Friendship makes our life worth while,
The chronicle of Friendship's tear, or smile,
For future man to keep and read again,
Is worthy subject for your worthy pen.
'Tis plain you generous are, as well as wise,
And know the objects that all men most prize
Are those in which themselves with toil have wrought
The precious product of their own hard thought,
So you have kept a store of pages white,
'Whereon each one of us may paste, or write, –
Mayhap of interest to himself alone –
The things that really make the Book his own,
So now, though I have dared to criticize
You see 'tis but the view of friendly eyes.
CHARLES HAYWOOD STRATTON.
Washington, D.C., May 27, 1921. [55]

The list of Omarians who traveled far to attend the meetings of the Club or simply composed poems and, in so many cases, prose in the spirit of Khayyamian thought is too extensive to be included here, but a few more examples should be sufficient to show the breadth and depth of this tradition in America. William B. Scofield, an Omarian, composed and dedicated the following prose to Charles D. Burrage, the founder of the Club. The text, one of the three he read, addresses Khayyam's regret for seeing his friends vanish in the wheel of life and death. He read it at the Omar Khayyam Club of America on April 2, 1921.

> He is often happy whose one thought is for friends. He shall know full days of willing sacrifice; and yet his friends may turn from his sweet ministry and then how shall he, rejected, face the coming days?[56]

George Rowe from San Antonio, Texas, also composed some quatrains, but formed his own style consisting of five and six stanzas.

> Sad, severed from the sea, a raindrop sighed,
> And, smiling gently, thus the sea replied,
> "*A part* of God are we, but we seem *apart*
> When Alif, moving, doth our union hide.

Finally, Stephan Magister composed a long poem consisting of several pages called "A Sage's Console." Each section varied in length and discussed social and political injustices of his time. A full analysis of his poems is beyond the scope of this work, but a quatrain with which he began the chapter is as follows:

> Maintain thy stature in men's eyes. If driven,
> On Fortune's breakers hope not to be shriven.
> Crimes, vices, follies, these may be condoned;
> Misfortune only may not be forgiven.

As the result of the international alliance of Orientalists, Khayyam's *Ruba'iyyat* and his other works were destined to be spread throughout America and Europe. Several major international Orientalist societies decided to hold annual meetings so the latest research on various aspects of the Orient could be shared among major European powers and America. The purpose of these meetings was not always to share the wisdom of the East, but as Edward Said wrote in his work, *Culture and Imperialism*, "Knowledge and exploitation were thereafter tied to the discourse (and acquisition) of empire."[57] It is for no other reason than the colonization of the Orient that, around 1870 and thereafter, we see a rise of geographical societies as well as many other disciplines culminating at the

International Colonial Congress (1889 and 1894) or specific groups such as the International Congress of Colonial Sociology in 1890.

To share the knowledge of the Orient, the American Academy of Arts, the American Oriental Society, Société Asiatique and the Royal Asiatic Society began a series of meetings, the first one being held in London in 1919, the second in 1920 and the third in 1921 in Boston, where the Omar Khayyam Club of America played an active role.

Even though the spirit of such conferences was primarily political, on the fringes of these meetings, literary and philosophical ideas were exchanged, and in all likelihood, the aspirations of the Omarian literary circle were transmitted through such meetings. Whereas what exactly transpired among various Orientalists at these meetings concerning Omar Khayyam is not known, by virtue of the active participation of the members of the Omar Khayyam Clubs of America and London we can conclude that Omar Khayyam was discussed in detail at some level. We know, for example, that Professor Lanman of Harvard, who was an active member of the Club and a member of the Académie des Inscriptions et Belles-Letters of the Institut de France, attended many of these meetings. On June 24, 1921, a meeting of Class III of the Academy was devoted entirely to philosophy, theology, and literature of the Orient; and we know that a number of the members of the Omar Khayyam Club of America as well as European scholars participated in this session.[58]

In subsequent meetings of the French Society in 1922 and then the British Society in 1923, we see the continued presence of members of the Omar Khayyam Club of America. Such notable figures as Charles D. Burrage, founder of the Club, and Arthur E. Cowley of Oxford, the head of the Bodleian Library, where the story of Khayyam in the West began, were among the active participants.

And now, thanks to the hard work of a few, so many throughout the world have come to know of one of the jewels of Persia. It is as a token of our appreciation and a debt of gratitude, as well as a demonstration of how widespread followers of Omar Khayyam were in America, that a brief mention of some of the members of the

Club is included here. The list, as it appears in the *Omar Khayyam Club of America* under the title "A Toast to the Dead," is as follows:

Members of the Omar Khayyam Club of America

A TOAST TO THE DEAD

April 2, 1921

To our members who have passed beyond the veil that hides the Infinite, and solved the last great mystery of Life.

Edward H. Clement
Gracious man of letters, ready writer, for many years Editor of the Transcript, a genial companion, lover of good books, a keen appreciator of the genius of Edward FitzGerald.

Edward Livingston Davis
A representative citizen of Worcester, ardently and sympathetically interested in literature and the Fine Arts.

Richard Henry Winslow Dwight
A patriotic American, and a profound student of history.

Frank Palmer Goulding
Charter member of this Club, great lawyer, a leader at the Worcester and Massachusetts Bars, a most generous and knightly gentleman, a devoted friend to the poor and oppressed, brilliant orator and advocate, a delightful and polished writer, untimely taken from us, mourned without ceasing.

Edward Palmer Hatch
Clean-souled, brave and loyal, a friend to all, generous, loving, greatly loved, one of Nature's noblemen.

Col. Thomas Wentworth Higginson
An heroic National figure, commander of a colored regiment in the Civil War, an eloquent and persuasive Unitarian Minister, and apostle of liberty, a famous essay writer and nature lover, student, scholar and powerful moral preacher, friend and co-equal of FitzGerald, Norton, Holmes, Longfellow, Lowell, Thoreau, Sanborn, Whittier, Dana, Margaret Fuller, one of the pillars of our Club whose meetings he never missed.

John E. Hudson
Genial, book loving, well-read, a Prince among business men, a great corporation lawyer-manager.

Andrew Lang
Non-resident member of London, famous English poet, author and critic, admirer of Omar, friend of FitzGerald, known and loved by all the world.

Charles F. Libby
Great lawyer, leader of the Main Bar, President of the American Bar Association, lover of books, a faithful attendant to our meetings for many years, a tried and true friend.

Arthur Macy
Charter member, loved and loving, a rare and radiant soul, a wise and faithful follower of old Omar, a graceful poet and brilliant author.

Charles Hardy Meigs
Non-resident member of Columbus, Ohio, who with infinite skill and pains produced the Miniature Omar now so treasured.

J. Russel Marble
Merchant Prince, high minded citizen, a practical and generous man of affairs.

Prof. M. H. Morgan of Harvard
Keen, incisive, with a great passion for learning, most companionable of men, a lover of Omar.

Bernard Alfred Quaritch
Non-resident member of London, whom we of this Club delighted always to meet as man, bon vivant and scholar, a brave and loyal friend, world figure in the book marts and exchanges, a great book genius, a worthy son of a great father, who was FitzGerald's publisher and friend.

William F. Bitssell
A quiet old-fashioned English gentleman, who easily won our hearts, a man of the world, versed in the ancient and mystic lore of Clubs and in the manners and customs of the Orient, a valued member.

Prof. H. Morse Stephens
Of the University of California, a great teacher and author, loved as few teachers are, a power for good on the Western shore.

Ross Turner
Charter member, Vice-President of this Club for fifteen years, great painter and artist, ardent and enthusiastic flower and book lover, gentle, refined and true, whose illuminated Omar ranks as among the most beautiful of all.

In enduring memory of these friends and comrades we annually, with humble and contrite hearts, in solemn appreciation of the glorious beauties of their lives, speak the seven hundred-year-old lament of Omar in FitzGerald's magnificent rendering,

> "For some we loved, the loveliest and the best
> That from his Vintage rolling Time hath prest,
> Have drunk their Cup a Round or two before,
> And one by one crept silently to rest."

CHARLES DANA BURRAGE.

Between 1906 and 1921, the Omar Khayyam Club of America published eighteen works,[59] most of which dealt with the *Ruba'iyyat*. Whereas it appears that the Club continued its work for a few more years, the death of its key members, contributors and patrons brought the demise of the Club, which withered away to obscurity and oblivion. The other reason for the decline of the Club may have been that it achieved its purpose, which was to introduce Omar Khayyam to Americans. This task was fully achieved by the 1930s, since Khayyam and his *Ruba'iyyat* had become household names in America and had left an indelible mark upon the spiritual landscape of the American Society.

Let us now turn to notable American literary figures and examine the extent of their intellectual investment in Khayyam and his *Ruba'iyyat*.

MARK TWAIN AND THE *RUBA'IYYAT*

Given Mark Twain's sense of humor, sarcasm and skepticism concerning free will and determinism as well the great personal

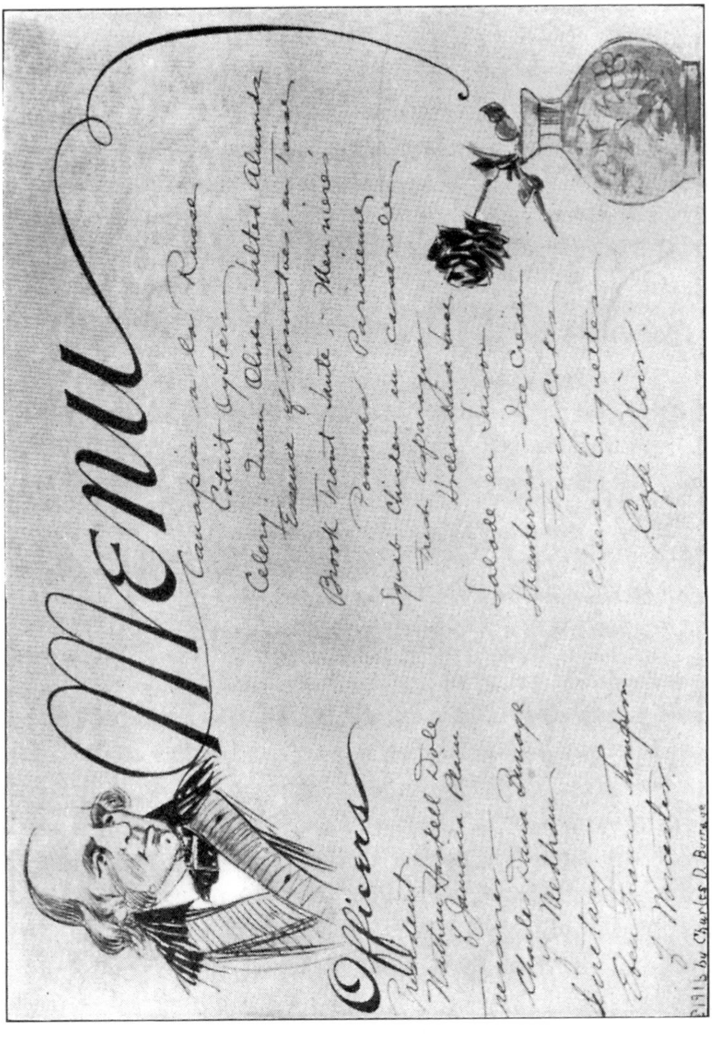

Reverse side of the Ellis menus

tragedies which he suffered, it is not surprising that he found in Khayyam what FitzGerald had found earlier – a familiar voice of discontent and a refusal to give into the urge to make sense of it all. Reverend Conway, in a lecture he once delivered, said:

> I remember once conversing on the subject with Mark Twain – a humorous man and a man of great power as well – and he startled me, as I had not associated him with such poetic ideas. By saying that he regarded one quatrain of Omar Khayyam's – the famous and the bold one beginning: 'O thou, who man of baser Earth did make' – as containing the most far-reaching and grand thought ever expressed in so short a space in so few words.[60]

Mark Twain himself, who was familiar with English poetry and quoted from the works of Tennyson, often expressed his utmost reverence for the *Ruba'iyyat*. It is with regard to the following quatrain that he says, "No poem had given me so much pleasure before," and in 1907 he added, "it is the only poem I have ever carried about with me; it has not been from under my hand for 28 years."[61]

> Oh Thou, who Man of baser Earth didst make
> And ev'n with Paradise devise the snake
> For all the sun where with the Face of Man
> Is blacken'd – Man's forgiveness give – and take![62]

Mark Twain's interest in poetry, though marginal compared to his prose, is a neglected area of scholarship. It is said that he had composed 120 poems from which Arthur L. Scott collected 65 of the less "embarrassing ones" and published them in *On the Poetry of Mark Twain with Selections from His Verse*. Mark Twain's poetry deals with the same themes that he discusses in his prose, and his sense of humor also comes through. Mark Twain came to know of the *Ruba'iyyat* and FitzGerald's translation sometime around the 1870s through Reverend Joseph H. Twichell, who drew his attention to several *Ruba'iyyat* in the *Hartford Courant*. In a letter to his friend, William Dean Howells, on November 26, 1876, Mark Twain stated, "It is no harm to put these words into wise Omar Khayyam's mouth, for he would have said them if he thought of it."[63]

Mark Twain developed an intense interest in the *Ruba'iyyat* and began to collect various copies of them. On May 19, 1884, he acquired the Osgood edition and on April 10, 1899, he ordered a half-crown copy of the *Ruba'iyyat* from Chatto Windus of London and a copy in 1900 from Philadelphia. It was in October of 1898 that, under the influence of FitzGerald's translation, and having suffered numerous personal tragedies, Mark Twain began to write the *Ruba'iyyat* of his own. Since several members of his family had died from various illnesses, these *Ruba'iyyat* inevitably grapple with age, disease, and the gradual decaying of the human body. He composed 45 quatrains and integrated them with two of FitzGerald's stanzas entitled *AGE-A Rubaiyat*.[64]

Mark Twain's *Ruba'iyyat* were a burlesque version of FitzGerald's; as Gribben says in his work, *The Mark Twain's Rubaiyat*, "Mark Twain mimicked the prosody of what is called the Omar Khayyam quatrain ... and tried to duplicate these features."[65] "How then Is Old Age better than the threatened Hell?"[66] becomes a theme that Twain embraces both in a prose format such as in "the five books of life" and in the poetic form. Twain plays with Khayyam and attributes sayings to him sarcastically. For example, such as some people are "able to govern kingdoms and empires but few there be that can keep a hotel."[67]

By October of 1898, the devastating effect of his daughter Susie's death had subsided, and his much-improved financial situation brought Mark Twain some degree of calm. But the question of old age and decay remained an insoluble problem for him. It is at this juncture that Mark Twain wrote, *AGE-A Rubaiyat,* a work that walks a fine line between satire and serious reflection on the cruelty of life. Gribben suggests that Mark Twain "could not decide whether he wanted to write a winking, mocking satire on revered old age, or a savage assault on the universal injustices of man's transient existence and unwelcomed fate."[68]

Gribben and MacDonnell, in their *Mark Twain's Rubaiyat*, have argued that *AGE-A Ruba'iyat* has several recurring phrases. First, there is the temporality of life and pleasures therein. Then one finds advice concerning acceptance of old age and how to come to terms

Individual club menus, 1916. Designed and presented by Albert W. Ellis.

with it. Mark Twain's lifetime had coincided with the discovery that our bodies consist of germs and bacteria, and this preoccupied him for some time. How our bodies are germ-ridden becomes a theme in Twain's *Rubaiyat*. The effects of old age and disease are the next recurring theme; for Twain the horror of old age replaces "the Honor of Old Age." Perhaps it is an attempt to retain our dignity against the insult of old age or to give into the alluring temptation of wanting to make sense of humiliation inflicted on us by the merciless forces of nature that prompts us to rely on the honor of old age.

Next comes death, or what Gribben, the illustrious biographer of Mark Twain, calls "the deepest, the darkest pit in this chamber of horrors, adumbrating the gloomy line of thought."[69] The horror of death ironically becomes praise of death, for it is death that ends it all. In December 1905, in an essay entitled "Old Age,"[70] Mark Twain visits this theme and states, "Yes, it is disappointing ... you say 'is this it? – this?' "

Mark Twain then turns to the theme of sex and hedonism, and to what he calls "the long past orgies" as images of sexual pleasure. His references to his various sexual experiences and utter frustration for his inability to enjoy sex in old age may have been why, in a letter to his friend Andrew Chatto, he refers to his *Rubaiyat* as "Omar's Old Age" and instructs him to "burn them at once." In this letter, Mark Twain states:

> Confound it, this seems to be the right time to privately publish my *"Omar's Old Age,"* written two or three months ago, but I've written only about 50 quatrains and am not ready. Besides, I am playing a game—no, thinking of it. An American friend said, "Try a new thing. Make a rare book for collectors—limited edition: 500 copies at $50 a copy, or 30 copies at $1,000 a copy; if the latter I will buy one copy and place 5 for you."
>
> Come—is it a wild and vicious scheme?
>
> Samples enclosed. Read them, then *burn* them at once; don't let any see them or hear about them.
>
> In writing me, don't use a title, but speak of the work as "ABC."
>
> Ys sincerely,
> SLC[71]

After Mark Twain's death, Albert Bigelow Paine had come to possess many of his manuscripts, poems, and memorabilia. Paine decided not to include Mark Twain's *Rubaiyat* in the official biography of his life, *Mark Twain: A Biography*, published in 1912; and thus few came to know of his *Rubaiyat*. Paine remarked,

> Mark Twain was not a good versifier – the demands of rhyme and meter were too much for him, as a rule though at times he seemed to overcome his difficulties. These quatrains offer a fair example both of his successes and his failures. Some of the stanzas are not for delicate readers. These of course were not intended for print.[72]

Gribben, who estimates the composition date of the *AGE-A Rubaiyat* to have been around the autumn of 1898, considers Mark Twain's *Rubaiyat* to be the work of his "brooding late phase" and adds that "the poem affords glimpses of the plunging depth of his emotional states that otherwise would never be documented ... Mark Twain may have meant *AGE-A Rubaiyat* to constitute his angry *In Memoriam*."[73]

The poetic license which allowed Khayyam and FitzGerald to express man's deepest existential discontent against a fundamentally cruel and unjust world also provided Mark Twain with the same relief. Inclusion of Twain's 45 *Rubaiyat* is beyond the scope of this work but in what follows, several examples of his *Rubaiyat* indicate his deep emotional and intellectual investment in Omar Khayyam. The following two quatrains express his frustration and outrage with the age:

34

And those who husbanded their golden Youth,
And those who flung it to the Winds, forsooth
  Must all alike succumb to Age
And know the nip of his remorseless Tooth.

39

Next, Deafness comes, and men must Shout
Into a foolish Trumpet, leaving out
The Gist of what they want to say—and still
O'er what they *have* said hangs a crippling Doubt.

And the following *Rubaiyat* indicate how Mark Twain played with FitzGerald's translations and made a burlesque version of them:

MARK TWAIN	FITZGERALD
1	1
Sleep! For the Sun scores another Day Against the Tale allotted You to stay, Reminding You, is Risen, and now Serves Notice – ah, ignore it while You may!	Wake! For the Sun, who scatter'd into flight The Stars before him from the Field of Night, Drives Night along with them from Heav'n, and strikes The Sultán's Turret with a Shaft of Light.
2	3
The chill Wind blew, and those who stood before The Tavern murmured, "Having drunk his Score, Why tarries He with empty Cup? Behold, The Wind of Youth once poured, is poured no more.	And, as the Cock crew, those who stood before The Tavern shouted – "Open then the Door! "You know how little while we have to stay, "And, once departed, may return no more.
3	7
"Come, leave the Cup, and on the Winter's Snow Your Summer Garment of Enjoyment throw: Your Tide of life is ebbing fast, and it Exhausted once, for You no more shall flow."	Come, fill the Cup, and in the fire of Spring Your Winter-garment of Repentence fling: The Bird of Time has but a little way To flutter – and the Bird is on the Wing."
27	32
There was the door whereof I had The Key, The Landlord too, who double seemed to me – Some heated Talk there was – and then, ah then But Rags and Fragments were we – Me and He.	There was the Door to which I found no Key; There was the Veil through which I might not see: Some little talk of ME and THEE There was – and then no more of THEE and ME.

The Eliots

Love and admiration for the *Ruba'iyyat* of Omar Khayyam seemed to have run deep in the Eliot family beginning with T.S. Eliot's grandfather, William Greenleaf Eliot (1811–1887) and then his cousin, Charles Eliot Norton – who introduced the *Ruba'iyyat* in a review article – the other cousin, Charles William Eliot, and finally T.S. Eliot himself. After his retirement from being a Unitarian minister, William G. Eliot became the chancellor of Washington University

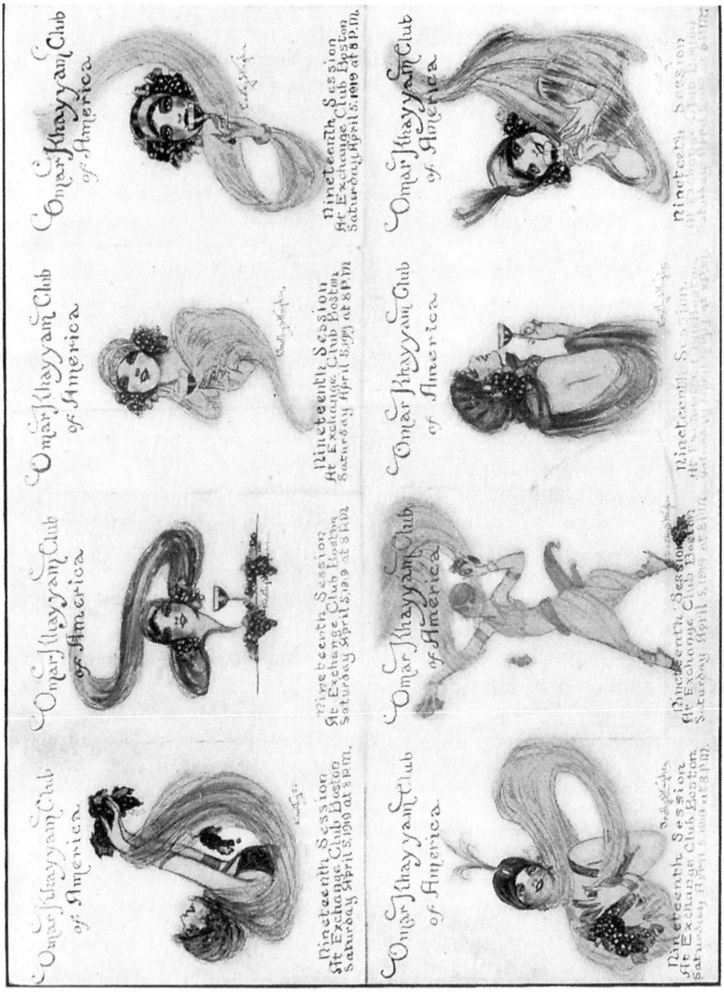

Individual club menus, 1919. Designed and painted by Dorothy S. Hughes.

and a civic leader. While William G. Eliot's moral stance on the *Ruba'iyyat* clearly fell in line with the spirit of Puritanism, he must have been keenly interested in them. In 1879, Rev. S.J. Barrow wrote an essay entitled, "Omar Khayyam," published in the *Unitarian Review* in which he sarcastically refers to William G. Elliot. He remarks, "A ministerial friend of ours had already read the *Ruba'iyyat* sixty times."[74]

William G. Eliot's relationship with the *Ruba'iyyat* was somewhere between his admiration for a rational theology and his awareness of and concern with the rise of skepticism and moral decay in America and Omar Khayyam's possible contribution in this regard.

Charles Eliot Norton, who was a pioneer in introducing Khayyam to the American audience, was a relative of T.S. Eliot and an Emeritus Professor at Harvard. It was he who wrote a review of the *Ruba'iyyat* in 1869 but, ironically, did not know FitzGerald was the translator since the latter, as was discussed earlier, published his translation anonymously. It was in England in 1868 that Norton met Burne-Jones, a literary figure who was ecstatic to have discovered the *Ruba'iyyat* and gave a copy of them to Norton who brought them back to America.

Norton, who saw unity of thought in the *Ruba'iyyat,* not only viewed Khayyam as a materialist but described his character as "moral," "shrewd," "inquisitive and independent," "penetrating imagination," and "a manly independence."[75] Norton's review sparked much interest in the *Ruba'iyyat* in America. Surprised by the reception, he said it was just "a little craze" for the book.[76]

The other cousin, Charles William Eliot, president of Harvard University, was asked in 1890 to lead a committee of 50 people to investigate the activities of the Demons Association with whom Khayyam was being identified. His conclusion was that the affiliation was "half baked."

The impact and influence of Omar Khayyam and his *Ruba'iyyat* on T.S. Eliot, a giant among American-British literary figures, was even more profound than it had been on Mark Twain. It would be fair to state that perhaps Omar's spirit of discontent was more admired by Eliot than the message of the *Ruba'iyyat.*

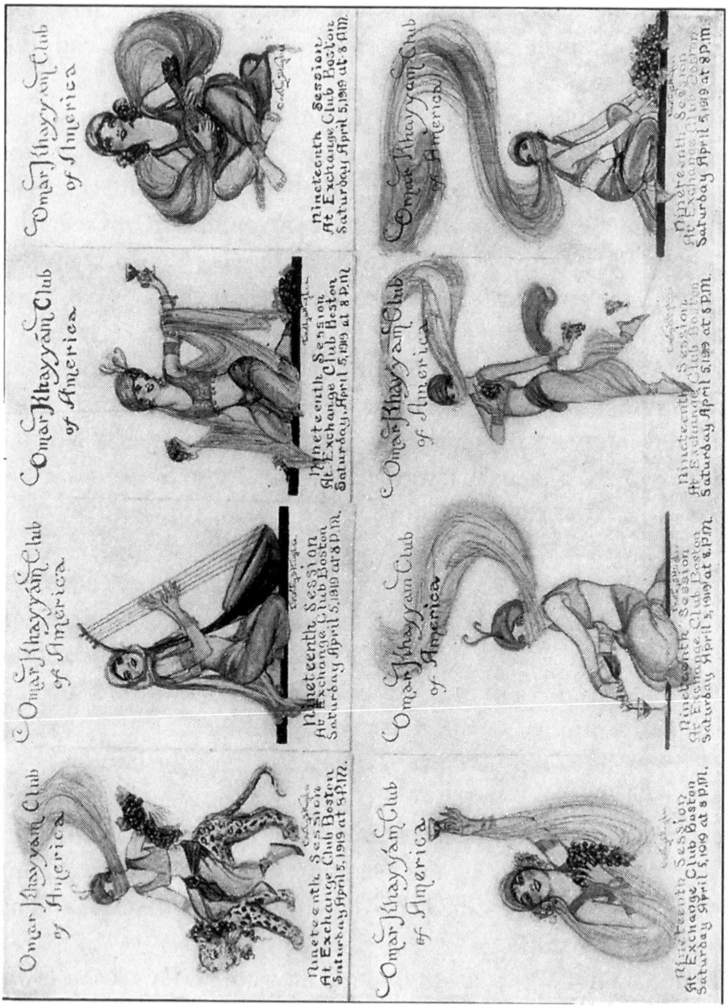

Individual club menus, 1919. Designed and painted by Dorothy S. Hughes.

Eliot was the son of the St. Lewis's founding Unitarian minister. The young Eliot, at the age of fourteen, read the *Ruba'iyyat*. The effect was so profound that, as Eliot indicated, he became a poet instantly for the rest of his life:

> I can recall clearly enough the moment when, at the age of fourteen or so, I happened to pick up a copy of FitzGerald's *Omar* which was lying about, and the almost overwhelming introduction to a new world of feeling which this poem was the occasion of giving me. It was like a sudden conversion; the world appeared anew, painted with bright, delicious and painful colours ...[77]

V.M. D'Ambrosio in her work, *Eliot Possessed: T. S. Eliot and FitzGerald's RUBAIYAT*,[78] elaborates on Eliot's spirit of rebelliousness based on those quatrains of Khayyam that Eliot quotes and the spirit that he includes in some of his works such as *Animula*. Eliot remarks:

> The heavy burden of the growing soul
> Perplexes and offends more, day by day;
> Week by week, offends and perplexes more
> With the imperatives of 'is and seems'
> And may and may not, desire and control.
> The pain of living and the drug of dreams
> Curl up the small soul in the window seat
> Behind the *Encyclopœdia Britannica*.[79]

Eliot's relationship with Khayyam and his *Ruba'iyyat* was far too complex and profound to merely imitate him and compose quatrains that copy the style of the *Ruba'iyyat*. Eliot went on to incorporate the "message" into his poetry and other writings. Eliot, who refers to his encounter with the *Ruba'iyyat* as having been "absorbed," a feeling that brings in his soul a "crisis," appears in *Animula* where a youth hides his feeling of love and absorption from his family because, like Khayyam, he too respected reason. Eliot admires Khayyam and he was also faced with the same choice, the sobriety of reason identified as self-control and the drunkenness of wine associated with "drug," a vehicle of freedom and forgetfulness from the world.

Some individual painted menus, Worcester, June 5, 1920. Presented by Henry Harmon Chamberlin.

Eben Francis Thompson. President of the Omar Khayyam Club of America.

The late Ross Turner. Vice-President of the Omar Khayyam Club of America 1900–1915.

Whatever the source of Eliot's pain and anguish, like Khayyam he takes refuge in many things. For Khayyam it was love, the beloved, and wine, while for Eliot, the *Encyclopedia Britannica.* Omar Khayyam and T.S. Eliot shared a common spirit, that of dismay and discontent for authority and control.

Eliot goes so far as to defend Khayyam against some of the critics such as Charles Whibley, who had become alarmed by Omar's popularity and exclaimed, "We had pictured to ourselves the honest citizen returning from his toil with a legful of masterpieces and discussing with his family circle, Stevensonianism, Omarianism, and other strange cults."[80] To the above, Eliot responded, "Whibley ... whether he was opposing the act of a government ... or the Omar Khayyam Club, he modulated his thunders according to the tree, shrub, or weed to be blasted."[81]

Eliot not only uses themes and concepts that reverberate throughout the *Ruba'iyyat*, but structural similarities appear between the works of these two men. The *Ruba'iyyat* and *The Waste Land* both begin with a tavern scene and proceed to offer an illustrated depiction of spring.[82]

OTHER LITERARY MOVEMENTS AND FIGURES

Thomas Bailey Aldrich, a prolific Orientalist and author of *The Sultan Goes to Ispahan*,[83] wrote a review in 1878 of the *Ruba'iyyat.* He said, "The world is very old to Omar and sentient with the dust of dead generations."[84] Aldrich admired Khayyam for the beauty of the form of the *Ruba'iyyat* and the simple and yet profound message of the quatrains, which he says, "has laws which are not to be broken with impunity," and it is an "instrument on which one may strike the highest or the deepest note, but it must be a full note."[85]

Unlike Eliot, Norton felt he had to defend the moral, spiritual, and religious aspects of the *Ruba'iyyat*, while Aldrich's attention had been focused more on the technical aspects and the very form of quatrains. In fact, Aldrich tells us that "unlike Ḥāfīz, Firdawsi, and

Professor Charles Rockwell Lanman. Vice-President of the Omar Khayyam Club of America.

the rest," Khayyam had little to say about love, and Aldrich never grasped what Khayyam meant by "beloved." Was it God, a mistress, or a friend? Despite Aldrich's interest in the formalistic aspect of the *Ruba'iyyat*, as the following suggests, he was not completely unaware of the message:

> Like those intaglios turned up from time to time in Roman earth. Omar Khayyam has shown us once more that a little thing may be perfect, and that perfection is not a little thing. But are these poems in any sense little things? Here and there the poignant thought in them cuts very deep. It is like a crevasse in an Alpine glacier, only a finger's breadth at the edge, but reaching to unfathomable depths.[86]

Among other American men of letters, James Whitcomb Riley, also known as the "Hoosier poet," became interested in Khayyam and wrote a book entitled, *The Rubaiyyat of Doc Sifers.*[87] Riley, a writer of notable distinction, embraced Khayyam's spirit of rationalism, humanism, and agnosticism; and speaking through a fictitious doctor named Sifers, he composed quatrains, though he changed the form from Khayyam's *aaba* to *aabb*. Among other notable followers of Khayyam, one can also name John Hay from the American mid-West, who gave a lecture in December, 1897, at the Omar Khayyam Club of London entitled, "In Praise of Omar," which was later published as a monograph. Reporting on the popularity of Khayyam and the *Ruba'iyyat* in America, he mentioned hearing a miner in the Rocky Mountains reciting the following quatrain of Khayyam:

> 'Tis but a Tent where takes him one day's rest
> A Sultan to the realm of Death addrest
> The Sultan rises, and the dark Ferrash
> Strikes and prepares it for another Guest.

John Hay was not only a respected literary figure, he was also U.S. Ambassador to England and Secretary of State under President McKinley. His interest in Persian literature and his political stature gave credence to the *Ruba'iyyat* for the public.

Referring to Khayyam as "a man of extraordinary genius," Hay went on to say that Omar "had sung a song of incomparable beauty and power in an environment no longer worthy of him, in a language of narrow range, for many generations the song was virtually lost." Referring to FitzGerald as "the twin brother" of Khayyam, Hay praised FitzGerald for singing the "forgotten poem, with all its original melody and force."[88]

It is refreshing to know that once upon a time, there was a Secretary of State who was also learned enough to appreciate literature and poetry and had this to say about the *Ruba'iyyat*:

> The exquisite beauty, the faultless form, the singular grace of those amazing stanzas, were not more wonderful than the depth and breadth of their profound philosophy, their knowledge of life, their dauntless courage, their serene facing of the ultimate problems of life and death.[89]

An attorney and advocate of revolutionary values, Clarence Darrow became a lover and proponent of the *Ruba'iyyat*. He wrote an essay called "A Persian Pearl," which, as part of a book, went into many editions. Darrow, who often quoted the *Ruba'iyyat* in his courtroom, praised Khayyam for he did not judge others because our fates are sealed and there is no room for judgment.

The other figure who should be mentioned is Ezra Pound, the eminent literary genius and a close friend of T.S. Eliot, who had developed a great admiration for Khayyam and his *Ruba'iyyat*, a reverence, which, unlike Eliot, lasted until the end. Questioning whether he should leave London for a different place, in a letter to his friend, William Carlos Williams, Pound paired himself with Omar Khayyam, asking:

> Whether self-inflicted torture ever has the slightest
> Element of dignity in it?
> Or whether I am Omar,
> Have I a country after all?[90]

And again, in a letter from Paris to his former professor, Pound wrote, "I am perhaps didactic; so in a sense, or different sense are Homer, Dante, Villon and Omar, and FitzGerald's translation of Omar is the only good poem of the Victorian era."[91]

To many critics, Pound's passionate interest in Omar Khayyam remains a mystery, one that James Miller reflected on by saying, "Omar Khayyam was one of the Pound's genuine weaknesses, a bizarre taste for one who shaped the modernity of modern poetry."[92] Ezra Pound's highest admiration for Khayyam, in addition to his extensive references to him as evidenced in his work, *Canto 80*, can best be seen in the fact that he named his own son "Omar Shakespeare Pound," and said, "Just note the crescendo."

Among the less notable figures we can name Elihu Vedder, who in 1884 made an illustration of the poem.[93] This work was closely affiliated with the sensuous theme of the Pre-Raphaelites. Vedder brought the *Ruba'iyyat* to life in drawing, while Isadora Duncan, an artist and sexual revolutionary, brought Omar and his *Ruba'iyyat* on stage.[94]

Finally, Ralph Waldo Emerson, a figure of great eminence must be mentioned, although his encounter with Khayyam was brief. Emerson, who was interested in Sufism and admired Persian Sufi poetry, read FitzGerald's translation on his trip to Europe and Egypt. Having taken keen interest in the *Ruba'iyyat*, he translated a few quatrains from German into English. His biographer, Ralph Rusk, writes, "During the voyage, Emerson read and reread Omar Khayyam forgetting that he had condemned it six months before."[95]

My endeavor to be inclusive and yet brief with regard to Western followers of Khayyam has been a frustrating one. Just as I thought all the Omarians of the Anglo-Saxon world had been accounted for, a few more appeared. Indeed, the subject of Omar Khayyam and the West can only be dealt with adequately in a separate work, but this much is sufficient to establish the extent of America's fascination with the old Persian master.

Anti-Omarians of the World Unite

At a time when the spirit of materialism was becoming prevalent in the West and the puritanical morality was in decline, there were those who sought a scapegoat. Khayyam's *Ruba'iyyat* was an easy target, for few poets outwardly advocated the meaninglessness of life embodied in hedonism, sex, and drinking as Khayyam had. This created what can be called "an anti-Omarian movement," which included intellectuals and preachers, statesmen and those concerned with the disintegration of the moral fiber of the society. D'Ambrosio purports that the angriest opponents of Omar Khayyam were not "satirists but sermonizers." They despised the *Ruba'iyyat* because they thought it contaminated the puritanical spirit of America's Protestant religion and contributed to its demise.

One of the early anti-Omarians was Paul Elmer More, who had strong Christian tendencies. More was a notable literary figure whose views on Khayyam and the *Ruba'iyyat* reflected the development of the humanist tradition in America in the three decades that followed the review of the *Ruba'iyyat* by Norton. Unlike Norton, however, whose approach to Khayyam was from a secular perspective, and unlike Aldrich's interest in the form of the quatrains, More was a "Christian humanist," who was highly critical of the *Ruba'iyyat*. He let this be known in his review of the *Ruba'iyyat* in 1899, although he later modified it into a less critical version.[96]

More's criticism of Khayyam was based on the latter's advocacy of determinism and the absence of free will, a criticism which More discusses in the context of femininity and masculinity. In a language that would be highly offensive to modern feminists, More identifies lack of will with the feminine and exercise of the will with the masculine. FitzGerald, who had said, "taste is the feminine of genius," described himself as a "feminine man."[97] In a statement reminiscent of Nietzsche, More criticized FitzGerald and stated, "Those who are feminine, do not possess the will to act." What follows, More concluded, is a "sham spirituality" and "allurements of the senses."[98]

D'Ambrosio in *Eliot Possessed: T. S. Eliot and FitzGerald's RUBAIYAT* considers More's reaction to the *Ruba'iyyat* to have come at the end of a cycle of response to Khayyam in America. She concludes that the works of Norton, Aldrich, and More represent the three phases of American response to the *Ruba'iyyat* from 1869 to 1899. It is D'Ambrosio's opinion that their work exemplifies a coherent and consistent unity in middle and late Victorian literature as it responds to the popularity of Khayyam's quatrains.

The term "cult" was increasingly used by some to describe the "Omarians" even by those who were ardent admirers of Khayyam. They had become alarmed by his immense popularity and the fact that the *Ruba'iyyat* had become elevated to the level of a new religion. Referring to the movement as "Omar Cult," Cowell expressed his admiration for Khayyam, but stated that "I cannot take him as a guide. In these matters, I prefer to go to Nazareth, not to Naishāpūr."[99]

Earlier in England, a retired "East-India man" had expressed the same concern by observing that the *Ruba'iyyat* had become elevated "to a position of almost a scriptural dignity."[100] The opponents produced a literary genre of their own; some utterly condemned Khayyam, such as Richard Le Gallienne in his "Fin de Siècle Cult of FitzGerald's *Ruba'iyyat* of Omar Khayyam."[101] Others evaluated the *Ruba'iyyat* from a religious perspective, such as *Ruba'iyyat of Omar Khayyam, translated into Christian.*[102] Richard Le Gallienne, having called Khayyam "the thinker-drinker" in 1897, wrote *Omar Repentant*[103] in 1908 and pronounced, "The Wine! The Grape! Oh, call it Whiskey and be done with it!"[104] And to these we can add *Quatrains of Christ*[105] and *Omar or Christ.*[106] Edgar Fawcett, a literary figure who was appalled by Khayyam's popularity in America, wrote in the *New York Journal*:

> Omar cult has been a silly "fad" and has illustrated the "hypocrisy of English ethics." He talked of the "ruffian heterodoxy" of "this Persian bon vivant." "The most pitiable stuff."... And the Omarian message was interpreted "Get drunk as often as you can, for there's nothing in life so profitable."[107]

Anti-Omarians generally attributed the popularity of the *Ruba'iyyat* to a shift and decline in Christian fervor. Bernard Holland attributed Khayyam's popularity to a shift in "the Anglo-Saxon race" and purports, "Christian wisdom is exactly opposite to that of Omar Khayyam."[108] Millar, in his article, "The Omar Cult," identified "the Omar cult on one side and the tenants of the Christian endeavourers whitening Muswell Hill on the other."[109] Most Anti-Omarians saw the deteriorating moral fiber of the West as the cause and Khayyam's popularity as the symptom of a disease. In his article, "The Popularity of Omar," Holland asks, "What is this philosophy of which Omar Khayyam is the father, and the spirit and the style of FitzGerald's is the mother?" He also adds in despair, "What is it in the present condition of the Anglo-Saxon world which has by late given so successful a career to this philosophy?"[110]

As the Anti-Omarians gained strength, even serious scholarly attempts were made to compare Khayyam to many intellectual figures such as Lucretius. C.D. Broad compared Khayyam to Schopenhauer and criticized the pessimism that emanated from them.[111] The perception of Khayyam's message as one of pessimism and hopelessness was becoming widespread, as is evident in an article entitled, "The Harm of Omar," which appeared in *T.P.'s Weekly*. The article states, "There is a real and deadly harm in Omar if he is taken too seriously ... there is harm in such hopelessness."[112]

Whereas for some it was the hopelessness of Khayyam's message that was disliked, for others, such ideas are to be shunned because they are the product of an inferior race. G.K. Chesterton called the message of the *Ruba'iyyat* "... a thing unfit for a white man, a thing like opium."[113] By this time, just about any social or moral decay was blamed on Khayyam. Even a decline in charity contribution to a church made a Scottish minister who knew Persian blame Khayyam for it. He remarked, "We confess, that we have hated this new patched Omar Khayyam of Mr. FitzGerald, and have at times been tempered to scorn the miserable, self-deluded, unhealthy fanatics of his cult."[114]

The criticism did not stop with Khayyam; FitzGerald, too, was scorned for having translated him. Havelock Ellis, in his major work, *Studies in the Psychology of Sex*,[115] calls FitzGerald a case of "Sexual Inversion" and goes on to demonize him. Ellis' work was banned in England, but a committee was formed to make its publication possible. The committee included several Omarians such as Grant Allen, Walter Crane, George More, Edward Allen, and the most famous member, George Bernard Shaw.

The type of literature that some of the Omarians produced fanned the flame of the Anti-Omarian movement. One such case was Edwin Arlington Robinson, a poet who was convinced that Khayyam's sense of determinism is true and our fate is sealed. Having developed an appreciation for what he considered Khayyam's pessimism, he wrote, "I'm afraid that I shall always stand in the shadow as one of Omar's broken pots."[116] Robinson was one of the few poets who versified in the Omarian tradition, embracing fatalism and pessimism; it was this type of literature that became the target of the Anti-Omarian movement. Another poet in the same tradition is A.E. Housman, whose 1896 work, *A Shropshire Lad*, embraced the pessimistic spirit of the *Ruba'iyyat* and became popular at Harvard University.

Finally, there were those who saw a revolutionary, anti-establishment, pro-social and moral chaos in Khayyam's message and wrote to denounce it. Several articles appeared identifying Khayyam as somewhat of a social anarchist. In this regard, Sylvanus Urban's article in the *Gentleman's Magazine*[117] and Willfred Meynell's article, "The Cause of Omar's Popularity,"[118] belong here as does Edmund Gosse in *Critical Kit-Kats*.[119] Allan, a philosopher and a novelist and an early member of the Omar Khayyam Club of America, considered Khayyam and Shelley as two radicals who called for revolution, and he wrote the following poem in their memory:

> A rebel our Shelley, a rebel our Mage
> That brotherly link shall suffice us;
> 'Tis in vain that the zealots, O Prophet and Sage,
> From his creed – and from thine – would entice us;
> We seek not to stray from the path you trod,
> We seek to widen its boarder;
> If systems that be are the order of God,
> Revolt is part of that order.[120]

Our discussion would remain incomplete without at least a cursory review of the Temperance Movement of Carry Nation, with its puritanical ethics, anti-drinking campaign and opposition to Omar Khayyam. To the Temperance Movement in the 1890, whose focal point was the advocacy of puritanical ethics and prohibition of drinking, the *Ruba'iyyat* was enemy number one, and Khayyam, a heathen poet or "The bibulous old Persian."[121] In Carry Nation's "saloon raid" on June 6, 1900, Nation smashed the glasses in a saloon shouting, "Glory to God!" This came to symbolize the anti-drinking campaign. Needless to say, Khayyam's prescription of wine as a remedy for all ills made him an easy target. Among the literature that examined Khayyam's *Ruba'iyyat* in relation to the Temperance

AND LOOK – UPON A BACTRIAN CAMEL, SEE
ONE WHO SPAKE LIGHTLY OF THE FAITH, AH ME!
HE MOCKED THE MASTER, MADE A GOD OF POSH–
SPIRIT OF OMAR, TELL ME, WHO IS HE?

Movement is "On Reading Omar Khayyam During an Anti-Saloon Campaign." The article went through several reprints, and the *New York Mail* published what they titled "The *Ruba'iyyat of Carrie Nation* " and " *Omar on the Wagon*," [122] which appeared in a Boston anthology.

The French, German and Dutch Scene

KHAYYAM IN FRANCE

Khayyam was also discovered on the continent in the nineteenth century, but unlike the Anglo-Saxon approach, which took interest in his *Ruba'iyyat*, the French first discovered his mathematical

A BOOK OF VERSES UNDERNEATH THE BOUGH,
A JUG OF WINE, A LOAF OF BREAD – AND THOU
BESIDE ME SINGING IN THE WILDERNESS –
OH, WILDERNESS WERE PARADISE ENOW

treatises. In 1851, M.F. Woepcke produced a critical edition of Khayyam's treatise on algebra and then translated it into French,[123] generating much interest among the Orientalists. It was following this introduction that Garcin de Tassy undertook the project of translating some of the *Ruba'iyyat* into French.[124] A decade later, J.B. Nicolas, who had learned Persian in Tehran, made a translation of a larger number of the *Ruba'iyyat* into French. Nicolas was a translator for the French Embassy in Tehran and in 1867 heard a reading of the *Ruba'iyyat* at the Persian court. He wrote a literal translation of a text lithographed in Tehran, which apparently became the basis for FitzGerald's newer edition containing 101 stanzas. The advantage of this translation was not only that it was done by an Orientalist who knew Persian quite well, but also that Nicolas had been affiliated with and influenced by the Sufis of nineteenth-century Persia. His interpretative translation clearly shows this Sufi leaning.[125] This work did not receive the attention it deserved, but an article by T. Gauthier on Nicolas' translation published in *Monitor de France* in 1867 introduced the work to the learned and literary circles. Among other French scholars interested in Khayyam were C.G. Salmon, whose short biographical article appeared in *La Grande Encyclopédie*[126] in 1861, as well as K.A. Barbier de Meynard.

Among other French scholars who expanded the existing research on Khayyam are C. Grolleau,[127] who compared Khayyam with figures such as Pascal, Heine, Budler, the British poet Swinburne, and C. Anet,[128] who collaborated with MīrzāMuḥammad Qazwīnī in a fine translation and introduction to the *Ruba'iyyat* from a scientific perspective. And finally, there is A. Guy[129] who discussed the technical aspects of quatrains and translated some of them into French. M.M. Foūlādvand, in his book,[130] tells us of a number of Iranian scholars who knew French well enough to have done major works on Khayyam.

OMAR KHAYYAM IN GERMANY

The reception of Omar Khayyam in Germany can be divided into two parts, pre- and post-FitzGerald Germany. The pre-FitzGerald period is limited to Joseph Freiherr von Hammer (1818) and

Friedrick Ruckert (1827), and the first post-Fitzgerald period begins with an article[131] that included 19 of Hammer's quatrains in addition to a German translation of the French translation of J.B. Nicolas. These initial translations gave rise to a flurry of activities in Khayyamian studies. In 1878, Adolf Friedrich Frafen von Schack translated 336 quatrains, of which 30 are from FitzGerald's English translation. Two years later, Friedrich Bodenstedt translated the entire *Ruba'iyyat* known to Germans at the time, and the 467 quatrains were published in 1880. With reference to them, Bodenstedt said,

> I have good reason to assume that, among a thousand readers, Hardly one knows about the peculiar man [Omar Khayyam], whose poetic heritage posthumously forms the contents of this book.[132]

Bodenstedt took issue with FitzGerald, whom he thought presented only the Epicurean side of Omar, and proposed the theory that Khayyam began as a skeptic when he was in his youth but matured into a Sufi master. To substantiate his theory, he arranged the *Ruba'iyyat* in such a way that showed Khayyam's progression from his youthful hedonism to a Sufi master.

In 1887, a volume appeared entitled, *Divan der Persischen Poésie*, edited by Jolius Hart in which 48 *Ruba'iyyat* from von Schack and 9 from Wollheim were included.[133] These works may have been an inspiration for Hermann Ethè, who translated eight quatrains and offered a commentary of his own which shows his thorough familiarity with FitzGerald. Ethè observed, "One could rightly call Omar's quatrains the memories of a radical free spirit." [134]

It is not until 1898 that Leon Kellner, a literary critic, wrote an article in *Die Nation*[135] in which he considered FitzGerald's poems and asked why, despite the popularity of Khayyam in America, he is so neglected in Germany. Kellner considered FitzGerald's translation a work of English literature independent of the original Persian. Three years later, Adalbert Meinhardt published another review in *Die Nation*[136] in which the philosophical impact of FitzGerald's Omar was discussed. Only two months later, Ferdinand Laban published an article in which he compared Omar Khayyam and

Giacomo Leopardi, arguing that Khayyam's perspective is fundamentally "anti-German."

> I might say the two poet-philosophers are regarded as curiosities that one might like to take a closer look at sometime, but whose essential core remains foreign to our blood.[137]

The period from 1898 to 1903 marked a German awakening to FitzGerald which included numerous books and articles, some of which are: Maurice Todhunter, who wrote several articles[138] on Khayyam and FitzGerald and Franz Blei, who saw the *Ruba'iyyat* as pessimism and described Khayyam as "a pessimistic-hedonist."[139]

German scholars were now set to provide an exhaustive translation of the *Ruba'iyyat*, an example of which can be seen in the translation of Maximilian Rudolph Schenck who reviewed other existing translations but offered a translation of 468 quatrains.

As the new century arrived, Khayyam's popularity in Germany rose to a new height with numerous articles presenting various aspects of Khayyam's thought appearing in popular journals. E. Wiedemann[140] had analyzed Khayyam's treatise, *On the Deception of Knowing the Two Quantities of Gold and Silver in a Compound Made of the Two,* and compared it to the work of other Muslim physicists such as Abū Manṣur Nayrīzī.

In 1909, a new translation of the *Ruba'iyyat* was made by Friedrich Rosen and published in *Deutsche verlags – Anstatt* of Stuttgart. Rosen had explained that his interest in translating the *Ruba'iyyat* began when he was a member of the Diplomatic Corps in Iran, but there was another reason for the translation. He says, "What especially encouraged me in this undertaking was the extraordinary popularity and diffusion that Omar's quatrains have had and still enjoy in the entire English speaking world due to their classical rendering by Edward FitzGerald."

Rosen corrected the mistakes of his predecessors both in terms of the content and form, which some had changed from *aaba* to *aabb*. After 1909, we see a new translation or an improved version of a previous one almost every year. In the 1910s Hector Preconi made a new attempt to retranslate all the *Ruba'iyyat* which appeared in

FitzGerald's second edition, plus 30 more. Preconi's work was published several times, including in an illustrated edition in 1911. In 1912, Curt Hamel Verlag in Berlin translated 184 of the *Ruba'iyyat* and published them as part of the second edition of Rosen.[141]

In 1917, a poet by the name of Alfred Henschke Klabund wrote 97 quatrains, a free interpretive translation based on FitzGerald's, and titled them, *Das sinngeditcht des Persischen zel Tmachers.*[142] And yet again, in 1921, there appeared another translation by Hans Bethge, who was influenced by FitzGerald. Of his own work, Bethge said, "The style in which I rendered Omar's proverbs rests on earlier German, French, and English models in both verse and prose, especially those of Schack, Rosen, Bodenstedt, Fitzgerald, and Nicolas."[143]

FitzGerald's influence on most German translators of Khayyam is evident, and few of them made a serious attempt to go directly to the Persian original. In 1927 however, Walter von der Porten relied on the Bodleian manuscript to translate 181 quatrains into German but kept FitzGerald's meter and poetic form. Porten rejected Nicolas' theory that Khayyam was really a Sufi, and Bodenstedt's view that Khayyam had gone from doubt to religious mysticism, choosing instead to side with FitzGerald's Epicurean understanding of Khayyam:

> In countless verses and in the most varied images he repeatedly invites his fellow humans to realize how short life is, how much suffering accompanies it, and yet at the same time how beautiful the world can be. Yet he stands in battle with the Islam that surrounds him; challenging, he praises wine; his finger points to the conflicting doctrine; he wants nothing to do with prayer and rites; his scorn castigates the hypocrite.[144]

Isolated scholarship on Khayyam in Germany became more organized in 1934, when the German version of the Omar Khayyam Club of London or America, the "Deutschen Ghajjam-Gesellschaft" was founded in Tübingen under the directorship of Professor Christian Rempis. The first major scholarly work of this club, which became popular in the intellectual circles in Baden-Württenberg, was a translation by Rempis entitled *Die Vierzeiler Omars in der Auswahl und Anordnung Edward FitzGerald.* While Rempis alluded to the beauty of FitzGerald's translation, as a scholar he was quite conscious of its shortcomings as well as the mistranslations of so many other works. In the introduction to the above work, Rempis said:

> There is no doubt that Omar Khayyam would not have become so widely known and famous in both the East and West without the free renderings of FitzGerald. Bearing witness to this are the translations of his quatrains into fifty-two languages.[145]

With the advent of Nazism in Germany in 1934, Omar Khayyam began to fall from the grace of scholarly circles, for the anti-authoritarian message of the *Ruba'iyyat* went against the doctrine of the Nationalist-Socialist movement. The Omar Khayyam Club of Germany (Deutschen Ghajjam-Gesellschaft) ceased to exist in 1937, and even the popular edition of Rosen published in the *Insel-Bucherei* series was withdrawn from the book stores. Omar Khayyam had been identified with the anti-Nazis, Rempis said in an interview on July 8, 1960, and added that, "Omar Khayyam's attitude towards life was not particularly compatible with Nazi doctrine."[146] In a fascinating statement, which reveals so much about Khayyam in Germany, Rempis noted, "Among this circle which was most interested in Omariana, Jews represented a great proportion. With the persecution of Jewish intellectuals after the Nuremberg laws of 1935, they are no longer able to take part in any of the Club's activities."[147]

The public perception of Omar Khayyam as an advocate of Epicureanism, hedonism, and cynicism toward life was directly opposed to Hitler's great promises in life. The Third Reich's exorbitant optimism considered Khayyam's pessimism unacceptable and thus forbidden. As it turned out, not only was Hitler vanquished, his atrocities vindicated Khayyam's view of the inherent temporality of life, suffering and pain of the human existence. Following the war, Khayyam, too, was liberated in Germany and regained some of his popularity, and Preconi's translation was reprinted in 1946, followed by a new translation by Rudolf Berger in 1948.[148]

Among other notable scholars of Khayyam were: Arthur Altschul,[149] who wrote a commentary on FitzGerald's translation; Hermann Jantzen, whose commentary[150] agreed with Kellner's interpretation of Khayyam as a pessimist; Joseph Steinmayer, who wrote a fine article titled, "FitzGerald and Omar Khayyam"; and Gustav Keyssner,[151] whose two articles dealt with the reasons for the prominence of Omar Khayyam and with the pertinence of his message to the present generation. In 1913, Walter Fränzel vehemently condemned Khayyam's world-view and his sense of pessimism, a theme that was also emphasized by Karl Zimmermann,[152] who argued it was Khayyam's nihilism that was appalling. Sol Gittleman states, "Zimmerman concluded that out of Omar's nihilism grew a hedonism which was the final expression of an intellect unable to cope with the riddle of existence."[153]

Henry W. Nordmeyer, in his article,[154] refutes the shallow understanding of Fränzel and Zimmerman and argues that "Omar's tragedy stems from the frustration of his Faustian search for knowledge ... Unlike Faust, who strives and because of this, finds salvation, Omar turned to wine."[155] Nordmeyer said, "Omar is an ironic enjoyer, one who knows that even enjoyment, in its deepest grounds, is without essence."[156]

In Germany, sometime during 1903–1932, there appeared seventeen translations of the *Ruba'iyyat*, some of which have already been mentioned. With the exception of a few, most were, in one way or another, renditions of or influenced by the majestic work of FitzGerald. As with the presence of Khayyam in the English speaking world and France, a separate work is needed to offer an exhaustive discussion of the reception of Omar Khayyam's *Ruba'iyyat* in Germany.

THE DUTCH OMAR KHAYYAM SOCIETY (HET NEDERLANDS OMAR KHAYYAM GENOOTSCHAP)

There appears to be a renewed interest in Europe in Omar Khayyam and his *Ruba'iyyat*. Whereas an exhaustive discussion concerning the subject matter is beyond the scope of the present work, the Dutch Omar Khayyam Society, whose members are currently from the

Netherlands and Belgium, is an example of this renewed interest in Khayyam.

The origin of scholarly interest in Omar Khayyam in the Netherlands goes back to 1891 when an article appeared in the Magazine *De Gids* (*The Guide*).[157] In the beginning of the twentieth Century quatrains attributed to Omar were translated by Dutch poets such as J.H. Leopold and P.C. Boutens, and there was an illustrated edition of the FitzGerald by Frank Brangwyn.[158] A number of other well-known poets in Holland followed this literary trend.

Interest in Omar Khayyam prior to World War II in the Netherlands had remained exclusive to certain intellectual circles, but in the post War period, several poetic translations were published. It was not until 1990 that a group of academics and men of letters established The Dutch Omar Khayyam Society. The original founders, Geert Bremer, Johan van Schagen, Dirk Jorritsma and Jos Biegstraaten met at Hotel Wientjes, in Zwolle, on February, 17, 1990. It was there that the Omar Khayyam Club was established and the founding members called themselves "Het Nederlands Omar Khayyam Gezelschap.

Jos Biegstraaten, a founding member, states the reason for his passionate interest in Khayyam to be as follows:

> These quatrains differed from the translations of the Dutch poets. I wanted to know why? This was the beginning of my search after Omar and his *Ruba'iyyat*. I compared the translations, and discovered two modern Dutch translations, by Johan van Schagen and Dirk Jorritsma. I found out where they lived and talked with them about their translations. I began to buy books dealing with the subject, and asked for publications about Omar and his *Ruba'iyyat* in a Dutch book magazine. That's how I came in touch with Geert Bremer, a professor of medicine in the University of Groningen, who phoned me, and told me he collected editions of Omar Khayyam's Rubaiyat. [159]

Since its founding in 1990, The Dutch Omar Khayyam Society has met twice a year, and in 1991, Jan Keijser, owner of "The Avalon Press", a very fine private press, joined the society. Three *Year Books* in Dutch (1992, 1995 and 2000) have thus far been published and a fourth edition is being prepared.

Presently, the society has fourteen members, four of them are academics associated with the prestigious Department of Oriental Studies at the University of Leiden and the rest are literary figures.[160]

The Dutch Omar Khayyam Society has organized two expositions, the first was in the Museum of the Book in The Hague in 1997 on "The Art of the Book." The second, in the Library of the University of Leiden in 2001, dealt with different aspects of Omar's life, Omar as a learned man, the poet, early translators, Dutch translators and their sources, FitzGerald and his associates, parodies, illustrations etc.[161]

EPILOGUE

Conclusion

The reconstruction of the life and thought of Omar Khayyam based on the existing textual evidence has been the central task of this work. This project however is not free from difficulty; one may argue that there lies an inherent dichotomy in the present work. On one hand I have argued, and justifiably so, that many of Khayyam's *Rubaï'yyat* are not his own and we do not know how many, if any, of them belong to him. On the other hand, throughout this work, I have used many of these inauthentic *Rubaï'yyat* to reconstruct who Khayyam was; in fact, I have analyzed and interpreted them as if they were Khayyam's to bring to light his intellectual orientation.

How and why, one may ask, would dubious evidence be used as a basis for the reconstruction of a figure about whom there are so many contradictory perspectives? In the final analysis, this is an insoluble problem if one were to adopt merely a historical-textual approach as most scholars of Khayyam have traditionally done. If it were true that the *Rubai'yyat* are inauthentic, the case is then closed and Khayyam remains at least partially veiled forever. While it is virtually impossible to know with absolute certainty which of the *Rubai'yyat* belongs to Khayyam, a careful analysis of most of the existing *Rubai'yyat* reveals that there is a strong "family resemblance" among most of them. A consistent and coherent message, a perspective on existential issues pertaining to the human condition and a way of life emanates from many of these quatrains.

It is precisely this family resemblance among so many of the *Rubai'yyat* that allows us to speak of a "Khayyamian school of thought." Such examples exist not only among other literary and poetic genres but also among artistic and philosophical schools of thought. For example, despite variations among the works of art in such schools as Impressionism, Cubism and Surrealism, there is a family resemblance among the works that belong to one school of art. Similarly, various language family groups such as Indo-European or Semitic, despite variations among them, bear fundamental grammatical similarities. The similarities among most of the *Rubai'yyat* are striking, from the most inauthentic ones to those that most scholars have agreed to have been Khayyam's, and one can see a common web of ideas and concepts.

Traditionally, large numbers of these immensely rich poems have been completely neglected by scholars simply because they are "inauthentic." It is almost like ignoring the aesthetic value of a beautiful work of impressionist painting because we cannot determine who the painter is! Does not a piece of art reveal much about the artist and the school of art to which it belongs? Just as an unknown work of Victorian poetry reveals much about poetry during the Victorian era, as well as the unknown author of the poem, the *Rubai'yyat* also tells us much about the Khayyamiam school of thought. It is time to suspend the search for the messenger and put the emphasis on the message – and therein lies a bit of historical Khayyam.

My applied method and approach for those scholars who believe that by sifting through the historical evidence the "real Khayyam" can be found, is nothing short of a nightmare. Their approach to Khayyamian study has ignored the immensely rich body of the *Rubai'yyat* simply because they are not authentic. However, are they not valuable in and of themselves? Does not the fact that their authors have attributed the poems to Khayyam say a great deal about who Khayyam was perceived to have been? May this perception not be valid at least to some extent? Even though I firmly believe that if only a fraction of the *Rubai'yyat* belongs to the real Khayyam, we can still deduce a great deal about the man and his ideas, ultimately there is some degree of speculation here.

Throughout this work, I have referred to "Khayyam" as a mysterious figure who is more than a historical personality and one who may or may not have written the *Rubai'yyat*. For me, Khayyam represents the bewilderment of those perplexed humans who spend their entire life going between reason and revelation, never resting in peace, and holding fast to the fundamentals of intellectual integrity with an uncompromising spirit.

To the critics who may argue "why attempt to reconstruct Khayyam based on dubious evidence," I say, "I am not alone in my endeavor to reconstruct a historical figure based on all the available evidence." Christianity among many other religions presents an excellent example. The lack of solid and indisputable evidence about the historical Jesus has not hampered the efforts of so many scholars in the last two thousand years to reconstruct the life of Jesus based on the existing evidence.[1] Similarly, even though the majority of the 1200 *Rubai'yyat* are clearly inauthentic, they remain part of a literary genre that provides a consistent and coherent message. In the interest of finding the "real" *Rubai'yyat*, the message has been all but ignored, it is time to dust off these rich and intriguing quatrains and study them as part of the Khayyamian school of thought, assuming that the true message of Khayyam permeates through them.

The second question which is even more pertinent than the problem of authenticity of the *Rubai'yyat*, and in a sense a by-product of it, is the question of "truth." Did Khayyam believe in a truth and if so, what was it he considered to be the truth? Clearly his philosophical writings and his *Rubai'yyat* are proponents of two different sets of ideas: the former indicates that Khayyam was a devoted Muslim who identified the truth with God, while the latter conveys agnosticism.

Those who have separated Khayyam the poet from the philosopher have naturally resolved this inherent contradiction, but in our case we have assumed that the two Khayyams are one and the same. Let us elaborate on this thorny question. One possible answer is to say that Khayyam was a hypocrite and that out of fear for his well-being he pretended to be a Muslim. The real Khayyam therefore is to be found in the *Rubai'yyat*, one who did not believe that there was a single "Truth" but instead believed in "truths." Fearing persecution, similar to so many other intellectuals, he too was forced to play the game of pretending to be a good Muslim. This is perhaps why he began and ended his philosophical treatises by praising God and the Prophet Muḥammad.

This theory is ludicrous for even a shallow reading of Khayyam's philosophical writings indicates that intellectually, he was operating well within an Islamic religious universe. There is nothing pretentious about his philosophical writings; they are wholly Islamic in intellectual texture, not to mention that his life-long adherence to the Islamic *shari'ah* provides additional evidence that his convictions were deep and real.

The other option, and one that I have argued for, is that Khayyam's concept of truth was as clear in his mind as his scientific views: for him Truth was God and God alone. Khayyam was a deist. Nowhere in his authentic *Rubai'yyat* or even those attributed to him did he ever question the very existence of God. Certainly he questions religion, chastises the orthodox, the religious laws and popular beliefs in various aspects of faith, but never what lies at the heart of religion: God. He questions anthropomorphism and even such divine attributes as justice, but never God's existence. Khayyam's satirical deconstructionism can in fact be construed as a defense of the heart of religion by shedding the façade that has developed around it. He puzzles over this God whose mysteries are allegedly unveiled for the orthodox. By alluding to the problem of evil and the uncertainty concerning hell and heaven, Khayyam questions the orthodox's eschatological arrogance, not the ineffable Reality of God.

The question of what Khayyam did believe by way of truth stems from one's fundamental inability or willingness to grant that it is possible for one to hold contradictory opinions simultaneously without being a hypocrite. To be a human is to undergo change and adopt different modes of thought, a phenomenon which in Islamic culture has a pejorative connotation. As indicated above, Khayyam was a deist whose belief in the existence of God constituted the fundamental axiom of his thought. He equates Truth with God, whose existence he has logically proven, at least to his own satisfaction. His rational scientific mind, however, did not and could not accept any of the standard religious answers to the major riddles of human existence. In fact, he went further to say that no one knows the Truth about such matters and thus there is no point in speculating upon them.

One may argue that Khayyam's adherence to the religious laws may have been because he was culturally a Muslim or out of fear of the orthodox jurists. It is my opinion that he did not see anything irrational about the religious laws of Islam (*Shari'ah*) and was convinced that they are a sensible set of laws to follow. It is not religious laws that he mocks but the zeal with which people become attached to them, the sharp point of his criticism being the orthodox and their historical record of stifling free thinking. The religious laws of Islam for Khayyam are a means to an end and are not to be taken seriously otherwise they become one and the same with the Truth. His criticism of religious formalism perhaps was intended to unveil the Truth and not to deny it.

Our Khayyam believed in the existence of one Truth which he identified with Allah and no other truth.

APPENDIX A

Translations of the Philosophical Treatises

1. On Being and Necessity (*Risālah fi'l-kawn wa'l-taklīf*)
2. The Necessity of Contradiction in the World, Determination and Subsistence (*Ḍarurat al-taḍād fi'l-'ālam wa'l-jabr wa'l-baqā'*)
3. The Light of the Intellect on the Subject of Universal Knowledge (*Risālah al-ḍiyā' al-'aqlī fī mawḍū' al-'ilm al-kullī*)
4. On the Knowledge of the Universal Principles of Existence (*Risālah dar 'ilm kulliyāt-i wujūd*)
5. On Existence (*Risālah fi'l-wujūd*)
6. Response to Three Philosophical Problems (*Risālah jawāb 'ān thulāth masā'il*)

INTRODUCTION

In what follows, a complete translation into English of the six philosophical treatises of Omar Khayyam is being offered for the first time. Swami Govinda Tirtha in the nineteenth century has offered a free and partial translation of three of these treatises.[1] Despite the beneficial nature of Govinda's translations, his project seems to have been to make them accessible to the educated reader. In doing so, however, the accuracy of the philosophical concepts has been compromised.

As is evident in these treatises, Khayyam is primarily providing us with a commentary on Avicenna's writings. Khayyam's views are consistent with traditional Peripatetic commentaries; he deals with most of the major issues of concern to Muslim philosophers such as essence, existence, emanation of different levels of being from the One, existence of evil and the problem of free-will and determinism.

Among the philosophical topics he discusses, his treatment of the problem of the priority of essence over existence is unique. In this regard, he deviates from the traditional Peripatetic view that existence is primary and essence secondary and advocates what is referred to as the "Principality of Essence" (*iṣālat al-māhiyyah*). The philosophical significance of this perspective remained unappreciated until Suhrawardī who lived not too long after Khayyam. The Principality of Essence was once again revived by Mīr Damād, the founder of the School of Iṣfahān in the seventeenth century. It is not known if Suhrawardī and Mīr Damād were in any way influenced by Khayyam, but the subject remains to be further studied. As I have indicated in Chapter Six of this work, Khayyam's philosophical writings are rather dense, and understanding them requires familiarity with traditional Peripatetic concepts and technical terminology. Those interested only in ascertaining a general understanding of Khayyam's philosophical ideas should refer to my elaborations in Chapter Six.

ON BEING AND NECESSITY
Risālah fi'l-kawn wa'l-taklīf [2]

Our gratitude is to God, bestower of all mercy and reward, praise be upon his selected servants especially Muḥammad, Peace be Upon Him, and his pure companions. Abū Naṣr Muḥammad ibn 'Abd al-Raḥīm al-Nasawī, the judge of Fārs province wrote in 476 AH to the master and proof of truth, the philosopher of the east and the west, Abu'l-fatḥ Omar ibn Ibrāhīm al-Khayyamī, May God sanctify his soul. [The letter] contains discussions on divine wisdom, exalted and high He is, creation of the world, man, and obligatory prayers. In that letter, he [Nasawī] included numerous poems but, except for the following few, nothing has remained.

Oh the wind of Ṣabā,[3] do justice to me and,
Take my greetings to Khayyam, the great man of wisdom
Kiss the ground by his door, humbly
A humility that is befitting of a wisdom such as his
He is a master philosopher from whose clouds of wisdom,
Rain comes like the fountain of life reviving degenerated bones
From the wisdom of Being and Necessity he brings forth,
Proofs that are free of questioning and doubt.

And thus Khayyam's response in his letter is as follows:

Oh, Learned brother and glorious master; may God grant you a long life, elevate your status and safeguard you against the evils of life. Your knowledge is superior to the knowledge of my companions, you are more virtuous than they and your soul more pure than theirs. You know more than they, that the problem of "being" and "necessity" is among the most complex problems and to possess an understanding of its subtleties is complex even for those who have reflected upon it previously.

These two topics can be divided into two types and each one requires complex reflections which rest upon numerous propositions about which the learned disagree. Being and necessity are among the ultimate subjects of the sublime nature, which is metaphysics. The opinions of the theologians with regard to this matter differ significantly and therefore make commenting upon them rather difficult. However, now that you have honored me by your request for a commentary concerning these matters, I have no choice but to briefly reflect upon them based on what I and masters who preceded me have concluded.

I am also well aware that your keen intelligence and comprehension of truths – may God protect your eminence – do not require that I elaborate on this subject too extensively.[4]

First, there is the subject of "whether a thing is," a question that pertains to the existence of a thing, such as when we say, "What is the reality of the intellect?" The answer to this is either through a definition or description or through elucidation of a noun. These matters do not limit the ability of one who responds to only negative or positive, rather the respondent can reply on the basis of what he considers to be a definition or description.

The third question is "why." This concerns a cause for which a thing has come into existence such that, had it not been for that cause, the thing [in question] would not exist. For example, we say "why does the intellect exist?" and this too does not limit the answer of the respondent between two contraries (negative or positive). Rather, it leaves the answer to the respondent; his reply, however, does not treat the question of "whatness" but addresses where the question of essence comes in.

The relationships between the subject matter of "what" and "why" have been dealt with adequately in the *Kitāb al-Burhān*,[5] a work on logic. Each of these subjects is divided into many subdivisions that we need not discuss here. The subject of "what is it" with regard to the first subject "whatness" is itself divisible into two parts. Due to the difference of opinions among philosophers, we inevitably embark upon its analysis. First, there is the "whatness of reality." This questions the reality of a thing, and in terms of a succession of topics, is prior to whether a thing exists (*hal*) since until the existence of something is falsified for us, we cannot discuss its essence or its non-existence which is devoid of real essence. The second subject is "what is it," which discusses the meaning of a noun that is attributed to a thing, and in the order of significance is prior to "whether a thing exists" (*hal*). This is because until we know what we mean by saying "does the griffin of the West exist or not" we cannot judge its deniability or verifiability and thus it is required that prior to an interrogative expression (*hal*), the noun has to be understood. Those logicians who have not understood the difference between these two types of "what" have become bewildered and have fallen into a quandary. Some of them have argued that "what" (*mā*) is posterior to the interrogative expression (*hal*) and have argued for the reality of it, while others have said that it is prior to *hal* and their purpose is to elucidate on "what is it." The notion of "why is it" however is posterior to the other two subjects because until we know the reality of something, we cannot know the cause for which the thing has come into existence.

In addition to the above subjects there are other categories such as whether, how, how much, when and where, all of which are accidental and discuss the reality of the accidents of an object and the proof concerning the very existence of these accidents. Realizing that these subjects are implied in the essential and real subjects [we have discussed], there is no need to discuss them here.

There is no being about which "whether it exists" cannot be asked and what is devoid of "I-ness" and verifiability is non-existent while we have assumed it to exist and this is impossible. Likewise, an existent cannot be devoid of its true reality, which distinguishes it from "other than itself". That which is not distinguishable from "other than itself" is non-existent (*'adam*); however, if we do assume it to exist, it is an impossibility. There are, however, beings that are devoid of "whatness" and they are the Necessary Beings. It is impossible for them not to exist, and if we were to assume that they do not exist, a contradiction arises. Something that in reality is of this nature has no cause or "whyness" and thus is a Necessary Being in and of itself. He is the ever singularly living eternal being from whom comes the existence of all existents, and from His wisdom – mighty and exalted are His names – emanates every good and just thing. There is a problem, however, in this subject matter but it is beyond the scope of our discussion.

If you reflect upon all existents and their "whatness", you would conclude that "whatness" of all things leads to a "whyness," a cause or means for which there is no "whyness," [that is another] cause or means (*asbāb*). The proof for this problem is as follows: if they ask why is there A, we say because of B, and if they ask why B, we say because of C, and if they ask why C, we say because of D ... inevitably a discussion concerning causality leads to a Cause for which there is no cause, otherwise an [infinite] succession or circularity will emerge and this is impossible.

Thus, it is true that the cause of all existents leads to a cause which has no cause. It is clarified in theology that there is a cause without having been caused and that it is He who is the Necessary Being in essence and unified in all aspects and is without any deficiency, and all things lead to Him and become existent because of Him.

Therefore it became obvious that the question "why does it exist?" lacks universal application to everything, rather it applies to those that, if they were to be assumed to be non-existent, no logical contradiction arises. This is not the case for the Necessary Unified Being.

Now that we have laid down the introductory principles and have briefly commented upon them, we can return to the main purpose of our discussion, namely being and necessity. The word "being," due to its commonality, has many different connotations; those concepts which are far from our purpose and intention, we can set aside. Being, in the sense that was discussed here, refers to the contingent beings such that if we think of them as non-existing, logical contradiction does not arise.

Regarding the subject of "does it exist?" (*hal*) if the question is whether the existents that can be referred to through its attributes do exist, the answer is positive. If we seek the proof for the existence of such existents through reason, they become very obvious because empirical observations and rational principles prove this such that we need no other requisite, for all the existents that are present to us belong to this category. Our bodies and dispositions are referent to non-existence.

As to how the Absolute Being from whom all things emanate in an orderly fashion and in a descending order in a latitudinal and horizontal manner [they are] from the First Origin. Generosity and true giving purely belong to God from whom all contingent beings benefit and thus it is the generosity and compassion of God, the Most High, which is the cause of existents. Therefore, if they ask us about the "whyness" of God's existence, we say, His existence does not have a reason for its existence, for He is Necessary. Just as one cannot ask about the "whyness" of the essence of the Necessary Being nor are His existents and all of His attributes subject to "whyness."

What remains from among the most important and difficult problems [to solve] is the difference among the order of existents. Their order of nobility is a problem that most people are perplexed by, to the point that one cannot find anyone who is rational and wise and is not bewildered in this regard. Perhaps I, and my teacher, the master of all who have proceeded before him, Avicenna, have thoughtfully reflected upon this problem and, to the extent that it is satisfactory to our intellects, we have understood it. What has satisfied us is either inwardly reprehensible and outwardly foolish, or is inherently stable and (true). It is from this aspect, which we have come to accept [the conclusion of this discourse].

Now, in an allegorical manner, I will elaborate on an aspect of the problem. Thus we say, the true and certain proof establishes that God has not created all existents simultaneously, rather he has created them from his own presence sequentially, and therefore the first thing God created was pure intellect. Since the first origin (intellect) has the highest proximity to God, it is the noblest of all existents and this order of nobility continues to the less noble. It is in this way that the creation of the existents has taken place – the lesser [noble] emanates a lesser [noble] until the lowest of all existents which is the nature of corruptible corporeals. [God] then has begun an ascending succession towards and ending up with man who is the noblest of all compound existents and who is the last to reach the world of generation and corruption. Therefore, among creatures, whatever is closer to the First Origin is more noble and the furthest from nobility is the nature of compounds. God, the Blessed and Most High, has determined that compounds be created at different times: it is impossible for the sum of objects that are contradictory and contrary [to be created simultaneously].

If it is asked why God created things which are contradictory and which cannot come together in a thing [e.g. good and evil], we say "to avoid a great amount of good in order to avoid some evil is itself a great evil." The wisdom, generosity and munificence of God, the Most Exalted, has bestowed on all existents their inherent perfection without reducing the dignity of a single one of them, except where every existent being differs in its proximity and distance [to God]. This is not due to God's lack of generosity but is what the perennial wisdom [of God] has deemed necessary.

This was a summary of the problem of being according to the opinion of some philosophers even though I have discussed it by way of transmission. It is with reflection upon its principles and with the assistance of reason your journey will lead to the certitude.

Perhaps the problem of "necessity" is simpler to treat than the problem of "being" and what I offer in this regard, I do so to benefit you. The term "necessity" has many connotations but philosophers have discussed these issues which I bring forth here.

Necessity emanates from God, Who is Most High, so that people be directed towards those perfections that bring about corporeal and spiritual perfections and prevent them from oppressing others, committing immoral acts, acquiring shortcomings (of character) and insisting on following one's bodily desires which prevents one from following the intellectual power.

Regarding the interrogative nature (*hal*) of necessity, it is implied in the question of "whyness" since why things are is contingent upon them being [first]. So in regard to the why of necessity we say that God Most High, created man such that it is not possible for him to submit and reach perfection unless it is through mutual assistance and cooperation. Until food, clothes and a home which are essentials of life are prepared, the possibility of the attainment of perfection does not exist. It is not possible for a man by himself to be responsible for all the necessities of life. In this regard, every man can release and liberate his fellow man from shouldering all the burden of life by himself.

Since this is the case, it is necessary that everyone follow those traditions and laws on the basis of which justice is established. The tradition [culminates] in one whose intellectual faculty is stronger than all others and the purity of his soul is superior to everyone else. From material goods, except the essentials and what one needs in life, he has not preoccupied himself with and hopes that what one intends is not the fulfillment of carnal desires; rather his intention is to obtain the approval of God the Most High. [It is He] who commands one to form the just rules, which do not place some above others and implement the divine laws without any discrimination. This is a reality which, through the intermediary of revelation and a vision of the angel [Gabriel], descends upon him; the lower orders however do not benefit from this. This individual, because he alone is worthy of obedience, is distinguished from others and this distinction is due to the signs and miracles that are indicative that they come from his Lord, Most Exalted.

It is apparent that humans vary in accordance with their susceptibility to good, evil, vices and virtues and this is because of the bodily disposition and the form of their souls. Since most people prefer their rights over the rights of others and, in rectifying [their rights] exaggerate and do not see other's rights, and because each one sees himself to be superior to others and more worthy to be in a position of mastery, it is therefore necessary for he who implements the divine laws to be so aided and supported by God so he may not fail to implement the laws among the majority of people. Some [are persuaded] through preaching, others through reason or emotion, and some by inducing fear and warning, and yet some through hardship, war and even killing can be swayed to remain within the confines of divine laws.

Since such a prophet does not exist at all times, it is necessary for these divine laws to remain valid for a specific time, meaning until such time that they are meant to be there and then be abrogated. Divine laws and rules are just, but unless people are continuously reminded of God, they will not remain stable. It is therefore incumbent upon them to perform those prayers in which the Prophet Muḥammad and God, the Most Exalted, are invoked and it is necessary for them to repeat it until, due to the continuous repetition, such names become ingrained in the heart.

Thus, in Divine and prophetic command and prohibition, there are three benefits. First, through obedience, the soul is cleansed by means of asceticism and bodily desires are reduced, and thus the power that causes intellectual powers to diminish is prevented. Second, to make the reflection upon Divine and eschatological matters become habitual, and through this, one observes prayers and prevents vanity so he may contemplate upon the incorporeal domain. This is so that the Divine names are glorified within him, meaning He who has brought all the existents into existence, Glory be upon Him and Sacred are His Names, and to know that there is no deity except God. Existents through an orderly succession have emanated from Him and His wisdom has been verified through analogies that are not illusory or sophistical. Third, through verses, He admonishes and promises what is necessary for the implementation of religious laws, and he who is to implement the *Sharī'ah* should inform the people in order that the principle of justice and coexistence may best be put into place, so that the order of the universe as the wisdom of God, Most High deems necessary may remain so.

These are the benefits of necessity and the spiritual wonders of prayer for he who acts upon them, and acquires spiritual rewards. Look upon the wisdom of the living God and His compassion; see them in a way whose wonders would dazzle your eyes. This summary came to me extemporaneously and I offer this treatise to you, the learned master, so you may complete its shortcomings and correct its fallacies. You may reward me by granting me to visit your eminence and to hear your soul-nourishing words, which soften my soul.

God knows best what is right and wrong and praise be upon God, in the beginning and the end, inwardly and outwardly.

THE NECESSITY OF CONTRADICTION IN THE WORLD, DETERMINISM AND SUBSISTENCE
Ḍarurat al-taḍād fi'l-'ālam wa'l-jabr wa'l-baqā'[6]

A discussion concerning the necessity of contradiction and your request to elaborate upon it brought me glory and fame and for that reason I thank God Most High with a sincere gratitude – it did not occur to me to pose such questions in the manner elucidated and to cast doubt upon them as fervently as I have here. The necessity of contradiction [implies that] a contingent being must have a cause and this causal series comes to an end with the Necessary Being. If the contingent being exists necessarily, [then it must] exist in its essence, then there comes a multiplicity in the essence of the Necessary Beings, but it is argued that the Necessary Being is One in all respects. Now, if the [first alternative] is possible, then it follows that the Necessary Being is its own cause and its own creator, but you have concluded that evil cannot emanate from such a Being.

In response, I offer the following: the attributes of things described are of two kinds. One type is essential and it is the one whose conception is only possible through primary description and it is necessary for it to be described not through a cause, such as animality in man, which is the essence that is prior to what is described. I mean, it must be the cause of what is described not its effect, such as animality and rationality which are attributes of man. In general, it can be said that all the constituent parts of a term are [its] essential attributes; these are meanings which are contained therein [in a term].

The other type is accidental and the opposite of what preceded. It is possible to conceive of an object without first conceiving its accidental attributes and that description is not the cause of what is described; neither does it precede in the order of existence or nature. This type is divisible into two categories: either it is necessary and inseparable, such as man's potential to be a thinker, a wonderer and a jester; or it is separable through imagination, not through existence, such as the blackness of a crow, since blackness of the crow can be separated in imagination but not in [external] existence; or they are separable both in the imagination and in the external world as man being either a writer or a peasant. These are the primary categories of attribution.

Then the necessary attributes of the existing objects can again be primarily and intellectually divided into two classes: either they are necessary through an intermediary and have a cause, such as laughter which by necessity is an actuality for man just as [the sense of] "wonder" is also by necessity an actuality for man. So this sense of wonder depends upon some other cause, this other cause is either necessary or separable. It is impossible for a separable attribute to be a cause of a necessary attribute such that this other attribute [separable one] be also necessary. If the necessity of that cause is due to another cause, which continues *ad infinitum*, then these causes are either in succession *ad infinitum* and this is impossible to prove, or it is circular with the cause being the cause of the cause and this also is obviously impossible. Or its cause leads to a cause for which there is no cause and this is the cause, which is the attribute of the Necessary Being, e.g. the attribute of thinker, which necessarily belongs to man. Indeed some of these attributes have been presented.

Let us now return to our primary inquiry, which is as follows: existence is an abstract matter which denotes two meanings by way of gradation, not by way of pure succession, nor by way of common sense. The difference between the three terms is clear from the rudimentary rules of logic and those two means are [first]; being in reality which is existence *par excellence* according to the general opinion. Secondly, there is existence in itself such as sensory perception, the imaginary, the conjectural, and the intellectual faculties.

This second meaning is exactly the same as the first meaning, for the knowledge and conceivable concepts, in so far as they are knowable and conceivable, are found in reality; and the knowing self is a real thing among other real things. It is clear that an attribute that is found in one of the real things is also found in all the other real things, except that the object which is conceptually understood, such as its representation, image and design may perhaps not exist in reality, such as our concept of Adam. So the conceived notion of Adam is a meaning found both in itself [in abstraction] and in reality since the "self" is a type of reality. However, the meaning of Adam is found in his representation, but his image is non-existent in reality. This is the difference between the two existences. It becomes clear that between the two, one is more correct; the primary, which precedes and succeeds, is known as gradation [of being], not in the common sense.

This problem is undoubtedly very subtle and deep and requires much elucidation. This is not hidden from anyone, like the attribute of animality, which exists in man, or the sum of all the three angles of a triangle, which are equal to two right angles. Here, by existence we do not mean existence in reality, but only existence in and of itself. This is because, intellectually, it is not possible to conceive of man except by conceiving of him as an animal since necessarily the meaning of animal is obtained through the meaning of man, just as oneness is necessary for threeness, since it is not possible to think and conceive of threeness, except by ones. Nothing can be conceived or thought of except through one of its attributes; therefore, that attribute becomes necessary for that thing [in order to be conceived of]. That is to say, it is not through a cause that the Necessary Being exists. Hence, [just as] singularity is necessary for the existence of threeness, so is animality necessary for the existence of man. All these attributes are essentially necessary for the existence of that which needs the attribute [to exist].

Among them [attributes] is a thing's necessity of being due to the precedence of another attribute, which is the Necessary Being, and among them are [also] a thing's necessity of being not due to the precedence of another attribute, which is the Necessary Being. Moreover, all that is necessary [i.e., attributes] are inseparable from the Necessary Being. This includes what is [necessary] due to another necessary [attribute], which precedes it, and what is not caused by a thing except by that whose essence is necessary. The proof has been presented in the foregoing discussion. Oneness is a [necessary] attribute of threeness, but then, the attribute of necessity belongs to the Necessary Being [only], [it then follows that] it can not exist in and of itself in reality, only the Necessary Being [can exist] in reality. The contingent essence of a thing, which is obtained for the thing [to be] and what is obtained in reality [i.e. accidents, are two different] things.

Non-existing attributes in reality may exist in the self and the intellect since [they are] non-existing attributes in reality. It is not possible to say that they are in reality; the same way one says void is a natural and extended dimension in which corporeal entities are extended and move from one position to another. So, these attributes exist in the intellect [only such as], void, which is conceivable in the intellect alone and does not exist in reality. So the existence of the attributes for what is described is that [it comes to be when it is] intended primarily in the self and the intellect and is not obtainable nor is it in reality. If it is said that such and such an attribute is necessary for a being, then what is meant by it is that existence is in the intellect and in the self but not in reality. Moreover, if it is said that it is a contingent being, then what is meant by it, is that existence is in the self and in the intellect. You know the difference between the two of them, whatever the attribute might be; existence in reality is different from the existence of a thing due to gradation, as we have already demonstrated.

It has been argued that the Necessary Being and all of its attributes in reality are One in every aspect and He is the cause of all existent beings coming to reality. You already know that existence in the self is also existence in reality through gradation and He is the Supreme Being and the cause of all things having become existent.

Non-existents and their causes are apparent to those who inquire. I do not wish to lengthen the discussion since it has already been shown that if it is stated that oneness is necessary for the existence of threeness, then we mean threeness is not due to [an independent] cause, nor made by a maker. Moreover all the essentials and necessities are as such due to another essential cause and that is necessary due to another necessary cause. From all this it should be clear that when it is said that the existence of oneness is necessary for threeness, what is meant is that it is so, not on account of some other cause, and is not due to the act of some other doer. Similar is the case with all other essential and necessary attributes. It is quite possible that an essential and necessary attribute might become the cause of some other essential and necessary attribute, and thus lead to an essential or necessary attribute for which there is no cause.

Thus an essential attribute may become a cause of existence in some sense. This view, however, does not negate the proposition that the Necessary Being in and of itself, is one in all respects, since here existence means existence in reality and the Necessary Being is one in reality as has been shown previously. This existence, therefore, is attained through a thing with regard to which existence in reality or in the self [can be apprehended]. In general all the existent beings existing in reality are contingent and nothing else, except the necessity of the One Being.

An analysis of this problem, generally, is that existents are contingent beings, which have emanated from the Sacred Being, by way of gradation and order. Some of these beings are not necessarily contrary and are not the result of the action of some actor, so that whenever that being is found, its opposite is also found necessarily, and if the opposite is found by necessity, then non-existence is also found by necessity. Again, if non-existence is found, evil is also found necessarily. It is quite correct to say that since the Necessary Being created blackness or heat, He thereby created the opposition, for if A̲ is the cause of B̲, and B̲ is the cause of C̲, A̲ is necessarily the cause of C. Here we are led to a particular end, the Necessary Being created blackness, hence opposition is found therein necessarily, but there is no doubt about the fact that the Necessary Being created this opposition in real things not by its own essence but by accident. He did not create blackness as the opposition of whiteness but as an essence existing contingently. All essences existing contingently are made necessary by the Necessary Being, for existence itself is good. But blackness is an essence, which can only be the opposition of something else. So whoever created blackness on account of its being a contingent existence created its opposite accidentally.

Evil therefore cannot be attributed in any way to the creator of blackness, for the primary purpose of the Eternal Being was the creation of the primary and good, but this particular form of species of good cannot possibly be devoid of evil and non-existence. It follows from all this that evil cannot be attributed to Him except by way of accident. The discussion here is not about accidents, but it is about essentials. I recommend that every philosopher I know exonerate Him [God] from evil and oppression.

Through elaboration and study arises another subject, which due to the inability of language, cannot be expressed; the intuition, which is obtained from the spirit of the perfect soul (*al-nafs al-kāmilah*) is not content but experiences an intense intellectual pleasure.

Here arises another pointed question with regard to a particular subject in theology, and that is: why did He create a thing, which He knew would be necessarily accompanied by non-existence and evil? The answer is that in blackness, for instance, there are a thousand good and only one evil. To abstain from wanting a thousand good for the sake of a single evil is itself a great evil, for the proportion of the good [that comes from] blackness to its evil is greater than the relation of a million to one. If that is the case, then it is shown that evil exists in the accidents and not essences of God's creatures, and that evil according to the primary wisdom of creation was very little which qualitatively or quantitatively is not comparable to the good [present in creation].

As to the second question about which of the two views, free will and determinism, is nearer to the truth, apparently, the determinist is on the right path, but in reality he [often] talks nonsense, for sometimes he is very far from the truth.

Some people say that duration and subsistence are matters, which have caused strife among some ignorant people because they can neither understand nor grasp the truth, since duration is only an attribute of a thing in addition to its other attributes for a given period of time. However, existence is not considered in terms of duration but that duration has an existence, which includes length of time, so that existence is more general in meaning than duration. Hence, there is no difference between existence and duration except in terms of generality and particularity. Therefore, one wonders about the statement of he who admits that existence and the existent have one and the same meaning in reality, even if the two of them are different in themselves, for one may be led astray when one deals with duration.

But the following argument of the dialecticians always leads them to impossibilities. They are asked: is there anything here that has the attribute of subsistence? If they answer no, then they are saying there is no subsistence. Hence, One creates and preserves the existents, as you may believe through succession or creation in recurring moments in spite of the fact that the [theory of] the existence through recurring moments has been falsified. For prudence sake we grant it. If on the other hand, they say that this creator through succession does not bring subsistence, they are faced with the worst kind of impossibility. If they refrain from saying that and reply that there is a thing here, which subsists, we say that this enduring thing endures on account of a duration, which is additional to its own self. Now this duration will either subsist, or it will not. If it subsists, then it subsists through subsistence, and this subsistence subsists through another, and *ad infinitum* and this is impossible. If, on the other hand, the subsistence does not subsist, how then can the subsisting thing subsist? This means that subsistence, on account of which the thing subsists, itself does not subsist. This is also impossible.

These dialecticians, in fact, commit the fallacy of asserting that the subsisting thing subsists on account of the continuous and contiguous durations in recurring moments, and hence they require an explanation, which is quite simple. They are asked, "What is the meaning of those recurring durations?" If they have any meanings, the subsisting thing will subsist. Hence these meanings must subsist with the subsisting thing for a duration, during which, the subsisting thing is described as subsisting. Otherwise, subsistence and that which subsists are meaningless. If they are two-bipartite existences, it is clear that existence and subsistence have the same meaning. Subsistence is nothing but the perpetuation of existence, or the existing thing having the attribute of existence for a period of time. It is possible for the absolute existence to be in a moment of time, but it is not possible for subsistence to be except in time. This then is the direction of their discourse and truth is with us and it shows us whose intellect is veiled from understanding the intelligibles.

This much comes to mind presently but only God knows the truth entirely.

THE LIGHT OF THE INTELLECT ON THE SUBJECT OF UNIVERSAL KNOWLEDGE

Risālah al-ḍiyā' al-'aqlī fi'l-mawḍū' al-'ilm al-kullī [7]

Indeed the subject of metaphysics is about universal knowledge upon which all sciences are conceptualized, such that its conception, is not contingent upon conceiving another thing. It most resembles the source of [all] conceptions, i.e., all objects and also the object which appears in conception. While it is necessary for existence to be in and of itself, non-existence *is* in actuality, for it is due to the principle of the gradation of [beings] that it is not possible for something to be existent unless it is completely knowable, namely that its [non] existence is not in reality. It is therefore necessary that it [existence] be an existent in itself, because something necessitates existence; otherwise, it would not be either of the two existents (abstract and real) and so something necessitates that it be a thing.

Nothing exists unless it is necessarily one of the two existences [abstract or real] since "thingness" is among the accidents of the realities of objects, so you may attempt to conceive a thing as an existent. If it were otherwise, you would fall into a cycle of impossibility. If both an existing thing and an object are universal, then the existing thing is prior [to existence] in that it is the subject of universal knowledge and it is conceptually more apparent. The "thingness" of the object is just like what is added to a thing, an attribution, and if a thing is added to the essence of the existent being, it necessitates that it exists in reality or in itself. If the existence of the existent exists in reality, then the existent exists, since it is judged that every existent requires existence and such is the succession. Moreover, if existence is an added attribute to the essence, there is no doubt that existence is an accident no matter how it is conceived – be it in reality or in itself. [Existence] then is the existential cause of the substance because the substance becomes an existent for existence and as long as its existence does not exist, it is not possible for it to exist. So it [becomes] necessary that an accident is the cause of the existence of the substance, but it [substance] is unchangeable. If each accident is the cause of the existence of a substance – because it becomes real by an accident – [this is] indicative that non-existence becomes the case necessarily. Moreover, if existence were an added thing to the essence of an existent, the existent through this would become an existent, [it would then follow that the] existence of God is also something which is added to His essence. I mean this existent is the opposite of non-existence about which we are speaking. Hence, Almighty God's essence is One, and it is impossible for this to be a multiplicity.

If a thing exists either abstractly or in itself, then it must be the case that everything has a reality specific to itself [and through it, it is distinguished from other things]. This first principle is not contrary to reason, since intellect is a reality. If something is derived from the effect of a reality in the intellect, then intellect, its reality, and [its] essence are attributed to the form that is found in reality. Hence, existence is in reality a category added to the essence or quiddity.

Reality is not a thing added to the essence of an existent being since existence in reality, is not an essence. Essence cannot exist in the same manner [as an existent] since the intellect comprehends only through intellectual abstraction [which conceives] through the accidents that are attributed to an existent being. It is not possible for this abstraction to take place externally, even though this is believed by those who are weak-minded, who think that intellectual [abstraction] quiddity, becomes an existent reality in the same manner. It is [their] firm belief that existence and the existent are things created in reality, impossibilities are not [well] understood [by them]. One principle that is necessarily impossible is that existence is added to the essence of an existent being; it is necessary for the existent to be in itself an existent through existence and that existence exists in itself through another which this succession continues *ad infinitum*.

Among the proofs contained in the arguments for this discourse, of [whether this is] the true path, is one in which the opponent asks, does this existence which is added to the essence of the existent, exist in reality – or does it not exist in reality? It is the opinion of some that it is not an existent in reality. If one inquires, then he is told that it has been established that this existence, which is added to the essence of the existent, exists in reality. Hence either it exists in itself or it does not. If it is stated that it is an existent in itself, then the claim is qualified. But if it is stated that it is not existent in itself, prior to saying that it is not existent in reality, at that point it is absolute non-existence for which there is no declarative proposition or judgment. It is necessary then to acknowledge the falsity of this judgment. It is true and clear that existence is an added attribute to the essence and quiddity of existence in itself, and not in reality. I mean, if existence, existing in reality [is] the same as itself, it is then meaningless for existence to be added to it, except when intellect considers the attribute intellectually and after one's intellect has attained the intelligible's quiddity.

The truth of this opinion is highly doubtful and it is the subject of great discussion. If we ask whether absolute existence is an intellectual quiddity or not, and state that it is not quiddity in the intellect, then the statement is impossible [to be true]. If it is not a quiddity in the intellect, existing in itself, then it is impossible for us to say that the existence in reality is a thing added to the essence of the thing. If we say that quiddity is in the intellect, having already judged that quiddity in the intellect requires that existence be added to it, then the quiddity of existence requires another intelligible existence in order for it to be existent. The answer to this problem is that intelligible quiddity requires intelligible existence in order for it to be existing in reality, not in itself because if you say that quiddity is an existent in itself, it requires that existence be an existent in itself. Having emanated from the First Source, as I said, the existent requires existence.

There are those who say that if the existence of Zayd[8] is not existent in reality, then how can Zayd exist? This argument is pure sophistry and impossible to understand from either of the following two aspects. One states that if Zayd's existence is not existent, then how can Zayd exist? A person could say that the existent exists because of an existence emanating from the errors of the Primal Origin. The second of the two arguments is that Zayd's existence in the intellect is a matter which is intelligible in and of itself. Hence the fallacies do not differentiate between the two existences, i.e. existence in reality and existence in itself [abstractly].

If one was to state that since Zayd is a particular, sensible and intelligible, his existence is a thing added to his quiddity. We answer by stating that to predict the universal predicate on [a particular] subject is impossible, since it exists through knowing [it as an] intelligible. Existence is a universal principal, which cannot be predicated upon a subject, except after it has been intellectually imposed upon the intellect at the time of one's intellection, singularly and not plural, just as the Almighty did not impose it [universally] either.

However, the proposition that says pure intelligibles are not with us and that it is not possible for them to be in essence, rather, they are intelligible through the imagination as one can only imagine them through the particulars. So perhaps imagining something is an act of the intellect in which there is an action. I mean intellection is an abstraction of the specific accidents and is not understood in itself but is thought of as being a particular.

There is no synthesis of the intelligibles with the imagination nor do they amalgamate with one another. Most of what is objected to in this regard is impossible when [it is understood that the] intellect imposes what is intellected upon a singular thing. The addition of singularity to what is intellectualized and its synthesis with imagination, is thought to be a particular being since it has been demonstrated that the truth of the existent in reality and its existence are a single unit. However, this multiplicity is attained through reflecting upon it and it's being an intelligible essence added to the concept of what is intellectualized, that is referred to as existence.

As the master of the learned [Avicenna] – blessing be upon his soul – has discussed in some of his teachings, perhaps the existence which is the quiddity of the First Truth comes by necessity, indeed, he stated that [this follows] because Absolute Necessity has no partner in any way. He also stated that existence is opposite of non-existence when one reflects upon all things, that is one of the necessities of a quiddity. This concept is the subject of how multiplicity comes from unity, which is the essence of the Almighty – May He be glorified.

Regarding the stance of the perplexed, much discussion remains, but also much has been gained and achieved. By way of unity, it is from the hand of the Almighty God that success comes. This much is possible for the intellect [to know] and we seek success from God to attain perfection. Only God knows best at all times.

ON THE KNOWLEDGE OF THE UNIVERSAL PRINCIPLES OF EXISTENCE
Risālah dar 'ilm kulliyāt-i wujūd[9]

First Section

So says Abu'l-Fatḥ 'Umar ibn Ibrāhīm al-Khayyam that once I had the honor to be in the presence of the just king, Fakhr al-Malik (The Honor of Nation) and closeness was granted in his exalted gatherings and his eminence requested that I compose a treatise with regard to the knowledge of the universals; thus this treatise was composed in accordance with his request so the companions of knowledge and wisdom may judge that this summary is more useful than volumes. May God Most High make our intention possible. With his [King] permission and generosity this discourse begins.

(1) Know that all the existent beings except the essence of God Most High are a genus. A substance (*jawhar*) is of two types, corporeal (*jism*) and simple (*basiṭ*). Of the words which imply "universal," first is the word for substance and once you divide them into two parts, one word is corporeal [compound], and the other simple and universals have no other meanings than these two. Except the essence of God, Most High, an existent being is this [a compound substance]. Some universals are divisible and others are indivisible, that which is divisible is corporeal and what is indivisible is simple and the divisible and the indivisible differentiate [from one another] in terms of hierarchy. What is simple from the perspective of their differentiation is of two universal types: one type is called "intellect" and the other is the "soul," each of them are different types. The universal intellect and its particulars have no limit. First, there is the active intellect, which is the effect of the First Cause due to its relationship with the Necessary Being that is the cause of all the existents that are below it and [Necessary Being] dominates all existents. The second intellect is the ordainer of the highest sphere and the third intellect is the ordainer of the sphere of spheres and the fourth sphere ordains the sphere of Saturn and the fifth sphere ordains the sphere of Jupiter and the sixth sphere ordains the sphere of Mars, the seventh sphere ordains the sphere of the Sun, and the eighth ordains the sphere of Venus; the ninth sphere ordains the sphere of Mercury; and the tenth, of Moon's sphere.

Each of these intellects has a soul for there is no intellect without a soul and soul without an intellect, and these intellects and souls are the ordainers of the spheres and the movers of each of their mass – what is of the soul moves by virtue of being a mover (*fā'ilī*) and what is of the intellect moves by virtue of the beloved for whom it had a yearning. It is for this reason that intellect is higher and more noble than the soul and for this reason it is closer to the Necessary Being.

(2) It should be understood that when we say the soul is the mover of the spheres by way of being the mover (*fā'ilī*) and intellect is the mover of the soul by way of the beloved [God], it is because the soul seeks its own likeness and desires to arrive at unity with it and because of the attraction which the soul has with the intellect.

Motion occurs in the heavens and these motions cause multiplicity to occur among the spheres, numerals are those which are universal and a universal number is infinite by necessity since every number that is finite is a particular to a [universal]. Numbers are of two types, even and odd [if even, it is succeeded by odd] and if odd, it is succeeded by even, since odd and even are parts of numerals; thus is the reason why no universal is finite and a universal number undoubtedly is among the universals.

Now, it has to be understood that universal existents are permanent for they are the effects of the Necessary Being. First, there is the active intellect and that is the universal intellect and then there is the universal matter and matter is of three types: spheres (*aflāk*), elements (*umahhāt*), and creatures (*mawālid*); each of them are divisible and their parts are not limited in terms of generation and corruption. The spheres and the heavens are those in whose parts there is no generation or corruption and below them are the elements which are: fire, air, water, and earth. As to creatures, first there are inanimate objects and then vegetables and then animals and man who is among the animals from the aspect of *Jinnis*[10] but also from the aspect of rationality which is superior to animals.

The sequence of beings is like the sequence of the letters of the alphabet, each of which is derived from a different one which is above it and each is a derivative of the other. For example, *Alif* (letter A) is not derived from anything because it is the first cause of all letters and the proof is that nothing precedes it but things proceed it and if one were to ask what is the lowest of the numerals we say it is number two since one is not a number for a number is that which has a predecessor and a successor. For example, they say one multiplied by one is none other than one and multiplied by two is none other than two and one by three is the same. But two by two is four because one precedes two and three succeeds it, three and one make four. The same is the case with all numbers and therefore the Necessary Being is One, not numerically, for one is not a number since nothing proceeds or succeeds it and the First Cause is One by necessity. The effect of it [First Cause] is the intellect and the effect of the intellect is the soul and the effect of the soul is the sphere and the effects of the sphere are the elements and the effects of the elements are creatures and each of these has a causal relationship with that which is below them. What is the effect of something perhaps is the cause of something else and this principle is called the "succession of gradation" (causal chain). Humans are humans when they are cognizant of gradations and know that everything is an intermediary since the spheres, elements, and creatures are the causes and effects of His existence but are not of his genus; Glory and Majesty are His. Now, that intellect and soul are the noblest things it is apparent that they must have been the same in the beginning. Those who know the beginning and the end know that a seeker has to seek proximity with [God] for the nature of His intellect and genus are one and the same. The first [created order] is the universal intellect and universal soul, but these are intermediary and alien from Him and He is alien to them. Therefore, the [intermediaries] should endeavor to attain his genus so that he may not remain far apart from his kindred souls, because perdition is a static condition.

It is known that a compound entity has no relation with the simple and the reality of the essence of man is simple and indivisible and matter is divisible. Matter is thus defined as that which has length, width, depth, and other accidental qualities such as lines and surfaces, which can be made to be perpendicular to it. The definition of simple is that which has no length, width, or depth receptive to all things and the impression of knowledge, it is neither a point nor a line, nor body, nor is it among other accidental qualities such as quality, quantity, relation, place, time, position, possession, action, passion; it is none of them. It is a substance that subsists by its own essence and the proof that it is a substance is that it is receptive to the impressions of knowledge and knowledge is an accidental category and accident does not subsist upon accident but upon substance. It is true that it [simple] is not a corporeal substance since matter, while it is receptive to divisibility, it is not [necessarily] divisible for what is receptive to divisibility is not [necessarily] divisible. Hence, the substance [man's self] should be kept pure from the attributes of corporeality. By "attributes" is meant the purpose of proximity which it has with the bodies – a proximity which it should not have except with its own genus for that will be the cause of its own destruction. God knows best.

Second Section

(3) Know that the intellect through understanding the intelligibles is engaged with itself and in order for the soul to understand the reality of the intelligibles it requires the intellect. Nobility is among the necessities of the soul and because of this, it continuously analogizes itself to the intellect and the proof is that no soul ever envies the intellect when it apprehends because the soul regards its ability more than that of the intellect at the time of perception, but its ability to understand is rather an approximation and not real.

The semblance of the soul with the intellect is inherent and its effect becomes evident in the sensibles and because the soul is more noble than the body, it [the body] is not without ignorance, in either case body is not devoid of ignorance for a body is a synthesis of matter and form, which has quality. Its quality gives the soul the universals and in particular gives a corporeal cause to particulars, which are its effect. What we have said here about particulars requires explanation. Just as the universal soul bestows on a particular soul, so spheres emanate from the elements and give the creatures and man who is part of all creatures – the quality of which part is [man's] constitution which bestows on a soul and the spheres and the elements and creatures. The ignorance of man is greater than those of other things.

(4) Know that the ancient [philosophers] have not pondered upon [the problem of the] particulars because the particulars are transient, impermanent and they [ancient philosophers] have expressed their views on the universals since universals are immutable and the knowledge that is founded upon them is permanent. Whoever discloses the universals, particulars become known through them.

Know that universals are five types: genus, species, differentia, particularity (substance)[11] and accident, each of these is a universal by itself. For example, genus is a singular universal term, which comprises of many universals just as matter and substance, each of whom are universals in themselves, which are comprised of multiplicity, just as substance is a term that implies all the knowables except God; and substances are of two types, verbal and non-verbal. The verbals are of two types, animate and inanimate, an animate is of two types, rational and non-rational. Now, one may find a genus such that, above its species, there is no species and that is the rational animal and the rest are intermediaries and each of the intermediary species in relation to what is above them are species and with what is below them are genus. Where there are species there are particulars to a universal and therefore each of them are universals and particulars. For instance, substance which is a genus to its species and its species is animate and inanimate and animate which is a genus to its species, is rational and non-rational.

Know that substance is universal for all the genus that are existent are all part of it and differentia is universal by virtue of which genus cannot be separated from genus and species from species. For instance, animal is a universal term and its different types are both rational and non-rational, non-rational and rational are differentia for man since it is through rationality that man can be distinguished from other animals and other things follow the same [process of] reasoning.

Particularity is an accident that neither in imagination nor intellectually can be abstracted from its substance; for example take wetness and water: if wetness is separated from water, it is not water and the same with heat and fire, dryness and earth, softness and air, and such like.

General accidents are of nine types: quality, quantity, relation, place, time, position, possession, action, passion, and all these are the accidents. Quantity deals with "how many" and quality with "how" and relation with "proportionality" – something to something else – and this is of a spatial matter and time has to do with "when" and position involves how it is laid and possession implies "will" and action with "deed" and passion with the "power of the doer."

(5) Know that actions that emanate from people are of two types and both are accidents, which are: present (*ḥāl*) and the habitual (*malikah*). The present action is that motion or repose produced in a man which is the result of change or emotion or desire and these are of two kinds, virtuous and non-virtuous. For example, anger and

malice are both non-virtuous and compassion and love are both virtuous. Whatever comes and soon disappears, is present action, and whatever lasts longer is called habitual, such as reading a book, which takes longer to forget; virtuous and non-virtuous characteristics remain with people but when they become non-existent, in the domain of possibility, it becomes an accident which no longer is an inherent part of the nobility of man.

In proving the existence of a creator much non-sense has been uttered since all that man has been capable of thinking are of three types: necessary, contingent or impossible. Necessary is that which cannot not be and possible is that which can be and contingent is that whose existence may or may not be and once it is proven that something is contingent [has a necessary cause] by necessity, possibility becomes necessary. Once it is said that something exists, in the imagination of the masses, its existence appears impossible. Thus, due to His existence, all paths necessarily lead to God, His Name be Exalted. All whose existence is contingent, pertains to all beings except the very essence of God, Exalted is He, and what is impossible cannot be contingent. God knows best.

(6) Know that existence is of two types, one is the Necessary Being and that is God Most High and the other is a contingent being. [The latter] is of two kinds, one substance and which is every existent that is self-sufficient from a subject and second, is accident which is not independent of a subject. Substance is of two types, one is inanimate and the other animate and objects are equal in their corporeality. The effects of objects however vary, some are cold, some hot, some vegetative, and some mineral and it would not be plausible that there be a common body for all these different effects for it is the presence of form and animating power in objects that cause the appearance of differences among them.

Philosophers have called some of those forms properties ...[12] and there is no doubt in it. Just as a magnet stone attracts a piece of iron, and fire has the potential such that from one of its flames, a hundred thousand flames appear while in [the original] fire there occurs no shortcoming. Fire is visible and due to seeing it numerous times, one loses its sense of wonder otherwise the fibers of fire are the strangest and the most wonderful of all things. Just as people are not bewildered at what fire does and know that in fire there is the power of ignition and heat, one should think that in the body of a magnet, there is the power whose disposition is to attract the iron. *He who truly understands the meaning of this, is freed from many problems.*

Third section
[On Different Types of Knowers]

(7) First, are theologians (*mutikallimūun*) who are content with theological arguments and consider this much knowledge of God, Exalted is His Name, to be sufficient. Second are Philosophers and sages who have relied on rational arguments to know the principles of logic as a way of knowing and have not been content with that as satisfying to oneself. They too however have not remained faithful to the principles of logic and have become helpless with it. Third are the Ismāʿīlīs and instructionalists (*taʿlimiyyūn*) who said how can knowledge be obtained other than through authentic instruction, for in proofs concerning knowledge of the Creator, His essence and His attributes, there are many difficulties. The reasoning of the opponents [is false] and their intellects are bewildered and helpless and therefore, it is better to seek the truth from the truthful person. Fourth are the Sufis who do not seek knowledge intellectually or discursively but by the cleansing of their inner self and through purgation of their morals, they have cleansed their rational soul from the impurities of nature and incorporeal body. When that substance [soul] is purified and becomes a reflection of the spiritual world, the forms in their status are truly unveiled without any doubt or ambiguity. *This path is the best of them all.* For it becomes known to the servant of God that there is no perfection better than the presence of God, [in the soul] and in that state, there are no obstacles or veils. For all that man lacks, is due to the impurity of nature, for if the [spiritual] veil is lifted and the screen and the obstacle is removed, the truth of things as they really are becomes apparent. The master of the creation [Prophet Muḥammad] upon him be peace and praise, has alluded to this and said, "During the days of your existence, divine grace comes from God. Do you not want to follow them?"

ON EXISTENCE
Risālah fi'l-wujūd[13]

Praise be upon Him to whom belongs glory, and sacred are His names. "He granted creation to all things and then guided them" and "accounted for all things."

1. Division of Attributes

Attributes that describe things are of two types; some are said to be "essential" and some "accidental." The accidental attributes are not to impose necessity upon that which is described and some of them [attributes] are not necessary, rather it is possible for them to be detached from it [essence] either in abstraction alone or in abstraction and in real existence. Then each one is of two types, essential and accidental which are divided into two types, one said to be abstract and the other existential (*wujūdī*).

2. Elucidation on Types of Attributes

As to the existential type, it is like describing an object, which is black because it possesses blackness. Blackness is the existential attribute, meaning it is an extra thing added to the essence of black, which exists in reality and whenever blackness is an existential attribute, then it becomes an attribute of existence. This type of existence does not need proof, for it is rather self-evident before the intellect, imagination, and the senses.

As to the type of an abstract accident such as the definition of two as half of four, if two being half of four is added to its essence, two would have so many meanings in addition to its specific meaning that could go on *ad infinitum* numerically and proof is indicative of its impossibility. As to the type that is abstract and essential such as the description of black as color, it can be said that colorness is an essential part of black.

3. Offering Proof that Color is Not an Added Attribute to the Color Black in Reality

Proof that color, due to its attribute is not added to the essence of blackness in reality, is that if it were an accident, black would also have to be an accident. How then can an accident be the subject of another accident? If the attribute of blackness be an attribute of color, then color is the attribute of the subject of blackness and neither blackness nor color are existent in reality. [If they did, then] essences [would have to] by necessity [exist in reality] and that is impossible.

4. Elucidation on Abstract Attributes

The meaning of our discourse is this: an abstract attribute is that which when the intellect reflects upon a concept intellectually, it deciphers what is intellected upon and offers an intellectual elucidation [of the subject matter] and considers its various aspects. All the existing accidents in reality may come to be the attributes of the concept, which is simple, and not compound. It is then known that indeed the attributes are from the aspect of abstraction and not due to existence in reality, since it is not possible for a simple entity to exist in reality [unless] it is in a compound entity. It has become known that accident does not become the subject of another accident and it has also become known that the subject of an accident cannot be the subject of the attribute by which an accident is described.

5. The Reason for the Perplexity of Some [Philosophers]

While most of these introductory issues are apparent, some of them however are not clear to the learned. These concepts are devoid of the knowledge of what is sublime and divinely universal, and those who have not understood these abstract attributes concerning the subject, [under the discussion] are deeply in error, such as some of the recent perplexed figures who have placed color, accident, existence and the like in a secondary state which cannot be described either through existence or through non-existence.

6. Neither with Existence nor with Non-existence: Why did the Perplexed Go Astray?

The doubt, which has led to this error, has been greatest and most obvious with regard to the primary propositions, that is, there is no intermediary between negative and affirmative [propositions] and it is obvious that there is no need for us to discuss its shortcoming or its solution.

7. How is it Possible for Them Not to Fall into Error?

If they paid attention to abstract attributes, this great disaster would not have happened, rather they say color is not found in reality and it is something different from blackness, indeed its definition is intellectually [abstract], that is, it is attained in the soul while the essence of blackness is conceived in the intellect as well as the elaborations of their various states and participation in whiteness in some cases, and such is existence and unity.

8. Why Some of the Seekers of Truth are Perplexed Regarding Existence and What is Their Perplexity?

Intellection upon existence is more difficult than upon other accidents and a group of people who seek the truth have become perplexed by it. They say, "man is one who can reflect upon truth and essence and can define existence. It is thus plausible for the intellect to conceptualize the meaning of [the concept of] man without thinking whether it is existent or non-existent." So, necessarily it is impossible for the notion of existence to have become a necessity from outside of its essence. They [perplexed philosophers] say, existence belongs to man, which means he has attained it from outside of himself, namely animality and rationality, which belong to his essence, not because someone has placed it there and not due to an intermediary of a cause. So God, glory be upon Him, has not made man [the concept of] corporeal, rather created him as an existent and thus it is impossible for a man not to be, except to exist corporeally. They said: if that were the case, necessarily, the concept of existence would become an added concept to man in reality. How could it not be [the case], and the concept [of existence] is externally endowed and nothing else.

9. Proof Concerning the Abstract Concept of Existence, Not an Added Concept in Reality

Before we try to resolve this ambiguity, we will offer a proof that existence is necessarily an abstract concept. We say: if existence was an added concept to reality, existence would be an existent, and it is said, every existent is an existent by having existence. Therefore, existence is an existent through existence and thus its existence continues *ad infinitum* and that is impossible.

10. Exposition of a Problem and its Refutation

If it is said that existence is a concept that cannot be described through existence by negating the attribute, that is [to say]: not to negate either of the two sides even if it is said, "either it is an existent or a non-existent in reality." We ask them, moreover, that both sides be negated and we say, "is existence an existent in a reality or is it non-existent in reality?" So, if the answer is positive, it becomes necessary for what is axiomatic to become impossible, and if the answer is negative, then existence is not existent in reality and this position is false.

So, we greet a companion and ask him again, "is existence an attribute which can be comprehended through the essence of the existent or not?" If the answer is positive, it is then necessary for him to confess that existence is an abstraction, and if the answer is negative, existence is non-existing both in reality and in the intellect. It is clear that the learned do not accept such things.

11. Exposition of Another Problem and its Refutation

Some of them have said, "an attribute of existence does not need another existence, in order for it to be existent, rather it is existent without another existence."

Response: the speaker wants to rid himself of [the problem] of succession but he does not succeed, rather he has fallen into a number of other impossibilities. We say, that this existence to which we are referring, is it existent or not? If the answer is negative, he has argued with us and contradicted himself. If the answer is positive, we say to him, "does that existent exist through another or not? If the answer is positive, succession to *ad infinitum* occurs which does not solve the problem and necessarily is impossible." If the answer is negative, we say, "this existence which has come upon it, is it some thing that has an essence or not?" If the answer is negative, then it is hallucination and is impossible. If the answer is positive, we say to him, "you have accepted the essence of an existent which has no existence, so why do you not accept this to be the case in all existents and in every essence, so you may free yourself from these contradictions; why are these [implications] impossible?"

Then if your original words are true, an existent whiteness needs an added existence [to be white] and so that too requires another added existence and this is impossible.

12. Refutation of the Perplexity from Another Aspect

Some of them are ignorant with regard to the contradictions [involved] and are engaged in vicious sophistry; we discontinued our discussion with them and began to refute them from another aspect. If the attribute of an existent being is existent because of its essence, not due to the existence of something else, which is affiliated with essence, then essence becomes existent with it; this is the case of a particular, which becomes predicated upon a compound entity, which is impossible. If this be the case, it is not that essence has become existent, rather it has become concomitant with the existent being. When the attribute of a particular is predicated upon the compound such as whiteness, which is white in its essence, and when it is associated with an object, the compound does not become whiteness, rather it becomes white. If whiteness be white because of its essence, the object does not become white, rather it becomes concomitant with a white object.

13. There is no Contention with Regard to Popular Opinion

People call whiteness white and they say, "this color is white," however this is by way of metaphor and is not truly the case. If existence is said to be existent metaphorically and not truthfully, this judgment is metaphorical and there is no point in contesting it.

14. The Self-Evident Nature of This Problem and Response to Their Sophistry

Know that this is a general problem for all sciences and no truth becomes evident for a scholar unless he is informed of its fallacy. I heard from one of them who said, "Existence is existent and does not need another existence, just as man is a man through 'man-ness' and 'man-ness' does not need another 'man-ness' to become man-ness."

He who says this does not differentiate between 'man-ness' and man. Were it not for 'man-ness' to be attributed to man, of course there would have to be another 'man-ness;' rather it is attributed to that which is man-ness. So, why has he [the opponent] not said the same of existence? That existence is not the attribute to the existent, which needs existence [to exist], rather, it is that which exists and nothing else, so this may refute this impossibility.

15. Exposition of the Perplexity of the Seekers of Truth

As for the solution to the perplexity of the seekers of truth, existence is that notion which is secondary and nothing else. If it is a concept, which is secondary, and nothing else, how is it possible for it to be an added concept in reality while it [existence] remains an attribute?

16. Solving the Perplexity of the Followers of Truth that Either Essence is Secondary or Existence

If something is secondary its essence comes from other than itself, for the essence was non-existing but then came to be. So essence is secondary and does not require existence nor is it related to existence; if essence, prior to existence, was non-existing, how would a thing [that does not exist] need a thing [in order to exist] prior to its existence? Indeed, requiring some thing among things is [a characteristic] of existent beings and not non-existence. The soul, which intellectualizes the essence and considers its states and elaborates upon it rationally, offers diverse descriptions – some of them are essential and some accidental.

17. Existence is a Concept that is Added to the Intelligible Essence

So one can see the imprint of existence in all objects such as accidents, and there is no doubt that existence is a concept that is added to the intelligible essence. There is no question in this regard, rather, our discourse is concerning existence in reality.

18. How the Intellect Realizes The Essence of Man-ness and its Existence

Once the intellect comprehends the essence they call "man-ness," it knows that animality and rationality, for him, are due to his essence and not because one has placed it there and existence for it is extrinsic to it. This means, if the essence be non-existent and not the subject of existence, the necessity of the attribute of existence has come to it extrinsically.

19. Perfection of the Soul is Attained Through Asceticism and Success Comes from God

For the learned, in accordance with their status, intelligibles are unveiled. He who learns about his soul from those who are ignorant in this regard, should know that because of their ambivalence they are in error. They must practice austere forms of asceticism and ask God for assistance for He alone can fulfill [their demands]. However, considering these matters and inquiry into spiritual states are among the most important subjects for discussion.

20. On the Essence of the Necessary Being and His attributes

The Necessary Being, may glory be upon Him, is He whose essence is not possible to be conceived of except as an existent. So, the attribute of existence present in the intellect is intrinsic to its intellectual essence and not because one has placed it there. If the attribute of existence is a notion that is added to its essence, indeed in the essence of the Necessary Being, there will be multiplicity. While it has been argued before that the Necessary Being is a unity in all its aspects and in no way can multiplicity enter into it unless multiplicity is [in its] abstract sense in which case it is numerically infinite. Essence in the abstract sense of multiplicity does not become multiple.

Generally, all the attributes of the Necessary Being are abstract in their essence and they are all devoid of any existence.

21. The Knowledge of the Necessary Being

His knowledge is existential (*wujūdī*), meaning, the form of the intelligibles is attained in His essence, and that they all are contingent and necessary for it. Discussion concerning this has been brought forth extensively elsewhere, so search for them there.

22. Non-Existence and its states

Once you know that existence is abstract, such as unity and other abstract things, then you have [also] known non-existence and its states from an abstract perspective and what kind of an existence is non-existence except that it [non-existence] is an intelligible concept and all intelligibles are in the soul. Therefore, the essence of non-existence, I mean its meaning, exists in the soul.

Discussion concerning whether non-existence is essentially intelligible or accidental is beyond our discussion here, the truth is that it is intelligible in accident.

23. What is the Relation of Essence to the Attribute of Existence and Non-existence?

After these concepts are explored, know that every existent is a contingent being whose essence can only be thought of intellectually without the attribute of existence becoming associated with it [leading to the idea] that the attribute of existence comes to it extrinsically and if the attribute of existence comes to it extrinsically, it is necessary that the attribute of non-existence be intrinsic to it. An attribute which belongs to a thing's essence prior to an attribute, belonging to it extrinsically, has priority in nature.

24. Proof that it is Not Possible that the Essence of a Contingent Being Be the Cause of a Necessity

We say, it is impossible that the essence of a contingent being is the cause of necessity unless there are intermediaries or other things which are contingent beings. If A is possible, then A must be the cause of B and it is known that B is a contingent being and no contingent being comes into existence unless its existence becomes necessary. So B has becomes a Necessary Being while A is not a Necessary Being. So from one aspect B is a contingent being and from another aspect it is a Necessary Being, except that the possibility of existence comes from its essence and its result is the necessity of existence.

So A is possible for it is A that is the efficient cause of the existence of B, while it is known that B is a Necessary Being. Every contingent being does not exist unless its existence becomes necessary. So, B becomes a Necessary Being while A is not a Necessary Being. Thus, from one aspect it is a contingent being and from another aspect it is a Necessary Being; unless the possibility of existence belongs to it from its own essence, the result is the necessity of existence. So A becomes the cause of the necessity of the existence of B and nothing else while A is a contingent to B. Therefore, the essence of a contingent being becomes the efficient cause of the necessity of existence and this is impossible. Therefore, it is not permissible that the essence of a contingent being [be the cause of necessity].

25. Objections Concerning This Proof

There are discussions and doubts concerning this proof, that is, A is the cause of the necessity of B, yet it is necessary just as fire is the cause of burning wood due to its heat. Then other attributes of fire do not enter into the act of burning and this I have stated by way of example.

26. Reply to the Objection

The answer: heat is the cause of burning, not the essence of fire; it is not possible for heat to exist except in a subject such as fire. So, heat has been added to fire, for it is the carrier of the efficient cause not because it is the efficient cause and if the essence of fire is the efficient cause then all its attributes would have to participate in the act of burning, especially essential or necessary attributes from which the essence of fire cannot be separated.

27. Return to the Previously Elaborated Proof

As we have said, "the essence of A in the sense that it is necessary, is the cause of B." So, if we speak from the aspect of its necessity, its necessity is the condition of the cause of A and not the cause of itself. Thus, there is a difference between a condition with which a cause is a cause and what causes itself, for what causes itself brings the necessity of B and that is the essence of A with a condition therein. This condition, meaning the abstractness of the necessity of A which [of necessity] comes to it from other than itself, does not take away from it the possibility of its essence. How is it possible to take away essential attributes?

So, the essence of A which is contingent with regard to the condition of its necessity is the cause of the necessity of B and therefore possibility enters in the completion (*tatmīm*) of necessity by bestowing existence. How could this not be the case that it is the necessities of the efficient cause that are involved in the completion of the essence of A? How can this not be the case with regard to things whose cause is A? If from the essence of A which is a Necessary Being, possibility could be taken away [abstractly], then this proof is falsified for this possibility belongs to its essence and is not possible to be taken away [from it] in any way.

28. Another Objection

If one were to say, and a doubter were to doubt, that the necessity of A is the cause of the necessity of B, then the necessity of A is not possibly found in a subject and the subject of A is like heat to the cause of fire in that it is not possible for it to be found except in a subject. If the necessity of A is the cause of the necessity of B then the essence of A necessitates possibility, possibility which is necessary for the subject of the necessity of A, this does not participate in the completion (*tatmīm*) of necessity.

29. Reply to this Objection

So, this is the answer: the necessity of A is not a thing that could exist in reality but it is a reality that is [comprehended] through intellectual abstraction. An abstract matter is existent in itself and non-existent in reality, so how can the cause of the essence of an existent be in reality? This is not like heat to fire in that heat is existent in the reality of fire. Burning which is the result of heat is not a matter of existence, rather it is non-existence and we will know the elaboration of this discourse after this chapter.

Moreover, if the necessity of the existence of A which is thought to be the cause of the necessity of B, exists in reality, then the possibility of the essence of A which is its subject, makes the completion of existence possible. This is because the agent cause (*al-fāʿil*) in its existence needs matter, it lacks action unless it participates with matter. Matter, which necessitates A, is the essence of A and so it is the essence of A which participates in the completion of necessity. What becomes essential here is that possibility and non-existence [equally] participate therein and this is impossible.

30. Emanation of the Essence from the Essence of the Transcendental Origin

Indeed, all the essences and quiddities emanate from the Essence of the Transcendental Origin, the First Truth, glory be upon Him, in accordance with an order and succession.

31. The Essences are Entirely Good

They [essences] are entirely good and there is no evil in them in any way. Indeed, evil is that which is non-existent or what necessitates it [and that follows] from the necessity of contradiction. This you know from what has already been elaborated upon.

32. God Most High, is much more exalted than what the oppressors and heretics state. There is no change or power unless it comes from Him. He is sufficient for me and the best of guides. Praise be upon Allah for He is the First Origin and the peace of Allah be upon our master [Muḥammad] and all of his pure companions.

RESPONSE TO THREE PHILOSOPHICAL PROBLEMS
Risālah jawābān lithulth masā'il[14]

In the Name of God, the Most Merciful and Compassionate.

Regarding the first matter, if the rational soul survives death and is resurrected together with the physical body, with their respective cause and effect, then each of the two, by way of truth, must be endowed with its own existence, specificities, and realities. This issue then is a proposition which is conditionally true.

If each of the two [soul and body] has its own specific existence, then it is necessary for the sum of them to be a unit. This also is a problem among the philosophers. Then, it is stated that as long as they are a unit, that unit must be finite because every finite unit is actualized – may God's Grace persist. This discussion is not new or original, among the Greek predecessors such as Pythagoras and the followers of the Atomists this [view has been] advanced. Every corporeal body is divisible *ad infinitum* in actuality, and they [philosophers in this regard] differ in their views.

Ibrāhīm al-Naẓẓām is a follower of them [atomists] in that the atom in its particles is composed of an infinite number of parts in actuality. Hence, there is no doubt that there can be an infinite number of entities, even if this [entity] is a primary matter. This view is not permissible, nor is it permissible for what is needed by way of its opposite to falsify this opinion. This proof is well known but definitely not clear to most people; rather, what is known by most of them is the opposite of what the majority believe, for what falls outside of the knowledge of infinite space is called a vacuum. This subject matter is imaginary and does not distinguish between the primaries except through proofs. Nonetheless, imagination does reside in this proof by certainty of action and the proof rests totally upon [the reliability of] sensible objects and dimensions. Imaginary infinity, as long as it is one of the intelligibles and is the essences of units and even though it is sequential in the intellect, essentially has a natural order. The first precedes the second, and the second, the third, and the third, the fourth. These are priorities in essence, such as the succession of causes and effects; and it is not conceivable that they be infinite either. There are many proofs, even if they fall outside the realm of understanding of its hypothetical nature. As long as they are among the intelligibles, essences of numbers [for example] even if the order of the numbers is intrinsically sequential, [the concept] does not rest on a necessary finitude. Indeed, the actualization of finitude and infinity is of this nature and this is impossible, as it has become clear among the seekers of knowledge.

Rejecting the apprehension of the soul from this aspect is impossible and the proofs concerning these concepts have been clarified in the works of the master, Avicenna, making it clear that every rational being who conceives something, does so potentially with infinite characteristics. That is because it is not possible for the intelligible concept to be, except as a universally abstract [form detached] from all the external attachments and accidental attributes, whether [they be] necessary or not, its particulars are infinite in potentiality. So, if the universal intellect conceives of infinite objects from the aspect of non-sequential numbers in a higher order, as we said, it then appears that the Necessary Being is singular from all aspects. We have shown that the world in its essence is knowledge and one does not know anything unless one knows Him. He is the unity of all the contingent beings since it is necessary that He be infinite, [if one argues] then there is no argument with us upon this matter. One could deviate after embracing His unity and the fact that He is the generator of all existence to infinity and that He knows His essence and that He creates. If you embrace these[15] conditional propositions, then it is necessary for us [to accept] that His knowledge is infinite and it is necessary to argue in favor of modifying the conditional propositions when they are true. The form of analogy is correct in that its conclusion is correct by necessity and misperception about that should be removed. When misperception is not removed, the intellect knows by its likeness [i.e. analogy], and that likeness of knowledge is false. There is no origin for a previously imaginary cause, and the intellect is not always able to analyze the analogies and comparisons through the principles of logic, such as the first example in the problem we presented. One suspects that everything known about it [infinite] is finite and every known finite thing has the right form [to be deciphered] by analogy. However, the conditional propositions [may be] false because one may say that every known, which is inclusive of it, is abstract and figurative. There is no proposition, which encompasses this topic such that it has a [abstract] meaning except when it encompasses what can be corporeally perceived through the senses and that is a common or figurative name. A figurative and abstract term is used [to describe things], as for this proposition and all that it encompasses, it is finite. It is the greater one. If a proposition states that all knowledge is finite, then it is the same argument, [namely], how is it then possible for a conditional proposition to serve as proof of itself?

So [what] one really means [by this is] that every "encompassing" is finite in that the encompassing is figurative and abstract. Hence, the greater one is in falsehood, as in the case of one who represents these false analogies [as true, the more] the intellect is corrupted with doubts about the true results. The true conditional propositions must be supported by logical principles through discourse or reflection, which are science and proofs, especially in regard to the problems of the science of metaphysics, and transcendental wisdom which is the ultimate goal of the philosopher [Avicenna] in order for the student of *Al-Najāt* [to learn] with regard to the afterlife and eschatological matters.

As for the second issue, contingent events come to be through a unified means and also through a succession in order to reach the

Necessary Being, falsehood of what is naturally possible [follows] if one disregards the discourse of the sages. The answer [of sages], may God sustain their blessing, [is that] all existents are necessary beings but necessity divides them into two [types], i.e., either the Necessary Being is in His essences or it is a necessary being through others. The necessary being through others, is considered as such, because of a necessary cause and if it is considered to be non-existent [it is] because of a cause which is necessarily non-existent. His essence is considered to be non-differentiated from the causes of existence and non-existence. So its existence or non-existence is not necessary and is therefore contingent. This name [necessity] must be understood in this context. As for the contingent categories of the universal and particular, and the particular of the particular (differentia) and the propositions previously treated in logic, we say what is contingent is either universal, necessary or impossible. Concerning abstract issues, contingency has no existence at all in reality, nor does it in non-existence. Also the two abstractions [necessity and contingency] have been exhaustively commented upon through this discussion, and in the discourse of our opponents.

This treatise [has been composed] for the chief justice of Fārs province, Abī Ṭāhir, in the land of Fārs in the seventy-third year. A copy of this treatise is in Iṣfahān, Fārs and Baghdād, and the adjacent areas but I have no copy of it, otherwise, I would have offered it to your eminence immediately. That goes without saying. These concepts and states [of being] are many and my time is limited, I am disabled and suffer from a terrible illness, which causes my handwriting and speech to falter. May God grant us and our brothers a good ending.

As for the third issue, it has been proven that the existence of time is due to motion and the limited amount of motion of the heavenly bodies. Then it was ordained that motion is not sufficient to end the problem, the answer is not at hand and this is a grand question, difficult to conceive. The opinions of the theologians in this regard are varied. Some of them deny that time exists and that it needs to be proven by the philosophers, as mentioned at the beginning of the problem, and to discuss the proofs of those who bestow on it an eternally self-sustaining existence.

Then there are those who argue that [time exists] and bestow an existence upon it, which is not self-sustaining, but [they] place it in a time-bound event. Most people are weak-minded, except philosophers who believe that the discourse of motion and its quantity is a natural time as the philosopher [Avicenna] mentions it in the beginning of the natural science, I mean in the book of *al-Samāʿ al-Ṭabiʿī*. The foundations of knowledge are not among that science; rather, they are of a more transcendental science. Indeed, the discourse about the two of them is of the universal knowledge pertaining to the four sciences, I mean, the universal knowledge of every philosopher who begins with the natural science, which includes the sum of all sciences and different types of existents and it refers back to that which exists. The subject of this science is the existent. Then there is the science of theology, which in Greek is treated in *Enneads* and Aristotle has gathered these sciences in *Metaphysica*;[16] it is the science which transcends [existents] because of its participation in [metaphysical concepts], I mean because of its metaphysical nature.

Then comes the science of mathematics followed by the natural sciences, the meaning of their principles and their enumeration are necessary and prove what is possible for them. So regarding motion and its quantity in the book *al-Samāʿ al-Ṭabiʿī* the claim that time is an eternal essence has been falsified in that the Necessary Being is a unity from all aspects and there is no multiplicity in Him and His attributes, [nor is] there time in any of His attributes, neither is any attribute of the Necessary Being in time. As for the falsehood of the statement of he who says, "An accident is created in time through the impossibility of creation in a time prior to the creation of time," indeed, creation is creation in essence. As for the falsehood of the claim of he who refutes it, indeed it has been exhaustively discussed in the book of *al-Samāʿ al-Ṭabiʿī* of the *Kitāb al-shifāʾ*. Hence, no more needs to be said about it here. One can make the statement that a name [i.e. time] is a noun, an expression of our imagination through an absence which we are unable to imagine through the non-existence of time. Indeed, time is that whose non-existence cannot be imagined. How then does one argue regarding the proof of what we have previously mentioned in regard to the beginning of the problem, which is imagining the impossible. What necessitates this impossibility is that which [could] also not require it to be impossible.[17]

This is then the answer to the three issues and the first of them brings a great deal of benefit and great returns. Time does not allow us to answer the remaining questions here, but God willing, if I live long enough, I will begin to answer the rest if my stamina and intellect allow. The opinion of our master [Avicenna], whose perfect [treatment] of the concept of time in all aspects serves and honors [us] with an answer [to the problem of time], includes the beauty of his treatment and the sublimity of his goals which are to bestow upon us [wisdom], to the extent that one is receptive. May God Most High grant you and those who follow rightful guidance, peace.

Know that every existent either exists by the necessity of its essence or by other than its essence. Rather, it [existent] has a creator that has given it priority in essence. Moreover, [all things] end [in their natural] elevation to a creator who is a Necessary Being in and of Himself, not added to any other thing. Even though it is impossible to prove that there can be infinity in actuality, this [type of] existence has been explained as the most noble in reality and it has been shown that He has no equal in existence. We have explained that numbers are finite because they are part of the genera of existence. Know that things are hidden until the intellect comes to know of them through the knowledge that is axiomatic because [the axioms] make [knowledge to be like] preliminaries in order for the truth, which is sought from what is known primarily. Since every number can be doubled and there is nothing infinite in actuality, which is possible to double, but what is infinite is impossible to be a thing greater [than something else], so there is no number that is infinite in actuality. This is the first type of the second form of the sentential analogies. If it has been shown that the existent [does not exist] in and of itself but is [contingent upon] another thing, it leads to the essence of that which necessarily exists in and of itself. We say that it is impossible for the existent to be existent in itself other than that which is caused by the One: [this is] because it is between the first existent, which has no existence with a means or a cause, since if there was a cause, it would be prior [to itself] and this is without the status of existence. It is a self-evident truth that between every two [identical units] there is no essential or accidental difference. If the two are proved to exist primarily and singularly, then the difference would not be the thing that they both share in it, so the constituent [elements] of one of the two cannot be one of the two in which the other shares. What distinguishes the second is its existence through cause and effect with a cause in existence, this is not a primary truth, but this is an impossibility and it has been demonstrated that existence of the essence of the Necessary Being exists in itself and is sanctified without an equal partner and that is God Almighty.

As for what the perplexed ones say about the great sublime One, it has been shown that there is no [other] creator because its essence would have had to be other than a Necessary Being in and of itself and that is the most remote form of possibility. Hence, corporeal existence is a cause because it is a compound made of matter, form, and quiddity; the [latter] two have priority in the intellect. They exist by necessity in the intellect [in a manner] whose existence benefited from another and none is equal to Him in necessity, [nor is] His existence through an intermediary. That which does not have an intermediary is the noblest and most perennial in existence. He is praised as having no opposite, hence the meaning of the two opposites is the distinction of the two from each other and each of the two has been falsified by the other. So, if He had an opposite, it would not be visible. Hence, [what follows] is that there is no Necessary Being but there is a Necessary Being, and [their opinion] is impossible. The non-existence of His opposite is the cause of His existence and therefore, for Him to be known is impossible.

Praise Be Upon He Who is One.

APPENDIX B

The Ruba'iyyat[1] *Edward FitzGerald's Translation*

My translation will interest you from its Form, and not also in many respect in its Detail: Very unliteral as it is, many quatrains are mashed together; and something lost, I doubt, of Omar's simplicity, which is so much a virtue of him.

EDWARD FITZGERALD

FitzGerald's translation is a work of a poet inspired by a poet; not a copy, but a reproduction, not a translation, but a redelivery of a poetic inspiration.

CHARLES ELIOT NORTON

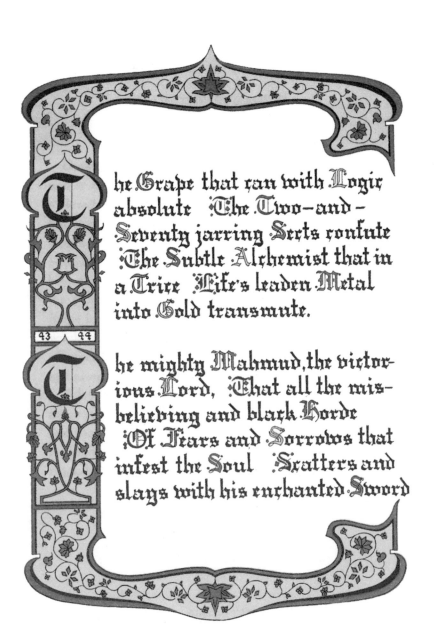

43

The Grape that can with Logic absolute
The Two-and-Seventy jarring Sects confute:
The Subtle Alchemist that in a Trice
Life's leaden Metal into Gold transmute.

44

The mighty Mahmud, the victorious Lord,
That all the misbelieving and black Horde
Of Fears and Sorrows that infest the Soul
Scatters and slays with his enchanted Sword

1

Wake! For the Sun, who scatter'd into flight
The Stars before him from the Field of Night,
Drives Night along with them from Heav'n, and strikes
The Sultān's Turret with a Shaft of Light.

2

Before the phantom of False morning died,
Methought a Voice within the Tavern cried,
"When all the Temple is prepared within,
Why nods the drowsy Worshipper outside?"

3

And, as the Cock crew, those who stood before
The Tavern shouted--"Open then the Door!
"You know how little while we have to stay,
"And, once departed, may return no more."

4

Now the New Year reviving old Desires,
The thoughtful Soul to Solitude retires,
Where the WHITE HAND OF MOSES on the Bough
Puts out, and Jesus from the Ground suspires.

5

Iram indeed is gone with all his Rose,
And Jamshyd's Sev'n-ring'd Cup where no one knows;
But still a Ruby kindles in the Vine,
And many a Garden by the Water blows.

6

And David's Lips are lockt; but in divine
High-piping Pehlevī, with "Wine! Wine! Wine!
"Red Wine!"--the Nightingale cries to the Rose
That sallow cheek of hers to' incarnadine.

7

Come, fill the Cup, and in the fire of Spring
Your Winter-garment of Repentance fling:
The Bird of Time has but a little way
To flutter--and the Bird is on the Wing.

8

Whether at Naishāpūr or Babylon,
Whether the Cup with sweet or bitter run,
The Wine of Life keeps oozing drop by drop,
The Leaves of Life keep falling one by one.

9

Each Morn a thousand Roses brings, you say;
Yes, but where leaves the Rose of Yesterday?
And this first Summer month that brings the Rose
Shall take Jamshyd and Kaikobād away.

10

Well, let it take them! What have we to do
With Kaikobād the Great, or Kaikhosrū?
Let Zāl and Rustum bluster as they will,
Or Hātim call to Supper--heed not you.

11

With me along the strip of Herbage strown
That just divides the desert from the sown,
Where name of Slave and Sultān is forgot--
And Peace to Mahmūd on his golden Throne!

12

A Book of Verses underneath the Bough,
A Jug of Wine, a Loaf of Bread – and Thou
Beside me singing in the Wilderness--
Oh, Wilderness were Paradise enow!

13

Some for the Glories of This World; and some
Sigh for the Prophet's Paradise to come;
Ah, take the Cash, and let the Credit go,
Nor heed the rumble of a distant Drum!

14

Look to the blowing Rose about us--"Lo,
Laughing," she says, "into the world I blow,
At once the silken tassel of my Purse
Tear, and its Treasure on the Garden throw."

15

And those who husbanded the Golden grain,
And those who flung it to the winds like Rain,
Alike to no such aureate Earth are turn'd
As, buried once, Men want dug up again.

16

The Worldly Hope men set their Hearts upon
Turns Ashes--or it prospers; and anon,
Like Snow upon the Desert's dusty Face,
Lighting a little hour or two--is gone.

17

Think, in this batter'd Caravanserai
Whose Portals are alternate Night and Day,
How Sultān after Sultān with his Pomp
Abode his destined Hour, and went his way.

18

They say the Lion and the Lizard keep
The Courts where Jamshyd gloried and drank deep:
And Bahrām, that great Hunter--the Wild Ass
Stamps o'er his Head, but cannot break his Sleep.

19

I sometimes think that never blows so red
The Rose as where some buried Caesar bled;
That every Hyacinth the Garden wears
Dropt in her Lap from some once lovely Head.

20

And this reviving Herb whose tender Green
Fledges the River-Lip on which we lean--
Ah, lean upon it lightly! for who knows
From what once lovely Lip it springs unseen!

21

Ah, my Belovéd, fill the Cup that clears
TO-DAY past Regrets and future Fears:
To-morrow!--Why, To-morrow I may be
Myself with Yesterday's Sev'n thousand Years.

22

For some we loved, the loveliest and the best
That from his Vintage rolling Time hath prest,
Have drunk their Cup a Round or two before,
And one by one crept silently to rest.

23

And we, that now make merry in the Room
They left, and Summer dresses in new bloom,
Ourselves must we beneath the Couch of Earth
Descend--ourselves to make a Couch--for whom?

24

Ah, make the most of what we yet may spend,
Before we too into the Dust descend;
Dust into Dust, and under Dust to lie,
Sans Wine, sans Song, sans Singer, and--sans End!

25

Alike for those who for TO-DAY prepare,
And those that after some TO-MORROW stare,
A Muezzīn from the Tower of Darkness cries,
"Fools! your Reward is neither Here nor There."

26

Why, all the Saints and Sages who discuss'd
Of the Two Worlds so wisely--they are thrust
Like foolish Prophets forth; their Words to Scorn
Are scatter'd, and their Mouths are stopt with Dust.

27

Myself when young did eagerly frequent
Doctor and Saint, and heard great argument
About it and about: but evermore
Came out by the same door where in I went.

28

With them the seed of Wisdom did I sow,
And with mine own hand wrought to make it grow;
And this was all the Harvest that I reap'd--
"I came like Water, and like Wind I go."

29

Into this Universe, and Why not knowing
Nor Whence, like Water willy-nilly flowing;
And out of it, as Wind along the Waste,
I know not Whither, willy-nilly blowing.

30

What, without asking, hither hurried Whence?
And, without asking, Whither hurried hence!
Oh, many a Cup of this forbidden Wine
Must drown the memory of that insolence!

31

Up from Earth's Centre through the Seventh Gate
I rose, and on the Throne of Saturn sate,
And many a Knot unravel'd by the Road;
But not the Master-knot of Human Fate.

32

There was the Door to which I found no Key;
There was the Veil through which I might not see:
Some little talk awhile of ME and THEE
There was--and then no more of THEE and ME.

33

Earth could not answer; nor the Seas that mourn
In flowing Purple, of their Lord forlorn;
Nor rolling Heaven, with all his Signs reveal'd
And hidden by the sleeve of Night and Morn.

34

Then of the THEE IN ME who works behind
The Veil, I lifted up my hands to find
A Lamp amid the Darkness; and I heard,
As from Without--"THE ME WITHIN THEE BLIND!"

35

Then to the Lip of this poor earthen Urn
I lean'd, the Secret of my Life to learn:
And Lip to Lip it murmur'd--"While you live,
Drink!--for, once dead, you never shall return."

36

I think the Vessel, that with fugitive
Articulation answer'd, once did live,
And drink; and Ah! the passive Lip I kiss'd,
How many Kisses might it take--and give!

37

For I remember stopping by the way
To watch a Potter thumping his wet Clay:
And with its all-obliterated Tongue
It murmur'd--"Gently, Brother, gently, pray!"

38

And has not such a Story from of Old
Down Man's successive generations roll'd
Of such a clod of saturated Earth
Cast by the Maker into Human mould?

39

And not a drop that from our Cups we throw
For Earth to drink of, but may steal below
To quench the fire of Anguish in some Eye
There hidden--far beneath, and long ago.

40

As then the Tulip for her morning sup
Of Heav'nly Vintage from the soil looks up,
Do you devoutly do the like, till Heav'n
To Earth invert you--like an empty Cup.

41

Perplext no more with Human or Divine,
To-morrow's tangle to the winds resign,
And lose your fingers in the tresses of
The Cypress--slender Minister of Wine.

42

And if the Wine you drink, the Lip you press,
End in what All begins and ends in--Yes;
Think then you are TO-DAY what YESTERDAY
You were--TO-MORROW you shall not be less.

43

So when that Angel of the darker Drink
At last shall find you by the river-brink,
And, offering his Cup, invite your Soul
Forth to your Lips to quaff--you shall not shrink.

44

Why, if the Soul can fling the Dust aside,
And naked on the Air of Heaven ride,
Were't not a Shame--were't not a Shame for him
In this clay carcase crippled to abide?

45

'Tis but a Tent where takes his one day's rest
A Sultān to the realm of Death addrest;
The Sultān rises, and the dark Ferrāsh
Strikes, and prepares it for another Guest.

46

And fear not lest Existence closing your
Account, and mine, should know the like no more;
The Eternal Sākī from that Bowl has pour'd
Millions of Bubbles like us, and will pour.

47

When You and I behind the Veil are past,
Oh, but the long, long while the World shall last,
Which of our Coming and Departure heeds
As the Sea's self should heed a pebble-cast.

48

A Moment's Halt--a momentary taste
Of BEING from the Well amid the Waste--
And Lo!--the phantom Caravan has reach'd
The NOTHING it set out from--Oh, make haste!

49

Would you that spangle of Existence spend
About THE SECRET--quick about it, Friend!
A Hair perhaps divides the False and True--
And upon what, prithee, may life depend?

50

A Hair perhaps divides the False and True;
Yes; and a single Alif were the clue--
Could you but find it--to the Treasure-house,
And peradventure to THE MASTER too;

51

Whose secret Presence, through Creation's veins
Running Quicksilver-like eludes your pains;
Taking all shapes from Māh to Māhi; and
They change and perish all--but He remains;

52

A moment guess'd--then back behind the Fold
Immerst of Darkness round the Drama roll'd
Which, for the Pastime of Eternity,
He doth Himself contrive, enact, behold.

53

But if in vain, down on the stubborn floor
Of Earth, and up to Heav'n's unopening Door,
You gaze TO-DAY, while You are You--how then
TO-MORROW, You when shall be You no more?

54

Waste not your Hour, nor in the vain pursuit
Of This and That endeavour and dispute;
Better be jocund with the fruitful Grape
Than sadden after none, or bitter, Fruit.

55

You know, my Friends, with what a brave Carouse
I made a Second Marriage in my house;
Divorced old barren Reason from my Bed,
And took the Daughter of the Vine to Spouse.

56

For "Is" and "Is-not" though with Rule and Line
And "Up-and-Down" by Logic I define,
Of all that one should care to fathom, I
Was never deep in anything but--Wine.

57

Ah, but my Computations, People say,
Reduced the Year to better reckoning?--Nay,
'Twas only striking from the Calendar
Unborn To-morrow, and dead Yesterday.

58

And lately, by the Tavern Door agape,
Came shining through the Dusk an Angel Shape
Bearing a Vessel on his Shoulder; and
He bid me taste of it; and 'twas--the Grape!

59

The Grape that can with Logic absolute
The Two-and-Seventy jarring Sects confute:
The sovereign Alchemist that in a trice
Life's leaden metal into Gold transmute:

60

The mighty Mahmūd, Allah-breathing Lord,
That all the misbelieving and black Horde
Of Fears and Sorrows that infest the Soul
Scatters before him with his whirlwind Sword.

61

Why, be this Juice the growth of God, who dare
Blaspheme the twisted tendril as a Snare?
A Blessing, we should use it, should we not?
And if a Curse--why, then, Who set it there?

62

I must abjure the Balm of Life, I must,
Scared by some After-reckoning ta'en on trust,
Or lured with Hope of some Diviner Drink,
To fill the Cup--when crumbled into Dust!

63

Oh, threats of Hell and Hopes of Paradise!
One thing at least is certain--This life flies;
One thing is certain and the rest is Lies;
The Flower that once has blown for ever dies.

64

Strange, is it not? that of the myriads who
Before us pass'd the door of Darkness through,
Not one returns to tell us of the Road,
Which to discover we must travel too.

65

The Revelations of Devout and Learn'd
Who rose before us, and as Prophets burn'd,
Are all but Stories, which, awoke from Sleep
They told their comrades, and to Sleep return'd.

66

I sent my Soul through the Invisible,
Some Letter of that After-life to spell:
And by and by my Soul return'd to me,
And answer'd "I Myself am Heav'n and Hell:"

67

Heav'n but the Vision of fulfill'd Desire,
And Hell the Shadow from a Soul on fire,
Cast on the Darkness into which Ourselves,
So late emerged from, shall so soon expire.

68

We are no other than a moving row
Of Magic Shadow-shapes that come and go
Round with the Sun-illumined Lantern held
In Midnight by the Master of the Show;

69

But helpless Pieces of the Game He plays
Upon this Chequer-board of Nights and Days;
Hither and thither moves, and checks, and slays,
And one by one back in the Closet lays.

70

The Ball no question makes of Ayes and Noes,
But Here or There as strikes the Player goes;
And He that toss'd you down into the Field,
He knows about it all--HE knows--HE knows!

71

The Moving Finger writes; and, having writ,
Moves on: nor all your Piety nor Wit
Shall lure it back to cancel half a Line,
Nor all your Tears wash out a Word of it.

72

And that inverted Bowl they call the Sky,
Whereunder crawling coop'd we live and die,
Lift not your hands to It for help--for It
As impotently moves as you or I.

73

With Earth's first Clay They did the Last Man knead,
And there of the Last Harvest sow'd the Seed:
And the first Morning of Creation wrote
What the Last Dawn of Reckoning shall read.

74

YESTERDAY This Day's Madness did prepare;
TO-MORROW's Silence, Triumph, or Despair:
Drink! for you know not whence you came, nor why:
Drink! for you know not why you go, nor where.

75

I tell you this--When, started from the Goal,
Over the flaming shoulders of the Foal
Of Heav'n Parwīn and Mushtarī they flung,
In my predestined Plot of Dust and Soul.

76

The Vine had struck a fibre: which about
If clings my Being--let the Dervish flout;
Of my Base metal may be filed a Key,
That shall unlock the Door he howls without.

77

And this I know: whether the one True Light
Kindle to Love, or Wrath-consume me quite,
One Flash of It within the Tavern caught
Better than in the Temple lost outright.

78

What! out of senseless Nothing to provoke
A conscious Something to resent the yoke
Of unpermitted Pleasure, under pain
Of Everlasting Penalties, if broke!

79

What! from his helpless Creature be repaid
Pure Gold for what he lent him dross-allay'd--
Sue for a Debt he never did contract,
And cannot answer--Oh the sorry trade!

80

Oh Thou, who didst with pitfall and with gin
Beset the Road I was to wander in,
Thou wilt not with Predestined Evil round
Enmesh, and then impute my Fall to Sin!

81

Oh Thou, who Man of baser Earth didst make,
And ev'n with Paradise devise the Snake:
For all the Sin wherewith the Face of Man
Is blacken'd – Man's forgiveness give--and take!

82

As under cover of departing Day
Slunk hunger-stricken Ramazān away,
Once more within the Potter's house alone
I stood, surrounded by the Shapes of Clay.

83

Shapes of all Sorts and Sizes, great and small,
That stood along the floor and by the wall;
And some loquacious Vessels were; and some
Listen'd perhaps, but never talk'd at all.

84

Said one among them--"Surely not in vain
"My substance of the common Earth was ta'en
"And to this Figure moulded, to be broke,
"Or trampled back to shapeless Earth again."

85

Then said a Second--"Ne'er a peevish Boy
"Would break the Bowl from which he drank in joy;
"And He that with his hand the Vessel made
"Will surely not in after Wrath destroy."

86

After a momentary silence spake
Some Vessel of a more ungainly Make;
"They sneer at me for leaning all awry:
"What! did the Hand then of the Potter shake?"

87

Whereat some one of the loquacious Lot--
I think a Sūfi pipkin-waxing hot--
"All this of Pot and Potter--Tell me, then,
"Who is the Potter, pray, and who the Pot?"

88

"Why," said another, "Some there are who tell
"Of one who threatens he will toss to Hell
"The luckless Pots he marr'd in making--Pish!
"He's a Good Fellow, and 't will all be well."

89

"Well," murmur'd one, "Let whoso make or buy,
"My Clay with long Oblivion is gone dry:
"But fill me with the old familiar Juice,
"Methinks I might recover by and by."

90

So while the Vessels one by one were speaking,
The little Moon look'd in that all were seeking:
And then they jogg'd each other, "Brother! Brother!
"Now for the Porter's shoulder-knot a-creaking!"

91

Ah, with the Grape my fading life provide,
And wash the Body whence the Life has died,
And lay me, shrouded in the living Leaf,
By some not unfrequented Garden-side.

92

That ev'n my buried Ashes such a snare
Of Vintage shall fling up into the Air
As not a True-believer passing by
But shall be overtaken unaware.

93

Indeed the Idols I have loved so long
Have done my credit in this World much wrong:
Have drown'd my Glory in a shallow Cup,
And sold my Reputation for a Song.

94

Indeed, indeed, Repentance oft before
I swore--but was I sober when I swore?
And then and then came Spring, and Rose-in-hand
My thread-bare Penitence apieces tore.

95

And much as Wine has play'd the Infidel,
And robb'd me of my Robe of Honour--Well,
I wonder often what the Vintners buy
One half so precious as the stuff they sell.

96

Yet Ah, that Spring should vanish with the Rose!
That Youth's sweet-scented manuscript should close!
The Nightingale that in the branches sang,
Ah, whence, and whither flown again, who knows!

97

Would but the Desert of the Fountain yield
One glimpse--if dimly, yet indeed, reveal'd,
To which the fainting Traveller might spring,
As springs the trampled herbage of the field!

98

Would but some wingéd Angel ere too late
Arrest the yet unfolded Roll of Fate,
And make the stern Recorder otherwise
Enregister, or quite obliterate!

99

Ah Love! could you and I with Him conspire
To grasp this sorry Scheme of Things entire,
Would not we shatter it to bits--and then
Re-mould it nearer to the Heart's Desire!

100

Yon rising Moon that looks for us again--
How oft hereafter will she wax and wane;
How oft hereafter rising look for us
Through this same Garden--and for one in vain!

101

And when like her, oh Sākī, you shall pass
Among the Guests Star-scatter'd on the Grass,
And in your joyous errand reach the spot
Where I made One--turn down an empty Glass!

(TAMAM)

APPENDIX C

Arabic Poems[1]

If I be satisfied through gambling with language
Which is attained laboriously through my hand
I would feel safe from the vicissitudes of all events
But o' my life, you are just a moment among moments
And for me, above the two firmaments, there are homes
Lift me high in the heavens between the two bright stars
Is it not the destiny of the heavens to turn every glory
And to turn every good into evil?
Be patient o' soul for your place of rest indeed
Is none but to tumble from top to bottom
When your world draws nearer, it is still too far
Now that the product of life is none but death
The fate of those hard at work and those not, are the same

* * * *

If religion and the heavens, seven
Bow before me now,
I fast from sin, inside and out
Breaking my fast, the Lord's praise I shout
For those from truth lost,
May my soul's presence be truth's cost
As if my straight path brings insights to be
As bridges built spanning the divide of mystery

* * * *

I spent my life looking for a brother I can trust,
One who will stand by me if others betrayed me,
I befriended many but found how unworthy they are,
Changed companions but failed to find true friends
I said to myself "cease your search for in this life,
You shall not find a true human you can trust."

* * * *

Poverty has not brought me to you
My pride has not allowed me to know poverty
It is the attainment of honor that I seek
A virtue that belong to the free and great nations
If the world had given me free will;
And had flowed along my desires
I would have rushed and returned
To be with you and spend the rest of my life

* * * *

Have the night winds remained calm?
Or have their eye-lids closed in sleep?
Have the spheres complained or their part become worn out;
So they have become weary and lost their guided paths?
It is as though the revolving stars have stopped
Moving, and have missed their goals!
In the heart of Bahram, there is moaning and pain,
While Kiwan is blind and does not heed the observation towers!
That is why the Turkish state has gone too far
And the Turkish people have started seeking ascent to heaven!

* * * * *

The intellect wonders when it comes to possess it,
Wonders at the sight of those who depend on fate;
For its gifts are changing like the wind,
And its blessings are as transient as the shade!

Notes

INTRODUCTION

1. All dates hereafter will be given first in the Persian-Islamic calendar followed by the Common Era.
2. Perhaps an exception is Swami Govinda Tirtha, *The Nectar of Grace: 'Omar Khayyam's Life and Works*, Allahabad: 1941 in which a thorough analysis of his poetry is offered. This work, however, is too technical for the general reader and lacks the substantial research that has been done since then. Also see Kasra's introduction to *The Rubaiyat of 'Umar Khayyam*, New York: 1975 and Elwell Sutton's expanded edition of translation and notes of Dashti's *In Search of Omar Khayyam*, New York: 1971. Minovī, one of the most eminent scholars of Khayyam, reports that up until 1929, there were nearly 2000 books written on Khayyam. Of his poems, there have been 32 translations into English, 16 in Urdu, 12 in Arabic, 5 in Turkish, 2 in Danish. Notably, Edward FitzGerald's translation into English has been reprinted 139 times.
3. N.H. Dole, *Flowers From Persian Poets*, New York: 1901, p. 81.
4. Within the same general vicinity there is the tomb of Imāmzadeh Maḥrūq, the brother of Imām Riḍā, the eighth Imām of the Shi'ites. A few yards away one finds the tomb of Farīd al-Dīn Aṭṭār, the famous Sufi of the late fifth/eleventh century as well as the tomb of the thirteenth/nineteenth century master painter Kamāl al-Mulk.
5. M. Muḥit Ṭabāṭabā'ī, *Khayyam ya Khayyāmī*, Tehran: 1370 AH.
6. An example of this perspective is the recent article by M.R.J. Nā'inī, "Khayyām-ī nayshābūrī khayyam-i shā'ir nist," *Rahāvard Journal of Persian Literature*, 57(2001):20, Summer, 20–24.
7. *Risālah dar 'ilm-i kulliyāt-i wujūd*, in *Dānish nāmah-yi Khayyāmī*, ed. R.R. Malik, Tehran: 1377. pp. 389–90.
8. For more information on this type of literature see A. Irānī, *Payām-i falsafi-yi Khayyam*, Los Angeles: 1991.

9. For an example of the type of work which defends Khayyam against heretical thought and puts him completely among the faithful, see Sadiqī Nakhjāvanī, *Khayyam Pendarī*, Tehran: 1347 AH.
10. Johnson Brigham, *Many Sided Omar*, Des Moines: 1924, pp. 14–15.
11. The account of this conversation has been conveyed to me by Seyyed Hossein Nasr who was present at that meeting.
12. For a detailed discussion on different editions, their chronological order and their authenticity see Ibid. pp. 153–98.
13. For more information on the question of theodicy, see Eric L. Ormsby, *Theodicy in Islamic Thought*, Princeton: 1941.

CHAPTER ONE

1. Ahmad Sa'idi, *Ruba'iyat of Omar Khayyam*, Berkeley: 1991, p. 125.
2. While the exact date of his birth is not known, Swami Govinda Tirtha in his impressive calculation in *The Nectar of Grace: Omar Khayyam's Life and Works* (Allahabad: 1941, p. XXXII), mentions 439 AH, while R. Tabrizī in his *Tarabkhāneh* mentions 455 as the likely date. Most scholars seem to accept 439 as the probable date.
3. 'Abd al-Raḥmān Khāzenī in his *Mizān al-ḥikmah* which he wrote in 515 refers to Khayyam as "peace be upon his soul," a clear indication that he must have been dead by then. Tabrizī in *Tarabkhāneh* (p. 97) states the date of his death as 515. For more information on his death, see *Mujmal-i faṣiḥī* and also *Majma' al-fuṣahā* where the date is set as 517. Thomas Hyde in his work *Veterum Persarum et Parthorum et Medorum Religionis Historia* (Tehran: 1976) states that on the basis of an unpublished manuscript (he does not mention which manuscript) the date of his death was 517. In an unpublished manuscript in Paris (suppl Pers. 1366, p. 393,) written in 1010, the date of his death is said to be 510 while the author of *Tarikh alfī*, tells us his death occurred in 509.
4. Abu'l Ḥasan Bayhaqī, *Tatimmah ṣiwān al-ḥikmah*, Lahore: 1351, pp. 116–17.
5. Raḥīm R. Malik, *Omar Khayyam: Qāfilah sālār-i dānish*, Tehran: 1377, p. 184.
6. Fakhr al-Dīn Muḥammad ibn Omar al-Rāzī, *Tafsir mafātiḥ al-ghayb*, Beirut: 1421 AH.
7. Bayhaqī, *Tatimmah ṣiwān al-ḥikmah*, pp. 116–17.
8. Omar Khayyam, *Fi'l-kawn wa'l-taklīf*, in R.R. Malik, *Dānish nāmah-yi Khayyamī*, Tehran: 1377, p. 325.
9. For more information see A. Samarqandī, *Chahār maqālah*, ed. M. Mo'īn, Tehran: 1348, pp. 100–101.

10. For an account of this encounter see Ẓāhir al-Dīn Bayhaqī, *Ḥukamā-yi Islām*, ed. J. Lippert, Leipzig: 1903, pp. 243–4.
11. A.A. Ḥalabī, *Tārikh-i falasafa-yi Iran*, Tehran: 1373, pp. 294–353.
12. Ṣafadī, *al-wafī bi'l-wafiyāt*, Istanbul: 1964, v. 2, p. 142.
13. Qoṭb al-Dīn Maḥmūd Shirāzī, *Tuḥfat al-shāhiyyah*, p. 2. Also see Abbās I. Ashtiyānī, "Rāji' ba aḥwāl-i omar khayyam nayshāburī," in *Majmu'a-yi sharq*, no. 8, series 1, pp. 403–4.
14. While there is some skepticism regarding 'Ayn al-Qoḍāt Hamadānī having studied with Khayyam, there is an account of it in *Tarabkhāneh* (p. 155) which states, 'Ayn al-Qoḍāt first studied with Khayyam and then with Shaykh Abu'l Sa'id Abu'l Khayr. This is also mentioned in Shahrazūrī's *Nuzhat al-arwāh* (53/2) and Bayhaqī's *Durrat al-akhbār* (A Persian Translation of *Tatimmah ṣiwān al-ḥikmah*). It is entirely likely that upon his return from Mecca, Khayyam stayed in Hamadān for a while where Avicenna is buried and 'Ayn al-Qoḍāt's father was a prominent man. It may have been there that the young 'Ayn al-Qoḍāt studied with Khayyam. For more information regarding Khayyam's students, see *Durrat al-akhbār* (pp. 73–84). N.J. Pourjavādī in his authoritative work on the teachers of 'Ayn al-Qoḍāt Hamadānī does not mention Khayyam as one of his teachers. See *'Ayn al-Qoḍāt Hamadānī wa ustādān-i ū*, Tehran: 1374.
15. Javād Maqṣūd, *Sharḥ-i ahwāl wa āthār wadu-baytihāy-i bābā ṭāhir-i 'uryān*, Tehran: 1354.
16. Hamid Dabashi, *Truth and Narrative: the Untimely Thoughts of 'Ayn al-Quḍāt al-Hamadhānī*, Richmond: 1999, p. 86.
17. There were twenty-seven major universities (*madrasahs*) in Nayshābūr and over 6000 scholars have come from there. See M. Farzāneh, *Mardī az nayshābūr*, Tehran: 1349, p. 14 ff.
18. There are several accounts of this story in Z.M. Qazwīnī, *Athār al-bilād wa akhbār al-'ibād* and Tabrīzī in *Tarabkhāneh* and an abbreviated version of it by Shams al-Dīn Tabrizī in his *Maqālāt*. For a detailed discussion on Khayyam's relationship with Ghazzālī see J. Humā'ī, *Ghazzālī nāmah*, Tehran: 1368, pp. 342–4. For an intellectual analysis of their relationship see "al-Ghazzālī wa 'Umar Khayyam," *al-Thaqāfa*, Cairo: 1945, 363: 24–28 and for an imaginary discussion of their relationship see Jamshid Edulji Saklatwalla, "Imaginary Conversations Between Omar Khayyam and Ghazzālī," Bombay: 1937, series no. 15. Also see J. Soroushyar, "Khayyam wa Ghazzālī," *Yaghmā*, 27(1353): 152–3.
19. For a complete text of this letter, see "Nāmah-yi sanā'ī be khayyam," *Yaghmā*, ed. M. Minovī, 3(1329): 5.

20. In the text, he asks for a *qaṣidah* or *ghazal*, different poetic forms based on tripartite hemistiches.
21. Rashidī Tabrizī, *Tarabkhāneh*, as cited in R.R. Mālik, *Dānish nāmah-yi Khayyamī*, p. 46.
22. For more information see M. Farzāneh, *Naqd wa barrasi-yi ruba'iha-yi Omar Khayyam*, Tehran: 1356, pp. 27–30.
23. This story is mentioned in Al-Badaonī, *Muntakhab al-tawārikh*, Delhi: 1973, p. 230 and *Jahangushā-yi Juwaynī*, vol. 1, Leyden and London: 1912, p. 128. It is from this source that other authors have adopted this story and assumed it to be true.
24. For a full account of this see A.M. 'Abdus al-Jahshiyarī, *Kitāb al-wuzarā'*, Cairo: 1980, p. 96.
25. Rashīd al-Dīn Faḍlallāh in *Jāmi' al-tawārikh*, Leyden: 1329, p. 203. For a detailed analysis of this story see E.G. Brown, "Yet More Light On 'Umar-i Khayyam," *Royal Asiatic Society*, 8 (1899) 409–420.
26. The Gregorian calendar, widely used in Europe, misses one day every 3330 years whereas Khayyam's calendar misses one day every 5000 years. For more information on this see A.P. Youschkevitch, "AL-KHAYYAMI" Dictionary of Scientific Biography, ed. Charles C. Gillispie, vol. VII, New York: 1973, p. 324.
27. Al-Qifṭī, *Tārikh al-ḥukamā'*, Leipzig: 1903, pp. 243–4.
28. *Risālah jawābān lithulth masā'il*, in *Dānish nāmah-yi khayyāmī*, ed. R.R. Malik, p. 419.
29. For an account of Khayyam's last day, see Abu'l Ḥasan Bayhaqī, *Tatimmah ṣiwān al-ḥikmah*, pp. 116–7. This work has been translated by N.'A.M. Munshī Yazdī into Persian as *Durrat al-akhbār wa lum'at al-anwār* in 730 AH. There are some differences of the account of Khayyam's death between this and the original version of it reported by Bayhaqī.
30. Niẓāmī 'Aruḍī Samarqandī, *Chahār maqālah*, pp. 100–101.
31. To see the text and a thorough discussion of this treatise see R.R. Malik, *Dānish nāmah-yi Khayyamī*, Tehran: 1377, pp. 50–60.
32. A copy of the original text with notes that states this book is the hand written edition by Khayyam himself exists in Leiden, No. 199. This copy was moved to Berlin library in the 1940s. In 1912, the Introduction was translated into German by E. Wiedeman and G. Jacob and published as "Zu Omar-chajjam" in *Der Islam*, no. 3, pp. 42–62. This work has been translated into English by A.R. Moez as "Discussions of Difficulties in Euclid by Omar Khayyam" in *Scripta Mathematica*, vol. 24, no. 4, pp. 272–303.
33. For a detailed discussion and the text of this treatise, see R.R. Malik, *Dānish nāmah-yi Khayyāmī*, pp. 66–70.

34. Ibid., pp. 154–7.
35. For an English translation, see A.R. Moez, "A Paper on Omar Khayyam" in *Scripta Mathematica*, vol. 4, no. 26, pp. 323–37, and for a French translation, see Rushdī Rāshid and Aḥmed Jabbār in *Rasāi'l al-Khayyam al-jabriyyah*, Halab: 1981.
36. *Dānish nāmah Khayyāmī*, ed. R.R. Malik, p. 190.
37. Ibid., p. 192.
38. Ibid., pp. 188–241.
39. See ibid., pp. 288–304.
40. Ibid., pp. 303–17.
41. Ibid., pp. 321–42.
42. Ibid.
43. Khayyam's response is offered in the quotation by Imān Muḥammad Baghdādī at n. 29 of this chapter.
44. Ibid., pp. 344–68.
45. Ibid., pp. 367–75.
46. Ibid., pp. 378–90.
47. Ibid., p. 381.
48. Ibid., pp. 389–90.
49. B. Hāshemipour, "Goftārī dar bāra-yi risālah-yi dar 'ilm-i kulliyāt-i wujūd," *Farhang*, vol. 2, 14 (1380): 3–4, p. 58.
50. R.R. Mālik, *Dānish nāmah-yi Khayyamī*, pp. 412–22.
51. M. Minovī, "az khazā'in turkiyyah", *Majalla-yi dānishkadeh adabiyyāt*, 4 (1335): 2, pp. 42–75 and no. 3, pp. 53–89.
52. Ibid.
53. For a detailed discussion and the text of this treatise, see R.R. Malik, *Dānish nāmah-yi Khayyāmī*, pp. 424–38.
54. Ibid., p. 427.
55. As quoted in A. Dashti, *Damī bā Khayyam*, pp. 92–3.
56. Ibid., p. 92.
57. Ibid., p. 95.
58. Ibid., pp. 95–6.
59. Translated by the author, ibid., p. 94.

CHAPTER TWO

1. Ahmad Sa'idi, *Ruba'iyat of Omar Khayyam*, Berkeley: 1991, p. 212.
2. For a Sufi interpretation of Khayyam, see S.H. Nasr, "The Poet-Scientist Khayyam as Philosopher," in *Mélanges Luce Lopez-Baralt*, Series 9, No. 8, pp. 535–53; and "Omar Khayyam: Philosopher-Poet-Scientist" in *The Islamic Intellectual Tradition in Persia*, ed. M. Aminrazavi, London: 1996, pp. 175–78.

3. For more information on *Malāmatiyyah*, see M. Aminrazavi, "Antinomian Sufism and Ethical Relativism," *Journal of Henry Martin Institute for Islamic Studies*, 4: 1&2 (1995): pp. 17–24.
4. For an interpretation which exonerates Khayyam from "heretical ideas" completely, see S. Nakhjavānī, *Khayyam pendārī*, Tehran: 1347 AH.
5. Abu'l Majd Majdud ibn Ādam, also known as Sanā'ī Ghaznavī was an eleventh-century CE Sufi poet from Ghaznayn who was at the court of Masoūd Shāh and Bahrām Shāh. Among his major works can be named *Ḥadiqat al-ḥaqiqah, kārnāmah-yi balkh* and *Ṭariq al-taḥqīq* (the latter may not be his work).
6. Qur'an, 2: 129.
7. Legend has it that Imām 'Alī, the founder of Shi'ism, had a bisected sword (Zulfaqār) known for its effectiveness and sharpness.
8. Sanā'ī Ghaznavī, "Letter to Khayyam," *Dānish-nāmah-yi Khayyāmī*, ed. R.R. Mālik, pp. 13–16.
9. 'Abd al-Raḥmān Khāzenī, *Mizān al-ḥikmah*, Cairo: 1947, p. 36.
10. Zamakhsharī, *Al-Zājer lilṣighār 'an mu'ariḍāt al-kibār,* as cited in Raḥīm R. Malik, *Omar Khayyam*, Tehran: 1377, p. 18.
11. 'Aruḍī Samarqandī, *Chahār maqālah*, pp. 100–101.
12. Z.A. Muḥammad ibn al-Ḥusayīn al-Bayhaqī in *Tatimah ṣiwān al-ḥikmah*, pp. 116–17.
13. These three lines only are the translation of Swāmi Govinda's, *The Nectar of Grace*, section L, Introduction: ix.
14. It is not clear why Bayhaqī refers to Ghazzālī as "Abu'l Ḥasan Ghazzāl," but they are the same person.
15. Ibid.
16. T. Govinda Tirtha, *The Nectar of Grace*, p. 266.
17. Avicenna defends himself against the charge of heresy in his famous poem, saying:

    In the world there is one like I and if that be a heretic,
    There is thus no Muslim left in the world.

18. See Abū Ḥāmid Ghazzālī, *The Incoherence of the Philosophers*, trans. M.E. Marmura, Provo: 1979.
19. 'Imād al-Dīn Kātib Iṣfahānī, *Kharidat al-qaṣr*, Tehran: 1378 AH, vol. 2, p. 85.
20. Omar Khaṭṭāb was the second of the four Rightful Khalifahs who succeeded the Prophet Muḥammad and was known for his austere sense of piety and justice. Given the dates of Khāqānī and Khayyam's birth and death, it is highly unlikely that the two may have known each other. It is noteworthy that both Khayyam and Khāqānī went to the city of Ray where Khāqānī fell ill for sometime.

21. Khāqānī Shervānī, *Munsha'āt-i Khāqānī*, ed. M. Roushan, Tehran: 1362, p. 333.
22. Qur'an, 2: 22.
23. Qur'an, 50: 6.
24. Fakhr al-Dīn Rāzī, *Tafsīr mafātiḥ al-ghayb*, Bulaq: 1289.
25. Fakhr al-Dīn Rāzī, *Risālat fi'l-tanbih 'alā ba'ḍ al-asrār al-maw'dah fī ba'ḍ al-surah al-Quran al-'azīm*, as cited in Rahim R. Malik, *Omar Khayyam*, Tehran: 1377, p. 105.
26. A. Sa'idi in *Rubai'yyat of 'Omar Khayyam*, Berkeley: 1994, p. 35, modified by the author.
27. Qur'an, 95:4, 5.
28. See "On Theodicy and Providence," trans. by Sh. Inati, in *An Anthology of Philosophy in Persia*, ed. S.H. Nasr and M. Aminrazavi, New York: 1999, pp. 237–41.
29. For "theology of protest," see David R. Blumenthal, *Facing the Abusing God: A Theology of Protest*, Louisville: 1993; and for the "post-death of God" theology, see the works of Paul M. Buren.
30. Shahrazūrī, *Nuzhat al-arwāḥ*, p. 312.
31. *Al-mu'azzatayīn* is referring to the two *surahs* of taking refuge from evil, Qur'an: 113 and 114.
32. Shahrazūrī, *Nuzhat al-arwāḥ*, trans. by M.A. Tabrizī also known as *Madinat al-ḥukamā'*, Tehran: 1365, pp. 394–97.
33. Abū Bakr Rāzī, *Mirṣād al-ibād min al-mabda' ila'l-ma'ād*, Tehran: 1366, p. 31.
34. Qur'an, 7: 179.
35. From the *Mirṣād*, translated by the author.
36. A. Sa'idi, *Ruba'iyyat of Omar Khayyam*, p. 88, modified by the author.
37. Al-Qiftī, *Tārikh al-ḥukamā'*, pp. 243–4.
38. A. Afīfī, *Malāmatiyyah, ṣufīyyah and futuwwat*, Persian trans. N.A. Frouhar, Tehran: 1376.
39. A. Dashtī, *Damī bā Khayyam*, Tehran: 1364, pp. 103–32.
40. Translated by the author.
41. Shams Tabrīzī, *Maqālāt*, ed. M.A. Muwaḥḥid, Tehran: 1377, 2nd edn, pp. 301–2.
42. Ibid., pp. 301–2.
43. Ibid., p. 649. Shams dictated the *Maqālāt* in Konya or in Tabrīz, but in either case, he would have been a long way from Nayshābūr.
44. For more information on Shams' life and thought, see N. Ṣāḥib al-Zamānī, *Khat-i siwwum*, Tehran: 1351 AH/1960 CE.
45. Zakariyā' Muḥammad ibn Maḥmud Qazwīnī, *Athār al-bilād wa akhbār al-'ibād*, Beirut: 1973, p. 318.
46. Aṭṭār, *Tadhkirat al-uliyā'*, Tehran: 1336 AH/1957 CE.

47. *Mukhtaṣar fī dhikr ḥukamā' al-yūnānīyyīn wa'l-malliyyīn*, as cited in R. R. Malik, *Omar Khayyam*, Tehran: 1377, pp. 37–8.
48. Naṣr Mustawfī Qazwīnī, *Tārikh Gozideh*, ed. E. Brown, London: 1910, vol. 1, pp. 817–8.
49. It is not certain when this work was written, but Sanjarī al-Ansārī died in 749 AH/ 1458 CE.
50. Farīd al-Dīn Aṭṭār, *Manẓumah-yi ilāhī nāmah*, Mashhad: 1351, p. 25.
51. Āzar Bigdelī, *Ātashkadeh*, ed. Nāṣerī, Tehran: 1338, vol. 2, pp. 674–85.
52. Riḍā Qolikhān Hidāyat, *Riyāḍ al-'ārifīn*, ed. M.A. Gorgānī, Tehran: 1344, pp. 317–8.
53. Riḍā Qolikhān Hidāyat, *Mujma' al-fuṣaḥā*, ed. M.A. Gorgānī, Tehran: 1344, pp. 184–5.
54. "Fi'l-barāhīn 'alā masā'il al-jabr wa'l-muqābilah," in *Dānish nāmah-yi Khayyāmī*, ed. R.R. Malik, Tehran: 1377, pp. 94–241.
55. Ibid., p. 71–112.
56. Ibid., p. 71.
57. Ibid., pp. 324–33.
58. In *Dānish nāmeh-yi Khayyāmī*, ed. R.R. Malik, p. 342.
59. Ibid., p. 398.
60. Ibid., pp. 371–75.
61. Translated by the author.

CHAPTER THREE

1. A *Ruba'i* translated by the author; this may be an authentic quatrain.
2. For more information on Nayshābūr, see M. Farzāneh, *Mardī az nayshābūr*, Tehran: 1349 AH.
3. 'A. Bayhaqī, *Tārikh-i Bayhaqī*, ed. Kh. Rahbar, Tehran: 1378, vol. 3, pp. 942–3.
4. *Yon Palace* refers to the ruins of the ancient palace of the Sāsānian kings at Ctesiphon, a city on the left bank of the Tigris river in Iraq, destroyed by the Arabs after the battle of Qādasiyyah in 637 CE.
5. A. Sa'idī, *Ruba'iyyat of Omar Khayyam*, Berkeley: 1991, p. 150; "*coo-coo*," in addition to being the characteristic sound of a type of dove, in Persian it also means "where is it?" Here Khayyam is referring to the lost empire and emperors.
6. See S.H. Nasr, *Science and Civilization in Islam*, Lahore: 1983.
7. M. Fakhry, *Philosophy, Dogma and the Impact of Greek Thought in Islam*, VARIORUM, UK: 1994, and D. Gutas, *Greek thought, Arabic Culture*, London: 1998.
8. Dh. Ṣafā, *Tārikh-i 'ulūm-i 'aqlī dar tamadūn-i islāmī*, Tehran: 1371.

9. Ibid., pp. 37–134.
10. D. Gutas, *Greek thought, Arabic Culture*, London: 1998, p. i.
11. For more information see 'A. Badawī, *Madhāhib al-islāmiyyīn*, 2 vols, Beirut: 1973.
12. Ibid., p. 144.
13. Dh. Ṣafā, *Tārikh-i 'ulūm-i 'aqlī dar tamadūn-i islāmī*, p. 140.
14. Ibid., p. 144.
15. Yāqut al-Ḥamawī, *Mu'jam al-udabā'*, vol. 4, Cairo: 1936, p. 161–73.
16. Abū Ḥāmid Ghazzālī, *Fātiḥat al-'ulūm*, Cairo: 1322, p. 56.
17. *Rasā'il ikhwān al-ṣafā'*, Beirut: 1957, vol. 4, p. 95.
18. A. Sa'īdī, *Ruba'iyyat of Omar Khayyam*, p. 200. This may be an inauthentic quatrain.
19. Govinda Tirtha, *The Nectar of Grace*, p. 209.
20. Ghazzālī, *Iḥyā' al-'ulūm al-dīn*, trans. M. Khwārazmī, Tehran: 1378, p. 211.
21. Govinda Tirtha, *The Nectar of Grace*, p. 125.
22. Ibid., p. 234.
23. Qāḍī 'Abd al-Jabbār, *Sharḥ al-uṣūl al-khamsah*, Cairo: 1965, p. 139.
24. Govinda Tirtha, *The Nectar of Grace*, p. 26, modified by the author.
25. Ibid., modified by the author. This may be an inauthentic quatrain.
26. Ahmad Sa'idī, *Rubaiyyat of Omar Khayyam*, p. 88.
27. Qāḍī 'Abd Al-Jabbār, *Sharḥ al-uṣūl al-khamsah*, Cairo: 1965, p. 139.
28. Govinda Tirtha, *The Nectar of Grace*, p. 253, modified by the author.
29. Trans. by E.H. Whinfield in A.J. Arberry, *The Ruba'iyyat of Omar Khayyam*, London: 1949, p. 124.
30. Govinda Tirtha, *The Nectar of Grace*, p. 200, modified by the author.
31. Ibid., p. 251, modified by the author.
32. *Sāqī* in Persian means a female who serves wine.
33. Govinda Tirtha, *The Nectar of Grace*, p. 156, modified by the author.
34. Jabbār, *Sharḥ al-uṣūl*, p. 140.
35. E.H. Whinfield, *The Quatrains of Omar Khayyam*, p. 4, Ruba'i no. 424.
36. Qur'an, 3: 110.
37. Qāḍī 'Abd Al-Jabbār, *Sharḥ al-uṣūl al-khamsah*, p. 140.
38. A. Sa'idī, *The Ruba'iyyat of Omar Khayyam*, p. 71, modified by the author.
39. For a list of al-Kindī's works, see Ibn al-Nadīm, *Kitāb al-fihrist*, Cairo: 1990, pp. 371–79.
40. Abū Riḍā, *Rasā'il al-Kindī al-falsafiyyah*, vol. 1, Cairo: 1950, p. 97ff.
41. Al-Naẓẓām, *Encyclopedia of Islam*, New edn. VII, J. Van Ess,

1057–58. Also, *An Anthology of Philosophy in Persia*, ed. S.H. Nasr and M. Aminrazavi, vol. 3, London: 2004.

42. For Ibn al Rāwandī see S. Stroumsa, *Free Thinkers of Medieval Islam*, Leiden: 1999, pp. 73–86.
43. These three treatises may well be part of the same book. See ibid., p. 93.
44. As reported by Abū Ḥātim al-Rāzī, *A'lām al-nubuwwa*, ed. S. Al-Ṣawy, Tehran: 1977, p. 31. Trans. by S. Stroumsa.
45. Govinda Tirtha, *The Nectar of Grace*, p. 266. This may be an inauthentic quatrain.
46. For a partial translation of this treatise, see S.H. Nasr and M. Aminrazavi, *An Anthology of Philosophy in Persia*, vol. 1, New York: 1998, pp. 110–18.
47. M. Shahrastānī, *Al-milal wa'l-nihal*, ed. W. Cureton, vol. 2, London: 1842, p. 25cf.
48. For a survey of independent thinkers, often referred to as "free thinkers," see S. Stroumsa, *Free Thinkers of Medieval Islam*, Brill: 1999; and D. Urvoy, *Les Penseurs libres dans l'Islam classique*, Paris: 1996.
49. S. Stroumsa, *Free Thinkers of Medieval Islam*, p. 240.
50. Dh. Ṣafā, *Tārikh-i 'ulūm-i 'aqlī dar tamadūn-i islāmī*, pp. 137–8.
51. H. Ibrāhim Ḥasan, *Tārikh al-islām al-siyāsī wa'l-dīnī wa'l-thiqāfī wa'l-ijtimā'ī*, Cairo: 1965, vol. 3, pp. 168–9.
52. Translated by the author.
53. Ibid., p. 137.
54. For Islamic philosophical parables, see H. Corbin, *Visionary Recital*, trans. W.R. Trask, Princeton: 1988.
55. For philosophical parables of Suhrawardī, see *Oeuvres Philosophiques et Mystiques*, vol. 3, ed. S.H. Nasr, Institut d'Etudes et des Recherches Culturelles, Tehran: 1993.
56. Stroumsa, *Free Thinkers in Medieval Islam*, p. 241.
57. A.H. Al-Ṣarrāf, *Omar Khayyam*, Baghdad: 1949, pp. 19–20.
58. *Safar nāmah-yi Nāṣir Khusraw*, ed. M.D. Siyaqī, Tehran: 1375, pp. 18–19.
59. H. Jāvādī, "Khayyam wa abu'l-'alā' ma'rrī," *Khayyam nāmah*, Los Angeles: 1376.
60. O. Furough, *'Aqā'id-i falsafi-yi abu'l 'allā', filsuf-i ma'arrah*, trans. H. Khadiv Jam, Tehran: 1342, p. 236.
61. A. Sa'idī, *Ruba'iyyat of Omar Khayyam*, p. 132.
62. See H. Javādī, *Satire in Persian Literature*, Rutherford: 1988, p. 36.
63. O. Furough, *'Aqā'id falsafi-yi abu'l 'allā', filsuf-i ma'arrah*, p. 291.
64. A. Sa'idī, *Ruba'iyyat of Omar Khayyam*, p. 86, modified by the author.

65. For a thorough textual comparison between Ma'arrī and Khayyam see H. Shajarah, *Taḥqiq dar Ruba'iyyat wa zendegi-yi khayyam*, Tehran: 1320, p. 84–118.
66. M.T. Ja'farī, *Taḥlil-i shakhsiyat-i khayyam*, Tehran: 1365, p. 39.
67. For more information on Khayyam and Abu'l-'Alā' Ma'arrī see Omar Furough, "Abu'l-'Alā' Ma'arrī wa Khayyam," trans. H. Khadivjān, *Yaghmā*, 16(1342): 173–177; H. Kh. Nourī, "Khayyam wa Abu'l-'Alā'," *Mehr*, 4(1315) 913–920, 1021–1028, 1129–1138; A. Farzād, "Do usiyangar-i 'ālamsuz, Khayyam wa Abu'l-'Alā' Ma'arrī," *Negin*, 172(1358): 19–20, 51–52; 173(1358): 34–36.

CHAPTER FOUR

1. Ahmad Sa'idī, *Ruba'iyat of Omar Khayyam*, Berkeley: 1991, p. 62.
2. F.M. Shirvānī and H. Shāyegan, *Negāhī bar Khayyam*, Tehran: 1350, pp. 207–12.
3. A. Shahulī, *Ḥakīm Omar Khayyam wa zamān-i u*, Tehran: 1353, p. 39; and M. Farzāneh, *Naqd wa barrasi-yi rubāiha-yi Omar Khayyam*, Tehran: 1356 pp. 234–5.
4. M. Foulādvāndī, *Khayyam shināsī,* Tehran: 1379, pp. 73–5.
5. A. Dashtī, *Damī bā khayyam*, Tehran: 1377.
6. Ibid., pp. 143–5.
7. Ibid., p. 145.
8. Ibid.
9. Ibid.
10. See Ibid., pp. 149–50.
11. Ibid., pp. 150–51.
12. Ibid., p. 153.
13. These manuscripts exist at the Iranian Library of the Congress; see Ibid., p. 156.
14. Ibid., pp. 156–8.
15. Ibid., p. 158.
16. Ibid., p. 159.
17. Ibid., p. 161.
18. "Jam-i Jam" (Cup of Jam) refers to the crystal ball of the Persian King, Jam, through which he could see the future.
19. V.A. Zhukovski, '*Umar Khayyam and the Wandering Quatrains*, translated from Russian by E.W.D. Ross in *The Journal of the Royal Asiatic Society*, XXX, 1898.
20. A.E. Christensen, *Recherches sur les Ruba'iyyat d''Omar Khayyam*, Heidelburg: 1905.
21. For Brown's table see H. Shajarah, *Taḥqiq dar ruba'iyyat wa zendegi-yi khayyam*, Tehran: 1320, pp. 156–60.

22. For a detailed discussion on different editions, their chronological order and their authenticity, see Ibid., pp. 153–98.
23. For more information on Khayyam's relationship with the Epicureans, see O.B.S. Choubi, "Omar Khayyam, epicureans wa Charvakhā" in *Rad-i pā-yi falsafahā-yi hind dar sha'r-i fārsī*, trans. Sh. Mushirī, Tehran: 1378, pp. 129–36.
24. Translated by the author.
25. Translation by the author.
26. Translation by the author.
27. Translation by the author.
28. Qur'an, 2:156.
29. A. Dh. Qaraguzlū, *Omar Khayyam*, Tehran: 1379, pp. 127–28.
30. Translation by the author.
31. Quran, 26: 222–225.
32. Translation by the author.
33. Translation by the author.
34. A. Dashtī, *Damī bā Khayyam*, pp. 103–22.
35. Translation by the author.
36. Translation by the author.
37. Translation by the author.
38. Govinda Tirtha, *The Nectar of Grace*, p. 89.
39. Translation by the author.
40. Ibid., p. 231.
41. Ahmad Sa'idī, *Rubaiyyat of Omar Khayyam*, p. 180, modified by the author.
42. Ibid., p. 190.
43. Govinda Tirtha, *The Nectar of Grace*, p. 27.
44. Ibid., p. 209.
45. A. Sa'idī, *Ruba'iyyat of Omar Khayyam*, p. 184.
46. Ibid., p. 173.
47. Govinda Tirtha, *The Nectar of Grace*, p. 103.
48. Ibid., p. 144.
49. Ibid., p. 88.
50. Ibid., p. 90, modified by the author.
51. E.H. Whinfield, *The Quatrains of Omar Khayyam*, p. 30, modified by the author.
52. Ibid., p. 381.
53. W. Chittick, *The Sufi Path of Knowledge*, New York: 1989, p. 4.
54. Ibid., p. 380.
55. R. Otto, *The Idea of the Holy*, p. 25.
56. Ibid., pp. 6–7.
57. A. Sa'idī, *Ruba'iyyat of Omar Khayyam*, p. 88.

58. Ibid., p. 132.
59. Ibid., p. 123.
60. Ibid., p. 207.
61. Govinda Tirtha, *The Nectar of Grace*, p. 61.
62. Ibid., p. 71.
63. Ibid., p. 83.
64. Ibid., p. 229.
65. A. Sa'idī, *Ruba'iyyat of Omar Khayyam*, p. 158.
66. E.H. Whinfield, *The Quatrains of Omar Khayyam*, p. 393.
67. Nietzsche, *The Anti-Christ*, trans. R.J. Hollingdale, London: 1990, p. 125.
68. A. Sa'idī, *Ruba'iyyat of Omar Khayyam*, p. 153.
69. Ibid., p. 145.
70. Ibid., p. 163.
71. A. Sa'idī, *Ruba'iyyat of Omar Khayyam*, p. 181.
72. Govinda Tirtha, *The Nectar of Grace*, p. 249, modified by the author.
73. Ibid., p. 249.
74. A. Sa'idī, *The Ruba'iyyat of Omar Khayyam*, p. 208.
75. Quran, 3: 15, 4: 57, 37: 41–49, 38: 49–52.
76. A. Sa'idī, *The Ruba'iyyat of Omar Khayyam*, p. 183.
77. "hooris" are the angels usually perceived as young voluptuous females.
78. A. Sa'idī, *The Ruba'iyyat of Omar Khayyam*, p. 86.
79. Govinda Tirtha, *The Nectar of Grace*, p. 83.
80. A. Dashtī, *Damī bā Khayyam*, pp. 359–61.
81. A. Sa'idī, *Ruba'iyyat of Omar Khayyam*, p. 195.
82. Govinda Tirtha, *The Nectar of Grace*, p. 18.
83. Ibid., p. 29.
84. Ibid., p. 82.
85. Ibid., p. 83.
86. Ibid., p. 18.
87. Ibid.
88. Nāṣir-i Khusraw, *Safar nāmah*, Delhi: 1941.
89. S. Nakhjavānī, *Khayyam pendārī*, Tehran: 1347.
90. M. Ṭabāṭabā'ī, *Khayyam yā khayyāmī*, Tehran: 1370.
91. M. Khūrāsānī, "Maktab-i falsafi-yi shakkākān," *Armaghān*, vol. 32, no. 8, pp. 383–4.
92. Translated by the author.
93. Govinda Tirtha, *The Nectar of Grace*, p. 203, modified by the author.
94. Translated by the author.
95. Translation by the author.
96. Translated by the author.
97. By "five" Khayyam is referring to the five senses.

98. By "four" he means the four elements – water, wind, fire and earth.
99. *Sāqī* is a female who serves wine.
100. Translated by the author.
101. By "six" Khayyam is referring to the six directions, N, S, E, W, above and below.
102. The seven levels of the heavens are intended here.
103. Translated by the author.
104. The word "*ḥakīm*," which generally means "a wise man" in latter Islamic philosophy, became synonymous with a philosopher-theologian, a sage.
105. Translated by the author.
106. A. Sa'idī, *Ruba'iyyat of Omar Khayyam,* p. 76, modified by the author.
107. For more information on this, see M. Aminrazavi, *Suhrawardī and the School of Illumination*, London: 1996, pp. 64, 68, 85, 87, 153.
108. A. Sa'idī, *Ruba'iyyat of Omar Khayyam*, p. 58.
109. Ibid., p. 65.
110. Nietzsche discusses this in his *The Will to Power*, New York: 1968, p. 17.
111. S. Kierkegaard, *Concluding Unscientific Postscript*, Princeton: 1968, p. 182.
112. Govinda Tirtha, *The Nectar of Grace*, p. 65.
113. Ibid., p. 200.

CHAPTER FIVE

1. Govinda Tirtha, *The Nectar of Grace*, p. 131. This may not be an authentic quatrain.
2. Aḥmad Ghazzālī, *Risālah mu'iẓah*, ed. Nourbakhsh, Tehran: 1371.
3. S.H. Nasr, "The Poet-Scientist Khayyam as Philosopher" in *Mélanges Luce López-Baralt*, 9: 8 (2001), pp. 535–53.
4. H. Massé, *Anthologie Persane*, Paris: 1886.
5. V.A. Zhukovski, *'Umar Khayyam and the Wandering Quatrains*, trans. from Russian by E.W.D. Ross in *The Journal of the Royal Asiatic Society*, XXX, 1898.
6. A. Christensen, *Recherches sur les Ruba'iyat d' Omar Khayyam*, Heidelberg: 1905.
7. A.K. Qazwīnī, *Sharḥ-i ruba'iyyāt-i Khayyam*, ed. M.R.M. Chahārdehī, Tehran: 1379, p. 19.
8. Omar Khayyam, *Risālah fī kulliyāt al-wujūd*, in R.R. Malik, *Dānish nāmah-yi Khayyāmī*, pp. 389–90.
9. Abū Hāmid Ghazzālī, *Munqidh min al-ḍalāl*, in W.M. Watt, *The Faith and Practice of al-Ghazālī*, London: 1953, p. 26.

10. Shihāb al-Dīn Suhrawardī, *Ḥikmat al-ishrāq*, trans. by H. Zia'i and J. Walbridge, Utah: 1999, p. 8.
11. Govinda Tirtha in his *The Nectar of Grace* has cited below each *ruba'i* all those places and individuals who cited the same *ruba'i*, and has offered cross references as well.
12. Ibid., p. 1.
13. Ibid., p. 1.
14. Heron-Allen, *Omar Khayyam*, London: 1899, p. 89; modified by the author.
15. Bayhaqī, *Tatimah ṣiwān al-ḥikmah*, pp. 116–17.
16. Govinda Tirtha, *The Nectar of grace*, p. 2; modified by the author.
17. Ibid., p. 2.
18. P. Yogananda, *Wine of the Mystic: The ruba'iyyat of Omar Khayyam – A Spiritual Interpretation*, Los Angeles: 1990.
19. Ibid., p. 7.
20. E. FitzGerald, *The Ruba'iyyat of Omar Khayyam*, p. 141, no. 55; modified by the author.
21. Govinda Tirtha, *The Nectar of Grace*, p. 140; modified by the author.
22. Ibid., p. 139; modified by the author. Although this *Ruba'i* is consistant with the general theme of some of the *Ruba'iyyat,* it may well be inauthentic.
23. I have already referred to Qazwīnī's work, *Sharḥ-i ruba'iyyāt-i Omar Khayyam*. For Z. Daftary, see "Partaw-yi khirah kunandah-yi az nubugh-i khayyam," *Armaghān*, 32: 7–8, pp. 290–451.
24. A. Sa'īdī, *Ruba'iyyat Omar Khayyam,* p. 62.
25. Govinda Tirtha, *The Nectar of Grace*, p. 276; modified by the author.
26. A. Sa'īdī, *Ruba'iyyat Omar Khayyam*, p. 70.
27. "*Risālah fi'l-wujūd,*" ed. J. Nezhād Awwal, *Farhang*, vol. 12 (1378): 1–4, Winter, 1378, p. 111.
28. By "Magian Lane" Khayyam is referring to the neighborhood where Zoroastrians live.
29. The term Khayyam uses is "Allastum," a reference to the Qur'anic verse, "Am I not your Lord." Qur'an, 7: 172.
30. A. Sa'idī, *Ruba'iyyat Omar Khayyam*, p. 217.
31. Qifṭī, *Tārikh al-ḥukamā'*, pp. 243–4.
32. For more information, see J.S. Trimingham, *The Sufi Orders in Islam*, New York: 1998, pp. 12–13 and 187.
33. S.H. Nasr, *Sufi Essays*, Albany: 1972, p. 58.
34. A. Sa'idī, *Ruba'iyyat Omar Khayyam*, p. 232.
35. Govinda Tirtha, *The Nectar of Grace*, p. 131.
36. E. FitzGerald, *Ruba'iyyat of Omar Khayyam*, p. 122, no. 4; modified by the author.

37. For more information, see the three volumes edited by L. Lewisohn, *The Heritage of Sufism*, Oxford: 1999.
38. Govinda Tirtha, *The Nectar of Grace*, p. 131.
39. S.H. Nasr, *Sufi Essays*, p. 57.
40. E. FitzGerald, *Ruba'iyyat of Omar Khayyam*, p. 102.
41. Govinda Tirtha, *The Nectar of Grace*, p. 275; modified by the author.
42. Govinda Tirtha, *The Nectar of Grace*, p. 290; modified by the author.
43. M.A. Furūghī, *Majmu'a-yi maqālāt-i furūghī*, Tehran: 1375, p. 87.
44. A. Afīfī, *Malāmatiyyah, Ṣufīyah wa futuwwat*, trans. by N.A. Fruhar, Tehran: 1376, p. 16.
45. Ibid., p. 35.
46. M. I'timād, *Sha'r-i falsafī-yi khayyam*, Gilan: 1361, pp. 30–46.
47. Gh. Dinānī, "Ḥakim Omar Khayyam wa mas'alah-yi wāḥid wa kathīr," *Daftar-i 'aql wa āyāt-i 'ishq*, Tehran: 1380, p. 253.
48. Govinda Tirtha, *The Nectar of Grace*, p. 137; modified by the author.
49. A.M. Schimmel, *Mystical Dimensions of Islam*, Chapel Hill: 1975, p. 288.
50. Robert Graves and Omar 'Alī-Shāh, *The Original Ruba'iyyat of Omar Khayyam*, New York: 1968, p. 27.
51. Ibid., p. 18; for Biblical reference see Matthew: XXIII, v. 1.
52. Ibid., p. 34.
53. Ibid.
54. Ibid., p. 32.
55. L.P. Elwell-Sutton, "The Omar Khayyam Puzzle," *Royal Central Asiatic Journal*, LV 2, June (1968): pp. 176–9.
56. J.C.E. Bowen, "The Rubaiyat of Omar Khayyam: A Critical Assesment of Robert Graves' and Omar Ali Shah's 'translation'," *Iran: Journal of Persian Studies*, vol. XI(1973): pp. 63–73.

CHAPTER SIX

1. Ahmad Sa'idī, *Ruba'iyat of Omar Khayyam*, Berkeley: 1991, p. 102; modified by the author.
2. H.N. Iṣfahānī, "*Al-jawāb 'an thulāth masā'il*," *Farhang*, vol. 1, 12 (1378): 1–4, p. 155.
3. Rahim R. Malik, *Dānish nāmah-yi Khayyāmī*, p. 414.
4. Rashidī Tabrīzī, *Tarabkhāneh*, p. 144.
5. M. I'timād, *Sha'r-i falsafī-yi Khayyam*, Tehran: 1361, p. 21.
6. Gh. Dinānī, "Ḥakīm Omar Khayyam wa mas'alih-yi wāḥid wa kathīr," *Daftar-i 'aql wa āyat-i 'ishq,* Tehran: 1380, pp. 229–30.
7. "*Risālah fi'l-wujūd*," *Farhang,* vol. 1, 12(1378): 1–4, p. 113.
8. "*Fi'l- kawn wa'l-taklīf*," *Farhang*, vol. 1, 12(1378): 1–4, pp. 140–141.

9. "*Ḍarurat al-taḍād fi'l-'alam wa'l-jabr wa'l-baqā'*," *Farhang*, vol. 1, p. 175.
10. "*Risālah fi'l-wujūd*," *Farhang*, vol. 1, 12(1378): 1–4, p. 112.
11. Ibid., p. 112.
12. "*Al-jawāb 'an thulāth masā'il*," *Farhang*, vol. 1, 12(1378): 1–4, p. 166.
13. Ibid., p. 166.
14. Ibid., p. 166.
15. "*Risālah fi'l-wujūd*," *Farhang*, vol. 1, 12(1378): 1–4, p. 166.
16. Ibid., p. 167.
17. Abū Ḥāmid Ghazzālī, *Tahāfut al-falāsifah*, trans. M.E. Marmura, Utah: 1997, pp. 137–46.
18. "*Risālah fi'l-wujūd*," *Farhang*, vol. 1, 12(1378): 1–4, p. 112.
19. "*Fi'l-kawn wa'l-taklif*," *Dānish nāmah-yi Khayyāmī*, ed. Rahim R. Malik, p. 329.
20. Ibid., p. 335.
21. Ibid., p. 337.
22. Ibid., p. 336.
23. "*Ḍarurat al-taḍād fi'l-'alam wa'l-jabr wa'l-baqā'*," *Dānish nāmah-yi Khayyāmī*, ed. Rahim R. Malik, p. 358.
24. "*Fi'l kawn wa'l-taklif*," Ibid., p. 338.
25. It is not clear why Khayyam says this since the word should be "decreases" and not "increases." The possibility that the text is corrupted remains a viable explanation.
26. Ibid., p. 339.
27. "*Risālah dar 'ilm kulliyāt-i wujūd*," in Rahim R. Malik, *Dānish nāmah-yi Khayyāmī*, p. 381.
28. I.A. Netton, *Muslim Neoplatonists: An Introduction to the Thought of the Brethren of Purity*, London: 1982, p. 35.
29. For more information on these theological positions see *Al-Mabāḥith al-mashraqiyyah*, vol. 1, p. 128, *Al-Mawāqif*, p. 48, *Nihāyat al-marām*, vol. 1, pp. 37–45.
30. Ibid., p. 111.
31. For more information on the School of Iṣfahān, see S.H. Nasr, "The School of Iṣfahān," *A History of Muslim Philosophy*, vol. 2, ed. M.M. Sharīf, Weisbaden: 1966, pp. 904–32.
32. S.H. Nasr, "The Poet-Scientist Khayyam as Philosopher," *Mélanges Luce López-Baralt*, ed. A. Temimi, Series 9: 8, Mai 2001, pp. 535–53.
33. Gh. J. Nizhād Awwal, "Sukhanī dar bārah-yi risālah fi'l-wujūd," *Farhang*, vol. 1, 12(1378): 1–4, p. 88.
34. Ibid., p. 111.
35. "*Risālah fi'l-wujūd*," *Farhang*, vol. 1, 12(1378): 1–4, p. 111.

36. "*Risālah ḍiyā' al-'aqlī fī mawdu' al-'ilm al-kullī,*" *Dānish nāmah-yi Khayyāmī*, ed. Rahim R. Malik, p. 371.
37. "*Risālah fi'l-wujūd,*" *Farhang*, vol. 1, 12(1378): 1–4, p. 124.
38. Ibid., p. 124.
39. Ibid., p. 125.
40. "*Fi'l- kawn wa'l-taklīf,*" *Farhang*, vol. 1, 12(1378): 1–4, p. 140.
41. "*Al-jawāb 'an thulath masā'il,*" *Farhang*, vol. 1, 12(1378): 1–4, p. 165.
42. "*Ḍarurat al-taḍād fi'l-'ālam wa'l-jabr wa'l-baqā,*" *Dānish nāmah-yi Khayyāmī*, ed. Rahim R. Malik, p. 362.
43. "*Al-jawāb 'an thulath masā'il,*" *Farhang*, vol. 1, 12(1378): 1–4, p. 167–68.
44. Divine intentionality is inconsistent with the notion that motion cannot be introduced in Divine nature and this is the point Khayyam is alluding to here.
45. "*Ḍarurat al-taḍād fī'l-'ālam wa'l-jabr wa'l-baqā',*" *Farhang*, vol. 1, 12(1378): 1–4, p. 177.
46. Ibid., p. 177.
47. Ibid., p. 177.
48. "*Fi'l- kawn wa'l-taklīf,*" *Farhang*, vol. 1, 12(1378): 1–4, p. 152.
49. It is assumed that Qāḍī Nasāwī who had asked Khayyam to write *Fi'l-kawn wa'l-taklīf* had also asked Khayyam to respond to three questions one of which is determinism.
50. "*Ḍarurat al-taḍād fī'l-'ālam wa'l-jabr wa'l-baqā',*" *Farhang*, vol. 1, 12 (1378): 1–4, p. 169.
51. Ibid., p. 143.
52. Al-Fārābī, *Philosophy of Plato and Aristotle*, trans. M. Mahdi, in *Philosophy in the Middle Ages*, ed. A. Hyman and J. Walsh, New York: 1973, p. 224.
53. Ibid., p. 143.
54. Ibid., p. 143.
55. Ibid., p. 143.
56. Ibid., p. 143.
57. Ibid., p. 143.
58. "*Fi'l- kawn wa'l-taklīf,*" *Farhang*, vol. 1, 12(1378): 1–4, p. 141.
59. "*Risālah fi'l-wujūd,*" *Farhang*, vol. 1, 12(1378): 1–4, p. 111.
60. "*Fi'l- kawn wa'l-taklīf,*" *Farhang*, vol. 1, 12(1378): 1–4, p. 145.
61. "*Risālah fi'l-wujūd,*" *Farhang*, vol. 1, 12(1378): 1–4, p. 102.
62. Ibid., p. 103.
63. Ibid.
64. Ibid.
65. "*Ḍarūrat al-taḍād fi'l-'ālam wa'l-jabr wa'l-baqā',*" *Farhang*, vol. 1, 12(1378): 1–4, p. 164.

66. Govinda Tirtha, *The Nectar of Grace*, p. 262.This is an inauthentic quatrain.
67. Ahmad N. Tatavī, *Tārikh-i Alfī*, Tehran: 1378.
68. Govinda Tirtha, *The Nectar of Grace*, p. 200.
69. Ibid., p. 69.
70. F. Copleston, *A History of Philosophy*, vol. 1, New York: 1963, p. 31.
71. H.N. Iṣfahānī, "Hastī shināsī-yi ḥakīm Omar Khayyam," *Farhang*, vol. 2, 14(1380): 3–4, pp. 113–17.
72. Ibid., p. 113.
73. "*Risālah al-wujūd*," *Farhang*, vol. 1 12(1378): 1–4, p. 104.
74. "*Al-ḍiyā' al-'aqlī fī mawḍū' al-'ilm al-kullī*," *Farhang*, vol. 1, 12(1378): 1–4, p. 188.
75. "*Al-Jawāb 'an thulāth masā'il*," *Farhang*, vol. 1, 12(1378): 1–4, p. 165.
76. Ibid., p. 165.
77. "*dar 'ilm kulliyāt-i wujūd*," *Farhang*, vol. 1, 12(1378): 1–4, pp. 389–90.
78. "*Al-diyā' al-'aqli fī mawḍū' al-'ilm al-kullī*," *Farhang*, vol. 1, 12(1378): 1–4, pp. 187–8.
79. "*Al-Jawāb 'an thulāth masā'il*," *Farhang*, vol. 1, 12(1378): 1–4, p. 165.
80. "*Risālah-yi wujūd*," *Farhang*, vol. 1, 12(1378): 1–4, pp. 105–6.
81. "*Risālah al-wujūd*," *Farhang*, vol. 1, 12(1378): 1–4, p. 114.
82. "*Dar 'ilm kulliyāt-i wujūd*," *Farhang*, vol. 1, 12(1378): 1–4, pp. 389–90.
83. "*Risalāh al-wujūd*," *Farhang*, vol. 1, 12(1378): 1–4, p. 113.
84. Ibid., p. 112.
85. Ibid., p. 114.
86. "*Fi'l- kawn wa'l-taklīf*," *Farhang*, vol. 1, 12(1378): 1–4, p. 140.
87. "*Risālah al-wujūd*," *Farhang*, vol. 1, 12(1378): 1–4, p. 112.
88. "*Al-Jawāb 'an thulāth masā'il*," *Farhang*, vol. 1, 12(1378): 1–4, p. 161.
89. "*Risālah al-wujūd*," *Farhang*, vol. 1, 12(1378): 1–4, p. 112 and "*Al-diyā' al-'aqlī fī mawdū' al-'ilm al-kulli*," *Farhang*, vol. 1, 12(1378): 1–4, p. 189.
90. "*Fi'l- kawn wa'l-taklīf*," *Farhang*, vol. 1, 12(1378): 1–4, p. 141–2.
91. Ibid., p. 142.
92. Ibid., p. 142.
93. Ibid., p. 143.
94. "*Fi'l- kawn wa'l-taklīf*," *Farhang*, vol. 1, 12(1378): 1–4, p. 143.
95. "*Al-Jawāb 'an thulāth masā'il*," *Farhang*, vol. 1, 12(1378): 1–4, p. 169.
96. "*Fi'l- kawn wa'l-taklīf*," *Farhang*, vol. 1, 12(1378): 1–4, pp. 144–5.

CHAPTER SEVEN

1. A *Ruba'i* translated by the author.
2. S.H. Nasr "The Poet-Scientist Khayyam as Philosopher," *Mélanges Luce López-Baralt*, 2001, series 9, No. 8.
3. Ibid., p. 540.
4. Ibid.
5. Ibid.
6. Ibid., p. 541.
7. David M. Burton, *The History of Mathematics*, New York: 2003.
8. Ibid., p. 235.
9. R. Rashed and B. Vahabzadeh, *Omar Khayyam the Mathematician*, New York: 2000, p. 117.
10. Ibid., p. 6. This treatise is not extant.
11. Ibid., pp. 8–9.
12. Sharīf al-Dīn Ṭūsī, *Oeuvres mathématiques. Algèbre et Géométrie au XIIe siècle*, 2 vols. Collection "Sciences et Philosophie arabes-Textes et études," Paris: 1986, I.15.
13. R. Rashed and B. Vahabzadeh, *Omar Khayyam the Mathematician*, p. 20.
14. "*Sharḥ mā ashkal min muṣādirāt al-uqlidus*," *Dānish nāmah-yi Khayyāmī*, ed. Rahīm R. Malik, pp. 71–112.
15. Osman Baker, *Tawḥīd and Science*, Lahore: 1991.
16. Ibid., p. 159.
17. A. Rosenfeld and A.P. Youschkevitch, "Al-Khayyami," *Dictionary of Scientific Biography*, ed. Charles C. Gillispie, Vol. VII, New York: 1973, p. 327.
18. Ibid., p. 167.
19. David E. Smith, "Euclid, Omar Khayyam and Saccheri," *Scripta Mathematica*, vol. 3, no. 1, (1935), p. 8.
20. See D.J. Struik, "Omar Khayyam, Mathematician," *The Mathematics Teacher*, vol. LVI (1958), p. 284.
21. J.A. Chāvoshī, *Sayr dar afkār-i 'ilmī wa falsafī-yi ḥakīm Omar Khayyam Nayshābūrī*, Tehran: 1358, p. 279.
22. Ibid., p. 76.
23. For a discussion on the use of Khayyam's method by Muslim and European mathematicians, see Ibid., pp. 77–80 and also M. Hashtrūdī, "Khayyam, riyaḍidān-i shā'ir", *Yekān*, vol. 12, pp. 238–9.
24. J.A. Chāvoshī, "Omar Khayyam and the Arithmetical Triangle," trans. by Boozarjomehr, *Farhang*, vol. 2, no. 14 (1380), pp. 262–73.
25. Ibid., p. 273.
26. Translation by B.A. Rosenfeld and A.P. Youschkevitch, "Al-Khayyami,"

Dictionary of Scientific Biography," ed. Charles C. Gillispie, vol. VII, New York: 1973, p. 325.

27. "*Risālah fi'l- iḥtiyāj lima'rifat miqdārī al-dhahab wa'l-fiḍah fī jism murakkab minhā*," *Dānish nāmah-yi Khayyāmī*, ed. Rahīm R. Malik, p. 293.
28. For the translations, see M. Bagheri and S. Houshiyar, "Risālah-yi musiqi-yi Khayyam az didgāh-i riyāḍiyāt," *Rahpouyeh-yi honar*, 43(1376): 42–63; and T. Binesh, "Risālah-yi musiqi-yi khayyam yā khayyāmī," *Nashriyah-yi dānishgāh-i āzād-i islāmī-yi kirmān*, (1373): 1, pp. 92–101. For a critical edition see J.A. Chāvoshī, "Omar al-Khayyam wa'l-musiqī al-naḍariyyah," trans. M.M. 'Abd al-Jalil, *Farhang*, vol. 1, 14 (1378): 29–32 and 203–14.
29. S. Sapanta, "Khayyam wa musiqī-yi naḍarī," *Farhang*, vol. 2, 14(1980): 3–4, pp. 259–72.
30. See A.P. Youschkevitch, "Al-Khayyami," *Dictionary of Scientific Biography*, ed. Charles C. Gillispie, vol. VII, New York: 1973, p. 324.
31. Even though the author uses the word "*ahkām*," which literally means "principles," in this context he means predicting cosmic events, particularly predicting the weather, which Khayyam did not believe in.
32. 'Aruḍī Samarqandī, *Chāhār maqālah*, ed. M. Moin, Tehran: 1348, pp. 100–101.
33. For Farīd's comments, see J.A. Chāvoshī, *Ḥakim Omar Khayyam Nayshābūrī*, Tehran: 1358, p. 92.
34. 'Ālī R. Amīr Moaz, "A Paper of Omar Khayyam," *Scripta Mathematica*, 26 (1963), pp. 323–7.
35. Ibid.
36. The only copy of this work is at the Bibliothèque Nationale in Paris titled *Ancien fonds persan manuscript*, No. 169.
37. A. Özdurad, "Omar Khayyam and Architecture," *Farhang*, 14 (2002): 39–40, pp. 189–251.
38. For more information on his theory of postulates see H. Dilgan, "Al-Samarqandī," in *Dictionary of Scientific Biography*, vol. XII, p. 91.
39. For more information on al-Ruṃī see, H. Dilgan, "Qāḍī-zādeh al-Rumī," in *Dictionary of Scientific Biography*, vol. XI, pp. 227–9.

CHAPTER EIGHT

1. Charles D. Burrage, *Twenty Years of the Omar Khayyam Club of America*, Boston: 1921, p. 10.
2. Ibid., p.31.
3. *Omar Khayyam Club of America*, ed. Charles D. Burrage, Boston: 1922, p. 87.

4. This is a rare book; there is only one copy in Boston. The book also appeared in the *Calcutta Review* of March 1858.
5. Cowell reviewed them in the *Calcutta Review* of March 1858.
6. He is referring to Gore Ouseley's commission to Persia.
7. *Some Doings of the Omar Khayyam Club of America*, ed. Charles D. Burrage, Boston: 1922, p. 21.
8. E. FitzGerald, *Letters to Professor Cowell*, p. 282.
9. J. Brigham, *Many Sided Omar*, Boston: 1925, p. 5.
10. Moncure Conway, *The Omar Khayyam Cult in England*, 57 (1893): 1478, p. 305.
11. For a complete list of his Cambridge friends, see Walter J. Black, *Ruba'iyyat of Omar Khayyam*, New York: 1942, pp. 5–6.
12. Ibid., p. 7.
13. See his collected works in *Journal of the Royal Asiatic Society*, 1902, vol. VI.
14. Ibid., p. 8.
15. William Aldis Wright, *Letters and Literary Remains of Edward FitzGerald*, London: 1889.
16. J. Brigham, *Many Sided Omar*, p. 4.
17. Edward Heron-Allen, in his major work, *Some Sidelights Upon Edward FitzGerald's Poem: The Ruba'iyat of Omar Khayyam*, London: 1898, offers an extensive discussion on FitzGerald's translation-interpretation of the *Ruba'iyyat* based on the sources that FitzGerald had used or been influenced by. This may shed light on his lack of interest in exploring other aspects of Khayyam's thought beside his Epicureanism.
18. J. Brigham, *The Many Sided Omar*, p. 14.
19. Ibid., p. 4.
20. Ibid., p. 4.
21. Ibid., p. 15.
22. Ibid., p. 15.
23. *The Pre-Raphaelites and Their Circle*, ed. Cecil Y. Lang, Boston: 1968, p. xii.
24. William Michael Rossetti, *His Family Letters with a Memoir*, I, 135 in Ibid., p. xxii.
25. *The Pre-Raphaelites and Their Circle*, ed. Cecil Y. Lange, Boston: 1968, p. xx.
26. Charles D. Burrage, *Twenty Years of the Omar Khayyam Club of America*, Boston: 1921, p. 7.
27. Ibid., p. 7.
28. Moncure D. Conway, "The Omar Khayyam Cult in England," *Nation*, 57(1893), no. 1478, p. 304.

29. Ibid., p. 51.
30. Ibid., p. 52.
31. Ibid., p. 24.
32. Ibid., p. 25.
33. *The Book of Omar and Ruba'iyat*, New York & London: 1900, p. 39.
34. Ibid., p. 28.
35. Ibid., p. 43.
36. Ibid., p. 43.
37. Ibid., p. 43.
38. Ibid., p. 49.
39. Ibid., pp. 49–50.
40. E.B. Cowell, *Ruba'iyyat of 'Umar Khayyam*, London: 1908, p. xv.
41. Moncure D. Conway, "The Omar Khayyam Cult in England," *Nation*, 57(1893), no. 1478, p. 305.
42. *The Rubaiyat of Omar Khayyam*, Edward FitzGerald's edition, New York: 1942, poem no. 21, p. 128.
43. Ibid. poem no.15, p. 126.
44. Walter J. Black, *The Ruba'iyyat of Omar Khayyam*, p. 12.
45. *Some Doings of the Omar Khayyam Club of America*, ed. Charles Burrage, p. 17.
46. For a complete list of the officers see Ibid., p. 12.
47. Ibid., p. 21.
48. Ibid., p. 25.
49. Ibid., p. 22.
50. Ibid., p. 23.
51. The author writes *Ruba'iyyat* as "*Rubyhat.*"
52. Ibid., p. 24.
53. J. Brigham, *The Many Sided Omar*, Des Moines: 1924, p. 14.
54. *Some Doings of the Omar Khayyam Club of America*, ed. Charles Burrage, p. 34.
55. Ibid., p. 33.
56. Ibid., p. 8.
57. Edward Said, *Culture and Imperialism*, New York: 1993, p. 170.
58. For a complete list of the participants, see *Some Doings of the Omar Khayyam Club of America*, ed. Charles Burrage, p. 27.
59. For a complete list of the publications of the Club, see Ibid., pp. 38–40.
60. A.J. Arberry, *The Romance of the Rubaiyat*, FitzGerald's 1st edn., London: 1959, p. 34.
61. A. Gribben and K.B. MacDonnell, *Mark Twain's Rubaiyat*, Austin: 1983, p. 10.
62. Edward FitzGerald, *The Rubaiyyat of Omar Khayyam*, New York: 1942, p. 150, no. 81.

63. Ibid., p. 10.
64. A. Gribben and K.B. MacDonnell, *Mark Twain's Rubaiyat*, p. 14.
65. Mark Twain Papers at Berkeley, Notebook 40, TS, p. 47.
66. A. Gribben and K.B. MacDonnell, *Mark Twain's Rubaiyat*, p. 15.
67. This appears in the Appendix A of *A Tramp Abroad* (1880), see Ibid., p. 11.
68. A. Gribben and K.B. MacDonnell, *Mark Twain's Rubaiyat*, Berkeley: 1983, p. 17.
69. Ibid., p. 18.
70. *Mark Twain's Fables of Man*, ed. John S. Tuckey, Berkeley: 1971, pp. 441–2.
71. The original is in the archives of Chatto and Windus, Ltd., London, see A. Gribben and K.B. MacDonnell, *Mark Twain's Rubaiyat*, p. 27. The initials SLC stands for Samuel Clemens.
72. Ibid., p. 24.
73. Ibid., p. 24.
74. S.J. Barrow, "Editions Note Book,"*Unitarian Review and Religious Magazine*, 11(1879): pp. 384–6.
75. Charles E. Norton, "Nicolas's Quatrains de Kheyam," *North American Review*, 225(1869): 565–84. pp. 565–66.
76. A. K. Terhune, *The Life of Edward FitzGerald*, New Haven: 1947, p. 213.
77. T.S. Eliot, *The Use of Poetry and the Use of Criticism: Studies in the Relation of Poetry to Criticism in England*, London: 1985, p. 33.
78. V.M. D'Ambrosio, *Eliot Possessed: T.S. Eliot and FitzGerald's RUBAIYAT*, New York: 1989.
79. T.S. Eliot, *The Use of Poetry and the Use of Criticism: Studies in the Relation of Poetry to Criticism in England*, London: Faber and Faber Press: 1985, p. 33.
80. Charles Whibley, "Musings Without Method," *Blackwood's*, 170 (1903): p. 287.
81. T.S. Eliot, *Selected Essays*, London: 1951, p. 499.
82. In her "Table of Textual Comparison," D'Ambrosio clearly has shown some of these similarities; see V.M. D'Ambrosio, *Eliot Possessed: T.S. Eliot and FitzGerald's RUBAIYAT*, pp. 183–8.
83. Cited and discussed in Charles E. Samuels, *Thomas Baily Aldrich*, New York: 1965, pp. 55–8.
84. Thomas Baily Aldrich, "A Persian Poet," *Atlantic Monthly*, 41(1878): pp. 421–6.
85. Ibid., p. 424.
86. Ibid., p. 424.

87. James Whitcomb Riley, *The Ruba'iyyat of Doc Sifers*, illustrated by C.M. Relya, New York: 1897.
88. John Hay, *In Praise of Omar*, Portland: 1897, p. 5.
89. Ibid., p. 3.
90. E. Pound, *Letters of Ezra Pound*, London: 1951, pp. 158–9.
91. Ibid., p. 180.
92. James Miller, *T.S. Eliot's Personal Waste Land: Exorcism of the Demons*, Pensylvania: 1977, p. 154.
93. Elihu Vedder, *The Rubaiyat of Omar Khayyam*, Boston: 1884. This work with its many drawings was widely reviewed. See *Nation*, 39 (1884): 423 and *Atlantic Monthly*, 55(1885): pp. 111–16.
94. A report concerning this program appeared in "Illustrations: Omar Done into Dance by Isadora Duncan," *Critic*, May, 1899.
95. Ralph Rusk, *Life of Ralph Waldo Emerson*, New York: 1949, p. 478.
96. Paul Elmer More, "The Seven Seas and the Rubaiyat," *Atlantic Monthly*, 84(1899): pp. 800–808.
97. Edward FitzGerald, *Polonius*, Variorum, vol. 1, New York: 1903, p. 242.
98. Ibid.
99. E. Heron-Allan, *Rubaiyat of 'Umar Khayyam*, London: 1908, p. xv.
100. H.G. Keene, "Omar Khayyam" in Nathan Haskell Dole, *Rubaiyat of Omar Khayyam*, Boston: 1891, 2: p. 423.
101. Richard Le Gallienne "Fin de Siècle Cult of FitzGerald's *Ruba'iyat* of Omar Khayyam" in *Review of National Literature*, 2(1971): pp. 74–5.
102. Charles Potter, *A Bibliography of the Rubaiyat of Omar Khayyam*, no. 1066.
103. *Omar Repentant*, New York: 1908, n.p.
104. Richard Le Gallienne, *Rubaiyat of Omar Khayyam*, New York: 1897, p. 17.
105. Charles Potter, *A Bibliography of the Rubaiyat of Omar Khayyam*, no. 942 (1908).
106. Ibid., no. 668 (1914).
107. See A.H. Miller, "The Omar Cult," *Academy* 59(1900): p. 55.
108. Bernard Holland, "The Popularity of Omar," *National Review*, XXXIII (June, 1899), pp. 643–52.
109. A.H. Miller, "The Omar Cult," *Academy* 59(1900): p. 55.
110. Ibid., p. 647.
111. C.D. Broad, "The Philosophy of Omar Khayyam and Its Relation to that of Schopenhauer," *Review*, CLXVI (Nov., 1906): pp. 544–56.
112. "The Harm of Omar," *T.P.'s Weekly*, XVI (September 9, 1910): p. 340.
113. G.K. Chesterton, *Heretics*, London: 1906.

114. William Hastie, *Festival of Spring from the Divan of Jelalledin*, Glasgow: 1903, p. xxxiii, quoted in John D. Yohannan, "Fin de Siècle Cult of FitzGerald's *Ruba'iyat* of Omar Khayyam" in *Review of National Literature*, 2(1971): p. 85.
115. Havelock Ellis, "Sexual Inversion," in his *Studies in the Psychology of Sex*, 2 vols. New York: 1942, 1: pp. 50–51.
116. Edwin Arlington Robinson, *Untriangulated Stars: Letters of Edwin Arlington Robinson to Harry de Forest Smith*, 1890–1905, ed. Denham Sutcliffe, Cambridge: 1947, p. xxii.
117. Sylvanus Urban, *Gentleman's Magazine*, Old Series, CCLXXXIV (Jan–June, 1898): p. 413.
118. Willfred Meynell, "The Cause of Omar's Popularity," *Academy*, LXVI (March, 1904): p. 274.
119. Edmund Gosse, *Critical Kit-Kats*, London: 1895, pp. 65–92.
120. Printed in Edward Clodd's *Memories*, London: 1916.
121. "The Book Buyers Guide," *Critic*, 37(1900): p. 277.
122. Charles Potter, *A Bibliography of the Rubaiyat of Omar Khayyam*, nos. 1045, 1187, 1266, 1002.
123. F. Woepcke, *L'Algébre d'Omar al-Khayyam publiée, traduite et accompagnée d'Extraits de manuscripts inédits*. Paris: 1851.
124. Garcin de Tassy, J.H. *Note sur les Rubaijat d' Omar Khayyam*, Paris: 1857, p. 11.
125. *Les Quatrains de Kheyam*. Traduits du persan par J.B. Nicolas. Paris: 1867.
126. C.G. Salmon, "Biographie d'Omar Kheyyam", *La Grande Encyclopédie*. Paris: 1861.
127. *Les Quatrains d'Omar Khayyam*: Traduits du persan sur le manuscript de la Bodleian Library, Oxford. Introduction et notes de Charles Golleau. Paris: 1922.
128. *Les 144 Quatrains d'Omar Khayyam*. Traduits littéralement par Claude Anet et Mirza Muhammad Qazvini. Paris. 1920.
129. *Les Rubayat d'Omar Khayyam*. Texte persan et traduction en vers français, par A.G. I'tisam Zadeh. Teheran, 1310 AH/1931; Les Roba I d'Omar Kheyyam. Par Arthur Guy. Paris: 1934.
130. M. M. Foulādvāndī, *Khayyam shinasi*, Tehran: 1378, pp. 32–5.
131. Joseph Freiherr von Hammer-Purgstall, Grschichte der Schönen Redekünste Persiens, Vienna: 1818.
132. Friedrich Bodenstedt, *Die Lieder und Sprüche des Omar Chajjam*, Breslau: 1881 p. ix.
133. *Divan der Persischen Poésie*, ed. Jolius Hart, Halle: 1887, pp. 41–50.
134. S. Gittleman, *The Reception of Edward FitzGerald's Ruba'iyyat of*

Omar Khayyam in England and Germany, Ph.D. Diss., Univ. of Michigan, 1961, p. 169.

135. Leon Kellner, "Ein Unsterblicher Müssiggänger," *Die Nation*, XVI (Oct. 8, 1898): p. 24.
136. Adalbert Meinhardt, "Omar Khayyam," *Die Nation*, XXVII (April 5, 1902): p. 428.
137. Ferdinand Laban, "Ungelesene Bucher als zeichen der zeit," *Deutsche Rundschau*, 110–111 (June 1902), p. 436.
138. See Maurice Todhunter, "Edward FitzGerald Miscellanies," *Englische Studien*, XXXI (1902), pp. 126–9; and "Edward FitzGerald: More Letters," Ibid., pp. 142–5.
139. See Sol Gittleman, *The Reception of Edward FitzGerald's Rubaiyat of Omar Khayyam in England and Germany*, Ph.D. diss., Univ. of Michigan, 1961, p. 202.
140. E. Wiedemann, "Uber Bestimmung der spezifischen Gewichte," SPMSE (1906), 38: pp. 136–80.
141. Curt Hamel Verlag, *Die vierzeiler des neuen Omar Khajjam*, Berlin: 1912.
142. Klabund, *Das sinngeditcht des Persischen zel Tmachers*, Munich: 1917.
143. Hans Bethge, *Omar Khayyam Nachdichtungen*, Berlin: 1921, p. 140.
144. Walter von der Porten, *Die Vierzeiler des Omar Chajjam*, Hamburg: 1927, pp. 4–5.
145. Rempis, *Die Vierzeiler Omars in der Auswahl und Anordnung Edward FitzGeralds*, Tübingen: 1993, p. 7.
146. Sol Gittleman, *The Reception of Edward FitzGerald's Rubaiyat of Omar Khayyam in England and in Germany*, p. 192.
147. Ibid., p. 192.
148. Rudolf Berger, *Die Sinnsprüche O. Khayyams aus der Persischen*, Bern: 1948.
149. Arthur Altschul, *Rubaiyat von Omar Chajjam*, Dresden: 1910, p. 47.
150. H. Jantzen, "Omar Chaijam," *Anglia*, X (1911), p. 279.
151. Both articles appeared in Joseph Steinmayer, "FitzGerald und Omar Khajjam," *Süddeutsche Monatshefte*, Achter Jahrgang, June, (1911): I, p. 712.
152. Karl Zimmermann, "Drei Heilige," *Die Tat*, Achter Jahrgang, I (April–September, 1916): p. 38.
153. Sol Gittleman, *The Reception of Edward FitzGerald's Rubaiyat of Omar Khayyam in England and in Germany*, Ph.D. diss. 1961, p. 212.
154. Henry W. Nordmeyer, *Rubaiyat des Omar Khayyam*, Potsdam: 1926, pp. 1–20.
155. Sol Gittleman, *The Reception of Edward FitzGerald's Rubaiyat of*

Omar Khayyam in England and in Germany, Ph.D. diss. 1961, p. 216.

156. Friedrich Rosen, *Die Sinnsprüche Omars des Zeltmachers*, Stuttgart: 1909, p. 10.
157. See Potter, no. 568 (the 24 quatrains in Dutch mentioned there don't exist: they are in German).
158. Ibid., see Potter no. 419.
159. This quotation comes from a letter by Jos Biegstraaten to the author of this volume.
160. H. de Bruijn, J. ter Haar, A. Seyed-Gohrab and M.Goud.
161. An illustrated catalogue of this exhibition in 139 pages is available, in Dutch.

CONCLUSION

1. Jesus Seminar was a prestigious gathering of many eminent scholars of Christianity in order to determine how much of the Bible are actually the words of Jesus. The summary result was that only six verses of the Bible are the actual utterances of Jesus.

APPENDIX A

1. Swami Govinda Tirtha in his impressive calculation in *The Nectar of Grace: Omar Khayyam's Life and Works*, Allahabad: 1941, pp. LXXIX–CXXIX.
2. This translation is based on the critical edition of Behnaz Hashemipour, *Risālah fi'l-kawn wa'l-taklīf*, in *Farhang*, vols. 1–4, 12(2000): 29–32, pp. 137–45. For more information on different editions of this work see Ibid. 131–5.
3. "Ṣabā" is a wind that blows in the Spring from the north-east. It has come to symbolize a soul nourishing breath that has spiritual connotations in Persian literature.
4. The next five lines are prefatory statements and thus have been omitted.
5. This is a work by Avicenna.
6. This translation is based on the text of Rahim R. Malik, *Dānish nāmah-yi Khayyāmī*, Tehran: 1377, pp. 345–53. For more information on different editions of this text see Ibid, p. 344–5.
7. This translation is based on the text of Rahim R. Malik, *Dānish nāmah-yi Khayyāmī*, Tehran: 1377, pp. 371–5.
8. Zayd is in Arabic a generic name equivalent to "John Doe."
9. This translation is based on the text of Rahim R. Malik, *Dānish*

nāmah-yi Khayyāmī, Tehran: 1377, pp. 381–90. For more information on different editions of this text see Ibid.

10. *Jinnis* from which the word "Genie" comes from is originally a Qur'anic term usually understood as extra-terrestrial beings; they are above animals and on a par with man.
11. Khayyam uses the word "*khassah*" which literally means "particularity" but he really means "substance"; it is a rare usage of the word for substance which is traditionally referred to as *jawhar*.
12. The text contains the space and nothing is omitted here.
13. This translation is based on the text of Gh. J. Nezhad Awwal, *Farhang*, vols. 1–4, 12(2000): 29–32, pp. 101–118. For more information on different editions of this text see Ibid., pp. 85–100.
14. Perfunctory introduction not translated. This translation is based on the text of Rahim R. Malik, *Dānish nāmah-yi Khayyāmī*, Tehran: 1377, pp. 415–22. The text included here is a copy of the original hand-written manuscript and often not very clear.
15. The text is not clear here, the word appears to be "*al-hams*" which does not make sense in this context.
16. Khayyam along with many other Muslim philosophers thought that *Enneads* was actually Aristotle's *Theologia*.
17. The text is not clear.

APPENDIX B

1. The Rubaiyat of Omar Khayyam. Rendered into English by Edward FitzGerald, New York: 1942.

APPENDIX C

1. Translated by the author. For the Arabic version of these quatrains see Ali Dashti, *Dami ba Khayyam*, Tehran: 1368, pp. 93–7.

Bibliography

PRIMARY SOURCES

Omar Khayyam, *Risālah ḍiyā' al-'aqlī fī mawḍū' al-'ilm al-kullī Dānish nāmah-yi Khayyāmī*, ed. Rahim R. Malik, Tehran: 1377, pp. 370–375.

——, *Ḍarurat al-taḍād fi'l-'ālam wa'l-jabr wa'l-baqā'. Dānish-nāmah-yi Khayyāmī*, ed. Rahim R. Malik, pp. 346–53.

——, "*Dar 'ilm kulliyāt-i wujūd.*" *Farhang*, vol. 1, 12(1378):1–4, 389–90.

——, "*Fi'l-kawn wa'l-taklīf.*" *Dānish-nāmah-yi Khayyāmī*," ed. Rahim R. Malik, Tehran: 1377.

——, "*Al-jawāb 'an thulāth masā'il.*" Ed. H.N. Iṣfahānī, *Farhang*, vol. 1, 12 (1378):1–4, 163–70.

——, "*Risālah fi'l-wujūd.*" Ed. J. Nezhad Awwal, *Farhang*, vol. 1, 12 (1378):1–4, 102–166.

——, *Al-qawl 'alā ajnās al-ladhi bi'l-arba'ah.*

——, *Risālah fī sharḥ mā ashkāl min muṣādarāt kitāb uqlidus.*

——, *Risālah fī qismah rub' al-dā'irah.*

——, *Risālah fī barāhīn 'alā masā'il al-jabr wa'l-muqābalah.*

——, *Risālah fi'l- iḥtiyāj lima'rifat miqdarī al-dhahab wa'l-fiḍah fī jism murakkab minhā.*

——, *Khuṭbah al-ghurrā' Ibn Sīnā.*

——, *Risālah dar kashf ḥaqiqat-i Norūz.*

SELECTED BIBLIOGRAPHY

Afīfī, A. *Malāmatiyyah, Ṣufīyah wa futuwwat.* Trans. by N.A. Fruhar. Tehran: 1376.

Altschul, Arthur. *Rubaiyat von Omar Chajjam.* Dresden: 1910.

Aminrazavi, M. *Suhrawardī and the School of Illumination*. London: 1996.

Arberry, A.J. *The Romance of the Rubaiyat*. London: 1959.

——, *The Ruba'iyyat of Omar Khayyam*. London: 1949.

Aṭṭār, Farīd al-Dīn. *Manẓumah-yi ilāhī nāmah*. Mashhad: 1351.

——, *Tadhkirat al-uliyā'*. Tehran: 1336 AH/1957.

Avicenna. *On Theodicy and Providence*. Trans. by Sh. Inati, in *An Anthology of Philosophy in Persia*, ed. S.H. Nasr and M. Aminrazavi. New York: 1999.

Badawī, 'A. *Madhāhib al-islāmiyyīn*. 2 vols. Beirut: 1973.

Bayhaqī, Abu'l Ḥasan. *Tatimah ṣiwān al-ḥikmah*. Lahore: 1351.

——, *Tārikh-i Bayhaqī*. Vol. 3. ed. Kh. Rahbar. Tehran: 1378.

Berger, Rudolf. *Die Sinnsprüche O. Khayyams aus der Persischen*. Parnass-Bücherei, Bern: 1948.

Bethge, Hans. *Omar Khayyam Nachdichtungen*. Berlin: 1921.

Bigdelī, Āzar. *Ātashkadeh*. 2 vols. ed. Nāserī. Tehran: 1338.

Black, Walter J. *The Ruba'iyyat of Omar Khayyam*. New York: 1942.

Blumenthal, David R. *Facing the Abusing God: A Theology of Protest*. Louisville: 1993.

Bodenstedt, Friedrich. *Die Lieder und Sprüche des Omar Chajjam*. Breslau: 1881.

Brigham, J. *The Many Sided Omar*. Des Moines: 1924.

Burrage, Charles D., ed. *Some Doings of the Omar Khayyam Club of America*. Boston: 1922.

——, *Twenty Years of the Omar Khayyam Club of America*. Boston: 1921.

Burton, David M. *The History of Mathematics*. McGraw-Hill, New York: 2003.

Chāvoshī, J.A. *Ḥakīm Omar Khayyam Nayshābūrī*. Tehran: 1358.

——, *Sayri dar afkār-i 'ilmī wa falsafī-yi ḥakīm Omar Khayyam Nayshābūrī*. Tehran: 1358.

Chesterton, G.K. *Heretics*. London: 1906.

Chittick, W. *The Sufi Path of Knowledge*. Albany: State University of New York Press, 1989.

Christensen, A.E. *Recherches sur les Ruba'iyyat de 'Omar Ijayyam*. Heidelburg: 1905.

Clodd, Edward. *Memories*. London: 1916.

Copleston, F.S.J. *A History of Philosophy*. Vol. 1. New York: 1963, p. 31.

Conway, Moncure. "The Omar Khayyam Cult in England." *Nation* 57 (1893): 1478.

Corbin, H. *Visionary Recital*. Trans. W.R. Trask. Princeton: 1988.

Cowell, E.B. *Ruba'iyyat of 'Umar Khayyam*. London: 1908.

D'Ambrosio, V.M. *Eliot Possessed: T.S. Eliot and FitzGerald's RUBAIYAT*. New York University Press: 1989.
Dabashi, Hamid. *Truth and Narrative: The Untimely Thoughts of 'Ayn al-Quḍāt al-Hamadhani*. Richmond: 1999.
Dashtī, A. *In search of Omar Khayyam*. New York: 1971.
——, *Damī bā khayyam*. Tehran: 1377.
Divan der Persischen Poésie. Ed. Jolius Hart, Herausgegeben von Julius Hart. Halle: 1887.
Dole, Nathan Haskell. *Rubaiyat of Omar Khayyam*. Boston: 1891.
——, *Flowers from Persian Poets*. New York: 1901.
Eliot, T.S. *Selected Essays*. London: 1951.
——, *The Use of Poetry and the Use of Criticism: Studies in the Relation of Poetry to Criticism in England*. London: Faber and Faber Press 1985.
Ellis, Havelock. "Sexual Inversion." *Studies in the Psychology of Sex*. 2 vols. New York: 1942, 1:50–51.
Fakhry, M. *Philosophy, Dogma and the Impact of Greek Thought in Islam*. Variorum. 1994.
Faḍlallāh, Rashīd al-Dīn. *Jāmi' al-tawārikh*. Leyden: 1329.
Farzāneh, M. *Mardī az nayshābūr*. Tehran: 1349.
——, *Naqd wa barrasi-yi ruba'ihā-yi Omar Khayyam*. Tehran: 1356.
FitzGerald, Edward. *Polonius*. Variorum. Vol.1. New York: 1903.
——, *The Rubaiyyat of Omar Khayyam*. New York: 1942.
Foūlādvand, M.M. *Khayyam shināsī*. Tehran: 1378.
Furūghī, M.A. *Majmu'a-yi maqālāt-i furūghī*. Tehran: 1375.
Furūgh, O. *'Aqā'id-i falsafi-yi abu'l 'allā', filsuf-i ma'arrah*. Trans. H. Khadiv Jam. Tehran: 1342.
Le Gallienne, Richard. *Rubaiyat of Omar Khayyam*. New York: 1897.
——, *Omar Repentant*. New York: 1908.
Garcin de Tassy, J.H. *Notes sur les Rubanjat d'Omar Khayyam*. Paris: 1857.
Ghazzālī, Abū Ḥāmid. *Fātiḥat al-'ulūm*. Cairo: 1322.
——, *Munqidh min al-ḍalāl*. In W.M. Watt. *The Faith and Practice of al-Ghazālī*. London: 1953.
——, *Tahafut al-falāsifah*. Trans. M.E. Marmura. Utah: 1997.
——, *The Incoherence of the Philosophers*. Trans. M.E. Marmura. Provo: 1979.
——, *Iḥyā' al-'ulūm al-dīn*. Trans. M. Khwarazmī. Tehran: 1378.
Ghazzālī, Aḥmad. *Risālah maw'iẓah*. Ed. Nourbakhsh. Tehran: 1371.
Gittleman, S. *The Reception of Edward FitzGerald's Ruba'iyyat of Omar Khayyam in England and Germany*. Ph.D. Diss., Univ. of Michigan: 1961.
Gosse, Edmund. *Critical Kit-Kats*. London: 1895.

Gribben A. and K.B. MacDonnell. *Mark Twain's Rubaiyat*. Berkeley: 1983.
Gutas, D. *Greek thought, Arabic Culture*. London: 1998.
Ḥalabī, A.A. *Tārikh-i falasafa-yi Iran*. Tehran: 1373, 294–353.
al-Ḥamawī, Yāqut. *Mu'jam al-udabā'*. Vol. 4. Cairo: 1936.
Ḥasan, H. Ibrāhim. *Tārikh al-islām al-siyāsī wa'l-dīnī wa'l-thiqāfī wa'l-ijtimā'ī*. Vol. 3. Cairo: 1965.
Hastie, William. *Festival of Spring from the Divan of Jelalledin*. Glasgow: 1903.
Hay, John. *In Praise of Omar*. Portland: 1897.
Heron-Allen, E. *Omar Khayyam*. London: 1899.
——, *Rubaiyat of 'Umar Khayyam*. London: 1908.
——, *Some Sidelights Upon Edward FitzGerald's Poem: The Ruba'iyat of Omar Khayyam*. London: 1898.
Hidāyat, Riḍā Qolikhān. *Mujma' al-fuṣaḥā*. Ed. M.A. Gorgānī. Tehran: 1344.
——, *Riyāḍ al-'ārifīn*. Ed. M.A. Gorgānī. Tehran: 1344.
Humā'ī, J. *Ghazzālī nāmah*. Tehran: 1368.
Irānī, A. *Payām-i falsafi-yi Khayyam*. Los Angeles: 1991.
Iṣfahānī, 'Imād al-Dīn Kātib. *Kharidat al-qaṣr*. Tehran: 1378AH.
I'timād, M. *Sha'r-i falsafi-yi Khayyam*. Tehran: 1361.
Ja'farī, M.T. *Taḥlil-i shakhsiyat-i khayyam*. Tehran: 1365.
al-Jahshiyarī, A.M. 'Abdus. *Kitāb al-wuzarā'*. Cairo: 1980.
Javādī, H. *Satire in Persian Literature*. Fairlagh Dickenson Univ. Press. Rutherford: 1988.
Kasra. *The Rubaiyyat of 'Umar Khayyam*. New York: 1975.
Khāzenī ,'Abd al-Raḥmān. *Mizān al-ḥikmah*. Cairo: 1947.
Nāṣir Khusraw. *Safar nāmah*. Delhi: 1941.
Lang, Cecil Y., ed. *The Pre-Raphaelites and Their Circle*. Boston: 1968.
Lewisohn, L., ed. *The Heritage of Sufism*, 3 vols. Oxford: 1999.
MacDonnell, K.B. *Mark Twain's Rubaiyat*. Austin & Santa Barbara: 1983.
Malik, Raḥīm R. *Omar Khayyam: Qāfilah sālār-i dānish*. Tehran: 1377.
——, *Dānish nāmah-yi Khayyāmī*. Tehran: 1377.
Maqṣūd, Javād. *Sharḥ-i ahwāl wa āthār wa du-baytihāy-i bābā tāhir-i 'uryān*. Tehran: 1354.
Massé, H. *Anthologie Persane*. Paris: 1886.
Miller, James. *T.S. Eliot's Personal Waste Land: Exorcism of the Demons*. Pennsylvania: 1977.
Muḥammad, 'Abd al-Laṭīf, ed. *Rasā'il ikhwān al-ṣafā'*. Vol. 4. Beirut: 1957.
Nakhjavānī, S. *Khayyam pendārī*. Tehran: 1347.
Nasr, S.H. *Science and Civilization in Islam*. Lahore: 1983.
——, *Sufi Essays*. Albany: 1972.

Nasr, S.H. and M. Aminrazavi. *An Anthology of Philosophy in Persia*. Vol. 1. New York: 1998.
al-Naẓẓām. *Encyclopedia of Islam*. New edn. VII, J. Van Ess, 1057–58.
Netton, I.A. *Muslim Neoplatonists: An Introduction to the Thought of the Brethren of Purity*. London: 1982.
Nordmeyer, Henry W. *Rubaiyat des Omar Khayyam*. Potsdam: 1926.
Ormsby, Eric L. *Theodicy in Islamic Thought*. Princeton: 1941.
Otto, R. *The Idea of the Holy*. Oxford: 1958.
Potter, Charles. *A Bibliography of the Rubaiyat of Omar Khayyam*. London: 1929.
Pound, E. *Letters of Ezra Pound*. London: 1951.
Pourjavādī, N.J. *'Ayn al-Qoḍāt Hamadānī wa ustādān-i ū*. Tehran: 1374.
Qāḍī, 'Abd Al-Jabbār. *Sharḥ al-uṣūl al-khamsah*. Cairo: 1965.
Qaraguzlū, A. Dh. *'Omar Khayyam*.Tehran: 1379.
Qazwīnī, A.K. *Sharḥ-i ruba'iyyāt-i Khayyam*. Ed. M.R.M. Chahārdehī. Tehran: 1379.
Qazwīnī, Naṣr Mustawfī. *Tārikh-i Gozideh*.Vol. 1. Ed. E. Brown. London: 1910.
Qazwīnī, Zakariyā Muḥammad ibn Maḥmud. *Athār al-bilād wa akhbār al-'ibād*. Beirut: 1973.
Al-Qifṭī. *Tārikh al-ḥukamā'*. Leipzig: 1903.
Rashed, R. and B. Vahabzadeh. *Omar Khayyam the Mathematician*. New York: 2000.
Rāzī, Abū Bakr. *Mirṣād al-'ibād min al-mabda' ila'l-ma'ād*. Tehran: 1366.
al-Rāzī, Fakhr al-Dīn Muḥammad ibn Omar. *Tafsīr mafātiḥ al-ghayb*. Beirut: 1421 AH.
——, *Risālat fi'l-tanbih 'alā ba'ḍ al-asrār al-maw'dah fī ba'ḍ al-surah al-Quran al-'aẓīm*. As cited in Rahim R. Malik. *Omar Khayyam*. Tehran: 1377.
al-Rāzī, Abū Ḥātim. *A'lām al-nubuwwa*. Ed. S. Al-Ṣawy. Tehran: 1977.
al-Rāzī, Omar. *Tafsīr mafātiḥ al-ghayb*. Bulaq: 1289.
Riḍā, Abū. *Rasā'il al-Kindī al-falsafiyyah*.Vol. 1. Cairo:1950.
Riley, James Whitcomb. *The Ruba'iyyat of Doc Sifers*. Illustrated by C.M. Relya. New York: 1897.
Rosen, Friedrich. *Die Sinnsprüche Omars des Zeltmachers*. Stuttgart: 1909.
Rusk, Ralph. *Life of Ralph Waldo Emerson*. New York: 1949.
Ṣafā, Dh. *Tārikh-i 'ulūm 'aqlī dar tamadūn-i islāmī*. Tehran: 1371.
Ṣafadī, *al-wāfī bi'l-wafiyāt*. Vol. 2. Istanbul: 1931.
Safar nāmah-yi Nāṣir Khusraw. Ed. M.D. Siyaqī, Tehran: 1375.
Ṣāḥib al-Zamānī, N. *Khat-i siwwum*. Tehran: 1351 AH/1960.

Saidī, A. *Rubai'yyat of 'Omar Khayyam*. Berkeley: 1994.
Said, Edward. *Culture and Imperialism*. New York: 1993.
Samarqandī, A. *Chahār maqālah*. Ed. M. Mo'in. Tehran: 1348.
Samuels, Charles E. *Thomas Baily Aldrich*. New York: 1965.
Al-Ṣarrāf, A.H. *Omar Khayyam*. Baghdad: 1949.
Schimmel, A.M. *Mystical Dimensions of Islam*. Chapel Hill: 1975.
Shahulī, A. *Ḥakīm Omar Khayyam wa zamān-i u*. Tehran: 1353.
Shahrazūrī. *Nuzhat al-arwāḥ*. Trans. by M.A. Tabrizī, also known as *Madinat al-ḥukamā'*. Tehran: 1365.
Shajarah, H. *Taḥqiq dar ruba'iyyat wa zendegi-yi khayyam*. Tehran: 1320.
Shervānī, Khāqānī. *Munsha'āt-i Khāqānī*. Ed. M. Roushan. Tehran: 1362.
Shirvānī, F.M. and Shāyegan, H. *Negāhī bar Khayyam*. Tehran: 1350.
Shirāzī, Qoṭb al-Dīn Maḥmūd, *Tuḥfat al-shāhiyyah*. Cairo: 1937.
Steinmayer, Joseph. "FitzGerald und Omar Khajjam," *Süddeutsche Monatshefte*, Achter Jahrgang, June (1911): I, p. 712.
Stroumsa, S. *Free Thinkers of Medieval Islam*, Leiden: 1999.
Suhrawardī, Shihāb al-Dīn. *Oeuvres Philosophiques et Mystiques*. Vol. 3. Ed. S.H. Nasr. Institut d'Etudes et des Recherches Culturelles. Tehran: 1993.
——, *Ḥikmat al-ishrāq*. Trans. by H. Ziā'i and J. Walbridge. Utah: 1999.
Tabāṭabā'ī, M. *Khayyam yā khayyāmī*. Tehran: 1370.
Tabrīzī, Shams. *Maqālāt*. 2nd edn. Ed. M.A. Muwaḥḥid. Tehran: 1377.
Taṭavī, Aḥmad N. *Tārikh-i Alfī*. Tehran: 1378.
Tirtha, Swami Govinda. *The Nectar of Grace: Omar Khayyam's Life and Works*. Allahabad: 1941.
Trimingham, J.S. *The Sufi Orders in Islam*. New York: 1998.
Tuckey, John S., ed. *Mark Twain's Fables of Man*. Berkeley: 1971.
Ṭūsī, Sharīf al-Dīn. *Oeuvres mathématiques. Algèbre et Géometrie au XIIe siècle*. 2 vols. Collection "Sciences et Philosophie arabes-Textes et etudes". Paris: Les Belles Lettres 1986.
Urvoy, D. *Les Penseurs libres dans l'Islam classique*. Paris: 1996.
Vedder, Elihu. *The Rubaiyat of Omar Khayyam*. Boston: 1884.
Verlag, Curt Hamel. *Die vierzeiler desneuen Omar Khajjam*. Berlin: 1912.
Von der Porten, Walter. *Die Vierzeiler des Omar Chajjam*. Hamburg: 1927.
Wright, William Aldis. *Letters and Literary Remains of Edward FitzGerald*. London: 1889.
Yogananda, P. *Wine of the Mystic: The ruba'iyyat of Omar Khayyam – A Spiritual Interpretation*. Los Angeles: 1990.
Yohannan, John D. "Fin de Siècle Cult of FitzGerald's *Ruba'iyat* of Omar Khayyam" *Review of National Literature*, 2 (1971): 85.

JOURNAL ARTICLES

Aldrich, Thomas Baily. "A Persian Poet." *Atlantic Monthly*, 41 (1878): 421–26.

Aminrazavi, M. "Antinomian Sufism and Ethical Relativism." *Journal of Henry Martin Institute for Islamic Studies*, 4: 1&2 (1995): 17–24.

Amīr Mo'az, 'Ạlī R. "A Paper of Omar Khayyam," *Scripta Mathematica*, 26 (1963), 323–327.

Ashtiyānī, Abbās. "Raji' ba aḥwāl-i omar khayyam nayshāburī." *Majmu 'a-yi sharq*, no. 8, series 1, pp. 403–404.

Bagheri, M. and Houshiyār, S. "Risālah musiqi-yi Khayyam az didgāh-i riyāḍiyāt." *Rahpouyeh-yi honar*, 43 (1376): 42–63.

Barrow, S.J. "Editions Note Book." *Unitarian Review and Religious Magazine*, 11 (1879): 384–86.

Binesh, T. "Risālah musiqi-yi khayyam yā khayyāmī." *Nashriyah-yi dānishgah-i āzād-i islāmī-yi kirmān*, (1373): 1, pp. 92–101.

"The Book Buyers Guide." *Critic*, 37 (1900): 277.

Broad, C.D. "The Philosophy of Omar Khayyam and Its Relation to that of Schopenhauer." *Review*, CLXVI (Nov., 1906): 544–556.

Brown, E.G. "Yet More Light On 'Umar-i Khayyam." *Royal Asiatic Society*, 8 (1899): 409–420.

Chāvoshī, J.A. "Omar Khayyam and the Arithmetical Triangle." Trans. by Boozarjomehr, *Farhang*, vol. 2, 14 (1380): 262–273.

Chāvoshī, J.A. "Omar al-Khayyam wa'l-musiqī al-naḍariyyah." Trans. M.M. 'Abd al-Jalil. *Farhang*, vol. 1, 14 (1378): 29–32 and 203–214.

Choubi, O.B.S. "Omar Khayyam, Epicureans wa Charvakhā." *Rad-i pa-yi falsafahā-yi hind dar shi'ar-i fārsī*. Trans. Sh. Mushirī. Tehran: 1378, pp. 129–136.

Conway, Moncure D. "The Omar Khayyam Cult in England." *Nation*, 57 (1893), No. 1478.

Daftary, Z. "Partaw-yi khirah kunandah az nubugh-i khayyam." *Armaghān*, 32:7–8, pp. 290–451.

Dilgan, H. "Al-Samarqandī." *Dictionary of Scientific Biography*, vol. XII: 91.

——, "Qāḍī zādeh al-Ruṃī." *Dictionary of Scientific Biography*, vol. XI: 227–229.

Dinānī, Gh. "Ḥakim Omar Khyyam wa mas'alih-yi wāḥid wa kathīr." *Daftar-i 'aql wa āyat-i 'ishq*. Vol. I Tehran (1380): 229–230.

Duncan, Isadora. "Illustrations: Omar Done into Dance." *Critic*, May, 1899.

Farzad, A. "Do usiyangar-i 'ālamsuz: Khayyam wa Abu'l-'Alā' Ma'rrī." *Negin*, 172 (1358): 19–20, 51–52; 173(1358): 34–36.

Furūgh, Omar. "Abu'l-'Alā' Ma'rrī wa Khayyam." Trans. H. Khadivjan, *Yaghmā*, 16 (1342): 173–177.

Le Gallienne, Richard. "Fin de Siècle Cult of FitzGerald's *Ruba'iyat* of Omar Khayyam." *Review of National Literature*, 2 (1971): 74–75.

—— "Sānā'i Ghaznavī's Letter to Khayyam." *In Dānish-nāmah-yi Khayyāmī*. Ed. R.R. Mālik: 13–16.

—— "The Harm of Omar." *T.P.'s Weekly*, XVI (September 9, 1910): 340.

Hāshemipour, B. "Goftārī dar bāra-yi risālah-yi dar 'ilm-i kulliyāt-i wujūd." *Farhang*, vol. 2, 14 (1380): 3–4, 58.

Hashtrūdī, M. "Khayyam, riyāḍidān-i shā`ir." *Yekān*, vol. 12: 238–239.

Holland, Bernard. "The Popularity of Omar." *National Review*, XXXIII (June, 1899): 643–652.

Iṣfahānī, H. N. "Hastī shināsī-yi ḥakīm Omar Khayyam." *Farhang*, vol. 2, 14 (1380): 3–4, 113–117.

Jantzen, H. "Omar Chaijam." *Anglia*, X (1911): 279.

Jāvādī, H. "Khayyam wa Abu'l-'Alā' Ma'rrī." *Khayyam nāmah*. Los Angeles: (1376).

Kellner, Leon. "Ein Unsterblicher Müssiggänger." *Die Nation*, XVI (Oct. 8, 1898): 24.

Khūrāsānī, M. "Maktab-i falsafi-yi shakkākān." *Armaghān*, vol. 32, no. 8: 383–4.

Meinhardt, Adalbert. "Omar Khayyam." *Die Nation*, XXVII (April 5, 1902).

Meynell, Willfred. "The Cause of Omar's Popularity." *Academy*, LXVI (March, 1904): 274.

Miller, A.H. "The Omar Cult." *Academy* 59 (1900): 55.

Minovī, M. "az khazā'in-i turkiyyah." *Majalla-yi dānishkadeh-yi adabiyyāt*, 4 (1335): 2: 42–75 and no. 3: 53–89.

Mo'ez, A.R. "A Paper on Omar Khayyam." *Scripta Mathematica*, vol. 4, no. 26: 323–37.

—— "Discussions of Difficulties in Euclid by Omar Khayyam." *Scripta Mathematica*, vol. 24, no. 4: 272–303.

More, Paul Elmer. "The Seven Seas and the Rubaiyat." *Atlantic Monthly*, 84 (1899): 800–808.

Nasr, S.H. "The Poet-Scientist Khayyam as Philosopher." *Mélanges Luce López-Baralt*, Series 9, no. 8: 535–53.

——, "Omar Khayyam: Philosopher-Poet-Scientist." *The Islamic Intellectual Tradition in Persia*. Ed. M. Aminrazavi, London: 1996, pp. 175–178.

——, "The School of Iṣfahān." *A History of Muslim Philosophy*, vol. 2. Ed. M.M. Sharīf, Wiesbaden: 1966, pp. 904–32.

Nizhād Awwal, Gh. J. "Sukhanī dar bārah-yi risālah-yi fi'l-wujūd." *Farhang*, vol. 1, 12 (1378): 1–4, p. 88.

Nā'inī, M.R.J. "Khayyāmī nayshābūrī khayyam-i shā'ir nīst." *Rahāvard Journal of Persian Literature*, 57 (2001): 20.

Noūrī, H. Kh. "Khayyam wa Abu'l-'Alā'." *Mehr*, 4 (1315): 913–920, 1021–1028, 1129–1138.

Özdurad, A. "Omar Khayyam and Architecture." *Farhang*, 14 (2002): 39–40, 189–251.

Rushdī Rāshid and Aḥmed Jabbār in *Rasā'il al-Khayyam al-jabriyyah*. Ḥalab: Alturath al-'ilmī, 1981.

Salmon, C.G. "Biographie d'Omar Kheyyam." *La Grande Encyclopédie*. Paris: 1922.

Sapanta, S. "Khayyam wa musiqī-yi naḍarī." *Farhang*, vol. 2, 14 (1980): 3–4, 259–272.

Smith, David E. "Euclid, Omar Khayyam and Saccheri." *Scripta Mathematica*, vol. 3, no. 1 (1935): 8.

Soroushyar, J. "Khayyam wa Ghazzālī." *Yaghmā*, 27 (1353): 152–3.

Steinmayer, Joseph. "FitzGerald und Omar Khajjam," *Süddeutsche Monatshefte*, Achter Jahrgang, June (1911): I, p. 712.

Struik, D.J. "Omar Khayyam, Mathematician." *The Mathematics Teacher*, vol. LVI (1958): 284.

Todhunter, Maurice. "Edward FitzGerald Miscellanies." *Englische Studien*, XXXI (1902), pp. 126–129.

Whibley, Charles. "Musings Without Method." *Blackwood's*, 170 (1903): 287.

Wiedeman, E. and G. Jacob. "Zu Omar-chajjam." *Der Islam*, no. 3: 42–62.

Wiedemann, E. "Uber Bestimmung der spezifischen Gewichte." Beitr. Zur Gesch. Der Naturwiss., 8 SPMSE (1906), 38: 136–80.

Yohannan, John D. "Fin de Siècle Cult of FitzGerald's *Ruba'iyat* of Omar Khayyam." *Review of National Literature*, 2 (1971): 85.

Youschkevitch, A.P. "AL-KHAYYAMI." *Dictionary of Scientific Biography*. Ed. Charles C. Gillispie, Vol. VII, New York 1973: 324.

Zhukovski, V.A. "'Umar Khayyam and the 'Wandering' Quatrains." Trans. from Russian by E.D. Ross in the *Journal of the Royal Asiatic Scoiety*, (1898): xxx.

Zimmermann, Karl. "Drei Heilige." *Die Tat*, Achter Jahrgang, I (April-September, 1916), p. 38.

Index

For works of Omar Khayyam, page numbers for the translations given in the appendix are given in **bold** type.